Us against Them

LEXINGTON STUDIES IN POLITICAL COMMUNICATION

Series Editor: Robert E. Denton, Jr., Virginia Polytechnic Institute and State University

This series encourages focused work examining the role and function of communication in the realm of politics including campaigns and elections, media, and political institutions.

RECENT TITLES IN THE SERIES:

Post-9/11 American Presidential Rhetoric: A Study of Protofascist Discourse, By Colleen Elizabeth Kelley

Making a Difference: A Comparative View of the Role of the Internet in Election Politics, Edited by Stephen Ward, Diana Owen, Richard Davis, and David Taras

Seen and Heard: The Women of Television News, By Nichola D. Gutgold

Nuclear Legacies: Communication, Controversy, and the U. S. Nuclear Weapons Complex, Edited by Bryan C. Taylor, William J. Kinsella, Stephen P. Depoe, Maribeth S. Metzler

Conditional Press Influence in Politics, By Adam J. Schiffer

Telling Political Lives: The Rhetorical Autobiographies of Women Leaders in the United States, Edited by Brenda DeVore Marshall and Molly A. Mayhead

Media Bias? A Comparative Study of Time, Newsweek, the National Review, and the Progressive, 1975–2000, By Tawnya J. Adkins Covert and Philo C. Wasburn

Navigating the Post–Cold War World: President Clinton's Foreign Policy Rhetoric, By Jason A. Edwards

The Rhetoric of Pope John Paul II, Edited by Joseph R. Blaney and Joseph P. Zompetti

Stagecraft and Statecraft: Advance and Media Events in Political Communication, By Dan Schill

Rhetorical Criticism: Perspectives in Action, Edited by Jim A. Kuypers

Almost *Madam President: Why Hillary Clinton "Won" in 2008*, By Nichola D. Gutgold

Cracked But Not Shattered: Hillary Rodham Clinton's Unsuccessful Run for the Presidency, Edited by Theodore F. Sheckels

Gender and Political Communication in America: Rhetoric, Representation, and Display, Edited by Janis L. Edwards

Communicator-in-Chief: How Barack Obama Used New Media Technology to Win the White House, Edited by John Allen Hendricks and Robert E. Denton, Jr.

Centrist Rhetoric: The Production of Political Transcendence in the Clinton Presidency, By Antonio de Velasco

Studies of Identity in the 2008 Presidential Campaign, Edited by Robert E. Denton, Jr.

Campaign Finance Reform: The Political Shell Game, By Melissa M. Smith, Glenda C. Williams, Larry Powell, and Gary A. Copeland

Us against Them: The Political Culture of Talk Radio, By Randy Bobbitt

Us against Them

The Political Culture of Talk Radio

Randy Bobbitt

LEXINGTON BOOKS
A division of
ROWMAN & LITTLEFIELD PUBLISHERS, INC.
Lanham • Boulder • New York • Toronto • Plymouth, UK

Published by Lexington Books
A division of Rowman & Littlefield Publishers, Inc.
A wholly owned subsidiary of The Rowman & Littlefield Publishing Group, Inc.
4501 Forbes Boulevard, Suite 200, Lanham, Maryland 20706
http://www.lexingtonbooks.com

Estover Road, Plymouth PL6 7PY, United Kingdom

Copyright © 2010 by Lexington Books

All rights reserved. No part of this book may be reproduced in any form or by any electronic or mechanical means, including information storage and retrieval systems, without written permission from the publisher, except by a reviewer who may quote passages in a review.

British Library Cataloguing in Publication Information Available

Library of Congress Cataloging-in-Publication Data

Bobbitt, William R. (William Randy)
  Us against them : the political culture of talk radio / Randy Bobbitt.
    p. cm.—(Lexington studies in political communication)
  Includes bibliographical references and index.
  ISBN 978-0-7391-2639-4 (cloth : alk. paper) —ISBN 978-0-7391-2640-0 (pbk. : alk. paper)
  1. Radio talk shows--United States. 2. Radio broadcasting--Political aspects--United States. 3. Radio in politics--United States. I. Title.
  PN1991.8.T35B63 2010
  791.44'6—dc22   2010007002

∞™ The paper used in this publication meets the minimum requirements of American National Standard for Information Sciences—Permanence of Paper for Printed Library Materials, ANSI/NISO Z39.48-1992.

Printed in the United States of America

Contents

Preface		vii
Chapter 1	Hot Air	1
Chapter 2	The Audience: Who Listens and Why	17
Chapter 3	The Sponsors: Who Advertises and Why	29
Chapter 4	The Conservatives	39
Chapter 5	The Progressives	75
Chapter 6	The Libertarians	99
Chapter 7	The Women	111
Chapter 8	The Haters and the Shockers	123
Chapter 9	The Locals	145
Chapter 10	In Theory: Talk Radio and American Politics	165
Chapter 11	In Practice: Talk Radio and the 2008 Presidential Election	197
Epilogue	Talk Radio, the First Amendment, and the Fairness Doctrine	213
Notes		227
Sources		245
Index		257
About the Author		275

Preface

In October 2005, I was sitting in a small conference room at a major university, being interviewed by a group of professors and administrators attempting to fill a faculty vacancy. The conversation turned to my publishing record—I had published three books in the previous ten years—and my potential future colleagues inquired as to what my next book would be about. I had not thought that far ahead, and the question caught me off guard. But looking around the room, I saw on the far wall a large poster for a local talk radio station. Desperate for something intelligent to say, I blurted out, "I'm thinking about doing something about talk radio."

And that's how it started. On the plane ride home, I coincidentally picked up a news magazine in the seat pocket in front of me and found an article about the impact of talk radio on national politics. Throughout the article, there were numerous references to the dichotomous nature of talk radio programming. Liberals versus conservatives. Democrats versus Republicans. Blacks versus whites. Gay versus straight. Women versus men. The underlying theme, the article seemed to be saying, was "us versus them." What a great title for a book, I thought. When I got home and did a keyword search on the Internet, however, I found the title *Us vs. Them* was already taken by an author who had written a book about political debates in a more general sense. While *Us against Them* was also taken (by a sportswriter chronicling the history of the Ryder Cup golf competition), I preferred the ring of that title, and since my book was on a substantially different topic, an explanatory subtitle was all I needed to set my book apart.

This book will examine the dichotomous nature of talk radio, but will also examine the larger role that it plays in the American political process. One central question I wanted to research was the reason why people choose to listen to political talk instead of music. Do they listen to get objective information on both sides of political issues to help them make their own voting decisions, or do they seek out the hosts and content that simply validates their own beliefs? A few years ago, while researching my previous book, *Lottery Wars*, I interviewed the former governor of South Carolina and asked him about the role of the newspaper editorial page in the lottery issue. He told me that like in most other states, the editorial pages in South Carolina were "places for people who already agree on an issue to meet each other. . . . no one picks up the newspaper editorial page hoping to find information to help them make political decisions." When I began working on this book, I thought about that comment and began to wonder if the same question could be posed about the audience of talk radio.

Chapter 1 deals with the history of talk radio from its early days in the 1950s to the present landscape, including the 2008 presidential election. Chapter 2, titled "The Audience: Who Listens and Why," examines the audience by a number of factors, including demographic categories and listening habits. Chapter 3, titled "The Sponsors: Who Advertises and Why," will examine why some of America's largest companies choose talk radio as their primary advertising venue.

Chapter 4 profiles some of the most popular national talk radio hosts who identify themselves as conservatives, the most obvious being Rush Limbaugh, Sean Hannity, and Bill O'Reilly. Chapter 5 does the same for progressives, among them being Thom Hartmann and Ed Schultz. That chapter will also look at the failure of the Air America Network and other attempts at liberal talk radio. Chapter 6 will provide profiles of those talk radio hosts identifying themselves as libertarians, the most influential being Neal Boortz and Larry Elder. Chapter 7 profiles the leading women in political talk radio, and chapter 8 examines the role played by the more outrageous hosts who traffic in hate and shock. Chapter 9 will provide a sampling of some of the lesser-known personalities that serve local audiences.

Chapter 10 will take a theoretical look at how talk radio may or may have not impacted political issues and campaigns from the 1950s through the 2006 midterm election. Chapter 11 will examine the real impact of talk radio on the 2008 presidential campaign. The book closes with an Epilogue that examines the future of political talk radio in light of the newest threat to the First Amendment: the possible return of the Fairness Doctrine, a twentieth century law that once required broadcasters to provide politically balanced programming.

Like most other projects of this complexity, it would not have been possible without the help of numerous people. Specifically, I thank Rebecca McCary, Michael Wiles, and other members of the editorial staff at Lexington Books for their patience and guidance with this project.

I also thank the dozens of university professors, talk radio hosts, media ethicists, radio industry experts, and other individuals who gave so generously of their time for in-person, telephone, and electronic mail interviews. Especially helpful sources included Robert Thompson, founder of the Bleier Center for Television and Popular Culture at Syracuse University, as well as on-air personalities, program executives, and sales executives at radio stations in the panhandle regions of Florida and Alabama. At WNRP-AM in Pensacola: Rob Williams, morning host; Dave McBride, program director; and Dave Windsor, sales executive. At WCOA-AM in Pensacola: Alan Caudle, program manager; and Mike Mendelssohn, sales executive. At WFTW-AM in Ft. Walton Beach: Ken Walsh, morning host; and Brenda Franco, sales executive. At WEBY-AM in Milton, Florida: Mike Bates, general manager and afternoon host. At WNTM-AM in Mobile: Uncle Henry, morning host, and Dan Mason, program manager.

Chapter 1

Hot Air

Agree to Disagree

Like many aspects of American political culture, the value and impact of talk radio depends largely on who is making the assessment. Political conservatives, who make up a large percentage of the talk radio audience, view it as a sacred island in what they perceive to be a vast sea of liberally biased media. For them, talk radio is their free-speech outlet and their only viable alternative to network and cable television news, National Public Radio, and their favorite liberal-media villain—the *New York Times*. In contrast, many liberals view talk radio as a billion-dollar industry fueled by anger, intolerance, paranoia, and distrust of government.

Over its seven-decade history, talk radio has grown from a small-town curiosity and cheap advertising venue to a ubiquitous format for political debate that fits the definition of a modern-day town square. In academia, it is studied on a variety of levels, from undergraduate classes covering the history of broadcasting to doctoral-level seminars dealing with its role in public discourse—what sociologist Jurgen Habermas refers to as the "public sphere." In the real world, talk radio is viewed as an outlet for political discussion as well as an inexpensive (compared to television) conduit by which advertisers can reach their audiences. To fully understand the medium, however, one must go back to the beginning.

Gray and Pyne Create a New Radio Genre

The origins of talk radio can be traced back to 1945, when New York disc jockey Barry Gray became bored with playing music. He took a phone call from band-leader Woody Herman, and believing his listeners might want to hear the conversation, put the telephone receiver up to his microphone. Gray's engineer then found a more practical way for the host and callers to interact, and Gray never went back to playing music.

While broadcasting historians refer to Gray as the "father of talk radio," his focus was more on popular culture than politics, and his banter was seldom controversial. As a result, the birth of *political* talk radio did not take place until four years later. The founder of that genre was Joe Pyne, a twenty-three-year-old drama student who was putting himself through college by working at a number of part-time jobs at small radio stations in New Jersey. Upon graduating in 1949, Pyne abandoned the idea of a career in the theatre and instead sought to enter the world of radio news. He pitched an idea to one of his employers, WILM in Wilmington, Delaware, for a news program that would be based on opinion rather than objectivity. Station management gave the idea a chance, and Pyne's new show, *It's Your Nickel,* was the beginning of a new genre in radio—a program in which the host offered opinions on a variety of political topics and listeners could call in to agree, disagree, or suggest the next topic. Pyne spent the next eight years moving around the country for a series of similar short-term jobs in local talk radio. In 1957, he was working at a station in Los Angeles when the success of his show prompted station management to take the program nationwide, and by the mid-1960s his creation, simply titled *The Joe Pyne Show,* was carried by more than 250 stations.

Like the majority of hosts that followed him over the next four decades, Pyne was a conservative. He spoke with the authority and demeanor of a preacher, using his electronic pulpit to lash out against Communists, the women's movement, and opponents of the Vietnam War. Pyne's rhetoric was mostly an act—even judged against today's standards—but audiences and advertisers bought into it.

Pyne was followed by a number of hosts who approached their work from a variety of political perspectives, but for the most part, only the conservatives were successful. One of the most influential of the 1970s was Bob Grant, a former sportscaster who met Pyne when the two worked at WABC in Los Angeles in the late 1950s. One day in 1963, he reluctantly agreed to guest-host Pyne's political show, and after becoming enamored with that genre, he never went back to sports. Grant later moved to New York and became Pyne's East Coast counterpart.

The early success of political talk radio was fueled in part by the then-new technology of FM radio. FM was far better suited than AM to broadcasting music, and as a result, music programming made the move from AM to FM en masse. Left with hours of time to fill each day, AM station owners turned to the all-talk format. Another technological development that spurred the growth of AM talk was a mechanism that allowed for broadcasting programs on a seven-second delay, meaning that call screeners could cut off callers in midsentence for using profanities or making defamatory comments.

Following Pyne's death in 1970, Grant became the dominant talk radio host and held that distinction for much of the next two decades. He was joined on the national stage by Wally George and Michael Jackson, both conservatives based in southern California; and Alan Berg, a liberal based in Denver. But Grant remained the biggest name in talk radio until the late 1980s, when Rush Limbaugh took his place and prepared to lead the industry into a new era.

In the 1980s, FM music stations in major markets such as Chicago, New York, Philadelphia, Los Angeles, Miami, Atlanta, Dallas-Ft. Worth, Denver, and Seattle dominated the Arbitron ratings. AM stations in those markets were able to survive only because they switched to all-talk formats. Audience numbers were far below what they were for music and resulted in a corresponding drop in advertising revenue, but the decrease in production costs cancelled out those losses. With no music licensing fees to pay and talk show host salaries much lower than those of disc jockeys, station owners found the all-talk format to be a less costly and less competitive format than music.

National programs became possible with the advent of toll-free 1-800 telephone service in the 1980s, and the following decade they became even more successful with the popularity of cellular telephones.

Boston University political science professor Murray Levin believes the growth of talk radio in the mid-1980s was made possible by the historical and societal developments that occurred during the two decades that preceded it. Beginning with the assassination of President Kennedy in 1963 and extending through Vietnam and Watergate and climaxing with the Iran-Contra affair, Americans became more cynical about the government and the elected officials that were running it. The result, Levin wrote in his 1987 book, *Talk Radio and the American Dream*, was a "confidence gap" that proved to be a breeding ground for discontent, and far-right conservative talk show hosts such as Barry Farber and Bob Grant took advantage[1] (Limbaugh and Hannity were not nationally known at the time of Levin's book, but by extension they would be said to have also taken advantage). While much of the negative discourse about politics has found a new home—the Internet—talk radio continues to retain much of its role in this arena.

The Godfather

In 1984, Rush Limbaugh was a thirty-two-year-old public relations executive who became bored with his job with the Kansas City Royals. Before working with the Royals, Limbaugh had been a disc jockey with stations in Pittsburgh and Kansas City, but had never considered the talk format. But when he applied for a job at KFKB in Sacramento, California, that was the offer on the table. Limbaugh flourished in the new format, and for the next four years, he hosted a daily program on which he offered listeners his conservative views on local and state politics and challenged callers to debate him on the air. In 1988, Limbaugh's show caught the attention of ABC Radio executives, who brought him to New York and gave him a nationally syndicated program. Many years later, he would earn the nickname "The Godfather" for his role in ushering talk radio into a new era. Limbaugh's role in the success of political talk radio is discussed in detail in chapter 4.

The Perfect Storm

Except for the success of Limbaugh, talk radio struggled as an industry from the mid-1980s through 1992, due mostly to the political culture of the times. With America enjoying perceived economic and political prosperity, talk radio hosts struggled to find controversies to explore. Popular conservative presidents (Ronald Reagan and George H. W. Bush) were in the White House, communist governments were collapsing around the globe, and much of the world was at peace. Without controversy or discontent among the audience, talk radio was running out of fuel. Audience numbers were down, and as a result, so were the advertising dollars.

In 1986, Congress directed the Federal Communications Commission (FCC) to eliminate rules on radio ownership, allowing more monopoly ownership and allowing large networks to squeeze out smaller, independent stations. The following year, the Reagan administration directed the FCC to cease enforcing the Fairness Doctrine, a 1949 law that required broadcasters to cover both sides of controversial issues and allow the victims of personal attacks the opportunity to respond on the air. With that legal requirement no longer hanging over their heads, talk radio hosts could declare open season on public officials of both parties without the fear of causing trouble for their employers or networks. Some sponsors were reluctant to be aligned with the mean-spirited rhetoric, but for every one that cancelled, two more were waiting to take their places.

Those changes in the law laid the groundwork for the next historical development that added to talk radio's resurgence: the presidency of Bill Clinton. While still competing with each other for audience share and advertising revenue, conservative talk radio hosts were united in their hatred for the new president and first lady. Against the background of the Clinton presidency, Limbaugh's popularity skyrocketed, and a legion of Limbaugh wannabes emerged, the most significant of these being G. Gordon Liddy, Ken Hamblin, and Ben Ferguson.

For three or more hours each weekday, Limbaugh and his protégés stirred the passions of their massive conservative audiences. Talk radio had found a new target, and hosts blasted the Clinton administration on everything from its failed attempt at health care reform to the loss of American lives in the bombing of two embassies in Africa. When Clinton aide Vince Foster committed suicide in 1993, talk radio hosts and callers floated a variety of conspiracy theories. But the biggest issue on which the talk radio programs feasted was Clinton's affair with White House intern Monica Lewinsky.

For weeks after Clinton left office, talk radio kept up its anti-Clinton agenda, chastising the former president for his eleventh-hour pardoning of numerous Democratic Party supporters. When that furor died down and the controversial election of 2000 was resolved, it looked for a brief time that talk radio might be headed for another downturn. With a new conservative president (George W. Bush) in the White House and a lack of controversy in the first eight months of 2001, it appeared that talk radio might once again run out of fodder.

Then came September 11. Talk radio enjoyed yet another rebirth, this time fueled by hatred of the Muslim world, an almost bloodthirsty quest for retribution, and frustration with the inefficiency of the newly created Transportation Security Administration. The audience was back, and so were the advertisers. When the Bush administration went to war against Iraq in 2003, the rhetoric became more heated and the audience grew even larger.

During the course of the war, a major technological development split the talk radio industry into two segments. With the advent of satellite radio, talk programming was now offered in two formats: traditional radio, funded by advertisers; and satellite radio, funded by subscribers. While the audience for the latter would be smaller—at least at the beginning—there were a number of perceived advantages. Unlike traditional radio, which is subject to federal licensing and regulation, satellite radio would be hindered by neither. It would also be unfettered by the Fairness Doctrine, should Congress choose to reinstate it. In addition, with no advertisers to placate, hosts could be as controversial as they wanted to be.

Unlike traditional radio networks that offer their listeners mostly conservative hosts and programming, satellite networks offer a variety of political perspectives. Conservative views such as those offered by Liddy, Ferguson, Bill Bennett, Mark Levin, and Michael Reagan are balanced by the liberal views provided by Bill Press, Thom Hartmann, Ed Schultz, Randi Rhodes, Robert F. Kennedy Jr., and Stephanie Miller.

In July 2008, the two largest satellite services—Sirius and XM Radio—announced plans to merge, and the new network, calling itself Sirius XM, debuted on November 12 of that year, claiming more than 19 million subscribers.

Much of satellite radio's liberal programming comes from Air America, a network that began in 2004. Air America had a promising beginning, with the original idea being hatched by investment banker Sheldon Drobny and his wife, Anita, in 2002. The couple had lined up preliminary funding and secured comedian and political pundit Al Franken as the biggest name in the talent pool, but before the network could be launched, the Drobnys sold the network's assets to Evan Montel Cohen, owner of several advertising agencies and market research firms on the West Coast. The network was launched amid great fanfare, but its success was short-lived. In October 2006, the network filed for Chapter 11 bankruptcy and sought protection from its creditors. Green Family Media, a small media company run by a pair of New York real estate investors, purchased the network in March 2007. The network filed for bankruptcy again early in 2010.

America's Newest Town Square—Maybe

In the two decades that followed the weakening of the Fairness Doctrine, the talk show format grew from about 400 stations to more than 1,400. For a while, talk radio had the well-deserved moniker of "America's Newest Town Square," and communications theorists analogized it to town squares of the late 1700s, where townspeople gathered on a regular basis to debate political issues of the day. But by the late 1990s, many of those same theorists conjectured that talk radio would eventually have to share that distinction with the Internet, which included bulletin boards, discussion groups, and other venues for political debate. That belief grew in the following decade, when Internet functions such as MySpace, Facebook, and Twitter expanded their audiences from teenagers and young adults to include all age groups.

"Talk radio remains one of the most important forms of communication worldwide," says Carol Nashe, executive director of the National Association of Radio Talk Show Hosts. "Not everyone has access to the Internet and (social) networking sites. But almost everyone has access to a radio. Talk radio is like standing in the backyard leaning over the fence and talking to your neighbors. It is instant, interesting, informational, and personal."[2]

Mike Stern, an associate editor for news and talk at *Radio & Records*, believes that while talk radio can still be a forum for public debate, that is not the medium's most appropriate role. "Radio is a form of broadcasting that is defined as communicating from one to many," Sterns says. "Therefore, what talk radio does best is provide a place for a large audience of consumers to hear experts—which we call hosts—and provide context to news and current events of the day. Just like it would be considerably more difficult for talk hosts to effectively share their knowledge and insight through more focused one-to-one mediums, it is considerably more difficult to engage everyone in the audience in the type of discussion implied by the concept of being 'America's town square.'"[3]

The optimistic view that talk radio will remain a viable forum for political debate is supported by academics who study and teach in the field of political communication and related fields.

Lloyd Rohler, who teaches communication theory and popular culture at the University of North Carolina at Wilmington, says talk radio will survive as a venue for political debate because it provides more access than cyberspace. "Everyone has access to a radio, but not everyone has access to alternative media," he says. "The audience for talk radio is not the same as the audience for the Internet, or for Facebook, or for Twitter. I think this is largely due to its passive nature. You only have to turn it on; you don't have to be actively in command of it to get access. This is not true of the Internet. Also, radio has an advantage in that it is 'live' in the sense that the listener hears the host and can identify with his voice and mannerisms or his way of identifying himself. It seems more real than just reading text on a screen. Some people see the host as a 'friend' they can turn to each day."[4]

Wayne Munson, professor of communications at Fitchburg State College in Massachusetts, believes that the passive nature of radio gives it an advantage over newer forms of media. "The talk show can and will still be a venue for public debate—despite the newer media—because radio listening is an activity one can do while doing something else, especially certain jobs," he says.[5]

Robert Thompson, a Syracuse University professor who teaches courses in the history of television and radio, agrees. "In the past, when a regular person wanted to say something publicly, he or she had only two outlets—talk radio and the newspaper editorial page," Thompson says. "In both cases you had filters; in talk radio you have a call screener and on the editorial page you have gatekeepers as well. In the case of the Internet, anyone with a minimum amount of technical skills has the potential to reach an international audience."[6]

The problem with the Internet, Thompson adds, is that its potential is seldom realized. "Except for the occasional YouTube sensation or other viral video, few people who communicate on the Internet reach anyone outside of their own circle of friends," he says. "For all the talk we hear about the role of the Internet in the political process, the number of people who actually participate is very small." That takes Thompson back to the role of talk radio. "When we think about talk radio our first thought is the raving lunatics (hosts)," he says. "But that's the national picture. There are some very good local shows that have gotten past the anger and do some very good work."[7]

Michelle Williams, associate professor of political science and government at the University of West Florida, believes that talk radio will remain an important venue for public debate, but mostly for older demographic groups. "It's a generational thing," Williams says. "Younger people might express their political opinions on Facebook or Twitter, but for most older Americans, talk radio is still going to be their main outlet, both as listeners and callers. In my research I measure civic engagement by associational memberships and political activism, and talk radio is something that seldom comes up, especially with younger voters."[8]

Nicole Hemmer, a fellow at Miller Center for Public Affairs at the University of Virginia, agrees, pointing out social media such as Facebook and Twitter have been significant in the field of political organization rather than political debate. "In terms of political debate, the effect of the Internet and social media outlets have so far been additive rather than revolutionary," Hemmer says. "But it seems to me these changes don't diminish talk radio, but rather make it an even more powerful institution. The relationship between conservative talk radio hosts and conservative blogs and news sites is symbiotic: Limbaugh sources his material through Web sites such as Politico, Drudge, The Corner, and Human Events, giving his material credibility; they return the favor. Further, the growth of the Internet and the increased popularity of Internet-based social media haven't yet had any dampening effect on talk radio. Talk radio, at least among conservatives, is a well-financed, politically-powerful institution, and as such, seems unlikely to be allowed to peter out. Among conservatives, listening to talk radio is a fundamental behavior that expresses political identity. I suppose other conservative media could replace it, but for now, talk radio has little to fear from Internet-based debate."[9]

Talk Radio Today

Beginning in late 1989 and throughout much of the 1990s, talk was the fastest-growing format on the AM radio dial. Today, about 520 AM and FM radio stations across the country have adopted an all-talk format, with nearly all offering a combination of local and nationally syndicated programming. In addition, hundreds of local stations offer talk programming for at least part of their broadcast day, bringing the total number of talk outlets to more than 1,400 and the total audience to more than 100 million. According to Pew Research, approximately 17 percent of Americans listen to talk radio on a regular basis, giving it greater reach than any format other than country music. While trends in politics and popular culture has increased the number of listeners, the growth in the popularity of car telephones (and later handheld cellular telephones), has increased the number of callers.

Conservative host Michael Reagan insists that the advantage of talk radio over other media is the quality and quantity of both the information and the feedback. "Next time one of the national news anchors puts out a lie or a distortion, try picking up the phone and see if you can get through (to talk to them)," he wrote in his 1996 book, *Making Waves*. "And when the newspaper gets a story wrong, what's your redress? If you're lucky, a correction may appear in a half-inch box on page J-19. Or you can write a letter, which may or may not be printed in editorial form three weeks later when it no longer matters. But in talk radio, the quality of the information you get is very good because errors are usually detected and corrected in a matter of minutes."[10]

Talk radio is a frequent target for criticism and ridicule by television commentators, but talk show hosts claim that attitude is based largely on professional jealousy. Those same hosts claim that talk radio has been eating into the television ratings and newspaper readership for two decades, but the research is difficult to quantify. Reagan added that "talk radio embarrasses print and broadcast reporters by reporting stories they had ignored, and talk radio has broken the stranglehold of the liberal media."[11]

One prominent observer of the genre is Brent Bozell, who founded a watchdog group called the Media Research Center and wrote a 2004 book titled *Weapons of Mass Distortion: The Coming Meltdown of the Liberal Media*. Bozell reports that liberals often deny the "liberal bias" charge against other forms of media by citing the conservative slant of talk radio, but then clarifies that he and other conservatives have never claimed the media overall is liberally biased—just the *news media*. "Those conservatives on talk radio are commentators, not reporters," Bozell wrote. "None reports the news, but rather they react to it analytically and, by necessity, with prejudice. No conservative on talk radio denies his conservative stance, which puts them in juxtaposition with the liberals in the news media, almost all of whom deny their own bias."[12]

More than a dozen national radio networks are all-talk, the leaders among them being Premiere, Westwood One, Salem Radio Networks, and Talk Radio Network. Satellite networks such as Sirius XM offers a variety of programming in addition to talk, but report that talk is among their most popular offerings.

Most of talk radio programming falls into one of four categories: political, sports, consumer/financial advice, and personal/relationship advice. Political talk is by far the most popular among listeners and advertisers, with sports a distant second. Prior to 2008, the most popular topics for debate were the war in Iraq, illegal immigration, and national security issues such as domestic spying and treatment of suspected terrorists. The election dominated the conversation for much of 2008, and throughout 2009 the discussion focused on the new policies of the Obama administration—including the bailouts of the banking and automobile industries and proposed health-care legislation.

While Limbaugh remains the most popular and well-compensated talent in political talk radio, he has been joined on the national stage by fellow conservatives Sean Hannity, Mark Levin, and Michael Savage. Conservative Laura Ingraham, while far behind the top four, is the most popular and well-paid woman in the field. Bill O'Reilly once held a significant share of the conservative talk radio market, but he left the business early in 2009 and in many markets his show was replaced by one of two syndicated programs hosted by former republican presidential candidates: Mike Huckabee and Fred Thompson.

One of the fastest-growing subgenres of talk radio is late evening talk, which is often nationally syndicated and runs from 11 p.m. to 6 a.m. in the eastern time zone, and gradually earlier in the central, mountain, and pacific time zones. Although the topics tend to be the same, the tone is often thoughtful rather than vitriolic. The trend began in the early 1980s with Ray Briem, a conservative working out of Los Angeles, and Alan Berg, a liberal working in Denver. A decade later, Michael Reagan got his start in that format before shifting to daytime.

From the early 1990s through 2004, one of the stars of the overnight time slot was David Brudnoy, who was syndicated out of WBZ in Boston. "You might say the difference is night and day," Brudnoy said. "The evening format takes on a different sound and feel. The issues and personalities may be the same, but there is a greater opportunity to probe and explore topics after the rush of the day is over. All-night radio provides listeners with a relaxed, extended chance to consider questions because it is a less frenetic and hurried time. Unlike daytime talk, which tends to be rancorous, all-night radio is calmer and more deliberative."[13]

While the "kinder, gentler" format for late-night talk radio was common, it was not exclusive. Some local stations and national networks moved their most outrageous and controversial hosts to the overnight time slots. While their programs were not necessarily "indecent" as defined by the FCC, the move was somewhat analogous to the "safe harbor" rule by which the FCC required stations to limit indecent programming to late-night hours. In the 1980s and 1990s, some hosts believed their late-night time slots gave them leeway to shock and offend. Examples included liberal host Mike Malloy and conservative extremists Alfred Strom, Pete Peters, and Mark Koernke.

Another trend is "hot talk," which is sometimes called "rock radio without the rock music." It appeals mostly to men between the ages of twenty-five and forty-four—the demographic group heavily sought after by advertisers—but is appealing to women in the same age group as well. At the top of hot talk list are Howard Stern, Eric "Mancow" Muller, and Michael "Lionel" Lebron. Most of their programs air during morning drive time, with discussion topics covering both politics and popular culture.

During the latter years of the Bush administration, talk circulated in Washington about the possible return of the Fairness Doctrine or similar broadcasting regulation aimed at creating ideological balance on the airwaves. While politicians and industry experts generally agree that any legislation in that area would not be as draconian as the original doctrine, the idea is still quite controversial. Republicans and conservatives are against any regulation in that area, claiming it would likely violate the First Amendment. Supporters of the idea, mostly democrats and liberals, suggest the idea is not to dictate media content, but instead to provide a variety of viewpoints. Toward that end, they suggest alternatives such as one or more laws aimed at providing more diversity in media ownership.

Conservative Slant

A recent study by the Center for American Progress found that more than 90 percent of talk radio programming is conservative. The study compiled samples from 257 news and talk stations owned by America's five largest media conglomerates and found that combined, they offered 2,570 hours per week of conservative programming and only 254 hours of programming considered "liberal" or "progressive." Media critic Tim Rutten wrote in a 2005 column that talk radio is a "wholly owned subsidiary of the Republican Party" and its task during Bush's second term was to "explain a president whose poll numbers were in a freefall."[14] Recent polls taken immediately following recent presidential and midterm elections indicate that voters who regularly listen to talk radio voted for republican candidates by a 3-to-1 margin.

According to a 1996 study by the Annenberg Public Policy Center, conservative programming is more likely to focus on foreign affairs and military issues, whereas programming generally considered liberal or moderate focuses more on family and education issues. The same study found that media articles about talk radio greatly overstate the conservative nature of talk radio, with many newspaper stories treating it as nearly all far-right in ideology. While conservative ideology still dominates, it is not exclusive.

For much of the last twenty years, conservatives have complained about an alleged "liberal bias of the media." Although academic studies typically find that no such bias exists—claiming that the liberal orientation of working journalists is counterbalanced by the conservative ownership of newspaper chains and television networks—the charge continues to be made by talk radio hosts, conservative watchdog groups, and individual authors who use dubious sampling techniques and anecdotal evidence to support their point.

Media critic and author Kathleen Hall Jamieson claims that Limbaugh and other less prominent talk radio hosts made allegations of media bias "a mantra," pointing to studies that show the majority of journalists vote for democratic candidates. Those same hosts, according to Jamieson, ignore other studies that show that while journalists tend to be liberal on social issues, most are conservative on economic issues.[15]

A 2003 study by the Benchmark Company, a marketing research firm, found that conservatives were far more pleased than liberals with the ideological makeup of talk radio programming. More than 85 percent of conservatives responded they were happy with the programming exactly as it was, while 40 percent of liberals felt the programming "lacked balance."

Gloria Feldt, past president of Planned Parenthood, blames the conservative slant of talk radio on its corporate ownership and claims that many issues related to women (including abortion) suffer as a result. "The right wing, by and large, owns the airwaves," she wrote in her 2004 book, *The War on Choice*. "Much of the media concentration, and the right-domination of the airwaves, has come about because of the events that took place under (President) Ronald Reagan."[16]

Celebrating Ourselves among Ourselves

The talk radio industry has its own monthly trade publication, simply titled *Talkers*, the content of which includes profiles of talk show hosts and a mix of articles and editorials about the future of the talk format—almost evenly split between the optimistic view (ad sales are up and let's hope it continues) and the pessimistic (ad sales are up, but they can't possibly stay up).

More than half of the content is display advertising, most of it promoting up-and-coming talent looking for syndication deals as well as established hosts looking to expand their audiences. In the back of each forty-eight to sixty-four-page volume are classified advertisements from employers seeking new producers, sales executives, and on-air talent; and from established hosts wishing to change jobs and potential newcomers trying to break into the business. It's an expensive subscription—$75 per year—and its 11 by 14-inch format does not fit neatly into the mailbox, but within the industry it's considered required reading for station managers, sales executives, and hosts.

Talkers also sponsors an annual New Media Conference in New York City, at which industry leaders meet to discuss trends in the business as well as troll among the participants for new talent. The conference took the place of a similar event once sponsored by the National Association of Radio Talk Show Hosts. The NARTSH has undergone numerous structural and leadership changes since its founding in the 1980s, and while it no longer sponsors the conference, it claims to still promote and speak for the industry.

Back to the Future

Whether the platform is AM, FM, or satellite, talk radio audience numbers remain constant, and there is little turnover among advertisers. According to the Talk Radio Research Project, administered by *Talkers* magazine, the audience for political talk is mostly white, male, affluent, and politically conservative. Confronted with those numbers, however, station managers, hosts, and advertising sales executives are quick to point out what they believe is a changing demographic. While the numbers will never be closely representative of the general population, the industry claims to be making inroads among the younger, female, and less affluent listeners, as well as those identifying themselves as moderates and liberals. In addition, many media markets have at least one station identifying itself as "black talk" or "Hispanic talk."

Evolving technology is one factor that will keep talk radio relative. "The rap by some is that radio is yesterday's technology," said David Wharton, executive vice president for media relations for the National Association of Broadcasters. "But with radio moving onto the (World Wide) Web, and with the arrival of HD (high definition) radio, we're trying to position it as a futuristic technology."[17]

From a financial standpoint, one of the benefits of local talk radio over other formats is its low cost. Local stations can often produce a talk show with three staffers: a host, executive producer, and engineer. At the national level, staffing is a bit more complex, as more thorough hosts will also employ a staff of researchers and pollsters.

A December 2002 Gallup Poll indicated that 21 percent of Americans get their news from talk radio. While that poll is more than seven years old, there is little reason to believe that number as shrunk and anecdotal evidence that it may have grown.

Host as Opinion Leader

In his 2004 book, *The Politics of Misinformation*, political scientist Murray Edelman wrote that most political debate is based on falsehoods and exaggerations. "All but a small minority of such discussion and claims are based on false beliefs, false information, false premises, and false logic," he wrote. "And whenever one party to a political dispute begins to indulge in misrepresentation, the incentive is strong for all others to do the same."[18] Edelman's assertions raise questions about the role of talk radio hosts—do they allow falsehoods to continue, point out the weaknesses and fallacies of their arguments, or add to them?

"Facts are not terribly key to talk radio," wrote Chris Mondiacs, a political reporter in New Jersey, in a 1992 column. "There are many instances in which talk show hosts seize on an issue without fully understanding it. They come from a perspective of accusing anyone who holds a government office of being corrupt."[19] Media critic Peter Laufer comments that "aspiring talk show hosts find it easier to get on the air if they are willing to adjust reality."[20]

In 2005, the Annenberg Public Policy Center and the University of Pennsylvania conducted an in-depth study of American media and their influence on the political process. One of the startling findings of the study was that almost as many Americans (27 percent) labeled Rush Limbaugh as a "journalist" as they did *Washington Post* Associate Editor Bob Woodward (30 percent).

Beyond their own audiences on radio, many hosts find larger audiences for their messages when they are invited to be "contributors" on television talk shows on Fox News, CNN, and MSNBC.

"Rush has been driving the democrats crazy for years," wrote Ann Coulter in her 2004 book, *How to Talk to a Liberal (If You Must)*. "Liberals keep serving up their own dreary hosts, and the public keeps turning the dial back to Rush Limbaugh."[21]

Liberal talk show host Arianna Huffington says "it has become more difficult to ignore the likes of Bill O'Reilly, Sean Hannity, and Rush Limbaugh. They're no longer the lonely kooks wandering in the wilderness; they've got access to the halls of power, and they're staying for dinner."[22]

Even hosts themselves reluctantly admit the image of the industry is plagued by public perception that it is based largely on the hosts' contempt for political opponents as well as their callers. "Every time I turn on the radio, almost everything I hear is the host throwing some sort of vitriol on the party that they don't like," wrote Minneapolis host Jack Rice in a 2007 column in *Talkers*. "And then they talk over the sycophants who call in and agree or denigrate those who don't. As if the program simply becomes a vehicle to stroke the ego of the host. And these hosts have millions of listeners."[23]

The role of talk radio in the 2008 presidential election is a topic of debate and disagreement. Many republicans believe the genre is at least partially responsible for the party losing both the White House and Congress, first by opposing the candidacy of eventual nominee John McCain, then by its lukewarm support for McCain in the general election. Democrats downplay the role played by talk radio and claim that democratic candidate Barack Obama would have won regardless of the role played by the industry.

Looking at the future, many talk radio hosts believe some of their colleagues are making a mistake by affiliating themselves with specific political ideologies—and also by taking themselves too seriously.

Liberal talk radio host Stephanie Miller believes the move toward the extremes is dangerous for the industry. "It's entertainment, period," she says. It's not about right wing or left wing. The minute we think we're a political movement, we're dead."[24]

Conservative host Michael Gallagher agrees. "We're entertainers, and that's all," he said in a media interview. "Not news, not journalists. We're broadcasters and entertainers with strong opinions. But our job is to entertain, to be funny, and to be compelling."[25]

Michael Smerconish, a Philadelphia-based talk show host and author of a 2009 book, *Morning Drive*, believes that citizens who get their information from talk radio and cable television are getting an artificially dichotomous view of the world. "The only people that I meet who see the world entirely through conserva-tive eyes or through liberal eyes are people in talk radio and cable television," he says. "But in my day-to-day existence, it's a mixed bag."[26]

Show Business for Ugly People

Talk radio in itself is becoming a topic for attention by both news reporters and media critics. "Music doesn't make news; personalities make news, and most of the people on radio who have any sort of cultural impact are doing one form of talk radio or another," says Michael Harrison, publisher of *Talkers* magazine.[27] One late-night television host, commenting on the expanding waistlines and receding hairlines of Rush Limbaugh and his cohorts, once quipped that talk radio represented "show business for ugly people."[28]

The trend of talk radio hosts making news instead of just commenting on the news began in the 1990s, but the best examples have occurred recently. In the fall of 2006, for example, Limbaugh generated controversy when he accused actor Michael J. Fox of exaggerating the symptoms of his Parkinson's disease while appearing in television commercials supporting a political candidate who favors federal funding for stem-cell research. The following spring, Don Imus generated a two-week firestorm of negative publicity after making racially insensitive remarks about the Rutgers University women's basketball team on his CBS Radio show that was nationally simulcast on the cable television network MSNBC.

Both stories called attention to talk radio's pension for outrage and the tendency of its hosts to generate controversy rather than just discuss it. Limbaugh received hundreds of complaints by telephone, U.S. mail, and electronic mail. Imus, after his network and sponsors received similar complaints from audience members and civil rights advocates, was fired by his network. By comparison, Limbaugh and Imus got off easy: In 1984, controversial host Alan Berg, one of the few successful liberal hosts at the time, was shot to death by white supremacists outside his Denver, Colorado home.

Talk Radio as Fiction and Fact

The phenomenon of talk radio is rarely illustrated in popular culture, but those rare instances are worth noting.

In *The Turner Diaries,* the controversial 1978 novel by white supremacist Andrew McDonald, an unnamed Jewish radio talk show host is murdered as he stepped from his car in the driveway of his home. Six years later, that scene was played out in real life as Berg was murdered in similar fashion.

The first television program dealing with the genre of talk radio was *Midnight Caller*, a primetime drama which ran on NBC from 1988 to 1991. Its central character, played by Gary Cole, was a retired police officer exploring a second career in talk radio. The success of the show was short-lived, however, but a more successful television representation came two seasons later in the form of *Frasier,* a weekly situation comedy about the life and work of a radio-talk show host in Seattle. Although the title character portrayed by Kelsey Grammer was a Harvard-educated clinical psychologist who dealt with issues of the mind rather than politics, the show, one of the highest-rated situation comedies during its eleven-year run on NBC, was credited for introducing the concept of the radio call-in show to audiences who had little previous knowledge of the genre.

The most significant entry in this category, however, was the 1986 Broadway play simply titled *Talk Radio*, written by veteran playwright and actor Eric Bogosian. The play, and later a movie of the same title (featuring Bogosian in the lead role), featured a character named Barry Champlain, which was loosely based on the life and death of Berg. Bogosian described the Champlain character in explaining, "If the callers don't provide the drama, the host will. He is a skilled professional, sculpting each show from the raw material available. He adroitly cuts off callers as it suits him, while egging on others, knowing just what the audience wants. He is an actor as well, playing the part of a sincere, concerned, and sometimes angered observer."[29]

In 2005, Mark Gelbart published a novel with the same title, *Talk Radio,* but a much different story line. Gelbart's work told the story of Buck Bennett, an obnoxious right-wing local talk show host with a tumultuous personal life. Liberal but loyal caller Richard Schmitt decides that Bennett has humiliated him on the air one time too many, so he kidnaps the host and holds him hostage in a make-shift jail cell, where the two have a series of conservative versus liberal debates reminiscent of the movie, *My Dinner with Andre.*

The talk radio genre made it to the cable television market in 2006 when Home Box Office produced a ninety-seven-minute film, *Left of the Dial*, which documented the months preceding the start-up of Air America as well as its first year of operation.

Chapter 2

The Audience:
Who Listens and Why

Less News, More Talk

Prior to the early 1990s, political talkers had a hard time finding good time slots at their respective stations. Many general managers relegated political talk shows to late-night and graveyard shifts, where hosts shared time with psychics, self-help gurus, and financial advisors. That changed when Rush Limbaugh reinvented the talk genre.

Some media critics point out that the rise in popularity of talk radio coincided with the television networks' downsizing of their news operations. As television news became more expensive to produce and less profitable from an advertising standpoint, news operations became streamlined. But since Americans' interest in politics remained constant, they sought out new sources of information and found it in talk radio—and they didn't seem too concerned that talk radio content was not subjected to the same degree of editorial scrutiny as television news. For many listeners, the fact that talk radio was so overtly biased seemed to add to its appeal.

The Holy Book

For radio station owners, general managers, and advertising sales directors, the industry holy book comes in the mail every few weeks in the form of the Arbitron ratings, which uses the same formula of audience shares and ratings points used by Nielsen Media Research to quantify television audiences. Each ratings point represents a certain percentage of the total number of televisions or radios tuned in to a specific program, while "share" refers to the percentage of televisions or radios in use at the time. General managers use both numbers in making decisions regarding programming and on-air talent, and advertising sales departments use them to determine the price tags they assign to certain programs. The advantage that talk radio has over television news is its lower cost and tendency for its audiences to be more segmented. A television news program with a 2 percent audience share would likely be overhauled, while one with a 7 percent share would be just barely surviving. But those same figures applied to radio programming would be quite different: a 2 percent audience share would be successful in most markets, while a 7 percent share might make it number one in its time slot.

Lies, Damn Lies, and Statistics

Some local talk show hosts and station executives don't subscribe—either literally or figuratively—to what Arbitron says about their stations' audiences. Ken Walsh, host of a WFTS-AM morning talk show in Fort Walton Beach, Florida, believes the Arbitron books are inaccurate and that his station's listeners are generally older than the ratings books report. "I know that from the phone calls and emails we get," Walsh says.[1] Down the road in Milton, Florida, WEBY general manager Mike Bates agrees. "We don't subscribe to the scientific data, and for the most part we work off our qualitative data," he says. "We know that most of our listeners are over 35 people with money—doctors, lawyers, and business owners. That's all we really need to know."[2]

Some general managers and advertising executives are also skeptical about the figures provided by the Talk Radio Research Project (TRRP), a 2006 demographic survey commissioned by *Talkers* magazine. They contend that their audiences tend to be slightly older than the national figures provided by the TRRP. Bates claims, for example, that the TRRP's figure of 74 percent for voter turnout is low, and that at least 90 percent of his listeners vote.

The TRRP also estimated that 55 percent of the audience was male, but recent interviews with a number of station managers indicated the gender split was much closer to 50-50. The TRRP also found that 57 percent of listeners identify themselves as "independent," but many hosts and station executives believe those are largely "right-leaning independents."

According to a 2003 study by Pew Research, 48 percent of regular talk radio listeners identify themselves as conservative, 23 percent as liberal, and 30 percent as moderate—with each category being within a few percentage points of reflecting the population as a whole.

The results of the TRRP were far more detailed and somewhat different from the Pew Research findings. According to TRRP, almost half of the talk radio audience is between the ages of forty-five and sixty-four, and more than a third is between twenty-five and forty-four. Approximately 55 percent of the audience is male, and more than 65 percent is white. Slightly more than 38 percent of listeners describe themselves as "conservative" or "ultra-conservative," while 23 percent describe themselves as "moderate." By income, approximately 65 percent of the audience claims an annual income between $30,000 and $70,000, with 23 percent claiming to be above that bracket and 12 percent claiming to be below it.

Less than 14 percent of the respondents in the TRRP study described themselves as "liberal" or "ultraliberal," and 25 percent said their political leanings vary by issue. Many political scientists indicate that based on political ideology, the "varies by issue" group is one of the fastest-growing psychographic categories in America.

In addition to expanding in a general sense, political talk radio is experiencing exponential growth in terms of stations catering to specific demographic and psychographic groups. Black talk radio stations are growing in number and popularity in New York, Chicago, Washington, D.C., and Philadelphia, while Hispanic talk radio is on the rise in Miami. Christian talk radio is gaining popularity across the nation as well.

Bates uses the term "listener inertia" to describe the habits of his audience. "We know there are people out there that keep their dials set on a certain station all day and never listen to anyone else, but that's not the norm," he says. "They may have a favorite station, but most of the audience listens to other stations at some point in the day. But many of our listeners are loyal to specific hosts, and they don't like it when we make programming changes."[3]

Bates points to the example of a switch he made, early in 2009, when he awarded the 6 to 9 p.m. weeknight time slot to Bruce Williams, replacing Michael Reagan. "A lot of people didn't like it at first because they really liked Reagan and all of a sudden he wasn't there," Bates says. "But once they gave Bruce a chance, they realized that they liked him. It took a few weeks, but our local audience decided to stick with us."[4]

Michael Mendelssohn, sales director at WCOA-AM in Pensacola, says the talk radio audience differs greatly from those who watch television—not only in demographic makeup, but in degrees of loyalty. "With television, people have favorite programs but they don't have favorite stations," he says. "In talk radio, it's both. They turn on the radio first thing in the morning and it stays on that same station all day."[5]

In 1999, media researcher Barry Hollander found that the "audience loyalty theory" does not always hold up. In his comprehensive study of the talk radio genre, Hollander found the audience for talk radio is subject to constant turnover, meaning that at any one time there may be a large number of people listening, but over the long term the effect of the programming they listen to is minimal.

One of the criticisms of the media coverage of the talk radio industry is its portrayal of the audience as being homogenous or monolithic. In addition, many print and broadcast stories focus their attention on the role of the hosts—usually the most outrageous or outspoken—and portray the industry as a whole as dominated by the crude and offensive. Media researcher David C. Barker suggests that such misleading media coverage is at least partially responsible for the genre's negative perception among nonlisteners.

Over the years, the talk show audience has grown in total numbers but has also changed significantly in demographic and psychographic make-up. Studies from the 1980s suggested the audience for talk radio was skewed toward older, less affluent, and lesser educated white men who were sociologically and politically alienated from the mainstream of society. While that stereotype persists today, more recent studies—including those conducted by *Talkers* magazine—indicate a shift toward younger, better educated, and more affluent listeners. Listening to the banter between hosts and callers, however, listeners and media critics get the sense that political and social alienation is still a factor.

Washington Post media critic Jonathan Yardley refers to the listeners of conservative talk radio as "marginal Americans" who, when they call into their favorite programs, "bristle with discontent and resentment." He dismisses the talk radio audience as "Americans on the margin—people who have an excessive liking for the sound of their own voices, people with too much time on their hands."[6]

Media researcher Tom Lewis adds that many talk radio listeners "had parents who were secure in their knowledge that America was the greatest land of all and they had the cars, houses, jobs, and standard of living to prove it. Today, these disillusioned sons and daughters find they must work two jobs just to drive smaller cars and live in smaller homes. The stability of their youth is a fading memory. Jobs are no longer secure; marriages are crumbling; violence is unfettered; and people who have long lived on America's margins—homosexuals, blacks, and women who desire something other than a traditional family life—now get government help and preferential treatment to move into the mainstream. *Their* mainstream."[7]

Political scientist Murray Edelman concluded that many talk radio listeners are individuals "who lack very many sources of self-respect and pride and must latch on to the general ones that are taught to everyone, such as attachment to the nation and the institutions that characterize it."[8] Communication researchers Cameron B. Armstrong and Alan M. Rubin add that many individuals who are isolated from others look at talk radio as an alternative to interpersonal communication.

The negative stereotype of talk radio listeners is disputed, however, by many communication researchers, media critics, and industry executives. Writing in the early 1990s, for example, media critic Michael Weiskopf described the typical talk radio listener as "poor, uneducated, and easy to command,"[9] and while individuals outside the field may accept that stereotype as true, communication researchers believe that generalization no longer applies—and may never have.

While the old stereotype of Joe Sixpack—the low income, beer-drinking, gun-owning conservative—will always come to mind when one conjures up images of the typical talk radio listener, recent research indicates that a growing number of both listeners and callers and higher-income moderates and liberals representing a variety of professions.

"The stereotyped liberal view of the talk radio audience is that it's a lot of angry, uneducated white men," says Dan Shelley, a former news director at WTMJ, a news/talk station in Milwaukee, Wisconsin. "In fact, the audience is far more diverse. Many are businesspeople, doctors, lawyers, academics, clergy, or soccer moms or dads. Talk show fans are not stupid."[10]

In 1994, a group of six political scientists, led by C. Richard Hofstetter of San Diego State University, conducted a study of the audience for political talk radio and found it to be quite different from what was previously thought. The old stereotype of talk radio listeners, the authors wrote, was formed over a twenty-five-year period and was basically a stereotype consisting largely of "individuals feeling alienation, social and political isolation, and cynicism."[11] But Hofstetter and his coauthors found that the true audience was one that defied stereotypes and was so diverse in age, race, gender, and political affiliation that it defied easy categorization. Instead of concentrating on the demographic or psychographic characteristics of the audience, the researchers therefore explored the reasons why the audience listened.

One of the few factors that media researchers agree upon is that the majority of the talk radio audience is listening while driving an automobile or at work. They disagree, however, on why people choose talk radio over the most popular alternative—music radio. The idealistic view is that listeners are seeking objective information they can use to make political decisions. The more popular idea, however, is that they merely seek out the hosts and programming that supports beliefs they already hold. Beyond those two theories, other reasons included simple entertainment, escapism, relief for boredom, relaxation, and passing time.

Among the hosts who believe talk radio provides objective information is liberal host Thom Hartmann, who claims there is more than enough room on the radio spectrum for a diversity of political viewpoints. "People interested in politics want more than just information—they want context," Hartmann says.[12] Diane Rehm, host of a popular syndicated show originating at WAMU in Washington, D.C., calls talk radio "the epitome of participatory democracy."[13]

In 1999, Hofstetter teamed with SDSU colleague Christopher L. Gianos to conduct a second study of the talk radio audience. The researchers found that in most communities, even listeners who described themselves as political progressives nonetheless listened to conservative hosts as a way to keep in touch with local politics. They also determined that many listeners—especially those with long automobile commutes—found that the intellectual stimulation of the discussions outweighed the listeners' philosophical disagreements with the hosts. In other cases, they believe the apparent inconsistency between the conservative agendas of the hosts and the progressive leanings of the listeners was based on the fact that the latter group was listening in order to pass the time rather than obtain new political information. They also theorized that in many cases, the tendency of the hosts to make outrageous comments are experienced by the listeners as humorous or even cathartic, despite disagreement with the hosts. Regardless of ideological orientation, listeners find in talk radio one appealing feature—the spontaneous give-and-take banter between host and caller—that they could never find in the structured world of television news or interview programs.

One of the factors that talk radio hosts and listeners have in common is their belief that the "mainstream media" (the term is often used in a derogatory sense) is biased toward liberal viewpoints and downplays the beliefs and accomplishments of politicians who are republican and/or conservative. Sharing that viewpoint helps conservative hosts turn occasional listeners into fully devoted fans, convincing them that talk radio is a place to which they can turn for news that the mainstream press either distorts or ignores. Many convince their listeners that talk radio represents their *only* outlet for unbiased information, when in reality, it is just as biased as the forms of media they rail about—but it's the type of bias the listeners can live with.

The so-called liberal bias of the press has become talk radio shorthand for anything the host disagrees with. Media critic William McGowan believes that a rise in the popularity of talk radio among conservative listeners is partly due to the mainstream media's emphasis on diversity and the well-being of minority groups. "Talk radio's surge in popularity is one of diversity's unintended consequences," he wrote in a 2001 book. "While it may not always have its facts nailed down, this populist, largely conservative medium does get out the news that mainstream journalists have long ignored or suppressed. It also gives voice to ideas and perspectives that have been shunned or derided by traditional news outlets where diversity-driven orthodoxy has crimped the parameters of acceptable discourse."[14]

Talk radio listeners are therefore more critical of the mainstream media than nonlisteners, but it is not clear from the research how to answer the chicken-and-egg-cause-or-effect question: Are talk radio listeners skeptical about the mainstream media because they've been told to be skeptical by the hosts, or do they listen to talk radio because they were already skeptical about the mainstream media?

Ken Walsh adds two other smaller categories of listeners: the ones who purposely listen to hosts with whom they strongly disagree (sometimes at the expense of their blood pressure), while others listen to hosts of the opposite political persuasion in order to "report back" to their fellow conservatives (or liberals) about what is being said in the opposition camp.

Long-Time Listener, First-Time Caller

In addition to studying the motivations of audience members to listen to talk radio, researchers have also explored the reasons why so few listeners take the time to call and the vast majority does not. Multiple studies have shown that callers make up less than 5 percent of the listening audience, with some having it as low as 1 or 2 percent.

While talk radio *listeners* may be representative of the population at large, talk radio *callers* are not. Numerous audience research studies, and anecdotal evidence gleaned by sampling a variety of programs, indicate that the majority of callers tend to subscribe to the same political ideology as the host—meaning that most callers to Limbaugh's show tend to be conservative, while callers to Ed Schultz's show tend to be liberal.

One factor separating callers from noncallers is their motivation for listening. Audience members who listen for information and intellectual stimulation are also opinionated and engaged with the subject matter and are therefore more likely to call. Those who listen to pass the time tend to be less opinionated, less engaged with the subject matter, and therefore less likely to call. "Most people are reluctant to call, but once they get on the air one time they usually realize that it's not so bad," Walsh says. "Then after they get off the air they hear other people calling in who agree with them. That increases the likelihood that they will call again."[15]

Media scholar Ian Hutchby points out that callers and hosts approach the conversation with much different objectives. "Callers call in to discuss with a host topics of interest to them, or to complain about matters of interest to them, or to contribute to ongoing debates about issues for which they harbor some concern, and so on," he wrote. "Hosts, on the other hand, frequently and indeed routinely engage in overly argumentative talk, disputing points with the caller, undermining the rational grounds for a caller's case, taking up positions contrary to caller's avowed positions on issues in question, and so forth."[16]

Randall Bloomquist, Washington bureau chief and talk radio columnist for *Radio & Records*, concluded that callers to talk radio "either have too much time on their hands or they have a wildly passionate feeling one way or another about an issue. . . . What you're hearing on the air is a very, very small sample of the public, and it's just not statistically valid."[17]

Although nearly all hosts and call screeners deny that the purpose of call screening is to eliminate callers who disagree with the host, the perception among media critics is just that. And when contrary callers are allowed to get through, hosts often attempt to humiliate them and present them to their audiences as evidence that people who disagree with them are not just wrong—they're subversive, unpatriotic, or stupid. "Thank you for proving my point, sir," is a typical retort Neal Boortz gives callers who he believes have their facts wrong. "You're an idiot."[18] Boortz is a libertarian but falls in line with the conservatives on many issues; he is adamant about his support for the Iraq War and efforts to beef up homeland security. When callers' questions indicate their opposition to the war or dislike of President Bush, he patiently gives them a minute or two of air time, then lets loose with a tirade of corrections and insults.

Limbaugh, on the other hand, admits that callers who agree with him and shower him with praise get preferential treatment. Like most talk radio callers, those who get through to Limbaugh typically begin by telling him how long they've been a fan. "The primary purpose (of taking calls) is not to provide a forum, but to make me look good," he said in a 1993 interview.[19]

Bloomquist added that "what you hear on talk radio is no more a pure reflection of what the public thinks than the op-ed section of the *Washington Post*," he wrote. "What you hear on talk radio is manipulated and refined."[20]

Media researchers who have examined the frequency and content of talk radio calls report that the percentage of listeners who actually call vary greatly based on the size of the audience, what is happening in the news at the time, and the popularity of the host. On national programs, determined listeners will begin calling hours before air time and then remain on hold for an hour or more before speaking with a call screener and then another hour on hold before getting on the air. Because of the time commitment, callers tend to be either those who work at other hours or are unemployed. Many callers give up before getting on the air.

Media researchers estimate the number who attempt to call to be about 5 percent of the listening audience, and those actually getting on the air represent less than 1 percent. Callers to local talk shows have substantially better luck, with much shorter hold times and nearly all callers getting on the air. The percentage of the overall listening audience getting on the air, however, is estimated to be less than 4 percent.

Christine Craft, former host of a talk radio program in San Francisco, says some callers are simply up for a fight. "It's almost a test for them to see if they can get past the call screener and then get past the abuse from the host to make their point," she says. "Some of the people who call in are just natural born debaters."[21]

Boortz adds that "the 2 percent of our listeners who take the time to call in do so because they're angry, and the other 98 percent who just listen do so because they're curious."[22]

Many communication researchers provide anecdotal evidence that while callers who disagree with the host but do so with weak arguments are allowed more air time than those with stronger arguments, and that women and the elderly get less air time than younger male callers.

Peter Laufer, author of the 1995 book, *Inside Talk Radio*, speculates that many local hosts create the impression among listeners that their phone lines are jammed, but much of that impression is false. "A skillful talk radio host leaves the impression that an endless number of callers are clamoring for the opportunity to get on the air, but that often is not the case," Laufer wrote. "Even the nationally distributed shows at times suffer from a dearth of callers."[23] Peter Collins, a local host in San Francisco, told Laufer that he was sometimes puzzled by the patience of callers who waited on hold for hours to talk to him or other hosts. "What amazes me is that people put participation in talk radio so high on their life priorities and are willing to call a show when they know they're going to be on hold for five to forty minutes," Collins told Laufer. "They know they're only going to get two minutes to talk and they know, at least subconsciously, that it's all stacked against them, that the host will win, that I control the button that will terminate their call."[24]

At nearly every regional or national meeting of political talk show hosts and executive producers, conversation turns to the issue of the "problem callers" who dominate talk radio programs by both the length and frequency of their calls. On the local level, both conservative and liberal hosts (as well as their call screeners) admit that their shows tend to attract a small number of repeat callers. Some of the consistent callers are welcome, as the hosts and call screeners recognize the names of those who have something important to say. But far more often, hosts will roll their eyes when the call screener announces the name of a frequent caller. Some of those callers are on the line every day, either repeating the same negative comments or the latest conspiracy theories they gave gleaned from Internet blogs or other dubious sources. As a result, some stations limit callers to one call per week, but many persistent callers will get around the rules by calling from pay phones, changing their names, and disguising their voices. At stations will small audiences, call screeners find themselves putting repeat callers through to the host simply because there is no one else on the line.

"All local talk stations have the problem of repetitive callers," says Uncle Henry, a local host in Mobile, Alabama. "In most cases it's our own fault. We could limit our callers to once a week, but we've chosen not to. When the same caller brings up the same issue over and over again we'll cut them off, but if they can at least choose different topics each time, we'll let them go."[25] Unlike other local hosts, who give specific instructions to call screeners about what types of calls to take, Uncle Henry trusts his call screener to use his own judgment. "All I need to know is their first name, where they are calling from, the topic of the call, and their approximate attitude," he says. "Our best shows are the ones that are as unstructured as possible."[26]

Bates contends that listeners seem to be more concerned than hosts about repeat callers. "A lot of people ask me why we let the same people call in every day," he says. "We do get some repeat callers, but it's not as much as you might think. It doesn't seem to be a problem for us as much as it is for other people."[27]

Emiliano Limon, former producer of local host John Ziegler's show in southern California, says the repetitive callers fall into two categories. "For one, you've got the hard-core talk-radio callers who just like to hear themselves on the air," Limon told *Atlantic Monthly* in 2005. "These listeners will sometimes vary their first names and home cities to the screener, trying to disguise the fact that they call in night after night. And then there are the ones who just, for whatever reason, respond to the topic. Of these, a certain percentage are wackos, but some wackos actually make very good callers."[28]

While few hosts make the effort to ban specific callers, many have banned certain topics from their programs. Boortz, for example, became so exasperated over the abortion debate early in his career that he no longer allows it to be brought up on his nationally syndicated program. "I could alternate calls from pro-lifers and pro-choicers on every show for the rest of my career and would never run out of callers," Boortz told his audience in 2006. "And it would never change anyone's mind. It's pointless to talk about. It takes time away from topics on which we might eventually find some agreement among the audience. But abortion is one of those issues upon which our society will never agree."[29]

Many local hosts in southeastern states have banned any discussion of the Confederate flag, a policy that has been in place since the late 1990s controversy over that flag flying over the state capitol building in Columbia, South Carolina. "That's one of those issues that was the same twenty years ago and will be the same twenty years from now," says Uncle Henry. "There's no point talking about it."[30]

Robert Thompson, a Syracuse University professor who teaches courses in the history of television and radio, believes that talk radio programs will always be limited in the number of people who can call because many people listen while involved in some other activity. "So many people are driving their cars or doing something else that prevents them from calling in," Thompson says. "And there is another large segment of the audience that is perfectly happy to be listeners rather than callers. But that's not that different from the old notion of the town square. Back in the colonial days, when the townspeople would gather in the town square to debate politics, it was always far more people listening than talking."[31]

If there is a way to expand the number of callers, Thompson says, it's to deal more with local issues than national. "They could expand their base of callers—and get better callers—if they focused on what their school board is doing and what their mayor is doing," Thompson says. "There are a lot of ways to do a good local radio show without trying to imitate what the national guys are doing and without trying to being a provocateur."[32]

It is not uncommon for callers to blame their problems on the hosts. In July 2008, a female caller accusing Limbaugh of denigrating women on the air also blamed him for causing her high blood pressure. Other hosts hear stories about listeners blaming them for car accidents allegedly caused by the hosts' outrageous comments during their shows.

Chapter 3

The Sponsors: Who Advertises and Why

The Hands That Feed

When Air America filed for bankruptcy in October 2006, media analysts did not blame its failure on the lack of a listening audience, but rather the lack of advertising support. More than ninety companies had instructed their advertising agencies as well as ABC Radio—which carried much of Air America's products—that they did not want their spots played on any Air America programs. The largest advertiser to balk was Hewlett-Packard, but the list also included Microsoft, Wal-Mart, Exxon Mobil, Cingular, McDonald's, the United States Navy, and the U.S. Postal Service. Media critics noticed that all of those organizations were also frequent advertisers on Fox News (television) as well as conservative talk radio stations, but they denied they were coerced into choosing one over the other. Hewlett-Packard indicated it simply wanted to avoid "inappropriate or controversial programming environments."[1]

Unlike newspapers and magazines, which derive part of their revenue from home delivery and newsstand sales, and cable television, which generates income through subscriptions, talk radio (except for satellite services) is wholly dependent on advertising sales. That economic reality is apparent when comparing the success of conservative talk radio programming to its liberal counterpart. Long before Air America's difficult beginnings, libertarian host Neal Boortz blamed the failure of liberal talk radio on its inability to produce the audience numbers that in turn would generate advertiser support. "A liberal host can simply not generate the numbers and the ratings and the listener response and the business for the advertisers that a conservative can," he said in a 1999 interview.[2]

Great Expectations

Surveys of advertising content on local and national talk radio indicate that its roster of sponsors is somewhat different from the list of sponsors purchasing space and time in other forms of media.

A thirty-day sampling of talk radio advertising on several AM and FM stations in northwest Florida found that with few exceptions, both local and national sponsors advertised almost exclusively in that medium, to the exclusion of music radio, television, newspaper, magazine, and billboards. Some of those sponsors spend additional advertising dollars on Internet advertising, but even those companies still spend far more on talk radio.

The most often-heard ads aired during local talk programming (usually early morning and late afternoon) were for private schools, restaurants, and home improvement/construction suppliers such as plumbers, locksmiths, electricians, security system consultants, and retailers of lumber and concrete. Many of those spots were heard three or more times per hour and also aired on several competing stations. Ads heard less than three times per hour (often only once in a two-hour program) included those for karate and self-defense schools, automobile dealers, auto repair shops, a document storage and shredding company, a pawn and gun shop, and a computer repair shop.

Toward the end of the thirty-day sampling period, many counties in the listening area began seeing and hearing ads for local political candidates in other media outlets, including music radio, but political ads were rarely heard on talk radio. Several advertising executives commented that democratic candidates in the area would "never" advertise on a program that openly opposed their candidacies, and republican candidates tended to shy away for fear of being associated with some of the controversial hosts. At several stations, hosts had drawn the line and said there were enough nonpolitical advertisers available to preclude the need to accept political advertising. They feared that accepting political spots blurred the lines between advertising and commentary and created an in-studio climate in which they might be reluctant to criticize a sponsor. Advertising sales managers indicated they would have no problems with the potential perceptual problems (listeners believing the station or host was endorsing a particular candidate), but hosts believed otherwise.

National programming studied during the same thirty-day-sampling period featured advertising for companies offering a variety of financial services, including tax accounting, on-line postage, identity theft protection, and get-out-of-debt programs. Unlike local advertising, which seldom attempts to lure listeners to an advertiser's World Wide Web site, much of national advertising is designed to do just that. Advertisements for gold brokers, discount pharmacies, weight-loss programs, computer dating services, on-line legal services, hair loss remedies, and drug and alcohol treatment centers typically provided listeners with just enough information to pique their interest, then closed by encouraging them to go to the Web for more information.

Shortly after the 2008 presidential election, *The Sean Hannity Show* and other syndicated programs hosted by conservatives began carrying sixty-second spots for the Survival Seed Bank, a California-based on-line retailer specializing in preparing for nationwide food shortages. Under the new president, the ads implied, food will be scarce, and that will result in higher prices and empty store shelves. The spots make vague references to "a belligerent lower class demanding handouts" and "an emerging totalitarianism seeking control over every aspect of our lives." The company's most popular products include "enough seeds for a survival garden" for $149, a DVD explaining "food storage secrets" for $39.95, and a booklet titled "Preparing for a Crisis" for $20.00. The company existed long before the election, of course, but the victory by a liberal candidate helped with sales.

The More Things Change, the More They Stay the Same

A 1966 study commissioned by CBS Radio indicated that advertising on talk radio was twice as effective as the same amount of advertising on music radio, but for roughly the same cost. More than four decades later, executives with talk radio networks and advertising agencies agree that the same formula applies today, as the audience for talk radio tends to be slightly more affluent, and in urban areas the format tends to stand out in a market crowded with music stations.

Those executives contend that advertising on talk radio is more cost-effective than that on music radio because the audience is more engaged with the programming. Instead of passive background music in homes, cars, and offices, talk radio provides active, sometimes in-your-face programming that primes the listener to pay attention to the advertising as well.

"The big advantage is that the listeners who are engaged are *really* engaged," says Brenda Franco, senior account executive at WFTW-AM in Fort Walton Beach, Florida. "It's a small audience, but it's very loyal. Our advertisers get a lot more from their spots on talk radio than they would get from music radio."[3]

Dave Windsor, sales director at WNRP-AM in nearby Pensacola, agrees. "Radio is active," Windsor says. "People listen with a passion they're not going to find in the newspaper or on a billboard."[4]

Michael Mendelsohn, director of advertising sales at WCOA-AM in Pensacola, says that while all forms of advertising are most effective when stretched out over a long period of time, the rule is especially true for talk radio. When a potential client wants to purchase only a small number of spots (sometimes only one), he advises them to spend the money elsewhere. "For most clients we start with six-month commitments and work our way up to a year," he says. "We tell our advertisers that they need to be known long before they are needed, and in order to do that, they have to advertise with us for the long-term. For most of their customers, they hear the ads but there has to be a triggering event. For a jewelry store, they hear the ads every day for several months, and the triggering event is their wedding anniversary. For a lawyer, someone may hear the ads every day for several months, and the triggering event is a traffic accident or lawsuit. In those cases, they're more likely to call someone who they've heard advertising on the radio rather than going to the phone book."[5]

While much of talk radio advertising is aimed at individual consumers, many radio sales executives say their most successful form of advertising connects businesses to other businesses. "It's definitely B-2-B," Mendelssohn says. "A lot of our clients are small businesses attempting to advertise to other small businesses. Those small businesses put a lot of trust in us. They don't have a lot of dollars to spend, so every one has to count."[6]

Advertising time on talk radio can range from $50 to $70 per minute in small markets (populations under 100,000), $200 to $400 in midlevel markets such as Atlanta or Orlando, and $400 to $800 per minute in major metropolitan areas such as New York or Chicago. The major variables are time of day, personality of the host (in most markets, spots aired during Limbaugh's program cost twice as much as the hosts that come before and after him), and long-term commitment. Advertisers making a yearlong commitment can typically cut the per-minute cost in half.

Federal Communications Commission and Federal Elections Commission rules require that broadcasters provide equal access to all candidates and at the lowest rate paid by nonpolitical advertisers. That means that if a local car dealer makes a two-year commitment to a station to buy daily ads that average out to $5.00 per thirty-second spot, that station must offer political candidates the same $5.00 rate, even without the long-term commitment. Stations are also not allowed to raise their rates just for an election season.

Some stations have in-house production facilities and writers who can work with clients to develop their ads, but most advertising staffs prefer to work exclusively with advertising agencies. Most agencies have talented writers and access to high-quality production studios, while radio stations have the staff and facilities but seldom have the time. Stations rarely accept spots that have been written and produced by the advertisers themselves. "We get those requests from time to time," Mendelssohn says. "And we always say no. We sometimes ask them if they would perform surgery on themselves. They may be experts in how to run their business, but we're the experts in how to sell their business."[7]

Big Names, Big Bucks

While some advertisers are happy simply having their ads run during the Limbaugh program, others pay the extra money to have Limbaugh read them himself, but in exchange Limbaugh insists on a long-term commitment from the sponsors. Recently he added a third option: incorporating a mention of the advertiser's product or service into his banter. During the 2008 primary season, when a caller reported having voted for Hillary Clinton, Limbaugh responded with a comment about such a vote might warrant having to take two hot showers afterward—a task more pleasurable if the caller had purchased a Rinnai tankless water heater—one of Limbaugh's sponsors.

Some hosts go beyond simply reading the ads and overtly endorse products on the air. The most common beneficiaries are companies dealing with on-line legal services, weight-loss programs, and investment opportunities. In many cases the segues between the prerecorded, host-read advertisements and the regular content of the programs are so smooth that listeners struggle to tell the difference. This is a major difference between the ethical standards of talk radio hosts and those of more traditional radio and television journalists, whose employers would not allow such ventures into murky ethical areas. While Limbaugh, Boortz, and Hannity—three hosts who rake in thousands of endorsement dollars each year—see no ethical problems in such activity, that view is not shared by media ethicists and some practitioners.

Bill Press, a television commentator who occasionally fills in for Ronn Owens on KGO radio in San Francisco, agrees. "Frankly, even if they do own the product, I don't believe talk-show hosts should be doing personal endorsements," Press wrote in his 2001 book, *Spin This!* "In so doing, I think they damage their credibility. They should stick to being a good talk-show host, not a slick huckster."[8]

Michael Smerconish is one local host who learned the hard way what happens when a host's independence and stubbornness is in conflict with the station's advertising interests. One night in 1997, the popular host at WWDB in Philadelphia had booked an interview with journalist Lisa DePaulo to discuss a high-profile murder case she was covering for *George* magazine. At the last minute, the station's management cancelled the interview to make room for a one-hour paid infomercial in which Smerconish was asked to interview a local advertiser about a nonprescription cream that allegedly shrunk the prostate. Smerconish refused to do the interview and then boycotted his own show in protest—a tactic that kept him off the air for almost a month. He ended up at another station in town.

Lightning Rods

According to the advertising industry's premier publication, *Advertising Age*, the 2007 flap over Don Imus and his racially offensive remarks about the Rutgers University women's basketball team (discussed in more detail in chapter 8) illustrated the power that advertisers wield in determining program content and the job security of hosts. Within days, Procter & Gamble cancelled its advertising on MSNBC's cable television simulcast of Imus's radio show, and once it became apparent the company had the attention of both MSNBC and CBS Radio, other advertisers followed, including Geico, Staples, American Express, Sprint, PetMeds, General Motors, and GlaxoSmithKline.

A Procter & Gamble spokesperson claimed the company took action in order to "be accountable to customers. . . . this particular venue where our ads appeared was offensive to our target audience. And that's not acceptable to us."[9] A spokesperson for Sprint added, "We do not want our advertising associated with content which our customers and the public find offensive."[10] Several of the advertisers reported that their contracts with MSNBC specified only that the ads would run during the day but not specifically during Imus's three-hour slot. Once CBS Radio announced Imus's initial two-week suspension (before his eventual firing), Sprint and PetMeds requested that their ads not be included during the reruns of Imus's show that would be aired in his absence.

But the flack didn't begin with decisions made by advertisers; it actually began several days earlier when those advertisers were pressured to act by their customers and a number of civil rights groups. "Those events underscore what many pressure groups had proved in similar content controversies—that the best way to effect change in media is to go after the advertising dollars," wrote Andrew Hampp in *Advertising Age*. "There are so many media options today that it is easier for a marketer to pull out of a media outlet than put up with the negative publicity and the risk of a fall-off in sales."[11]

In 1993, pet food manufacturer Hartz Mountain contracted with the Westwood One network to advertise on a variety of talk radio programs but specifically instructed the network that the ads were not to run during Limbaugh's show. The following year, the Florida Citrus Commission came under fire from women's groups when it signed a million-dollar contract to advertise on Limbaugh's program. A National Organization for Women spokesperson called the decision "insulting, offensive, and unwise."[12] NOW organized a boycott of citrus products produced in Florida and took credit when the original six-month contract was not renewed.

While hosts such as Limbaugh and Bill O'Reilly earn the wrath of advertisers based on the overall tone of their programs, other sponsors cancel their advertising—or threaten to—based on specific incidents. Conservative host Michael Savage is the best example. In July 2008, Savage offended parents of autistic children by calling autism a "fraud" and claiming that "99 percent of autism cases were a result of lax parenting."[13] Unlike the massive defection of advertisers that led to the firing of Imus, only one advertiser—AFLAC—announced it would cancel its sponsorship of Savage's program. The previous year, however, more than a dozen advertisers withdrew their sponsorships after Savage's repeated comments about Islamic-Americans. The advertising boycott was organized by the Council on American-Islamic Relations.

Not only will some advertisers refuse to buy time during the programs of Limbaugh, Savage, or other controversial hosts, but some go as far as refusing to buy time on any station that carries a specific host, even if the sales staff can promise the ad in question won't be heard during that particular program.

Mendelssohn cites fast-food retailer Chick-fil-A, a company with strong Christian-based leadership and a squeaky-clean corporate history, as one example of a local advertiser insisting its advertising messages are heard only during noncontroversial programming. "Many of our advertisers have fundamental, moral, philosophical, or political differences with some of our programming," Mendelssohn says. "It's a juggling act."[14]

But Mendelssohn added that the reverse is much more common—advertisers asking for their slots to be aired only during specific programs. "Some of our clients will say 'only during Rush (Limbaugh)' or 'only during Sean (Hannity),' and they're very insistent about it," Mendelssohn says. "We do the best we can to accommodate them, but compared to other media, we're at a disadvantage. We have only twelve slots per hour, and once we run out we can't create more. A newspaper can print more pages and a billboard company can put up more billboards, but we work under limitations that we can't do anything about."[15]

There are fewer and fewer local stations that attempt to mix both music and talk into their programming. The reasons are largely economic—music stations have larger payrolls but corresponding higher advertising revenue, while talk stations have lower payrolls and less revenue. Stations attempt to mix the two formats find they don't work well together, and both listeners and advertisers shy away. In 2000, a Baltimore-area FM station abandoned the idea of a split schedule after advertisers became irritated with the station's controversial talk show hosts and asked, "Why can't you just play music?" Once the station dropped the talk part of its format, it told local advertising agencies that they "never again had to worry about your client's commercial airing next to controversy."[16]

Blurring the Lines between Advertising and News

Many talk stations offer local programming during the morning drive and begin their syndicated programming in the early afternoon. In between many offer thirty- and sixty-minute programs with titles such as "Ask the Experts," which feature advice on topics ranging from personal finance to automotive repair. In most cases the programs are hosted by one of the station's local advertisers that pay for the time, but station managers are reluctant to use the term "infomercial." The programs seldom do well in the ratings, but are an easy source of advertising revenue for the station and anecdotal evidence indicates the programs are popular with listeners and callers. Hosts find that callers interested in politics are often too busy to call in during that time of day, but the phone lines light up when the in-studio guest invites questions on home repair or financial planning. "Journalism purists might cringe at the idea, because it blurs the lines between news and advertising," says one local station manager. "But in tough economic times, you have to do what you have to do."[17]

Blurring the Lines between Advertising and Politics

The power of talk radio advertising to influence congressional legislation is best illustrated by the successful campaign to defeat President Clinton's proposed health care reform package in 1994. A coalition of interests representing the health care industry purchased advertising time on the talk shows of a number of conservative hosts. Not only did the advertisements themselves provide a 1-800 number for listeners to call, but hosts echoed their opposition to the legislation before and after the spots. During the week prior to the congressional vote, it was sometimes difficult to tell the difference between the paid ads and the subsequent one-sided discussion among the hosts and callers. On the other end of the 1-800 phone lines was a telemarketing firm employed by the health care industry to field the calls and pass them on to the callers' congressional representatives. According to consumer advocates John Stauber and Sheldon Rampton, "Those congressional staffers answering the phones had no idea those constituents had been primed, loaded, aimed, and fired at them by the radio ads, paid for by the insurance industry, with the goal of orchestrating the appearance of overwhelming grassroots opposition to health care reform."[18]

Chapter 4

The Conservatives

Multitaskers

Anyone doubting the role of talk radio in American politics and popular culture need only to conduct a brief keyword search on the Library of Congress' World Wide Web site. Between 1992 and 2007, more than two dozen books were published on the topic, most of them written by or about the genre's leading conservative personalities—including nine written by or about Rush Limbaugh. Another six were written by or about Bill O'Reilly, although most focused on his Fox News television program rather than his radio show. Radio hosts in general, and conservative talkers specifically, have become experts at multitasking: in addition to hosting their programs, they write books, do book-signings and other public appearances, and are sought out by television news interview programs for their perspectives on current events.

Limbaugh, along with fellow conservatives Michael Savage, Sean Hannity, and G. Gordon Liddy, often entertain their audiences by spreading conspiracy theories. In the past, their favorite tall tales have included those regarding the death of White House lawyer Vince Foster and unsubstantiated reports that the administration of President Bill Clinton had rewarded campaign contributors with burial rights at Arlington National Cemetery for the donors' family members who were not eligible for burial there.

James Fallows, in his 1996 book, *Breaking the News*, describes the "conspiracy theory" and "us against them" approaches as being crucial to talk radio's success. "When listeners tune into (Rush) Limbaugh each day, they know that he will fit the varied events of the preceding hours into the same dramatic structure he had established for them before," Fallows wrote. "This is the struggle of good versus bad, conservatives versus liberals, spokesmen for common sense versus enviro-wackos."[1] Other talk show hosts are equally adept at developing pictures of good and evil they can easily fit into any event.

Many conservative hosts believe that part of their responsibility is to provide an alternative to what they perceive as a liberally biased news media. Ultraconservative commentator Ann Coulter contends that conservative talk radio will always draw larger audiences than its liberal counterpart because it has a "built-in audience unavailable to liberals: people driving cars to some type of job."[2]

The criticism of talk radio for its perceived far-right-leaning stance on most social and political issues leads to occasional hyperbole. Poet Allen Ginsburg, writing in the liberal magazine *The Progressive,* for example, claimed quite seriously that if Limbaugh and other conservatives gained real power, the result would be "concentration camps and death marches."[3] Comedian-turned-liberal talk show host-turned-politician Al Franken claims that the perception of a "left-wing press" is a misnomer, but that the perception of a "right-wing press" is very real. "It's Fox News, the *Washington Times,* the *Wall Street Journal* editorial page," Franken says. "And of course, talk radio in general."[4]

Media critic Tim Rutten wrote in a 2005 column that talk radio is a "wholly owned subsidiary of the Republican Party" and its task during Bush's second term was to "explain a president whose poll numbers were in a freefall."[5]

The alleged tendency of conservative talk radio hosts to use inflammatory rhetoric and exaggerate or misstate the facts has created a cottage industry consisting of those scrutinizing or debunking their more outrageous material. Media watchdog groups such as Media Matters for America and Fairness and Accuracy in Reporting (FAIR) have had Limbaugh and O'Reilly in their sights for more than a decade.

One blogger wrote in 2008 that talk radio hosts are by nature "intellectually dishonest" and tend to overrely on dubious sources.[6]

Despite the large quantities of criticism dumped on conservative talk radio, the genre still draws praise from a number of credible voices. Former House Speaker Newt Gingrich cites three reasons behind the success of conservative talk radio. "First, they give people a place to ventilate and have a public dialogue rather than simply being lectured to by the elite communicators," he wrote in his 1995 book, *To Renew America.* "Second, they have created a unifying sense of confidence among millions of listeners that it is okay to be conservative and challenge the liberal wisdom. Third, when the elite media have tried to distort the news, the (radio) talk shows have a pretty good record of setting things straight over the following four or five days."[7]

Though they repeatedly denied it, during the Bush administration conservative talk show hosts received daily email updates from the White House, Republican National Committee, and GOP campaign operations. The "talking points" memos were collections of factoids that supported republican positions on the wars in Iraq and Afghanistan and an array of other international and domestic issues, including pending congressional legislation. In addition to those sources, many conservative hosts consult the Web sites of Limbaugh and Hannity, as well as those of conservative bloggers, for daily material.

"They (conservative hosts) are popular and powerful because they appeal to a segment of the population that feels disenfranchised and even victimized by the media," says Dan Shelley, a former news director at WTMJ, a news/talk station in Milwaukee, Wisconsin. "These people believe the media are predominately staffed by and consistently reflect the views of social liberals. This view is by now so long-held and deep-rooted, it has evolved into part of virtually every conservative's DNA. To succeed, a talk show host must perpetuate the notion that his or her listeners are victims, and the host is the vehicle by which they can become empowered. The host frames virtually every issue in us-versus-them terms. There has to be a bad guy against who the host will emphatically defend those loyal listeners."[8]

Many critics believe that conservatives' constant drumbeat about the "liberal media" is the equivalent of the "work the ref" strategy employed by basketball coaches. The idea, they say, is to complain long enough and loud enough that those media sources will eventually become self-conscious about their work and eager to disprove accusations of liberal bias.

In some cases, the conspiracy theories are offered by the callers rather than the hosts. While a handful of hosts challenge the callers to provide the sources of their information, the majority allow them to disparage public officials, political candidates, entertainers, and professional athletes with tales of alleged criminal behavior and sexual misconduct. Many victims of the negative and often untrue rhetoric respond to it the same way they respond to supermarket tabloids and Internet discussion boards—they ignore it.

Likewise, many media critics downplay the impact of the disparaging talk. In his 2009 book, *Bloggers on the Bus: How the Internet Has Changed Politics and the Press,* media critic Eric Boehlert wrote that it would be "unfair to judge conservative talk radio based on a few nutty callers."[9]

Open Mike

Barry Farber grew up in a Jewish household in Greensboro, North Carolina. His parents believed in exposing him to a variety of cultural experiences in school and various summer camps, and by the time he graduated high school he spoke five languages—Chinese, French, Spanish, Italian, and Norwegian—in addition to English. While attending the University of North Carolina he learned Russian, and shortly after college his world travels gave him the opportunity to learn Serbo-Croation and Indonesian.

As a newspaper reporter in the 1950s, he covered international issues, many of them related to the Cold War and the plight of Europeans wanting to emigrate to the United States. His radio career began when broadcasting executive William Safire hired him to be a producer at WINS in New York City. He soon began hosting his own show, which he called *Barry Farber's Open Mike*. In 1962, he moved to cross-town rival WOR-AM. After a brief attempt at politics—he lost to Bella Abzug in the 1970 race for the U.S. House of Representatives—he retreated to the radio booth for another seven years. After losing the 1977 New York City mayor's race to Ed Koch, he decided his future involvement in politics would be as a commentator rather than a candidate. In 1991 he was named "Talk Show Host of the Year," and today his show is syndicated by Talk Radio Network.

Farber's commentary is conservative but fairly noncontroversial, unlike that of Limbaugh, Hannity, and Savage. He also differs from those three in that he has resisted tempting offers from the publishing industry to capitalize on his radio success and move into the world of political books. He has written four books, but three of them deal with public speaking and one with learning foreign languages. His books on public speaking include *Making People Talk, How to Conceal Stupidity,* and *How to Not Make the Same Mistake Once.*

The Man You Love to Hate

Although some media historians would put Bob Grant's program in the category of "hate radio," most simply put him on the far right side of the dial—strongly conservative but not extreme enough to deserve sharing a category with Joe Pyne, the host who gave Grant his start.

Born Robert Gigante in Chicago, he got his start in radio while in high school, where his success in drama club productions left him yearning for a larger stage. He tried out for and earned a position with the school system's radio station, which meant that once every two weeks he was excused from class for an afternoon. He later attended the University of Illinois, where he worked at the campus radio station and pursued a degree in journalism. After graduation, he began working in radio at the news department at WBBM in Chicago in the 1940s. His superiors convinced him that he needed an "American-sounding" name, so he changed his name to Bob Grant. He later switched from news to sports and became sports anchor at KABC in Los Angeles, where he met Pyne, the station's controversial and hateful political talk show host.

On November 22, 1963, station managers feared what might happen if Pyne, an ultraconservative Kennedy hater were to do his regularly scheduled late-afternoon show following the president's assassination. They asked Grant to fill in, and he reluctantly agreed to do so. He never went back to sports.

Grant blossomed in the new format and relished his role in discussing political issues and candidates. He admitted in his autobiography, *Let's Be Heard*, that he was an admirer of 1964 presidential candidate Barry Goldwater but was forced to hide his support for fear of violating the Fairness Doctrine, a law that required broadcasters to cover both sides of political issues. While interviewing California gubernatorial candidate Ronald Reagan, Grant clearly outshined his guest in their relative grasps of the complexities of state politics. Toward the end of the show, the gap was so obvious that callers began to suggest the two change places, with Reagan hosting the show and Grant running for governor.

Eventually, Grant realized there would not be enough room for both him and Pyne at KABC, so he moved to New York to work at WOR. He later moved to WWDB in Philadelphia before returning to New York in 1984 to begin a twelve-year run at WABC, where his show became nationally syndicated.

In 1990, when New Jersey's more powerful conservatives were all backing Republican Christie Todd Whitman in her senatorial race against incumbent Bill Bradley, Grant declined to do so. He later said it was because he considered Bradley's re-election was a "done deal," but when Whitman made it a closer race than anyone expected, many of her supporters blamed the loss on Grant's silence. Three years later, Grant got the opportunity to atone for the slight by backing Whitman in her run for the New Jersey governor's office against incumbent Jim Florio. After several weeks of on-air criticism of Florio, the incumbent was quoted in a Philadelphia newspaper as asking the rhetorical question, "How can I win with Bob Grant beating my brains out every day?"[10]

Whitman won the election easily, and after publicly thanking Grant for his help on numerous visits to his show, within a year she was returning the slight from the previous campaign. "While Bob Grant has never used offensive or inappropriate language while I have been on his radio show, I am disappointed that he has begun to use his influence over the airwaves to spread hate or bigotry," she said in media interviews. "Consequently, I have decided to decline any future invitations to appear as a guest on Mr. Grant's show."[11] Grant responded that Whitman was "treating him like a pair of old shoes. . . . use them on a rainy day, and after the storm is over, you throw them in the trash."[12]

Throughout his career, Grant was skeptical of political correctness, critical of the animal rights and environmental movements, opposed to the Americans with Disabilities Act, and opposed to expanding laws to protect employees from sexual harassment in the workplace. On his show, he advocated gun ownership and more respect for law enforcement officers. In his only public position inconsistent with conservative traditions, he gave lukewarm support for abortion rights.

Despite his popularity, allegations of racism followed him through much of his career. In 1994, *New York* magazine published a cover story about Bob Grant titled "The Man You Love to Hate." Later that year, a second profile was titled "Why He Hates Blacks." The focus of the second article was on Grant's comments regarding Haitian refugees who had drowned attempting to get to Florida on substandard boats. Grant had told his listeners, "Well, if we stop picking them up, they would stop making those boats, and setting out from Port-au-Prince and risking their lives."[13] When a caller asked Grant what he would do about those who drowned, he replied, "If they drown, word would go back to Port-au-Prince and they would stop coming."[14]

Although he seldom used terms such as "black," civil rights leaders and other critics claimed that Grant used code words such as "inner-city residents" and "welfare mothers" (who he suggested should be sterilized after having two children) to relay racist messages to his audience. Grant railed against immigrants, referred to black churchgoers as "screaming savages," complained that basketball player Magic Johnson's HIV had not yet turned into AIDS, and suggested that rude taxi drivers be shot.[15]

He saved his most outrageous comments, however, for public officials. Among his favorite targets were President Bill Clinton, who he called "the Great Stain-maker," New York City mayor David Dinkins, an African American who he called "the men's room attendant," and New York governor Mario Cuomo, who he called by several Italian epithets understood only by other Italians.[16]

Grant's stint at WABC came to an end on April 3, 1996, when he was fired for commenting on the plane crash that killed Commerce Secretary Ron Brown. When preliminary news reports indicated that one person had survived the crash, Grant predicted on the air that the "lone survivor was likely Brown. . . . but I only say that because I'm a pessimist."[17] Grant's firing created an opening in afternoon drive time that was filled by a young radio rookie named Sean Hannity.

After leaving WABC, Grant moved across town to WOR, where he had worked a decade earlier. He replaced Barry Farber, the legendary host who quit to run for mayor of New York City. Grant continued his controversial banter with callers and criticism of public officials. His show was cancelled in 2003 due to declining advertising revenue, but he returned to WOR briefly to do a series of one-minute political commentaries—mostly tame in comparison to his earlier work—and also became a frequent guest on Hannity's WABC program.

WABC rehired Bob Grant in 2007, but the new show lasted only eighteen months. Today, he does fill-in work for other conservative hosts, including Mark Levin and Michael Savage.

Grant had been scheduled to receive a Lifetime Achievement Award from *Radio & Records* magazine in March 2008, but two months before the ceremony the magazine cancelled those plans, stating that his "past comments by him contradict our values and the respect we have for all members of our community."[18] Several talk show hosts, including Limbaugh and Hannity, protested the reversal and spoke out against it on their programs, and Neal Boortz protested by canceling his plans to attend that year's R&R conference.

Talent on Loan from God

Rush Limbaugh has been called the Babe Ruth of talk radio—the first host to generate such huge Arbitron ratings points and the first to warrant the high salary that goes with them. His domination of talk radio is difficult to deny. The typical Lexis-Nexis database search using the keywords "talk radio host" will return more articles about Limbaugh than the next fifteen to twenty hosts combined. For years, Limbaugh has been the second-most influential conservative voice in the media, and when William F. Buckley died in 2008, Limbaugh became the undisputed number one. As one media critic put it, "Limbaugh is to talk radio what Elvis Presley was to rock and roll."[19]

Many conservatives claim that Limbaugh's popularity stems from his political messages, but audience research indicates there are other factors in play as well. Fellow conservatives such as G. Gordon Liddy and Mark Levin espouse nearly identical messages, yet lag far behind Limbaugh in the ratings and advertising revenue generated by their respective shows. Instead, media researchers say, Limbaugh's popularity results from his ability to use to medium—what the host refers to as "talent on loan from God." Limbaugh, the researchers say, understands timing, voice inflection, emotion, and satire so well that he can generate audience numbers and advertising revenue that his competitors can only aspire to.

Limbaugh frequently cites statistics such as the number of stations carrying his broadcast and the latest Arbitron ratings—and expressing delight over the decline of his competitors' numbers. He has no reason to feel threatened by newcomers to conservative talk radio because the overall size of the talk radio audience is growing faster than the number of hosts. No one abandons Limbaugh for another conservative host, media researchers conclude, and for every new listener joining the audience of another host, one or more are joining Limbaugh's.

Limbaugh credits his success partly to his policy of not ridiculing or talking down to his callers, no matter how much he might be tempted. "These people (callers) consider themselves laughed at and made fun of on sitcoms and in the movies," Limbaugh said. "Here's a guy who doesn't condescend to them, doesn't make fun of people on the phone, considering every opinion they offer—for a little while, at least."[20]

Limbaugh bristles at being included on lists of hateful talk show hosts and shock jocks. "I'm not a hater, not one of the angry radio guys," he told *Time* reporter Margaret Carlson in 2001. "I'm an entertainer with a conservative agenda who wouldn't have twenty million listeners if I spewed venom. Yet the liberals lump me in with all the others."[21]

In addition to his radio program, he publishes the monthly *Limbaugh Letter*, for which he claims 400,000 subscribers, and a successful World Wide Website. His first book, *The Way Things Ought to Be* (1992), sold 2.5 million copies. His second book, *See, I Told You So* (1993) did almost as well.

Limbaugh is a member of Radio Hall of Fame, and in 2002 was named by *Talkers* magazine as the "greatest talk show host of all time."[22]

In 1956, Vice President Richard Nixon was visiting Cape Girardeau, Missouri and stopped into the home of Rush Limbaugh Jr., a former World War II fighter pilot who was a prominent local attorney and republican activist. There he met five-year-old Rush Limbaugh III, who would be one of the few members of the family not to go to law school. But his interest in politics was born on that day.

Limbaugh's grandfather, father, uncle, and four cousins became lawyers. His grandfather, Rush Sr., was still practicing law until his death at the age of 101. His father, Rush Jr., practiced law in Cape Girardeau while Rush's mother, Millie, ran the household and fed every stray cat in the neighborhood. His uncle, Stephen N. Limbaugh Sr., was appointed by President Reagan to serve as a federal judge in Missouri, and a cousin, Stephen N. Limbaugh Jr., serves as a judge on the Supreme Court of Missouri.

When Rush was sixteen, his father lent him the money for a summer course in radio engineering in Dallas. Limbaugh came home with a broadcasting license, which led to a job at a local radio station in Cape Girardeau. Soon he had his own show, working under the name Rusty Sharpe, and after that he never considered doing anything else. During his sophomore year of high school, Limbaugh quit the football and debating teams in order to spend more time at the radio station.

Although many biographical sketches report that he failed a college course in public speaking, in reality he received a D. His defense was that even though he enjoyed public speaking, he refused to prepare remarks in advance and opted instead to speak extemporaneously. Decades after leaving Missouri, nicknamed the "Show-Me State," Limbaugh was interviewed for one of the state's larger newspapers and said that everything he did after that was framed by "I'll show them." Limbaugh's mother added that "Rush didn't start talking until he was two years old. . . . and now he won't stop."[23]

Limbaugh took his radio act to Pittsburgh in 1972 and worked under the name Jeff Christie. He moved to Kansas City a few years later and worked a number of jobs in music radio before quitting in 1979 to take a public relations job with the Kansas City Royals.

In 1984, Limbaugh returned to radio, landing a job at KFBK in Sacramento, California, where he replaced the controversial Morton Downey Jr. In his first year at KFBK in Sacramento, Limbaugh's program tripled both the audience ratings and advertising revenue generated by his predecessor. Within a few years he earned the attention of Edward McLaughlin, president of ABC Radio, who moved him to New York City and gave him a national syndication deal.

Limbaugh launched the new show in August 1988, and in doing so went against conventional wisdom by scheduling it from noon to 3 p.m., eastern time—not in the morning or afternoon drive time, presumably the most lucrative slot for political talk. The noon television news and afternoon soap operas would be the preferred entertainment options, the experts told him. Within a few weeks, he proved the experts wrong, and over the next twenty years, Limbaugh's reach grew to more than 22 million listeners per week, tuning in on more than 600 stations.

By the early 1990s, Limbaugh was at the height of his popularity. In a move reminiscent of the days of *Amos 'n' Andy* broadcasts, when restaurants lured in customers with "radio rooms," many establishments today offer "Rush rooms" where customers can eat lunch while listening to their hero. Limbaugh encouraged his listeners to say "ditto" each time they agreed with him, and in time his listeners (some refer to themselves as his "followers") became known as "dittoheads."

Attacked by President Bill Clinton, Vice-President Al Gore, and other democrats and liberals, Limbaugh relished the attention and turned it to his advantage. Conservatives tuned in to worship their new hero, liberals tuned in to hear what outrageous things he would say next, and moderates turned into see what all the fuss was about.

On most political issues, Limbaugh takes the traditional republican and conservative positions: pro-national defense, antiabortion, and antigun control. But he saves much of energy for his opposition to entitlement programs and civil rights advances: he is against gay rights, affirmative action, and many other liberal ideas. "Life is not fair, folks, and if you spend your time trying to make the playing field even, you're never going to excel," he said at the 1992 commencement ceremonies at Cape Girardeau Central High School. "You have to accept life as it is."[24]

Limbaugh provided only lukewarm support for the first presidential campaign of George H. W. Bush in 1988, but after the win, he and Bush became friends. The talk show host spent a night in the Lincoln Bedroom at the White House as a guest of the president, and by the time Bush was ready for his reelection campaign, Limbaugh was on board.

At the conclusion of the Republican National Convention in 1992, Houston mayor Bob Lanier declared it "Rush Limbaugh Day" and presented the host with the key to the city at a festive downtown ceremony. Using the occasion to rail one more time about the alleged liberal bias of the news media, Limbaugh quipped, "You have fifteen thousand media people to cover the event, but only one of us telling the truth—me."[25] Despite Bush's loss to Bill Clinton, republicans in Congress showed their appreciation by naming Limbaugh an honorary member of Congress.

After Clinton won the election, Limbaugh had trouble hiding his contempt for the new president, but in media interviews and personal appearances, he tried to soften that perception by emphasizing that Clinton's policies were far more dangerous than his alleged personal behavior. But on the air it was a different story. It started soon after the inauguration, when Limbaugh began making constant remarks about Clinton's alleged marital infidelity and referred to his daughter, twelve-year-old Chelsea, as "the White House dog."[26]

Limbaugh's hatred for the Clinton administration became even more apparent as it unveiled its new proposal for health care reform. His program featured salvo after salvo of half-truths and distortions about the virtues of the plan. Interspersed throughout the program were advertisements critical of the plan that were paid for by the Coalition for Health Insurance Choices, a front group financed by the insurance industry. The ads featured a 1-800 number that individuals could call for more information. Callers were then connected to a telemarketer who offered to forward their calls directly to the appropriate congressional representative. As media critic John Stauber observed, "the congressional staffers fielding the calls typically had no idea that their constituents had been primed, loaded, aimed, and fired at them by radio ads on the Limbaugh show, paid for by the insurance industry, with the goal of orchestrating the appearance of overwhelming grassroots opposition to health reform."[27] When Clinton unveiled his first budget, Limbaugh urged listeners to call their congressional representatives, and so many did that the switchboard broke down briefly.

In June 1994, as members of Congress urged Clinton to fire Surgeon General Joycelyn Elders following numerous controversial comments attributed to her, Clinton responded on a St. Louis talk radio station by claiming, "After I finish this interview and get back on the plane, Rush Limbaugh will have three hours to say whatever he wants," Clinton told the host and audience. "And I won't have any opportunity to respond."[28]

As the investigation into the Clintons' financial affairs heated up in 1996, Limbaugh referred to Hillary Clinton as a "congenital liar," a phrase he picked up from a William Safire column in the *New York Times*. A few weeks later, the majority of those responding to a CNN/*Time* magazine poll said they believed that Hillary Clinton had been untruthful in her accounting of the Whitewater real estate deal.

During his commentary on Whitewater, Limbaugh speculated that Vince Foster was murdered in an apartment owned by Hillary Clinton and the body was moved to Marcy Park. Later, Limbaugh charged that "journalists and others working on or involved in Whitewatergate have been beaten and harassed in Little Rock. Some have died."[29] Those accusations prompted republican Congressman Bill Dannemeyer to call for congressional hearings on the "frightening" number of individuals in and around the Clinton White House to die under suspicious circumstances. "(Limbaugh) started to hammer us as self-indulgent, over-privileged yuppies who thought it was permissible to break the law if you were wealthy and went to Yale," wrote former White House Communications Director George Stephanopoulos in his 1999 book, *All Too Human*. "The attacks were effective, and unlike many of their later attacks against Clinton and our administration, not entirely unfair. Absent the grassroots firestorm that rightwing talk radio ignited, we might have gotten away with the (Zoe) Baird nomination (to be attorney general), but that's what it would have been—getting away with it."[30]

On his television program, Limbaugh often showed altered photographs showing Stephanopoulos's head on a baby's body. "Rush," he said to Limbaugh at a cocktail party, "don't you think it's time to get me out of diapers?"[31] Limbaugh agreed and soon began sharing with viewers of his television program altered photographs showing Stephanopoulos's head on the body of a toddler riding a rocking horse.

After Clinton left office, Limbaugh proved he could be controversial on topics other than national politics.

For the 2003 National Football League season, for example, ESPN hired Limbaugh to provide color commentary on its Sunday Night Football pregame show. The first few weeks of the season, Limbaugh's performance drew mixed reviews, but his brief television stint came to an end after he commented on the poor performance of Philadelphia Eagles quarterback Donovan McNabb. Limbaugh suggested that the media had gone overboard in defending McNabb against fan criticism because "they (the media) wanted a black quarterback to do well."[32] Although he repeatedly clarified that his comments were meant to be a criticism of the media rather than McNabb, civil rights activists considered his remarks racist. He eventually quit the show, saying he wanted to avoid his ESPN colleagues from enduring "additional discomfort."[33] Conservatives rushed to Limbaugh's defense, claiming it was yet another example of political correctness stifling public discourse and that Limbaugh was only stating what sportswriters and fans had been saying privately for several seasons.

In the fall of 2006, Limbaugh generated controversy when he accused actor Michael J. Fox of exaggerating the symptoms of his Parkinson's Disease while appearing in television commercials supporting a political candidate who favors federal funding for stem-cell research. While Fox admitted that he did not take his medication the morning the commercials were filmed, he denied that he did so to increase the effect of his tremors.

Limbaugh insisted that Fox exaggerated his lurching, facial movements, and other mannerisms in order to make a more dramatic case in support of stem-cell research and the candidacy of Claire McCaskill, a democratic senatorial candidate in Limbaugh's home state of Missouri, who made federal funding for that research a central part of her campaign platform. "It was clearly an act," Limbaugh told listeners. "If it was not an act, then I apologize."[34]

During the administration of George W. Bush, Limbaugh supported the war in Iraq and the president's efforts to fight terrorism around the world after the terrorist attacks of September 11, 2001. Limbaugh rejected allegations that American soldiers had abused detainees at the notorious Abu Ghraib prison in Iraq as nothing more than "boys will be boys" and "sort of like hazing, a fraternity prank. . . . sort of that kind of fun."[35] In a 2004 tirade on his show, Limbaugh said the photographic documentation of the alleged abuse looked like "good old-fashioned American pornography" and that the guards were "just having a good time. . . . just like anything you'd see Madonna or Britney Spears do on stage. . . . maybe something like you would see on stage at Lincoln Center, funded by an NEA grant."[36]

On other war-related topics, Limbaugh said that democrats in Congress had "aligned themselves with the enemy" and were "PR spokespeople for al-Qaeda."[37]

During his twenty-one years in syndicated radio, Limbaugh's frequent targets for on-air criticism have included democrats, liberals, feminists ("feminazis"), environmentalists ("environmental whackos"), Anita Hill, Jesse Jackson, Al Sharpton, Ted Kennedy, Mario Cuomo, Al Gore, Barack Obama (who he calls "Halfrican-American"), homeless advocates, dolphins, spotted owls, university professors, and the "art and croissant crowd."[38] He often enrages feminists with comments such as "I enjoy the women's movement—especially when I'm walking behind it."[39] He once called AIDS "a modern-day plague on homosexuals."[40] For a short time he cut off callers with whom he disagreed with "caller abortions," sound effects that included a woman's scream and the sound of a vacuum cleaner. He told offended listeners to consider how much worse real abortions were.

One of Limbaugh's favorite targets is academia, where he rails against the alleged liberal bent of university professors and what he describes as the "scourge of political correctness" on college campuses. "I'm not suggesting that we kill *all* of the liberals," he frequently tells his listeners. "We need to leave enough of them around so we can have two on each college campus, where they can be living fossils, so we will never forget what these people stood for."[41] Limbaugh described political correctness as "the greatest threat to the First Amendment in our history."[42]

When commenting on the television program *Survivor*, which features cross-country races among groups that are sometimes organized by ethnicity, Limbaugh commented that the black team would be the worst swimmers, the Asian team would have the most technical skills, and the Mexican team would likely win because they had more experience at covert travel.

Limbaugh is also critical of celebrities' involvement in antiwar activities, his favorite targets being Sean Penn and Martin Sheen. "It's beyond me how anyone can look at these protestors and call them anything other than what they are: anti-American, anti-capitalist, pro-Marxist, and communists," Limbaugh told his 20 million listeners.[43]

Some of Limbaugh's sharpest criticisms are directed at environmentalists. He labels scientists speaking about global warming "environmental alarmists" and "pseudo-experts."[44] On the subject of drilling in the Arctic National Wildlife Refuge (ANWR), Limbaugh commented that "if you put together a video of ANWR, you would see nothing but snow and rock. It is no place anybody's ever going to go. The wildlife that lives there wishes it didn't, but it's too stupid to figure out how to move anywhere."[45]

Defending the nuclear power industry while taking a cheap shot at one his least-favorite senators, Limbaugh once quipped that "more people have died in Ted Kennedy's car than have died in nuclear power plant accidents,"[46] referring to a 1969 tragedy in which a young woman drowned when Kennedy drove his car into a lake on Martha's Vineyard.

In 1990, Limbaugh got his first exposure on television as a guest host on Pat Sajak's late-night talk show. AIDS activists in the audience heckled him repeatedly because of his radio comments about gay rights and funding for AIDS research, and eventually the audience had to be removed. Two years later, he got his own television program, produced by Roger Ailes, but it lasted only four years.

Over the years, Limbaugh has used a number of musical pieces to introduce segments on his show, and those selections have both entertained and offended. When a *New York Times* reporter committed suicide by jumping from a tall building, Limbaugh introduced the story with a snippet from the Pointer Sisters song, "It's Raining Men." Prior to commenting on the plight of the homeless, he often uses "Ain't Got No Home." Discussions about AIDS are preceded by a snippet from Diane Warwick's "I'll Never Love This Way Again," and segments about the distribution of condoms in public schools are preceded with the Fifth Dimension's "Up, Up, and Away, in My Beautiful Balloon." During the early stages of the 2008 election campaign, his staff put together a musical parody of the song "Puff the Magic Dragon" and titled it "Barack the Magic Negro." Limbaugh said the intent of the song was not to be racist, but instead to ridicule the voters' belief that Obama was an omnipotent candidate who could save the country.

Other snippets are chosen to poke fun at his reputation for self-aggrandizement. Examples included samples from Tina Turner's "Simply the Best" and a Bo Diddley riff: "Come in closer, baby, hear what else I got to say . . . . You got your radio turned down too low. . . . Turn it up!"[47]

Limbaugh's role in politics and popular culture is a frequent topic for media researchers. In a 1997 book chapter, political scientist William Dorman blasted Limbaugh and other talk show hosts for their position that the media are liberally biased, claiming that "allowing Limbaugh to be a media critic makes as much sense as considering *Penthouse* magazine valid material for the study of women's issues."[48]

Media researcher Tom Lewis says that the hardest job at Limbaugh's operation is likely the person in charge of preparing transcripts of his show, because "it all comes out in, well, a rush. The words tumble forth in disarray to form incomplete sentences and muddled paragraphs. It is hard to punctuate the transcript because it is so difficult to know exactly when he pauses. But no matter how garbled his delivery may be, it works with stunning success—to the consternation of liberal listeners and many in the media."[49]

Communication researcher Jeff Land questions the way in which Limbaugh and his fans equate his Arbitron ratings with a sense of right and wrong. "For Limbaugh, what matters is how many people agree with him," Land concluded in a 2006 study. "If his ratings are high, he must be telling the truth. And his ratings tend to insulate him against criticism."[50]

Limbaugh is also frequently criticized by other members of the media. MSNBC commentator Keith Olbermann, for example, claims that Limbaugh is in it mostly for the money. "He doesn't believe half the junk he spouts," Olbermann wrote in his own 2006 book. "He's a quiet, almost colorless man who, if he could be guaranteed similar success in sportscasting, would sell out the sheep who follow his every word—and would do it by the end of business today."[51]

Newsweek contributor Evan Thomas described Limbaugh in a 2003 story as a "twice-divorced, thrice-married schlub whose idea of a good time is to lie on his couch and watch football. . . . he's the darling of red-state America."[52] *Time* magazine media critic Richard Corliss added that "Rush's program is a combination of C-Span, Comedy Central, and the Nostalgia Network."[53]

Media critics have also found plenty of fodder in Limbaugh's persona and presentation style.

E. J. Dionne, a political columnist for the *Washington Post*, notes that Limbaugh uses rock and roll and other counterculture trappings to sell traditional conservatism to baby boomers and younger generations. "His message is traditional, but his means are modern," Dionne wrote.[54]

"Limbaugh's fans are not country club Republicans," observes *Mother Jones* media critic Stephen Talbot. "They're Kmart conservatives who consider Rush one of them, even if he did make $25 million over the last two years."[55]

In a 1994 guest column in *USA Today*, NBC News president Michael Gartner wrote that "Limbaugh has only a passing acquaintance with the truth. . . . He's toying with you, folks, get you all riled up with a stew of half-truths and non-truths. . . . He's making fools of you, feeding you swill—and you're taking it in."[56]

Limbaugh has also earned both the respect and wrath of other talk show hosts. Fellow conservative Michael Savage describes Limbaugh as "a swell-headed bullfrog, feeding primarily on his own ego."[57] But Savage and other Limbaugh critics contend that Limbaugh owns much of his success to Clinton.

While he vehemently denies that he cares about comparisons to other talk show hosts, he bristles when media critics suggest that Sean Hannity, Michael Savage, or Bill O'Reilly are threatening his position. "Since when do I care what the media thinks?" Limbaugh mused. "Media polls are not the measure. Ratings and revenue are the measure. And it still ain't even close."[58] Limbaugh treats Hannity and Savage with what media critics call "condescending affection" and compared O'Reilly to fictional television newscaster Ted Baxter on *The Mary Tyler Moore Show*.

Limbaugh is a study in contradictions: He lauds the accomplishments of Ronald Reagan and considers the fortieth president his hero, yet he did not register to vote until he was thirty-five—well into Reagan's second term. Although he frequently talks about family values, he has been married and divorced three times, has no children, and rarely goes to church.

In 1977, Limbaugh married for the first time, but it lasted only a few months. His second marriage, in 1983, was to Michelle Sixta, a college student and usher for the Kansas City Royals. They divorced in 1990, and in 1994 he married Marta Fitzgerald, an aerobics instructor he met on the Internet. The wedding ceremony was held at the home of Chief Justice Clarence Thomas, with the justice presiding. Less than two years later, they divorced.

Limbaugh's weight has fluctuated over the years from 250 to 350 pounds, and he often jokes that he has the "perfect face for radio."[59]

In 2001, Limbaugh admitted to listeners that he had become deaf in his left ear and had only partial hearing in his right ear, the result of an autoimmune disease. Until corrective surgery could be scheduled that improved his hearing, Limbaugh struggled with timing on the air, at times leaving long pauses between a caller's comments and his response, and at other times cutting off a caller in midsentence.

Two years later, he admitted he had become addicted to pain killers Oxy-Contin and Hydrocodone, a problem that was unrelated to his ear surgery, but instead to prior struggles with back pain and related surgery. Having moved his show to his home in Florida, he was charged in that community with "doctor shopping" in order to find physicians to write additional prescriptions for the drugs. In early 2006, he reached an agreement with Florida prosecutors in which he would reimburse the state for the cost of the investigation ($30,000) and enter an eighteen-month supervised rehabilitation.

Although his hearing has been mostly restored and his legal problems are behind him, Limbaugh has become a bit of a recluse, broadcasting his show from his West Palm Beach estate, a 2.8-acre, $14.5 million property that includes 250 feet of private beachfront. He describes the complex as his "southern command" and "heavily fortified bunker."[60]

Limbaugh drives around the estate in a black Maybach 57S, a $450,000 luxury sports car. There are five homes on the property—all his—but he lives in the biggest one, a 24,000 square-foot house that includes a humidor to accommodate one of his two hobbies—fine cigars—and a patio that opens onto a practice putting green (to accommodate the other). He also owns a $54 million Gulfstream G500 airplane.

He seldom has in-studio guests, and to expedite communication while not on the air, he learned to read lips. He does fewer book signings and other public appearances than before. Insiders say he spends his spare time reading and watching television (mostly research for his show), and when he wants to see a movie, he buys it online rather than going to the video rental store.

In July 2008, Limbaugh signed a new eight-year, $400 million contract with Premiere Radio Networks. "I have said I shall not retire until all Americans agree with me," he said upon signing the new contract. "That is still operative."[61]

Depending on the venue, Limbaugh takes either partial or full credit for the discussion of the Fairness Doctrine's possible return. "Since I brought it up, there have been dozens of news articles and opinion pieces all across the fruited plain," Limbaugh wrote in his 1993 book, *See, I Told You So*. And virtually every television story and published piece discussing the Fairness Doctrine have put my name in the lead."[62]

In addition to being in the political news throughout much of 2009 for his criticisms of the Obama administration, Limbaugh also made sports headlines. He was part of a consortium of Missouri-based business interests attempting to purchase the St. Louis Rams football team, but after weeks of controversy, the consortium dropped him from their roster in order to improve their chances of having the purchase approved by other National Football League owners.

The Apple Doesn't Fall Far from the Tree

Michael Reagan is the adopted son of the late President Ronald Reagan and his first wife, actress Jane Wyman. His introduction to economics came in the early 1960s when his father, the future president, gave him a raise in his allowance. The increase from one dollar to five dollars per week was possible, his father said, because President John F. Kennedy had just cut taxes. The younger Reagan claims that he has been a believer in tax cuts ever since.

Reagan got his start in talk radio in 1983 when a family friend introduced him to George Green, general manager of KABC Radio in Los Angeles. After only a few minutes of conversation, Green invited him to do fill-in work at the talk radio station. Reagan had just started a career writing political nonfiction, so he limited his KABC work to part-time. That part-time job lasted five years, but then he met the general manager at KSDO in San Diego, who offered him more consistent fill-in work. He moved his family from Los Angeles to San Diego, but a few days before he was scheduled to start, another host left the station on short notice, so Reagan was promoted from part-time to full-time. That was January 1989, and much of the discussion for his first week on the job was related to incoming President George H. W. Bush. One of Reagan's first calls was from the outgoing president—his dad.

During the first Bush administration, Reagan frequently expressed opinions different from those of the new president as well as his own father. Among those issues was passage of the Brady Bill, a law intended to limit the sale of handguns. The law was named after James Brady, President Reagan's press secretary, who was injured in a 1981 assassination attempt. Michael Reagan also sparred frequently with Bush on tax policy, but one of the major areas of concern was government spending. Reagan overtly opposed the construction of a $656 million federal government office building in Washington, D.C., and was one of the first critics to point out the irony of naming it after his father—one of the most antispending presidents in history. "What was I supposed to do—support a government boondoggle just because they put my dad's name on it?" he asked his listeners. "Pork is pork is pork, whether it's democratic pork or republican pork. In fact, I denounced the project even more vehemently because I felt this wonderful white elephant was an insult to my dad's name."[63]

Unlike other conservative radio hosts, Reagan does not fancy himself a conspiracy theorist—but that doesn't stop him from providing them with radio airtime. One of his favorite guests is Larry Nichols, the former marketing director for the Arkansas Development Finance Authority who became an outspoken critic of the Clinton administration and frequently told tall tales about the misdeeds of Bill and Hillary Clinton when they were governor and first lady of Arkansas in the 1980s and early 1990s.

Nichols's vendetta against the Clintons continued once they reached the White House, and in Reagan, he found a sympathetic ear and a large audience, as he was a guest on Reagan's program more than thirty times. One of Nichols's conspiracy theories involves the controversy surrounding the July 20, 1993 suicide of White House lawyer Vince Foster. While not concurring with Nichols's claim that Foster was murdered, Reagan told his listeners (and later, readers of his second book), he believed that Foster did take his own life, but not in the manner described in official investigative records. In addition to scrutinizing the Foster story, Reagan and his guests also spoke about (and wrote about) the so-called Arkansas Flu—the suspicious tendency of those working for and around the Clintons to die under mysterious circumstances.

Except for Nichols's tales, Reagan seldom has patience for the many conspiracy theories floated on the Internet and espoused by his callers—including several that suggested Foster was murdered, either to end an alleged affair with Hillary or because of his knowledge of various White House scandals. But Reagan continues to suggest that the Clintons's attempts to block the release of critical details of the investigation raise suspicions. "Just a day or two after Vince Foster died, President Clinton stated publicly that it would 'remain a mystery' why his friend died," Reagan wrote in his 1996 book, *Making Waves*. "I thought that was a strange statement for Bill Clinton to make. I don't agree with the president's view that the death of Vince Foster *must* remain a mystery. And I certainly don't believe that it *should*."[64]

In 1994, Reagan openly opposed his stepmother, former First Lady Nancy Reagan, when he supported Oliver North in his run for the U.S. Senate seat representing Virginia.

Like Limbaugh, Michael Reagan was made an honorary member of Congress in 1994.

Three Hours a Day, Every Day—That's All We Ask

Sean Hannity grew up in New York City listening to talk radio hosts Barry Farber and Bob Grant. After graduating from high school, Hannity began to pursue his childhood dream of becoming a priest, but he dropped out of the seminary after less than a year.

Hannity recalls in his 2002 book, *Let Freedom Ring*, how he was moved to join the conservative movement (and the talk radio profession) while watching on television the 1986 congressional hearings related to the Iran-Contra scandal. "I found myself furious at the sight of congressmen excoriating a patriot like Ollie North," Hannity wrote. "I was so riveted by the hearings that I wouldn't go to work. I'd stay home and watch the hearings all day. I even taped them so I could watch them over again. The more I watched and listened, the angrier I got. And in my search to express my views—to hear a different viewpoint on the subject from what was available on TV—I began calling into radio talk shows to defend Ollie. I beat up on the sanctimonious congressmen and senators, and somewhere along the way, I found my calling in life."[65]

Hannity's first talk radio job was at the student-run station at the University of Santa Barbara in 1987. He claims he was fired for being too conservative. "The station was dominated by left-wing programming, including a gay and lesbian perspective show, a Planned Parenthood show, and multiple shows accusing (Ronald) Reagan and (George H. W.) Bush of being drug runners and drug pushers," Hannity wrote in *Let Freedom Ring*. "The left-wing management had zero tolerance for conservative voices."[66]

The specific incident that prompted Hannity's termination was an interview with an AIDS researcher who called gays "a subculture of people engaged in deviant, twisted acts." Hannity added that "anyone listening to this program that believes homosexuality is a normal lifestyle has been brainwashed. . . . It's very dangerous if we start accepting lower and lower forms of behavior as the norm."[67] After the firing, the local chapter of the American Civil Liberties Union intervened on his behalf, citing the free speech principles at stake. The station reversed its decision, but Hannity decided to leave anyway.

Unemployed and broke, Hannity dropped out of USB and scraped together enough cash to put an advertisement in a radio trade publication. After a brief telephone interview, he was hired by WVNN, a low-power AM station in Huntsville, Alabama. The station's management had no idea how young he was (twenty-six) or that he had never done a two-hour show five days a week. Hannity worried that his New York accent might not be welcome in the deep South, but he knew that the pyschographics of the audience would be to his liking—conservative, politically active, and family oriented. And the $19,000 per year salary was more than he ever dreamed of making.

In 1992, libertarian Neal Boortz left WGST in Atlanta for cross-town rival WSB. That created a vacancy for Hannity, who became an instant hit with Boortz's former audience and talk radio fans in general. He was able to get off to such a quick start partly because a noncompete agreement clause in Boortz's WGST contract kept him off the air at WSB for months.

On a visit to New York to appear on Phil Donahue's television program, Hannity visited the studios of WABC Radio, where he met Rush Limbaugh and his childhood idol, Bob Grant. Shortly after that visit, Grant was fired, and even though Hannity lobbied for Grant's job, that morning drive slot went to the more experienced Mike Gallagher. But Hannity soon found himself with a better job and time slot—WABC's afternoon drive program, which he named simply *The Sean Hannity Show*. His first day on the job was September 10, 2001. He had a routine first day on the job, but the events of the following day would make Hannity into a national superstar.

Today, Hannity has about 12 million listeners, giving him the second-largest talk radio audience behind Limbaugh. Prior to the 2000 election, one media critic described him as a "Long-Island raised, Irish-Catholic Manichean moralist"[68] who can turn even the most benign topic into a polarizing one. But since that election, Hannity seems to have mellowed somewhat.

Unlike other conservative hosts who often mock or insult their callers, Hannity may be the best at establishing rapport, or, as media critic Rory O'Connor describes it, "knocking down the walls that separate him from his callers."[69] He often refers to callers as "friends" and ends many calls by telling the caller, "You're a great American." His other signature line is "Three hours a day, every day—that's all we ask."

Hannity also differs from his fellow conservative hosts in another important way: instead of saying outrageous and politically incorrect things himself, he allows his guests to do so. Frequent guests include republican pundits Ann Coulter, Pat Buchanan, and Oliver North. But perhaps his favorite guest is Dick Morris, a former advisor to President Bill Clinton, who has turned his disdain for Bill and Hillary into fodder for numerous books and guest shots on television and radio.

One Hannity talking point with which constitutional scholars would strongly disagree is his insistence that there "is no place in the Constitution that says there should be separation of church and state."[70] While those last four words do not appear in the document, for almost the entire 220 years of the Constitution's existence, they have been considered a paraphrasing of the First Amendment's establishment clause, which reads, "Congress shall make no law respecting the establishment of religion, nor prohibiting the free exercise of."

Media critic Sharon Crowley ridicules the title of Hannity's 2004 book, *Deliver Us from Evil: Defeating Terrorism, Despotism, and Liberalism.* "It's as though each of these practices were equivalent to the others, and as though all were evil," she wrote in her 2006 book, *Toward a Civil Discourse.*[71]

Commenting on news reports that new Congressman Keith Ellison, a Muslim, was planning to be sworn into office on a Quran instead of the customary Bible, Hannity drew a parallel between Islam and Nazism, asking a guest on his show, "Would you have allowed him to choose Hitler's *Mein Kampf,* which is the Nazi bible?"[72] Hannity later attempted to backpedal and insisted that he was not equating the Quran with *Mein Kampf,* but media watchdog groups such as Fairness and Accuracy in Reporting continued to question the metaphor.

Even as President Bush's job approval ratings dropped below 30 percent during his second term, Hannity remained supportive of both the chief executive and the Iraq War. "I think he's a man of principle, a man of faith," Hannity told an Associated Press reporter in 2006. "He's got a backbone of steel and he's a real, genuine, big-time leader. He's a consequential figure for his time. We just don't see it right now."[73] Hannity has repeatedly questioned the patriotism of democratic Representative John Murtha of Pennsylvania, simply because he challenged Bush on the failings of the Iraq War.

In early 2009, during President Obama's fourth week in office, an Ohio newspaper poll reported that 81 percent of respondents indicated they would rather have a beer with Hannity than the new president.

Pinheads and Patriots

Bill O'Reilly's radio show debuted on 205 stations in the spring of 2002. By the time he left the air in February 2009, that list had grown to more than 400 stations. His prime-time Fox News television program currently reaches 2.3 million viewers. He denies accusations that both his radio and television programs are or ever were theatrical in nature, but media critics and political opponents differ. Among his critics is Comedy Central's Stephen Colbert, whose thirty-minute nightly comedy, *The Colbert Report,* is a thinly disguised parody of O'Reilly's television program.

O'Reilly has written one novel, *Those Who Trespass* (1998), and five works of nonfiction, most dealing with the same social and political issues dealt with on his radio and television programs.

O'Reilly is the Irish-Catholic son of a naval officer and grandson of a Brooklyn police officer. He grew up in the hardscrabble New York suburb of Levittown and attended Catholic schools, where he lettered in four sports. "That wasn't very much fun at the time," he said in a 2004 interview on National Public Radio (NPR). "But in retrospect it was for the better. If it hadn't been for Catholic school, I would probably be in a penitentiary right now."[74] O'Reilly says he has been an environmentalist since reading Rachel Carson's *Silent Spring* in high school.

O'Reilly graduated from Marist College in southeastern New York, then took a job teaching English and history at a private catholic high school in Miami. After a few years he was admitted to the journalism school at Boston University, where he earned a master's degree in broadcasting in 1976. He spent the next ten years working for a number of local stations in New England and on the West Coast and then landed a job as a correspondent for ABC News. Three years later, he was hired as lead anchor for the CBS investigative journalism series, *Inside Edition*, where he covered stories including the fall of the Berlin Wall and the 1992 Los Angeles riots. He left the program in 1995 to earn a second master's degree, this one from the John F. Kennedy School of Government at Harvard University. After receiving that degree, he was hired by the upstart television network Fox News and given his own program, *The O'Reilly Factor*. In 2002, he created a radio program of the same name, but he eventually renamed it *The No-Spin Zone*.

In 1994, O'Reilly changed his party affiliation from republican to independent, but today claims his political idol is democrat Robert F. Kennedy, the late attorney general and U.S. senator from his home state of New York.

He avoids using terms such as conservative and liberal, opting for "traditionalist" and "secular-progressive." The latter agenda, he claims, includes the expansion of gay rights and a more forgiving attitude toward alleged child molesters and criminal suspects. He frequently sounds the alarm about school principals who fail to instill discipline in their schools, suggesting those principals be fired; and judges who let accused sexual predators get off with light sentences, suggesting those judges be impeached.

His favorite targets for criticism on his radio show were celebrities in the news, including Britney Spears, Jessica Simpson, Sean Penn, Martin Sheen, Rosie O'Donnell, and Alec Baldwin. One segment of his show was called "Pinheads and Patriots." The daily Pinhead award typically went to a principal, judge, or celebrity as mentioned above, while the Patriot award often went to an American who had done something noteworthy, usually in support of veterans or active-duty military.

While O'Reilly often vilified sexual predators and judges who impose light sentences upon them, he also drew criticism for the occasional insensitive comment that implies the victims are partially to blame. In August 2006 he was criticized by women's groups after commenting that an eighteen-year-old New Jersey woman who was raped and murdered had invited the assault because she was drunk and provocatively dressed. Two years later, child advocates chastised him over comments about an eleven-year-old boy who was held captive and sexually molested for four years; O'Reilly commented that the boy did not attempt to escape because he was having "a lot more fun than he did under his old parents."[75]

O'Reilly railed against Jamie Lynn Spears, sister of singer Britney, criticizing her for being sixteen, unmarried, and pregnant at the same time. O'Reilly, who put more of the blame on Spears' "pinhead parents" than on the daughter, used the story as evidence to support one of his favorite points: that ineffective parenting skills leads to an increase teenage pregnancy, drug abuse, high school dropouts, and other problems.

Also on O'Reilly's list of favorite targets were the department stores that allegedly require their employees to say "Happy Holidays" instead of "Merry Christmas" and city and county governments that removed religious artifacts such as crosses and artwork featuring the Ten Commandments from public buildings. Throughout the 2007 and 2008 holiday seasons, O'Reilly devoted a large portion of his radio and television programs to such issues, claiming he was fighting back against the secular-progressives and their "war on Christmas."

O'Reilly once said that instead of hitting New Orleans, he wished that Hurricane Katrina had hit New York City and focused its wrath on the United Nations Building. "And I wouldn't have rescued any of them," he told his listeners.[76]

O'Reilly claims he is for the decriminalization of marijuana, against the death penalty, and for environmental safeguards, positions which he calls progressive rather than liberal. "My positions are based on problem-solving," he says. "I'm a problem solver—if the solution is on the left, I grab it. If the solution is on the right, I grab it."[77]

Like most conservative talk show hosts, O'Reilly accused the *New York Times* and other media outlets as having a "hard left, secular agenda." He called the American Civil Liberties Union "terrorists" who were "almost as dangerous as al Qaeda."[78]

On both sides of the radio microphone, O'Reilly earned a reputation as a curmudgeon. On both his television and radio programs, he was brusque with both guests and callers; and when being interviewed by other outlets, he often came across as arrogant and defensive.

The best example of the latter was an October 8, 2003, interview on the NPR program *Fresh Air,* hosted by veteran radio reporter and interviewer Terry Gross. O'Reilly said later that he expected the interview to focus on his new book, *Who's Looking Out For You?* Instead, he complained, Gross turned the interview into a discussion of his interviewing style and political beliefs and that he was immediately put on the defensive.

The interview opened with Gross pressing O'Reilly to defend himself against the accusations in Al Franken's book, *Lies and the Lying Liars Who Tell Them.* Fifty minutes into the interview, the content of Franken's book had garnered a larger share of the time than O'Reilly's book, so O'Reilly decided he had enough. He accused Gross of trying to trap him "into something that *Harper's* magazine can use." O'Reilly told Gross, "You should be ashamed of yourself. And this is the end of the interview."[79] With that, O'Reilly terminated the conversation.

A few days later, NPR ombudsman Jeffrey Dvorkin issued an on-air rebuke of Gross, saying, "I believe the listeners were not well-served by the interview"[80] and that he regretted that it might serve to confirm public belief in NPR's alleged liberal bias. A year later, O'Reilly was further annoyed when Gross published her own book, *All I Did Was Ask*, which featured her accounts of her more noteworthy interviews, including the one with O'Reilly. She made no mention of Dvorkin's commentary. When Gross later appeared on O'Reilly's television program, she said she disagreed with the ombudsman's criticisms but "did not know why they were left out of the book."[81]

O'Reilly gave his own account of the interview in his 2006 book, *Culture Warrior*. He said he regretted his behavior, calling it "demeanor foolishness." But he also regretted agreeing to the interview itself, calling it "another dopey move in an autumn full of them."[82]

The NPR interview came two months after O'Reilly had participated in a panel discussion with Al Franken at the August 2003 Book Expo in Los Angeles. Organizers had chosen to promote the session using a poster showing the cover of Franken's book, which featured O'Reilly's face and the word "liar." In the book, Franken called O'Reilly "a bully who cuts off anyone who disagrees with him."[83]

O'Reilly had been invited to plug his own book, *Who's Looking Out for You?* Against his own instincts, O'Reilly chose to follow through with his commitment to appear on the panel, even though he was annoyed by the poster; he knew about the book but had not previously seen the cover art.

O'Reilly went first, but he refused to take the bait that event organizers had laid out for him; instead, he limited his comments to current events and the content of his own book. When it was Franken's turn to speak, he paraphrased passages in his book in which he asserted that O'Reilly's childhood was spent in the affluent Long Island town of Westbury, New York, not the blue-collar Levittown as O'Reilly claimed in his books and on his radio show. When O'Reilly recalled the episode in *Culture Warrior*, he reproduced a copy of the deed to his parents' home—showing a Levittown address.

In 2004, O'Reilly was named in a sexual harassment lawsuit filed by one of his producers. The thirty-three-year-old woman claimed O'Reilly called her after hours to brag about his vast collection of sex toys and offered to take her on a vacation to the Caribbean. O'Reilly, claiming the woman was attempting to extort money from him, responded by filing a countersuit. Both cases were resolved out of court.

O'Reilly once had lunch with Al Sharpton at a Harlem restaurant, then commented on his show how surprised he was that the establishment was "exactly the same" as other restaurants in New York, even though "it's run by blacks."[84]

Upon leaving either his radio booth or television studio, many of O'Reilly's guests complain that the interviews were largely one-way and that they had little opportunity to say what they wanted to say. They cited O'Reilly's tendency to dominate the conversation, interrupt his guests in midsentence to ask the next question, and change the subject any time a guest seemed to be scoring too many points with the audience. As Marvin Kitman wrote in his biography, *The Man Who Would Not Shut Up*, trying to have a conversation with O'Reilly was "like trying to drink water from an open fire hydrant."[85]

Other critics have pointed out the irony and deception O'Reilly exhibited in subtitling his radio show *The No Spin Zone*, as the entire show is nothing but spin. Even other conservative talk show hosts lampoon O'Reilly, with one of them commenting that "O'Reilly has been playing O'Reilly for so long and has developed such a library of hooks, tics, and subplots, that he sometimes seems to be parodying himself."[86]

The liberal watchdog group Media Matters for America named O'Reilly its "Misinformer of the Year" in 2004 but said it was unable to come up with a total number of inaccuracies spread on his television and radio programs. "After a while," a group spokesperson said, "we just stopped counting."[87]

One feature of MSNBC political commentator Keith Olbermann's nightly commentary is the announcement of that day's "Worst Person in the World," a distinction given to whichever politician, journalist, celebrity, or radio talk show host raised his ire that day. O'Reilly is a popular choice: in an eleventh-month period from mid-2005 to mid-2006, O'Reilly earned the distinction twenty-seven times. Limbaugh was a distinct second with six mentions, while Bill Bennett and Neal Boortz were named twice each and Laura Ingraham and Glenn Beck were named once each.

O'Reilly is annoyed at media portrayals of him as a bully who interrupts his guests in midsentence. "I've said 'shut up' six times in twelve years, and they all deserved it," O'Reilly told *Time* magazine in 2008. "They were either bloviating, filibustering, or lying."[88] His most common complaint about reviews of his books is that the reviewers want to comment on his television and radio shows and interviewing style rather than the content of the book being reviewed.

Two of the more popular books written about O'Reilly are Peter Hart's *The Oh Really Factor: Unspinning Fox News Channel's Bill O'Reilly* and Joseph Amann's *Sweet Jesus, I Hate Bill O'Reilly*. A third book, Marvin Kitman's *The Man Who Would Not Shut Up*, took a more even-handed look at the man. Kitman, a self-professed "liberal TV critic," admits, "I don't agree with much of what he (O'Reilly) says, but I like the way he says it."[89]

Kitman spent five years on the book, which he based on more than two dozen interviews with friends, colleagues, and critics. O'Reilly was one of his primary sources, yet the author still refers to the book as an "unauthorized biography." The book focuses on O'Reilly's diverse employment history, including time spent as a school teacher, newspaper journalist, and of course, television and radio personality. He also deals at length with the sexual harassment lawsuit.

In addition to those volumes, O'Reilly's work is also the subject of research for professors and graduate students at numerous universities. The Annenberg School of Communication at the University of Pennsylvania conducted one such study in the mid-1990s, and in 2007 three professors at Indiana University devoted an entire twenty-seven-page paper to O'Reilly's rhetoric.

Sometimes the Sky Really Is Falling

Dr. James Dobson is a licensed clinical psychologist and evangelical Christian who founded a nonprofit organization, Focus on the Family, in 1977. He also used the name of the organization as the title for his radio program, which at first dealt mostly with spiritual matters but eventually expanded to include political issues. It was soon syndicated by more than 7,000 stations—almost all of them Christian in format—and is heard by more than 220 million people in 164 countries.

In 1983, Dobson founded the Family Research Council, a political organization opposed to abortion and same-sex marriage. His public comments on the latter—on his radio program, in media interviews, and newspaper columns—have served as effective fund-raising tools but have also drawn the ire of numerous gay rights organizations, including the We Are Family Foundation, an organization often confused with his. But the agendas of the two organizations couldn't be further apart. While the foundation provides literature and audiovisual materials to help public schools promote "tolerance and diversity," Focus on the Family contends those terms are "buzzwords for homosexual advocacy."[90]

Dobson's interest in overturning the 1973 Supreme Court ruling in *Roe v. Wade*—the landmark case that legalized abortion nationwide—is manifested in his constant monitoring of the Supreme Court docket and attention paid to presidential nominations to fill court vacancies, even at times when no seats are vacant or expected to be. In 2004 he led a unsuccessful campaign to block republican Senator Arlen Specter's bid to head the Judiciary Committee, the body which first evaluates presidential nominees for federal judgeships.

The following year, Dobson reportedly told six democratic senators behind closed doors that he would work to defeat them for re-election in 2006 if they blocked conservative appointees to the U.S. Supreme Court. To add credence to his threat, he reminded them of the role he played in the 2004 defeat of Senate Minority Leader Tom Daschle. During the 2008 presidential campaign, he warned listeners that if Barack Obama was elected, he would appoint the "most liberal Supreme Court justices we've ever had."[91]

But Dobson's support for conservative causes goes just beyond the issues of abortion and gay rights. In 2004, he took credit for getting out enough of the Christian vote to ensure the re-election of George W. Bush. Political observers say his opinion carries more weight than those of Jerry Falwell and Pat Robertson. Even though the latter have more name recognition and charisma, media critics believe their tendency to dilute their arguments with gaffes and hyperbole gives more credibility to Dobson, who can present similar viewpoints but in a more palatable and articulate tone.

The seventy-two-year-old Dobson has been criticized in recent years for focusing too much of the program's agenda on abortion and gay marriage while not paying more attention to broader political issues. He resigned from his post as chairman of Focus on the Family in February 2009, but pledged to continue hosting the radio show of the same name.

I Might Be Wrong, but I Doubt It

Growing up in Pennsylvania in the early 1970s, Mark Levin would often fall asleep listening to the radio. At sixteen, he cajoled Philadelphia talk station WCAU-AM into giving him a part-time job hosting his own show for an hour a day. He jumped from the eleventh grade into college, finished his undergraduate program in three years, and graduated from Temple University Law School at age twenty-two. He worked in several cabinet departments during the Reagan administration and at one point was chief of staff to Attorney General Edwin Meese. After Reagan left office, Levin formed a public interest law firm, and in

1995, he became an unofficial consultant to Rush Limbaugh, advising him on legal and constitutional issues.

In 2002, Levin began hosting his own show, working for free at WABC in New York. Within a few years, he had his own nationally syndicated show.

On his radio program and in his books, Levin rails against the Supreme Court and its decisions. In his 2005 book, *Men in Black: How the Supreme Court Is Destroying America,* he argues that the Court is made up of "activist judges" who "defy the principle of separation of powers and believe it is justifiable for the judicial branch of the federal government to seize power from the executive and legislative branches."[92] In the book, he also blasts the Court as a whole for its rulings that remove religion from public schools, defend gay rights, and hamper government efforts to investigate groups with suspected links to terrorist organizations. In addition to criticizing the justices for their liberal voting records, he also attacks many of them personally. In an early chapter, he described revered justices such as Stephen J. Field, Felix Frankfurter, William O. Douglas, Hugo Black, and Thurgood Marshall as "bumbling old curmudgeons" who stayed on the bench too long.[93] He chided several of them for their rumored (but never proven) sexual dalliances with subordinate employees. Reviews of the book were mixed; those published in media outlets with conservative biases praised it, while those with progressive leanings labeled the anecdotes used to support Levin's criticisms as exaggerated. One reviewer commented that readers will experience "overwhelming urge to shower between chapters."[94]

Levin blames much of society's problems on the "welfare state" and illegal immigration. He claims that a "modern liberal assault on Constitution-based values" began in the 1930s with President Franklin Roosevelt's New Deal and has "snowballed out of control ever since."[95]

Today, Levin has a nationally syndicated program hosted by the Landmark Legal Foundation, a nonprofit organization that advocates a strict constructionist view of the constitution. The show reaches 5.5 million listeners per week, making Levin the fifth-ranked host in the country, according to *Talkers* magazine. A staunch conservative in the mold of Limbaugh and Hannity, Levin rails daily against liberals, immigrants, gays, and feminists. He calls the National Organization for Women the "National Organization for Ugly Women."[96]

Taking the High Road Is Overrated

G. Gordon Liddy, who calls himself "the G-Man," is a former agent for the Federal Bureau of Investigation who was best known for his role in the 1972 Watergate break-in. In 1973, he was sentenced to twenty years in prison after being convicted for conspiracy, burglary, and wiretapping. He was paroled in 1977.

Today, his nationally syndicated show airs on the Radio America Network.

Liddy and his call screeners are known in the talk radio business as having a fairly low credibility threshold for determining who gets on the air. Callers are welcome to launch salvo after salvo of distortions, half-truths, and outright falsehoods about democratic politicians and liberal celebrities, often quoting allegations gleaned from tabloid newspapers and Internet blogs as though they came from a major wire service. Liddy seldom asks his callers clarifying or scrutinizing questions, and the more outrageous the callers' accusations, the more play they get—especially if they are passing along the latest unsubstantiated gossip about Al Gore or Bill or Hillary Clinton. Special "guest callers" claiming to be investigative journalists or former government officials are often interviewed either in the studio or over the telephone. Liddy refers to many of these guests' outrageous allegations and conspiracy theories as "breaking news," even though no corroborating stories are ever found in reputable newspapers or television news broadcasts.

On August 26, 1994, while discussing the federal government's raid on an isolationist compound in Waco, Texas, Liddy told his listeners: "Now if the Bureau of Alcohol, Tobacco, and Firearms comes to disarm you and they are bearing arms, resist them with arms. Go for a head shot; they're going to be wearing bulletproof vests. . . . They've got a big target on there, ATF. Don't shoot at that, because they've got a (bulletproof) vest on underneath. Head shots, head shots. Kill the sons of bitches."[97]

During the 1996 presidential election campaign, Liddy compared the two candidates, republican challenger Bob Dole and democratic incumbent Bill Clinton. Liddy sized up the difference by calling Clinton a "yellow coward who turned and ran, someone with his thumb up his ass instead of a bullet in his heart."[98]

Fellow conservative Michael Reagan draws a contrast between himself and Liddy: "I use my microphone to inform and motivate; Liddy uses his microphone as a cattle prod—*buzz-buzz, shock-shock*," Reagan wrote in his 1996 book, *Making Waves*. "And that's not a criticism of Liddy, just an observation."[99]

In 1994, Liddy created controversy when he attempted to raise funds for St. Jude Children's Hospital in Memphis, Tennessee, by selling a calendar that included photographs of lingerie-clad women armed with handguns. Hospital officials found the idea distasteful because their wards housed so many children with gunshot wounds. When asked about the mini-controversy, Liddy told reporters that the hospital's objections to the calendar were analogous to "banning advertisements showing children in station wagons because so many children are killed in station wagons."[100] The hospital issued a statement distancing itself from Liddy, and journalists were unable to learn how much money was generated and how much, if any, was donated to the hospital.

As a convicted felon, Liddy is prohibited by federal law from possessing firearms, yet he brags on his show about keeping guns to protect his home and for target shooting. According to ATF, possessing or firing a gun—even at a firing range—could earn an ex-con a ten-year prison sentence.

The Black Rush

Armstrong Williams is a black conservative who irritates liberals and civil rights activists with comments some consider backwards or racist. Many of his comments follow traditional republican talking points: anti-affirmative action, anti-abortion, and in favor of school vouchers. Some media critics refer to him as "the black Rush Limbaugh."

In addition to his radio work, Williams has written a number of books and today writes a weekly newspaper column and hosts occasional television specials, but it was his public relations work that brought him national attention in 2005. The controversy began when *USA Today* filed a Freedom of Information Act request with the U.S. Department of Education (DOE) as part of an investigation into its budgetary decisions. Almost by accident, the investigation revealed that the DOE had paid Williams $240,000 for promoting on his television and radio programs the No Child Left Behind Act (NCLBA), a package of government initiatives aimed at helping at-risk students achieve academically. Documents revealed that Williams was paid to urge Americans to contact their congressional representatives and express support for the legislation, encourage other black journalists to do likewise, and book Education Secretary Rod Paige as a guest on his television program.

The money did not pass directly from the DOE to Williams, however. The payment was part of a $1 million contract between the DOE and Ketchum Public Relations, which in turn passed the $240,000 payment to Williams's public relations firm, the Graham-Williams Group. Williams apologized for the lapse in judgment, saying that even though he was a commentator and not a journalist, he should abide by the same ethical standards. He refused to return the money, however, even after being urged to do so by numerous government watchdog groups, responding that the government "paid for a result, and got it."[101]

Opponents of the George W. Bush administration used the controversy to further their agenda, stating that the administration had violated both the letter and spirit of the Gillett Amendment—a federal law prohibiting the expenditure of taxpayer money for promotional purposes—and that it "deceived the public by concealing the role of taxpayer dollars in promoting partisan policies."[102] Numerous congressional leaders complained about the arrangement, and one even threatened to hold up the confirmation hearings for incoming DOE Secretary Margaret Spellings until the department thoroughly investigated the Williams affair. Bush, after denying any knowledge of the arrangement, said in media interviews that his administration would no longer "pay commentators to advance our agenda . . . our agenda should be able to stand on its own two feet."[103]

Media ethicists were also concerned about the implications of the arrangement and called it "political opinion disguised as editorial content." Even though Williams did not promote NCLBA in his newspaper column, Tribune Media Services dropped the Williams column from its offerings.

Child Prodigy

Ben Ferguson started listening to talk radio—usually Limbaugh—while riding in his mother's car on the way to school or tennis lessons in the late 1980s. "If not for Rush, I might not have developed such a love of undressing liberals in public by pointing out all the flaws in their arguments," Ferguson wrote in his 2002 book, *It's My America Too*. "I was always a very opinionated kid, so I was that much more interested in hearing Rush express his opinions, and I guess his enthusiasm for what he did rubbed off on me."[104]

After months of trying to call Limbaugh's show, Ferguson became frustrated with the constant busy signals. He called a local station that carried the show to ask for tips on how to get through. The only advice he received was to call other shows that did not receive as many calls. In 1991, at age twelve, he finally became a regular caller on a Memphis show hosted by Mike Flowers.

The following year, he became a regular caller to the nationally syndicated show of Ken Hamblin. Another Memphis host heard his frequent contributions and invited him to be an in-studio guest on his morning show. The interview was scheduled for ten minutes, but the show received so many calls that Ferguson stayed on for more than an hour. That experience turned into a regular weekly interview, and later into a part-time job in which Ferguson filled in for other hosts. Politicians lining up to be interviewed on Ferguson's show included Senate Majority Leader Bob Dole, House Speaker Newt Gingrich, Education Secretary (and former Tennessee governor) Lamar Alexander, Vice President Al Gore, and Missouri representative Richard Gephardt. Within two years, Ferguson was a full-time talk show host with a three-hour show that aired five days a week—all while still in high school.

I'm Not the President, But I Played One in the Movies

When Bill O'Reilly left the airwaves in February 2009, in many markets he was replaced by Fred Thompson, for former U.S. senator from Tennessee and for a brief time, a 2008 presidential candidate in the republican primaries. But he's actually better known for his work in prime-time television and the movies. For five seasons, he portrayed Arthur Branch, the grouchy district attorney on television's *Law & Order*. In movie roles he has played a president, a vice president, and a White House chief of staff. In a tongue-in-cheek reference to his failed presidential campaign, his radio signature line is "Why do you need to be president when you can host a radio talk show?"

Thompson's show is syndicated by Westwood One. In most markets, it airs live during the early afternoon, but like O'Reilly's, it is heard later in the day in some areas. And much like the man he replaced, Thompson has an approach to radio talk that is highly conservative with just a touch of curmudgeon. His co-host is his wife, Jeri.

The Best of the Rest

Lars Larson got his start in radio at age sixteen, spinning 45 rpm records at a small station in Tillamook, Oregon. Twenty-eight years later, he's moved only seventy-five miles to the east—to KXL-AM in Portland—but at the same time he's moved far right. He has a local show on weekday afternoons, on which he deals with both local and national issues; and a nationally syndicated show on

Westwood One, which is carried by 175 stations, weeknights from 7 to 10 p.m. eastern time.

On October 23, 2003, Larson was hosting a public event for the station's listeners while across town, documentary filmmaker and liberal rabble-rouser Michael Moore was drumming up support for his work at a rally at the Portland Convention Center. Moore reportedly asked the crowd to suggest which conservative in town most deserved to be harassed, and someone in the crowd responded with Larson's name and home phone number. Moore called the number and got a voice-mail message referring callers to his cell phone number, which Moore called as well. Moore announced the numbers to the crowd, and over the next few weeks, Larson and his wife were harassed at their home—and the wife was harassed at work—to the point at which they had to change both phone numbers and eventually move from their home. As the phone calls got uglier, Larson's station arranged for private security guards to accompany him whenever he went out in public.

For much of the 1980s, Ray Briem was the host of a popular conservative program, airing in the overnight hours, on KABC in Los Angeles—the same station at which Bob Grant was the primary daytime host. Briem's program was syndicated in major cities across the country. Briem was highly acclaimed for lining up the hard-to-get interviewees that other hosts could not, including his Russian counterpart, Vladimir Pozner, who did frequent reciprocal interviews with Briem live from his studio in Moscow.

Hugh Hewitt received his undergraduate degree from the University of Michigan, worked as a ghostwriter for former President Richard Nixon, then attended law school. He held several different jobs in the Reagan administration, then took a job overseeing construction of the Nixon Library in California.

Today, he hosts a talk show on Salem Radio Networks that airs in the early evenings. Hewitt is more thoughtful and less confrontational than other conservative hosts. Unlike Limbaugh and O'Reilly, who bully their guests and callers, Hewitt lets other people talk and seems generally interested in what they have to say. A softer version of Sean Hannity, he passes on the opportunity to name-call politicians and instead allows his guests to do so. He labels his show "National Public Radio for conservatives."

In the early stages of the 2008 presidential election campaign, he endorsed former Massachusetts governor Mitt Romney and authored a book titled *A Mormon in the White House: What Every American Should Know about Mitt Romney*.

Bill Bennett's first government job was as secretary of education during the administration of President Ronald Reagan. When Reagan left office, his successor, George H. W. Bush, appointed him as the first director of the Office of National Drug Control Policy (better known as "drug czar").

Today, his national show, *Morning in America*, airs on Salem Radio Networks. In 2005, during a discussion of the relationship between crime, drugs, and education, he told listeners, "If that (crime reduction) were your sole purpose, you could abort every black baby and your crime rate would go down."[105] Despite the controversial remarks, Bennett is still on the air today.

From 1987 to 2003, Ken Hamblin had a local show in Denver and was nationally syndicated for much of that time. As one of the few black conservative voices in talk radio, he adopted the signature line "just an unassuming colored guy," and the phone number for his show was 1-800-IM-ANGRY.

Hamblin was a former newspaper photographer and documentary film producer who came to the radio booth predisposed to be skeptical of the civil rights movement and affirmative action, claiming that those ideas have outlived their usefulness. He bristled at the suggestion that black physicians, attorneys, and other professional persons achieved their positions because of the affirmative action rather than hard work. He also criticized the welfare system and other public assistance programs for allegedly making poverty worse by providing incentives for black women to have more children and disincentives for seeking work.

Many liberals, both black and white, labeled Hamblin's beliefs as racist, even though they were tame compared to those of other national hosts. In 1993, a group of black legislators meeting in Denver heard Hamblin's show and threatened to instruct the Federal Communications Commission to review the station's operating license. They accused Hamblin of pandering to the station's conservative audience by choosing "material that will sell" instead of telling his listeners the truth.[106]

Fox News personalities Brian Kilmeade and Andrew Napolitano cohost the network's top-rated radio program, *Brian and the Judge*, which airs weekday mornings in most markets. Politics is the primary topic of the show, but the pair occasionally venture into other fields, such as sports, entertainment, and popular culture.

Kilmeade is a former sports journalist who made the transition into news and political talk following the terrorist attacks of September 11, 2001. Napolitano is a former superior court judge who is considered an expert on the U.S. Constitution.

While Kilmeade is a strict conservative, Napolitano is more of a libertarian, but together they have developed a rapport that works, both between themselves and their callers.

One of the newest entries in the conservative talk radio competition is former Congressman Mark Foley, a Florida republican who resigned in 2006 after the media reported that he sent sexually explicit electronic mail messages to several underage congressional pages. Foley had cosponsored legislation to protect minors from being exploited online, and while the irony was lost on him and his supporters, it was not lost on the national media or his congressional colleagues.

In September 2009, he began his talk radio career with a local program on WSVU in West Palm Beach, Florida. A statement released by the station called his show "conversational" and claimed that the email controversy was "not something for us to comment on. . . . as far as what he did with his personal life, that's not for us to say."[107]

Chapter 5

The Progressives

Darwinism and Political Talk Radio

Talk radio is, media critics claim, the perfect meritocracy because the hosts able to generate the largest audiences and the most advertising revenue will rise to the top, while those unable to do so will fail. And that's generally been the case with liberal or "progressive" talk radio programming. One media critic analyzing the prospects for Air America at its onset commented that "Al Franken's success as a comedian may not necessarily translate into success as a talk show host; instead of being given an audience by fiat, he will have to earn it, just as any other host of any political ideology would have to."[1]

Some stations have experimented with pairing a liberal host with a conservative, but such ventures have a better chance of succeeding on the local level, as opposed to programs that are syndicated nationally. Some national programs claim to pair a conservative with a liberal, but a closer examination of their positions reveals that a more accurate description is that of a conservative and a moderate.

Conservative host Michael Reagan says that liberal talk radio doesn't work because "liberals aren't fun. . . . Liberals have no sense of humor; they don't know how to laugh at themselves. The ability to do so is what made my father (former President Ronald Reagan) so popular."[2] Fellow conservative host Rush Limbaugh agrees and asks, "Who wants to listen to a bunch of people run down the country and run down the institutions and traditions that made this country great?"[3]

Lynn Woolley, a Memphis-area talk radio host and coauthor of a 2007 book, *The Death of Talk Radio*, offers another theory as to why liberal or progressive talk radio struggles. "My guess is that liberalism only makes sense in short sound bites," he wrote. "When a liberal host has three hours a day to explain kooky ideas such as nationalizing the healthcare system, his arguments collapse under their own weight. But when conservative ideas and values are stripped of emotion and analyzed with truth and logic, they stand up to the scrutiny."[4]

Another host, John Gambling, adds that, "Conservative talk radio is not pessimistic, it's optimistic; it's hopeful for the future. Liberal talk radio is whining and crying, and nobody wants to listen to that."[5]

Robert Thompson, a Syracuse University who teaches courses in the history of television and radio, believes that conservative talk radio hosts are more successful than their liberal counterparts because they've mastered the us-against-them approach to political debate. "The conservative hosts approach every debate by outlining for the audience a clear view of what is right and what is wrong," Thompson says. "It's an easy formula, because all they have to do is lay out their position in black and white terms and then watch the fur fly. Liberals tend to take a more open-minded approach and use qualifiers like, 'yes, but what about. . . .' and 'you also have to consider. . . .' That makes more sense from an intellectual standpoint, but it doesn't produce the fur-flying atmosphere that makes the conservative shows so popular."[6]

Long before the advent of Air America, liberal host Thom Hartmann lamented the domination of the talk radio airwaves by conservatives, and commented that national radio networks were missing a critical business opportunity by not pursuing progressive (his term for "liberal") programming. "Stations that take the plunge into progressive talk will serve democracy by offering a loyal opposition (which Americans always appreciate), and earn healthy revenues in an industry where it's increasingly difficult to find a profitable niche," he said. "And whichever network is first to realize this simple reality and provide stations with solid progressive or democratic talk programming will build a strong, viable, and financially healthy business."[7]

Media critic L. Brent Bozell claims that liberal talk radio has more potential to be successful at the local level than nationwide and would be best advised to stick to urban areas where progressive ideas are more likely to find friendly audiences. "San Francisco, Boston, or Washington, D.C. may embrace a local liberal talk show, but America will continue to reject the national ones," Bozell wrote in his 2004 book, *Weapons of Mass Distortion.*[8]

"Progressives have never fully embraced talk radio, and have instead gravitated to the free-wheeling transparency of online outlets," says Faiz Shakir, research director for the Center for American Progress. "Conservatives, on the other hand, seem to enjoy the experience of talk radio—they are more comfortable with ideological voices filtering and relaying only certain information that they want to hear. It seems highly unlikely that Limbaugh's influence is going to fade. If the Clinton years serve as any kind of lesson, his influence will continue to grow among conservative activists while a Democrat is in the White House. So in the near-term future, the next ten years or so, I think it's a safe bet to say that political talk radio will continue to be a major factor."[9]

Bill Hess, operations manager for Clear Channel's AM talk stations in Washington, D.C., believes the quality of liberal talk shows has been steadily improving over the last decade. He points to the success of *The Ed Schultz Show*, based at WWRC in Fargo, North Dakota. In most markets, Schultz competes against Limbaugh, but in a few cities his show airs on tape during the afternoon drive. "Schultz is a breakout talent," Hess said when Clear Channel expanded Schultz's syndication deal in 2006.[10]

In 2005, the Center for American Progress (CAP), a liberal Washington think tank, opened an in-house radio studio in the heart of the District of Columbia and encouraged radio talk show hosts to originate their broadcasts from there. The first week it was open, liberal hosts Ed Schultz and Stephanie Miller did remote broadcasts, and as of late 2009, the facility is in almost continuous use. While it is open to talk show hosts of all political camps, CAP staffer Andrea Purse reports that inquiries from conservative hosts are rare, as most are aware of the center's progressive leanings.

The following year, CAP joined forces with radio industry giants Clear Channel and Jones Radio Networks to organize a talent hunt for new liberal talk hosts. Organizers said the competition, conducted in the style of *American Idol*, was necessary because the audience for liberal talk was growing so much faster than the talent available. "Great talkers such as Ed Schultz, Bill Press, and Al Franken are hard to find," said Paul Woodhull, owner of a Washington-based radio management consulting firm, because "progressive talk has grown so big, so fast, that all of us in the industry are searching high and low for more great progressive talk radio talent."[11]

Industry consultant Jim Casale refers to National Public Radio (NPR) as a mirror image of conservative talk. "NPR and (conservative) talk radio have the same core values," he says. "They give people an in-depth understanding of the news that they can't get elsewhere. They also get perspective on the news—they get interpretation."[12]

Some media critics believe the failure of liberal talk radio is the underlying reason for speculation that congressional democrats will attempt to reenact the Fairness Doctrine. "Unable to compete in talk radio's free marketplace of ideas, the liberal media, leftist politicians, moveon.org, and Media Matters, have doubled their efforts to bring back the Fairness Doctrine," wrote Ronald Bush in a 2008 column in the *Pensacola News Journal*. "The Fairness Doctrine is straight from the communist manifesto because it would force radio stations to carry liberal talk show hosts. The truth is, liberalism does not sell, but conservatism does. That is the reason that one liberal talk show host after another fails when in direct competition with conservatives."[13]

As of early 2010, liberal talk hosts were doing well—not threatening Limbaugh or Hannity but successful enough to stay on the air—in Miami, San Diego, Denver, San Francisco, Seattle, and Portland. But in other major-market cities, liberal talk was difficult to find. In mid-market and small-market cities, it was nearly impossible to find.

"It is sad that liberal talk has not yet caught on," says Dan Mason, program manager at WNTM-AM in Mobile, Alabama. "But Rush invented the genre. The more popular programs are the ones that follow the leader."[14]

Conspiracies Real and Imagined

The birth of the "conspiracy theory" approach to talk radio can be traced to two of the earliest practitioners of liberal talk: Long John Nebel and John Henry Faulk. Nebel was an eighth-grade dropout who spent much of his twenties and thirties in a variety of occupations—theater usher, freelance photographer, and auctioneer—until finding his niche in talk radio at age forty-three. Despite his limited education, he was an avid reader who educated himself by spending almost all of his free time in public libraries and becoming conversant on numerous political and social topics. The nickname "Long John" had several possible origins, but the most popular assumption was related to his slender build: six-foot-four but never more than 160 pounds.

Nebel spent much of his radio career at WOR in New York, where he was eventually syndicated by the Mutual Radio Network. His show was broadcast live from midnight to 5:30 a.m. eastern time each weekday morning. His usual format was to interview a guest for the first ninety minutes, allow callers to ask questions of the guest for another ninety minutes, then spend the last two and half hours taking calls on other topics. Most of the guests and topics were related to politics, but he occasionally ventured into popular culture and entertainment news.

As his listeners' interest in politics and other traditional talk show material waned, Nebel ventured into oddball topics such as reincarnation, alleged government mind-control techniques, unidentified flying objects, voodoo, witchcraft, parapsychology, hypnotism, conspiracy theories, ghosts, and other subjects he referred to as the "strange and unexplained." After he married Hollywood starlet Candy Jones, she became his cohost and regaled listeners with her own tall tales of being a victim of Central Intelligence Agency mind-control experiments.

Sometimes the callers' comments were more outrageous than those offered by Nebel, so WOR engineers invented a technology that is still in use at most talk radio stations today: the seven-second delay. While it was intended to curtail obscene or otherwise offensive language used by callers, engineers would also use it when profanities were uttered by Nebel or his in-studio guests.

In 1962, Nebel moved to cross-town rival WNBC and earned a then-unheard of annual salary of $100,000. He stayed there until 1973, when the station switched formats. Nebel landed at WMCA in New York, where he stayed until his death in 1978.

Faulk was a folksy and populist radio host who had a brief career in the 1950s. His program was neither wildly popular nor successful; he was more famous for earning a spot on Senator Joseph McCarthy's infamous blacklist of alleged communist sympathizers and his legal battle to get his name removed. The legal decision in his favor eventually led to the dismantling of the list.

Faulk attended the University of Texas and entered the Merchant Marines. He later worked for the American Red Cross during World War II. After the war, he went to work in radio.

Faulk's broadcasting career included a stint at CBS Radio, where he worked with legendary radio and television figure Edward R. Murrow. His political problems began when a group investigating his background erroneously reported to CBS management that Faulk's work with his union, the American Federation of Television and Radio Artists, was connected to his belief in communist principles. Faulk lost his job as a result of the allegations, and he filed a defamation suit against the group that conducted the investigation. The result was a $3.5 million damage award, but on appeal that was lowered to $500,000—an amount nearly wiped out by the legal fees and debts incurred during his lengthy period of unemployment.

Faulk was successful in having his name removed from the blacklist, but radio work was still hard to find. He spent much of his later years visiting college campuses and speaking on topics related to the First Amendment and civil rights. He also wrote a 1963 book, *Fear on Trial*, in which he chronicled his legal struggles to have his name removed from the blacklist. In 1975, the book was made into a movie of the same title, with William Devane portraying Faulk. Faulk also had bit parts on the television skit comedy program, *Hee Haw*.

Rapping with Petey Greene

Ralph Waldo "Petey" Greene was an ex-convict who spent much of the 1960s on the radio airwaves at WOL-AM in Washington, D.C. He saw his job as "shaking up the establishment," as he used the show as a platform to rail against poverty and racism both in Washington and nationwide. By the standards of that decade, many labeled him a "shock jock." But compared to those who followed him, Greene's act was fairly benign.

Greene overcame years of drug addiction to become one of the Beltway's most prominent media personalities. Shortly after leaving prison following a lengthy sentence for armed robbery, Greene began his radio career with a show called *Rapping with Petey Greene*. His station manager was Dewey Hughes, then husband of Cathy Liggins Hughes, who later took over the station and became one of the most powerful women in radio.

In 1984, Greene died of cancer at age fifty-two. His autobiography, *Laugh If You Like, Ain't a Damn Thing Funny*, was published posthumously in 2003. In 2007, Greene was portrayed by veteran actor Don Cheadle in the 2007 biopic film, *Talk to Me*.

Mystery Man

When the Denver Broncos hired new head coach Dan Reeves in 1981, the public ceremony was held at Nichols Arena during the halftime festivities for a Denver Nuggets basketball game. Selected to emcee the brief program was one of the city's most controversial figures—Alan Berg, a local talk radio host who drew both cheers and jeers as he appeared on court to introduce Reeves. The coach, a newcomer in town who knew nothing about Berg's reputation, looked at him during the ceremony and asked, "And who are you?" For Berg, forty-six years old and struggling with alcoholism, depression, and career issues, the question was much more complex than Reeves had intended it. *Just who was Alan Berg?* Dan Reeves wanted to know. And so did Alan Berg.

Berg attended the University of Colorado for two years, then transferred to the University of Denver, then to the University of Miami, where his parents owned a winter home. He then transferred to Northwestern University in his hometown of Chicago, and finally graduated from DePaul University Law School. After graduation, he began working as a law clerk for a prestigious Chicago firm while his wife taught at a school for gifted children. When he set up his own law practice, his clientele included accused shoplifters, rapists, and deadbeat dads, as well as a buxom young woman charged with indecent exposure for appearing topless on a Chicago beach. He lost the case, but gave a vigorous defense, calling the female breast "one of God's most beautiful creations."[15]

He defended comedian Lenny Bruce against obscenity charges stemming from his appearances in Chicago, but his most lucrative clients were from Chicago's underworld—all of them, of course, wrongfully accused. His annual salary of $100,000—a lot of money in the late 1950s—improved his lifestyle but also increased his appetite for expensive homes, vehicles, and rare wines. The stress of Berg's workload left him with a sleeping disorder and mild epilepsy, which produced seizures at inconvenient times.

While still living in Chicago, he met Jewish comedian Jackie Mason, who suggested Berg consider a second career in stand-up comedy. But terrified at the possibility of a seizure while on stage, Berg froze during his audition and never attempted comedy again.

For Berg, the stress of his heavy caseload and dealings with unsavory characters worsened his seizures and drove him into alcoholism. He gave up his law practice and ended up back in Denver, running his own custom shirt business in leased retail space in the lobby of the upscale Albany Hotel. While operating the store he met two people who would figure prominently into his life. The first was Audrey Oliver, a young black woman who he helped obtain a small business loan to open a shoe store. They eventually had an affair, even though Berg was still married to and living with his wife. The second was Laurence Gross, host of a radio talk show on KGMC, who was impressed with Berg's ability to converse with him and other customers on a variety of topics. Gross offered him a Sunday afternoon show in the fall of 1971. When Berg explained his fear of freezing up or possibly having a seizure—the same fear that derailed his career as a stand-up comedian—Gross told him not to worry. "You're on opposite the Denver Broncos," Gross said. "No one will be listening to you anyway."[16]

At the beginning, Berg was terrible, even by his own admission. He talked too fast, slurred words together, trailed off at the end of sentences, and smoked while he was on air, which caused him to cough and wheeze. Not only were listeners turned off, but also the sponsors who were paying extra to have Berg read their ads live.

It took more than a year for Berg to settle into the job, and gradually the listeners, advertisers, and station management were pleased. While his on-air delivery had improved, his consumption habits were dangerous for the station's equipment; he frequently damaged microphones and other equipment by spilling soft drinks, and his habit of accidentally starting trash can fires with smoldering cigarettes became part of his legacy.

When the radio station was sold and the new owners asked Berg to avoid discussing controversial topics on the air, Berg protested by asking women in the audience to call in and share their favorite recipes. Berg resigned and moved across town to KHOW, but it was a poor fit because talk was only part of the station's programming, and the station's target demographics were substantially younger than what he was accustomed to.

In 1976 Berg was diagnosed with a brain tumor, and after surgery his seizures stopped. A change in station management caused him to move from KHOW back to KGMC, which had changed its call letters to KWBZ. In exchange for getting his old job back, he promised the station owners he would tone down his show.

That promise didn't last long. He was soon attacking white supremacists in general and the Ku Klux Klan specifically. Based largely on frequent mentions of his Jewish heritage, his support for interracial marriage and gay rights, and dislike for the KKK and other white supremacist groups, Berg lived under the shadow of constant death threats, received both by telephone and through the mail. In 1979, the leader of the local chapter of the KKK burst into his radio studio and pointed a gun at him, but the suspect quickly fled the building when he was told the police were on the way.

The death threats had prompted Berg to no longer have his home address and phone number listed in the local telephone directory, but one year the phone company published the information by mistake. In the last years of his life, he became almost overwhelmed by paranoia, always sitting facing the door while eating in a restaurant, taking different paths driving to and from work each day, and carrying a small pistol in his pocket or on the floorboard of his car.

Early in 1981 KWBZ switched its format to the country music format, and Berg was out of work again. But by this time his reputation was national, creating a bidding war for his services among Denver talk station KOA and other stations in Detroit and Oklahoma City. He opted to remain in Denver and took the job at KOA.

In and out of the radio booth, Berg was an odd character. He wore the same dark pants and plaid jacket nearly every day, yet he owned more than 150 pairs of shoes. His home was immaculate, based largely on the fact that he was seldom there. There were seldom groceries in his house except for coffee and food for Fred, his Airedale. He owned no dishes or silverware, as he ate out for almost every meal.

Biographer Stephen Singular described the six-foot-two Berg as "about a hundred and fifty pounds and held together by wire instead of bones. . . . He wore longish gray hair, a full whitish beard over his pock-marked face, and thick, eyebrow-level bangs."[17]

Some speculate the long hair and beard were to cover the scars from numerous plastic surgery procedures undertaken to appear closer in age to the much younger women he dated between (and sometimes during) his two marriages. According to Singular and numerous obituaries, Berg dealt with the stress of his life and his work by consuming a steady diet of caffeine, cigarettes, amphetamines, and antidepressants.

With each publication of the Arbitron ratings books, Berg consistently beat his cross-town rival at KNUS, Peter Boyles. In the era of the early 1980s, when many radio talk show hosts, both conservative and liberal, adopted the moniker of "the man you love to hate," Berg truly embraced the title. When a local newspaper took a poll in which it asked readers to identify their favorite and least favorite radio talk show hosts, Berg won in both categories.

Over the years the Federal Communications Commission (FCC) received numerous complaints about Berg, including many from surrounding states. Berg was still considered a local host, but the station's 50,000-watt transmitter allowed its signal to travel through the clear mountain air to more than thirty states. Luckily for Berg and station managers, he worked during a time of restraint by the FCC, and each complainant received a kind thank-you letter that included an explanation of the First Amendment values at stake. As long as Berg did not use obscenities, his program content was largely beyond the agency's purview.

On his afternoon show on June 18, 1984, Berg interviewed Colorado Congresswoman Patricia Schroeder about the upcoming Democratic National Convention in San Francisco, which his station was planning to send him to cover. He also took a few minutes to prepare for the scheduled topic of the following day's program: gun control.

Berg never got to work the next day. On his way home that night, Berg had dinner with his ex-wife and stopped at a grocery store to buy dog food for Fred. As he pulled into his driveway about 8:30 p.m. and stepped out of his Volkswagen, he was cut down by thirteen bullets from an assault rifle fired from a vehicle parked across the street. He was dead before the police arrived seven minutes later.

Within the hour, police informed coworkers at KOA of Berg's death, and Ken Hamblin, a conservative African American host who disagreed with Berg on nearly every political issue but nevertheless considered him a friend, was on the air at the time. He passed the microphone to Rick Barber, the station's top news reporter, who announced that Berg was dead. Hamblin didn't leave the studio for more than twenty-four hours—not out of fear for his life, as local journalists speculated—but in order to field phone calls from Berg's listeners. Fred was brought to the studio so Hamblin and other coworkers could look after him.

By the following day, the Federal Bureau of Investigation, which had monitored white supremacist groups in the area for years, began working the Berg case, along with more than sixty local law enforcement officers. After gathering physical evidence at the scene and interviewing neighbors—who remember seeing two men sitting in the car across the street—investigators pored through years of show tapes and personal letters that included threats. Some in the media commented that Berg had made so many enemies in the region and had received so many death threats that investigators wouldn't know where to start.

Police also looked into Berg's mafia connections back in Chicago, where his law practice required him to defend unsavory characters. They also questioned the man who had walked in the studio and threatened Berg with a gun five years earlier, wondering if he might have come back to finish the job. Other theories came and went, and hundreds of tips were called in to police headquarters, but investigators kept coming back to the primary suspects: a white supremacist group called The Order.

The Order was a splinter group affiliated with the Aryan Nation, whose members rotated among the group's hiding places in rural Colorado and Idaho. In the early 1980s, members spent much of their time attempting to threaten and intimidate judges, lawyers, and liberal journalists. They financed their operations using poorly printed counterfeit currency and money obtained by robbing banks, department stores, and armored cars. In early June 1984, they drew up a hit list for that summer's assassinations: television producer Norman Lear, who produced television programs advocating racial harmony; Morris Dees, a liberal lawyer who ran a white supremacist watchdog group; William Wayne Justice, a federal judge who ruled in favor of school desegregation; and Denver radio host Alan Berg. Berg's murder was the only one carried out.

Within hours of the shooting, members of The Order who had been involved in the murder had scattered across surrounding states. Several were apprehended while committing subsequent crimes, and the leader of the group was killed in a raid on one of The Order's hiding places.

As a result of the investigation and subsequent trial, several of the defendants were convicted of other crimes, including counterfeiting and murder of a Missouri state trooper. The search of one of the group's hideouts, however, produced an automatic rifle that was matched against the thirteen bullets found in Berg's body.

Meanwhile, as motorists in the Denver area burned their headlights in tribute to Berg and memorial services were held at the temple where he worshipped, talk show hosts around the country said they were starting to pay more attention to suspicious people they encountered, wondering if they might also be a target. Many applied for and received concealed weapons permits.

No one was ever formally charged with Berg's murder. Not only was it impossible to determine who among the four men present pulled the trigger, but the federal government chose to invoke the Racketeer Influenced and Corrupt Organizations (RICO) statute and file charges of conspiracy, which took priority over the state's murder case. According to Singular, who covered the case as a reporter for *The Denver Post*, the idea was to "throw the largest possible net over the largest number of suspects."[18]

Until the Jon Benet Ramsey case came along twelve years later, the Berg investigation garnered more attention than any other murder case in Colorado history.

Anything but Mickey Mouse

Jim Hightower was born in Denison, Texas, a small border town that was also the birthplace of future President Dwight D. Eisenhower. He earned a degree in government from the University of North Texas, and while at UNT, he developed an interest in politics while serving as student body president and interning at the U.S. State Department. After graduation, he worked as a legislative aide and worked on the 1976 presidential campaign of Oklahoma Senator Fred Harris.

After that experience, Hightower returned to Texas and established a liberal magazine called the *Texas Observer*. He failed in his first campaign for public office, losing the race for a seat on the Texas Railroad Commission. He was later elected to two terms as agricultural commissioner. When he ran for his third term in 1990, he was defeated by future Governor Rick Perry, whose campaign was orchestrated by Karl Rove. During the 1992 presidential campaign, he supported Senator Tom Harkin of Iowa, but eventually cast his superdelegate vote at the convention for Bill Clinton.

In the 1990s, Hightower became known as America's "most popular populist," hosting two radio shows and doing numerous public appearances. Political columnist Molly Ivins said of Hightower: "If Will Rogers and Mother Jones had a baby, Jim Hightower would be that rambunctious child—mad as hell, with a sense of humor."[19]

Hightower was a liberal and a democrat, but he earned a reputation for criticizing public officials of both major political parties as well as corporate icons. He once drew the wrath of Nike for his claim that the company violates health and safety standards for its workers in Malaysian factories and pays them far less than the minimum wage in the United States. He also encouraged his listeners to challenge public officials and hold them accountable; the phone number for his show was 1-800-AGITATE.

Hightower, whose national radio program was syndicated by ABC Radio, saw his program cancelled in 1996. While the network claimed the move was based on low ratings, Hightower and his fans believe he was let go because he criticized on his show the deal in which the Walt Disney Corporation purchased ABC Television and ABC Radio—a deal he referred to as "a Mickey Mouse affair."[20]

Hightower also criticized the Telecommunications Act of 1996, a massive bill that loosened many of the rules that limited media ownership. "We're not talking about a monopoly over toasters," he told his listeners. "We're talking about a monopoly over basic information, and it's a dangerous one."[21]

Since being let go by ABC, Hightower has spent much of his time writing. He is the author of numerous books on American politics, including *There's Nothing in the Middle of the Road but Yellow Stripes and Dead Armadillos* (1997), *If the Gods Had Meant Us to Vote They Would Have Given Us Candidates* (2001), *Thieves in High Places: They've Stolen Our Country and It's Time to Take It Back* (2003), *and Swim Against the Current: Even a Dead Fish Can Go with the Flow* (2008).

He considers his constituency for both his books and radio program to be consumers, working families, environmentalists, small business owners, and "just plain folks." He has been called a "modern-day Johnny Appleseed, spreading his brand of folksy populism across America."[22] Today, he offers daily two-minute essays that are broadcast on more than 150 commercial and public radio stations, on the Internet, and the Armed Forces Radio Network.

Learning Curve

Ed Schultz is a former quarterback at Moorhead State University in Minnesota. After a brief career in the Canadian Football League, he went to work as a radio sportscaster, then made the switch to conservative talk. In the late 1990s he met and dated a liberal activist and community volunteer who bristled at the insensitive way that he and other conservative talkers referred to the homeless on their programs. She invited him to have lunch at a Salvation Army shelter to meet some of the "bums" he criticized on his show. That was the beginning of the end for Schultz's conservative political stances. Today, he is one of the most successful liberal voices on the radio, and the girlfriend who took him to the homeless shelter is now his wife and assistant producer.

Schultz is widely regarded as the most successful liberal talk show host in the country, even though he prefers the label "progressive." His book, *Straight Talk from the Heartland: Tough Talk, Common Sense, and Hope from a Former Conservative,* was published in 2004.

Following Franken

Thom Hartmann developed his interest in politics at age thirteen while campaigning for republican candidate Barry Goldwater in the 1964 presidential election. By age sixteen, he had graduated from high school and was enrolled at Michigan State University. While at MSU he protested the Vietnam War and learned the radio business by working as a part-time news announcer at a local country music station. He never graduated from MSU, but later earned two degrees in herbology at other schools and a PhD in homeopathic medicine at Brantridge College in England.

From 2005 to 2007, Hartmann hosted a local talk show on KPOJ in Portland, Oregon, a station affiliated with Air America. On February 19, 2007, his show went into national syndication on that network.

Today, Hartmann's program is broadcast to more than 1.5 million listeners. In addition to his interest in politics, he is also a scholar of the history and textual analysis of the U.S. Constitution, attention deficit hyperactivity disorder, and a variety of environmental issues, including global warming.

Hartmann rejects suggestions that in order to broaden its audience, liberal talk radio needs to take off some of its edge. Some within the industry claim that in order to "succeed," programming needs to become "less about politics and more about movies, books, theatre, fashion, money, and sports," he says.[23] Hartmann's objections are based on the fact that no one would make the same suggestion to Limbaugh or any other conservative host. He analogizes the idea to asking country music deejays to talk about classical music or classical music hosts to talk about rap. "Radio listeners expect their programs to be true to their genre," Hartmann said.[24]

Redefining Liberal

Alan Colmes has his own radio talk show on Fox Radio, but is better known for being the liberal half of Fox News Channel's *Hannity and Colmes* prime-time television show that he cohosted with Sean Hannity. The hour-long program that ran from 1996 to early 2009 and featured newsmakers being cross-examined by the conservative and liberal hosts.

Today, Colmes has his own syndicated talk show and is one of the few successful liberals on the radio. He defines "liberal" as "someone who sees both sides" and attempts to walk the tightrope between conflicting viewpoints on his show.[25] Media critics assert that as long as Colmes insists on being fair to both sides, he will never overtake Schultz as the king of liberal talk. "He is so enamored with the idea of being fair-minded that he seems compelled to let his own side down just for the sake of it," wrote David Brock in his 2004 book, *The Republican Noise Machine*. "He's also dull as dishwater."[26]

Birth of a Liberal Network

In 2002, Chicago business investors Sheldon and Anita Drobny were upset that their favorite liberal host, Atlanta-based Mike Malloy, lost his national syndication deal and was no longer heard in the Chicago area. The Drobnys were seeking other investors to help Malloy find a new syndication deal when they met Bill Clinton and Al Gore, the former president and vice president, who pitched a more ambitious idea: the development of an entire radio network based on liberal ideology. Recommending that the new network aim high when recruiting talent, Gore reportedly introduced the Drobnys to comedian Al Franken, who became the lead talent for the new venture, along with comedienne Janeane Garofalo. The Drobnys named their new venture Air America.

Two weeks into the venture, Multicultural Radio, scheduled to operate the network's affiliates in Chicago and Los Angeles, claimed a check from the Drobnys had bounced and the network owed the company more than $1 million. Unable to pay the entire amount, Air America was ordered by a court to settle with Multicultural Radio for $250,000 plus legal fees.

After the Drobnys dropped out due to financing problems, the enterprise was taken over by Evan Cohen, a multimillionaire from Guam who had just survived a scare with brain cancer and decided to spend his money and time on worthy causes—one of them being liberal talk radio. He relaunched the network on March 31, 2003, with stations in five major markets: New York, Chicago, Los Angeles, Minneapolis-St. Paul, and Portland, Oregon. Within two weeks the stations in Chicago and Los Angeles dropped out because their sales staffs couldn't sell the time, and a week later the entire network folded. Critics on the right, led by Franken nemesis Bill O'Reilly, gloated. Franken insisted that the failure did not mean there was no audience for liberal talk (as O'Reilly had suggested); the venture just lacked a solid business plan and sufficient rainy day capital to persevere fluctuations in ad sales.

Atlantic Monthly media critic Joshua Green wrote in a 2005 article that while Air America claimed to be the kinder, gentler, and more rationale counterpart to conservative talk radio, its programming is just as angry, but in the opposite direction. "Taken as a whole, the network is already infected by the corrosive negativity, strutting egotism, and bizarre paranoia that marked much of what traversed the conservative airwaves in the late 1990s," Green wrote. "Much of what Air America carries is anger-laced polemic that plays to the furthest-left element of the electorate."[27] Green added that gaining a foothold in talk radio was an integral part of the democrats' master plan to retake Washington. "They are unified in their belief that they must build a political infrastructure to compete with the republicans, and many activists believe that liberal talk radio, though still in its infancy, is already the most mature component."[28]

According to media reports, Air America lost $9.1 million in 2004, $19.6 million in 2005, and $13.1 million in the first ten months of 2006. When the network went bankrupt in October of 2006, it had assets of $4.3 million and liabilities of $20.2 million, including $360,000 owned to Franken.

Later that year, Home Box Office produced a 97-minute film, *Left of the Dial*, which documented the months preceding the start-up of Air America as well as its first year of operation.

Green Family Media, a small media company run by a pair of New York real estate investors, purchased the assets of Air America in March 2007. The network returned to airwaves on May of that year, calling itself Air America 2.0. First-day interviewees included New York governor Eliot Spitzer, New York City mayor Michael Bloomberg, actor Paul Newman, and senators Hillary Clinton and Barack Obama. In January 2010, the network filed for bankruptcy for the second time.

Class Clown

Even though Al Franken has not been formerly associated with Air America since 2004, he was instrumental in its formative years.

Franken was an admitted class clown in high school and college. After winning multiple Emmy Awards for comedy writing and performing in the NBC program *Saturday Night Live*, Franken entered the world of political journalism with books such as *Rush Limbaugh Is a Big Fat Idiot* (1996) and *Lies and the Lying Liars Who Tell Them: A Fair and Balanced Look at the Right* (2003), the titles of which indicate their tone. Fox News sued Franken and his publisher over the subtitle of the latter, claiming trademark infringement over use of the network's signature line, "fair and balanced." A federal judge found the suit to be "wholly without merit," a phrase Franken later used to describe Fox News itself.[29]

Franken seemed to enjoy the publicity the case generated for the book and credited it with much of its rise to the top spot on the *New York Times* best-seller list. He told NPR interviewer Terry Gross that in retrospect, if he had known how much it would help sales, he would have sent Fox a letter at the onset saying, "please sue us."[30]

In 2004, Franken entered the world of talk radio, signing a one-year contract with the fledgling Air America network. Still relishing his legal victory over Fox News, Franken first titled his show *The O'Franken Factor* as a way to poke fun at the similarly titled show of O'Reilly, his conservative counterpart and nemesis.

Franken said the title of his first book (on Limbaugh) was hyperbole and was an "over-the-top ad hominem attack on a man who makes over-the-top ad hominem attacks,"[31] but that the irony was lost on most book reviewers and Limbaugh defenders. Franken often accused Limbaugh and other conservative talk show hosts as shilling for the Bush administration on issues related to national security and the war in Iraq. Apart from his dislike for Limbaugh, much of Franken's act is driven by his loathing of President George W. Bush and presidential advisor Karl Rove.

O'Reilly, discussing Franken in his own book, *Culture Warrior*, wrote that "Franken's modus operandi was to call people with whom he disagreed, like Rush Limbaugh, sophomoric names.... And when critics call him out for such vitriol, Franken would fall back on the defense that his work was intended to be 'satire.' Jonathan Swift would be made physically ill by the assertion."[32]

In 2003, Franken served as a fellow at Harvard University's Kennedy School of Government and was the first nationally syndicated radio host to visit American military personnel in Iraq, participating in five USO tours between 2003 and 2007. In 2008, Franken ran for the U.S. Senate seat in Minnesota against republican incumbent Norm Campbell, and for months following the November 4 voting, election officials in that state were involved in endless recounts. The election was finally settled in Franken's favor in April 2009.

Chapter Five

Looking for Lunch in All the Wrong Places

Many liberal hosts are former politicians seeking second careers. One such example is former California governor Jerry Brown, a far-left liberal whose political platform included opposition to the Vietnam War and advocacy of civil rights and campaign finance reform. As governor he also proposed placing in stationary orbit above the state a communications satellite that could be used in a statewide emergency. The latter idea earned him the nickname "Governor Moonbeam," a moniker that later became applied to other liberal politicians based on their quirky ideas.

In 1995, Brown was hired by the KPGA-FM, a Pacifica Network station in Berkeley, to host a local call-in talk show. Both the radio program and Brown's political action organization, based in Oakland, were called *We the People*. His programs, usually featuring invited guests, explored alternative views on a wide range of social and political issues, from education and health care to spirituality and the death penalty. He was an outspoken critic of both the Democratic and Republican parties, often referring to himself as a "recovering politician" (a phrase intended as an analogy to the term "recovering alcoholic"). As a talk show host, one of Brown's key issues was the inherent problems associated with mergers in the media and the conservative ownership of large radio networks. Brown's program lasted until 1999, when he ran for and was elected mayor of Oakland.

Brown was not the only former democratic officeholder to fail in political talk radio. Former Colorado senator and 1984 presidential candidate Gary Hart, Connecticut Governor Lowell Weicker, New York Governor Mario Cuomo, Virginia Governor Douglas Wilder, and New York City mayor Ed Koch made brief and unsuccessful attempts at talk radio in the 1990s, with many of them promoted by their networks as "The Liberal Answer to Rush Limbaugh."

One of the most unusual cases of a former officeholder switching careers and going into talk radio involves Ben Jones. Jones was the actor who played "Crazy Cooter" Davenport on the 1979-1985 television series *The Dukes of Hazzard*. When the series ended, Jones unsuccessfully ran against incumbent Pat Swindall for a seat in the House of Representatives, representing Georgia's Fourth Congressional District. Encouraged by his-better-than-expected showing, he challenged Swindall again in 1988, and that time won. He served two terms, but lost in the democratic primary in the 1992 election. By the 1994 election, a reorganization of Georgia congressional districts meant he would have to challenge republican Newt Gingrich for his seat. Gingrich easily won the election and went on the become speaker of the house.

Jones then began a six-year adventure in talk radio, much of it spent at WGST in Atlanta. In 1998, he broke with the Democratic Party over its support of President Bill Clinton, and instead called for Clinton to resign in the midst of political scandals. In 2002, with his legal residence now being in Virginia, he unsuccessfully challenged popular republican Eric Cantor for a seat in the House of Representatives, becoming one of the few politicians to seek elected office in more than one state. Despite earning the wrath of the party, Jones is still active in democratic politics. He no longer has his radio show, but writes op-ed pieces for local and national newspapers and has returned to acting part-time.

The Best of the Rest

From 1993 to 1999, Ray Suarez was host of NPR's *Talk of the Nation*, making him one of the few Hispanic talk show hosts in the country. In media interviews, he said that listeners always determined the topics of the program and that he doubts that anyone would attempt to call him a Hispanic Rush Limbaugh. "Listeners are driving the conversation," he says. "Anyone who calls the show and says, 'ditto, Ray' is just not enough."[33]

Today, Suarez is host of *America Abroad*, an NPR program that examines the role of the United States in international affairs. The show is also heard on Sirius XM satellite radio.

Jerry Williams grew up in New York City in the 1930s and adopted a liberal political viewpoint early in life, as his middle-class Jewish family benefited greatly from President Franklin D. Roosevelt's New Deal programs. Five decades later, he spent much of the 1980s as one of the few liberal voices in the Boston talk radio market.

A fan of the progressive social programs of presidents John F. Kennedy and Lyndon Johnson, Williams lamented that the best candidate the democrats could come up with in 1984 was Walter Mondale. He liked liberal social programs but not the high taxes that went with them, often referring to his adopted home state as "Taxachusetts."

Williams was on the air for more than thirty years in Boston, from the mid-1960s to the late 1990s. In the early days he was clearly a liberal, but in his later years he preferred the term "populist." Much of his later years were spent railing against governors Michael Dukakis and William Weld, referring to the latter as "that orange-headed WASP."[34]

Warren Ballentine is an African American attorney who grew up on Chicago's South Side. In his law practice, he defended cases involving murder, sexual assault, police misconduct, drunk driving, drug dealing, gang violence, and domestic relations, while arguing cases based on employment and housing discrimination. He began his talk radio career in 2007, and today his syndicated program is heard in thirty-seven markets via the Radio One Network. He calls on his listeners, who he refers to as "Truthfighters," to pursue solutions instead of just complaining about problems. He is also a frequent guest and correspondent for CNN and Fox Business News.

In 2007, Ballentine joined with fellow African American hosts Al Sharpton and Michael Baisden to organize the National Economic Blackout, a one-day campaign in which African Americans were to have avoided spending money in order to symbolically call attention to a number of economic issues affecting black America.

In an era in which many talk radio stations might have one progressive host and oftentimes none, KGO-AM in San Francisco at one time employed two of the best-known. During the twenty-two years in which their times at KGO overlapped, Bernie Ward and Ray Taliaferro gave the station a one-two progressive punch that reached far beyond the bay area.

Ward joined KGO in 1985 after a brief career in Catholic school teaching and as a member of Representative Barbara Boxer's congressional staff. At first, he was a fill-in host and full-time reporter, but he eventually gave up reporting to become a full-time political talk show host. One of his favorite foils was San Francisco Mayor Art Agnos, who denounced Ward at the beginning of almost every news conference.

In October 1997, the *San Francisco Chronicle* published a story speculating that KGO was allowing Ward's contract to expire. His listeners showed their support by flooding the station's lobby with donations of canned food for a local food bank, getting a headstart on the seven-year tradition that Ward had established. They also staged a midday rally outside of the KGO studios, and soon station executives reversed their decision and renewed Ward's contract.

In December 2007, however, Ward was fired following his indictment on charges of possessing child pornography.

Taliaferro has hosted *The Early Show* at KGO since 1977. His program consists of lively—and sometimes confrontational—discussion of contemporary issues in American politics, culture, and current events. Taliaferro began his broadcasting career in the 1960s. He started at KNEW-AM in San Francisco, then worked in several television jobs before being hired at KGO.

Taliaferro remains one of the most influential African American talk show hosts in the country. His nighttime talk show mainly deals with political issues affecting California as well as the nation. He describes himself as a "progressive democrat." As president of the San Francisco chapter of the NAACP from 1968 to 1971, he was arrested four times during protest rallies.

Michael Jackson, the son of a British soldier, began his radio career in South Africa, where his father was stationed. In the 1960s, the family moved to the United States and settled in California, and Jackson worked a number of radio jobs in San Francisco and Los Angeles, where his British accent was an anomaly. He was first hired at KEWB in Oakland, where he was a typical disk jockey on the overnight shift, but he became bored playing music and began talking at length with listeners who called in with requests. His show morphed into a talk show on which he and his callers bantered about family life and relationship issues. Because of the nature of the show, callers occasionally expressed suicidal thoughts, and with Jackson's permission, police regularly monitored his show and traced some of the calls. On at least one occasion, Jackson is credited with saving the life of a suicidal caller by keeping him on the line until police could intervene.

Today, Jackson's program is based at KGIL in Los Angeles, but is heard on several stations across the southern part of the state. He covers mostly popular culture and politics, and is known for his cerebral style.

Jackson is often praised by media critics for his policy of welcoming callers with opposing viewpoints. "If you have something to say, I don't care what your ideology is," he said in an interview.[35] Jackson is often critical of conservative hosts for not welcoming opinions inconsistent with their own.

Throughout the eight-year presidency of George W. Bush, Mike Malloy was one of his most vocal critics on the airwaves. In addition to ridiculing the president, he also went after republicans in general, fundamentalist Christians, and homophobes. While insisting he is still a registered democrat, he often criticizes politicians of that party as well, and admits that his true political leanings are often more in line with the Green Party. He was born into a Baptist household, but today is an atheist.

Malloy is a former Cable News Network copy writer who began his career in talk radio in 1990, working at WSB in Atlanta. He had a loyal following among Georgia liberals while in the evening time slot, but when the station moved his show to early afternoon to compete against Rush Limbaugh, whose syndicated show aired on cross-town rival WGST, Malloy's show proved to be no match. When WSB declined to renew his contract, he landed at WLS in Chicago, where he stayed until 2000.

Malloy then moved his show to the Internet, where it was moderately successful. In 2004, he was signed by Air America, but that stint lasted less than two years. When Air America went into bankruptcy protection, Malloy decided not to stick around during the reorganization. He then went through a series of syndication deals on second-tier radio networks that had financial problems of their own. Today he is self-syndicated, and his show airs weeknights from 9 p.m. to midnight.

Robert F. Kennedy Jr. is the son of former attorney general and U.S. Senator Robert F. Kennedy and the nephew of the late President John F. Kennedy and Senator Edward M. Kennedy. A graduate of the University of Virginia Law School, Kennedy briefly served as a prosecutor in New York County.

As a result of a 1983 charge of drug possession, Kennedy was sentenced to probation and 1,500 hours of community service. Through that service, he became associated with the Riverkeepers, an environmental group protecting New York's Hudson River. After his court-mandated service, he became the group's chief legal counsel and filed a number of suits against corporate polluters. He helped the group expand its role and today it is known as the Waterkeeper Alliance, which performs environmental watchdog work across the country. In addition to that work, he also teaches environmental law at the Pace University School of Law in New York.

Since 2004, he has cohosted *Ring of Fire,* a syndicated program airing on Air America. His cohost is Pensacola, Florida attorney Mike Papantonio, but for most programs Papantonio is at his home studio and Kennedy is in his office at the university.

Bill Press's first exposure to politics was as chief of staff to a republican state senator in California and later a staff member for Governor Jerry Brown. He began his broadcasting career at local television stations in Los Angeles, but he became nationally known in the 1990s for his political commentary on MSNBC and Cable News Network. At CNN, he was a frequent contributor on programs such as *The Spin Room* and *Crossfire.*

In 2005 he transitioned into talk radio, and today his national program is heard on Sirius XM Satellite Radio. He is also a prolific writer, with his books carrying self-explanatory titles such as *Spin This: All the Ways We Don't Tell the Truth* (2002) and *Bush Must Go* (2004). In his most recent book, *Trainwreck* (2008), Press argues that the recent failures of the Republican Party—and conservatives in general—are indicators that the liberal political philosophy is the best hope for the country's future.

Of all of the progressive talk show hosts discussed in this chapter, Alfred Charles Sharpton Jr. (better known as Reverend Al Sharpton) has the most diverse resume. Before going into talk radio, he worked as a Baptist minister, political candidate, civil rights leader, and judicial activist. Except for politics, Sharpton remains active in all of those fields.

Since January 2006, Sharpton has been the host of *Keepin' It Real*, which airs daily on the Radio One Network. He is also a frequent guest on Fox News, Cable News Network, and MSNBC.

Inside and outside his radio studio, Sharpton is a lightning rod for controversy. In his roles as civil rights and judicial activist, he often publicly defends criminal suspects he believes are wrongfully accused, despite overwhelming evidence to the contrary, and is always raising the possibility of police misconduct and racial profiling in cases where race is an issue. Many other talk show hosts, including Neal Boortz and Bill O'Reilly, have called Sharpton a "race-baiter" based on his tendency to introduce race in his discussion of national news stories, whether applicable or not.

In April 2007, Sharpton landed one of his biggest guests to date: disgraced fellow talk show host Don Imus. The interview took place shortly after Imus's controversial comments about the Rutgers women's basketball team, but before he was fired by CBS Radio.

Since early 2008, the Internal Revenue Service has been investigating his political group over its fund-raising and income reporting procedures. In addition, the state of New York has investigated Sharpton's business interests over alleged tax irregularities, but as of late 2009, no report has been issued in those cases.

Tom Joyner is the host of *The Tom Joyner Morning Show*, which airs weekdays on Radio One Networks.

Joyner is an Alabama native and graduate of Tuskegee Institute, one of the premiere historically black universities in the country. After graduation, he enjoyed a brief career in pop music and was a founding member of The Commodores, along with friend Lionel Richie.

Joyner began his broadcasting career in Montgomery, Alabama, and worked at a number of radio stations in the southeast before taking a job at WJPC-AM in Chicago.

For a while in the late 1980s and early 1990s, he worked simultaneously at two radio jobs: the morning show at KKDA in Dallas, Texas, and the afternoon show at WGCI in Chicago. Commuting between the two jobs every day for almost a decade, he earned nicknames such as "the Fly Jock" and "the Hardest Working Man in Radio."

In 1994, Joyner gave up the two shows to take a nationally syndicated job with ABC Radio. He dealt with a variety of topics, including politics, popular culture, and pop music. In 2005, he took the show to television, but it lasted less than a year.

Joyner is the author of two books. In *I'm Just a DJ, But It Makes Sense to Me* (2005), Joyner offers thoughts on historically black colleges and universities as well as the role of the African American consumer and the importance of fatherhood. In 2009, he authored *Tom Joyner Presents How to Prepare for College*, a book helping college-bound high school seniors and their parents prepare for the transition.

Joyner is an advocate for voter registration, a cause he promotes on his radio show and in public appearances. He created and promotes "Take a Loved One to the Doctor Day," an annual promotion to encourage preventive health screenings. He has also founded the Tom Joyner Foundation to provide financial assistance to students at historically black colleges and universities. Since 1998, it has raised more than $55 million to help African American students stay in school.

In 2004, Joyner was awarded the National Association of Broadcasters' prestigious Marconi Award, and in 1999 became the first African American to be inducted into the National Radio Hall of Fame.

Tavis Smiley was born in Mississippi, but he spent much of his childhood moving around the country as part of a military family.

While a student at Indiana University, he interned as an aide to Tom Bradley, the first African American mayor of Los Angeles. He returned to Indiana University after the internship and earned a bachelor's degree in law and public policy in 1986. Upon graduation, he returned to Los Angeles, where he once again worked for Bradley.

After an unsuccessful run for a seat on the Los Angeles City Council, Smiley became a radio commentator, producing one-minute daily segments titled *The Smiley Report* on a Los Angeles station. He eventually earned a full-time job, hosting his own show on race and politics, and is also a frequent guest on cable television news programs. In the late 1990s, he briefly hosted a talk show on Black Entertainment Television.

Today, Smiley hosts a television program simply titled *Tavis Smiley*, which airs on Public Broadcasting Service (PBS). He also hosts a weekly radio show on Public Radio International (PRI) stations.

In 1999, Smiley founded the Tavis Smiley Foundation, which funds programs that develop young leaders in the black community. In 2004, Texas Southern University honored him with the opening of the Tavis Smiley School of Communications and the Tavis Smiley Center for Professional Media Studies.

Roland Martin is a syndicated newspaper columnist, political commentator on the Cable News Network, and host of a radio talk show on WVON in Chicago. He earned a master's degree in Christian communications at Louisiana Baptist University and is one of the more influential African Americans in media. On his radio program he openly supported Barack Obama during the 2008 presidential campaign, but in his television commentary he subverted his views in order to provide a more balanced look at the democratic field.

Chapter 6

The Libertarians

Equal-Opportunity Skeptics

Although many libertarians bristle at the oversimplification of their philosophy, most practitioners tend to be fiscal conservatives and social moderates. Like conservatives, they believe in lower taxes, a balanced federal budget, and the reduction of spending for entitlement programs such as social security, welfare, Medicare, and Medicaid (some go as far as advocating the elimination of the federal income tax). Many also support the Second Amendment and the rights of gun owners. They don't go as far as liberals in advocating gay rights and access to contraceptives; they just believe a person's sexual behavior is none of the government's business. But their most important issues are the expansion of individual rights and a corresponding restriction in the role and scope of government. According to libertarians, the government that governs best is the one that governs least.

The popularity of the libertarian philosophy is borne out of Americans' growing dissatisfaction with the conservative-liberal dichotomy. That is reflected in the popularity of libertarian talk show hosts such as Neal Boortz, Larry Elder, Glenn Beck, Dennis Miller, and Todd Schnitt. Many libertarian hosts tell their listeners that they are equal-opportunity critics who are skeptical of both democrats and republicans.

You Shall Hear the Truth, and the Truth Shall Make You Mad

Neal Boortz was born in Pennsylvania, but as the child of a career Marine, he spent much of his childhood in California, Texas, and Florida. By his own admission, he was a mediocre high school student, but he went on to earn an undergraduate degree from Texas A&M University, where he worked at the campus radio station, hosting his own show using the pseudonym Randy Neal.

He later earned a law degree from John Marshall Law School in Atlanta, and while building his law practice, he supported himself as a speechwriter for Georgia governor Lester Maddox. He also became a fan of WRNG-AM talk radio host Herb Elliman. The day after Elliman committed suicide, Boortz showed up at the studio to lobby for his job. He quickly found his niche in talk radio, but continued to practice law until 1992, when he gave it up to concentrate on his radio show, which he moved to a cross-town rival station, WSB, in 1993.

In 1999, he became nationally syndicated through Cox Media and today is, by far, the most popular libertarian talk show host in the country. For a signature line, Boortz took the biblical verse, "You shall know the truth, and the truth shall set you free," and perverted it into, "You shall hear the truth, and the truth shall make you mad."

While still a local host in Atlanta, Boortz earned national notoriety in 1988 when he entertained listeners with stories of a new sport called cat-chasing. According to Boortz's explanation, the sport consisted of skydivers jumping out of airplanes in order to pursue cats tossed out a few seconds earlier. Boortz later admitted that he got the idea from the newsletter of a skydiving club in Arizona, but as the gag went along he added details such as the Georgia Cat-Chasing Championship being held in the southeastern corner of the state, with the winners advancing to the National Cat-Chasing Championship in Phoenix. Boortz expected groups such as People for the Ethical Treatment of Animals (PETA) and the American Society for the Prevention of Cruelty to Animals (ASPCA) to protest, but neither group was heard from; both knew it was a hoax. But many listeners bought it—some called requesting information on how they could become participants or spectators, and others called in outrage. Many of the latter group threatened to boycott Home Depot, one of Boortz sponsors, who took the threat seriously enough to cancel its advertising temporarily. Other listeners went as far as to complain to the Federal Communications Commission (FCC) and suggest that it revoke the station's license.

After admitting the hoax, Boortz put together a highlight tape related to the hoax and sold it; he attempted to calm angry listeners by donating the proceeds to local animal charities.

After more than three decades in talk radio, Boortz has built a wide audience, with research indicating his listeners include conservatives, liberals, and fellow libertarians. In most markets his program airs live from 8:30 a.m. to 1 p.m. eastern time, meaning he overlaps with Rush Limbaugh for the last hour of his show. In some markets, programmers avoid the conflict by airing Boortz on tape in the midafternoon or early evening.

Before taking calls, Boortz regales his listeners with a morning dialogue that often includes criticism of wasteful government spending and political correctness. His specific targets for ridicule are public schools (he refers to them as "government schools"), teachers' unions, liberals, smokers, the obese, welfare recipients (he often uses the term "welfare queens"), and those who insist on preserving the Confederate flag as part of their southern heritage (he calls them "flaggots"). He refers to the homeless as "urban outdoorsmen," public education as "taxpayer-funded child abuse," and attention deficit disorder and global warming as "liberal mumbo jumbo" and "scientific fraud."

Boortz also makes an almost-daily habit of informing listeners of which democratic public officials or civil rights leaders have angered him most recently. His favorite targets are Bill and Hillary Clinton, Senators Tom Daschle and Harry Reid, House Speaker Nancy Pelosi, and civil rights leaders Jesse Jackson and Al Sharpton.

But occasionally, even lesser-known names cross his radar screen. After African American Congresswoman Cynthia McKinney, who represents Georgia's Fourth Congressional District (which includes Boortz's hometown of Atlanta) was involved in an altercation with a Capitol Building security guard, Boortz pounced. He called her a "ghetto slut," said her hairstyle resulted from "an explosion at a Brillo factory," and that she looked like "what would happen if Tina Turner peed on an electric fence."[1] In his discussion of the February 2009 proposed economic stimulus package, Boortz referred to the three republican senators who voted in favor of it—Arlen Specter of Pennsylvania and Susan Collins and Olympia Snowe of Maine—as "the three stooges."[2]

Other times he chooses his targets for ridicule at random. One morning he asked listeners to find their copy of that day's *USA Today* and look at the photograph on a particular page. "Look at the man in the photograph wearing a tanktop and cut-off shorts," he told listeners. "The next time you get on an airplane, that's the fat-ass who will be sitting next to you."[3] But many times his humor is more benign, as when he suggested that someone should play a joke on airline pilots by purchasing a warehouse on the approach to Hartsfield-Atlanta International Airport and painting the message "Welcome to Birmingham" on the roof.

"Most talk show hosts use humor where it's appropriate; I use it where it's inappropriate," Boortz says.[4]

Boortz's first venture into book publishing was his 1997 book, *The Commencement Speech You Need to Hear*, which he wrote in the form of a hypothetical commencement address he hoped to deliver to college graduates if ever invited to do so. The general theme of the book was the importance of embracing personal liberty and rejecting the liberal approach to government, using examples from the administration of President Bill Clinton. The following year, he expanded on those ideas in his second book, *The Terrible Truth about Liberals*.

In 2005, Boortz collaborated with his friend, Georgia republican Congressman John Linder, to write *The Fair Tax Book*, a detailed proposal to abolish the Internal Revenue Service and replace the national income tax with a consumption tax that the coauthors claim would be fairer to all income levels and less vulnerable to fraud and evasion. The striking cover of the book features the abbreviation IRS with a red circle and line through it. The "fair tax" plan calls for levying a 23 percent sales tax on retail goods and eliminating taxes related to income, Medicare, Social Security, gasoline, and capital gains. The cornerstone of his plan, Boortz said, would be dismantling the Internal Revenue Service and replacing "nine million pages of gobbledygook with a 133-page tax guide."[5] In 2008, Boortz and Linder wrote a sequel, appropriately titled *Answering the Critics*, in response to the questions raised by the first *Fair Tax* book.

One of Boortz's best-settling books is *Somebody's Gotta Say It* (2007), a collection of essays about what he refers to as the "scourge" of political correctness.

In addition to his radio show and career as a political author, Boortz is also a private pilot who flies himself around the country for public appearances and book signings, and between his homes in Atlanta and Naples, Florida.

Boortz was severely criticized following the April 16, 2007 shooting spree at Virginia Technological Institute. Returning from a news break, the "bumper music" serving as a segue turned out to be from the Pat Benatar song, "Hit Me with Your Best Shot." Boortz argued for days that bumper music for each segment was chosen at random by a computer software program, but media watchdog groups, while believing the explanation, continued to criticize because Boortz refused to apologize for the unfortunate timing. Boortz compounded the criticism by suggesting that the answer to preventing shootings such as the one at Virginia Tech and similar incidents at suburban shopping malls was arming students and other citizens. "Instead of waiting for the government to come save them, the situation could have been handled by just one armed student who could have taken the guy out," he told his listeners.[6]

Boortz downplays the influence that all talk radio hosts have, especially himself. He bristles when callers refer to themselves as his "followers" ("I'm an entertainer rather than a cult leader, and therefore my audience consists of 'listeners' and not 'followers,'" he says).[7] Boortz disputes the FCC's claim of "publicly owned airwaves" and launches tirades at callers who use the term. Consistent with that view, Boortz is opposed to the possible return of the Fairness Doctrine. Midway through President Bush's second term, when speculation circulated in Washington that the doctrine might be on the table in a future legislative session, Boortz predicted that if a democrat was elected president in 2008—especially if it was Hillary Clinton—within six months his or her party would introduce legislation aimed at eliminating talk radio from the airwaves.

Boortz's gruff demeanor has earned him millions of listeners, including many who call to say they were so insulted by his commentary that they will "never listen again." Many call back a week later to say they are still listening and are still offended, but this time they "really mean it" when they say they will "never listen again."

"People on the left think I'm too right, people on the right think I too far left," he told a radio industry panel in 2008. "I love it that way; that's why I call myself a libertarian. I default to freedom on most issues."[8]

While many media critics label Boortz as a "Limbaugh wannabe," others take the comparison much further and harsher. One contributor to a media-oriented blog called Boortz a "small time nobody doing a fascist radio program and trying hard to break into the big time by making outrageous comments and sensational statements meant to stir controversy so he can get on the Limbaugh gravy train."[9] Another blogger added, "Boortz just makes statements his listeners accept as fact without verification. . . . It's really a simpleton's primer for politics. Any good political science major in college can take apart most of Boortz's arguments handily, but they never make it onto his show."[10]

When enthusiastic callers gush about their affection for Boortz or comment on the depth of his knowledge or role in influencing politics, Boortz deflects the compliments with lines such as, "I don't know anything more than my callers or anyone else. . . . I just happen to have a microphone."[11] He is also modest and self-deprecating when comparing his clout to that of Limbaugh and Sean Hannity. "On the grand pecking order of talk radio hosts, I'm one of the smallest peckers there is," he told listeners early in 2009.[12]

He likewise makes no apologies for his demeanor or even his appearance, quipping on the air that he has turned a "nasty behavioral disorder into a successful career" and that he had the "perfect face for radio." His college-age daughter uses a fake last name, a decision that Boortz refers to as "a very good idea."[13]

The Black Ann Coulter

African American radio host Larry Elder was born in Los Angeles to parents of opposing political persuasions. Growing up, he and his older brother were subjected to constant Vietnam-era political debates at the dinner table. He wrote in his 2003 book, *Showdown*, that while his democratic mother could "out-debate (my) republican father in facts, figures, and historical facts, (my) father made more sense I grew older."[14]

Today, Elder is the host of *The Larry Elder Show*, which originates from KABC-AM in Los Angeles and has consistently been the top-rated program at the station since 1994. The nationwide syndication rights make him the second-highest-rated libertarian on the radio (behind Boortz). He also writes a column for *Investor's Business Daily* and a syndicated column that appears in a variety of newspapers around the country.

Like most libertarians, Elder is a conservative on most fiscal issues and a liberal on many, but not all, social issues. He summarizes the dichotomy by saying he favors smaller government and lower taxes and wants the government to "stay out of my wallet and out of my bedroom."[15]

His first book, published in 2000, was titled *Ten Things You Can't Say in America* and served as an expose of the evils of political correctness. As the title indicates, the book lists ten precepts about American politics and race relations that would be risky for politicians, journalists, or celebrities to contradict in public.

But not Elder. He counters those misconceptions with his own opinions, including (1) blacks are more racist than whites, (2) the "glass ceiling" that allegedly prevents women and minorities from advancing in business and politics is not as pervasive and generally believed, and (3) the federal government's "war on drugs" and "war on poverty" are making those problems worse rather than better. "The truth is, race relations in America have never been more cohesive," he wrote. "Considering the staggering diversity of its people, racism in today's America is approaching insignificance. But if you are white and say this, you're a bigot. If you're black and say this, you're an Uncle Tom. Besides, there's good money in yelling 'racism.'"[16]

In his 2008 book, *Stupid Black Men*, Elder attacks ideas such as racial quotas (while stopping short of advocating a complete ban on affirmative action), reparations for slavery, and an obsession with political correctness that requires white journalists and politicians to gingerly tip-toe around the issue of race. Elder echoes the sentiment of one listener who emailed him and said, "Larry, I'd be happy to pay reparations for slavery—just tell all the ex-slaves to come over to my house and line up at the door."[17]

In 2009 Elder published his fourth book, *What's Race Got to Do with It?* It continues on the same theme of his previous books: black Americans should stop using race as an excuse for their failure to be successful, and white Americans should stop making excuses on their behalf. Elder refers to liberal bias of the press—a consistent theme in all four of his books—as a form of "media malpractice."[18] His outspokenness has earned him the nickname of "the black Ann Coulter," given to him by fellow talk show host Al Sharpton.

In September 2003, Elder attempted a television version of the radio program, but it was cancelled after less than two years due to low ratings. He has had considerably more success elsewhere on television, having played himself in *Spin City* and other situation comedies.

An Inconvenient Radio Show

Glenn Beck began his radio career at age thirteen, winning in a contest a one-time, hour-long shift as a disk jockey at a Seattle radio station. In high school he took an after-school job at a Christian radio station, a stint that ended when his mother and brother both committed suicide.

Beck was admitted to Yale University based largely on a letter of recommendation from Connecticut Senator Joe Lieberman. He began studying theology but stayed only one semester.

In 2000 he discovered the Mormon Church, remarried, and settled into a radio job in Tampa, Florida. Two years later his show became syndicated, and in 2006 he began hosting a nightly news-talk program on CNN Headline News. In 2008 he moved his television program to Fox News, while his radio show reaches 8 million listeners and is heard on more than 400 stations. He credits his religion and second wife with resurrecting his career.

Beck is syndicated by Clear Channel Communications, which some critics refer to as a "front" for conservatives and the Republican Party, as most of its personalities are located on the far right of the political spectrum.

Beck clarifies that he is a libertarian, not a republican, and on his television and radio shows he attacks republicans and democrats with equal fervor. His issues include Islamic terrorism, illegal immigration, and global warming. On the latter issue, he doesn't focus as much on the cause—claiming he doesn't know enough about it to determine whether the blame should lie with industry or natural factors—as he does on possible solutions.

During the 2008 presidential primary season, Beck called Hillary Clinton "comrade" and a "liberal fascist" and John Edwards a "communist." He quipped that if Clinton sincerely believed in affirmative action, she should "concede 5 extra percentage points to Obama in every opinion poll."[19]

Beck has labeled Clinton as a "stereotypical bitch," speculated that the wife of Ohio Representative and presidential candidate Dennis Kucinich "must have been on a date rape drug" when the couple married, and described television host Rosie O'Donnell as "a fat witch with blubber pouring out of her eyes."[20]

Beck once joked that he wanted to strangle documentary filmmaker Michael Moore and called Michael Berg, who criticized the Bush administration after his son Nicholas was beheaded in Iraq, as "despicable" and "a scumbag."[21]

Beck's presentation style has drawn comparisons to those of Rush Limbaugh and even Father Charles Coughlin. In a 2009 profile, *Time* magazine called him the "hottest thing in political rant, left or right," and hinted that his admitted attention deficit hyperactivity disorder (ADHD) contributes to his fondness for hyperbole and outrageous comments.[22] Horror novelist Stephen King refers to Beck as "Satan's mentally challenged younger brother."[23]

Beck is one of numerous talk-show hosts to perpetuate a false news story that made the rounds on the Internet for more than two years: that the federal government was drafting plans for a "NAFTA Superhighway" stretching from Mexico to Canada and that eventually the three countries that comprise North America would become one. The *Time* profile accused Beck of having "a knack for stitching seemingly unrelated data points into possible conspiracies."[24]

Beck's first book, *The Real America*, is a semiautobiographical collection of essays on politics, celebrity culture, and the decline in personal responsibility. His 2007 book, *An Inconvenient Book*, takes a lighthearted approach to issues such global warming, computer dating, media bias, political correctness, child molesters, the minimum wage, the United Nations, and illegal immigration. The title was a spoof on the title of Al Gore's book, *An Inconvenient Truth*. His third book, *Arguing with Idiots*, was published in 2009. Beck is also publisher of a monthly magazine titled *Fusion*, which offers commentary on politics and popular culture written by Beck and a variety of contributors.

Career Change

One of the newest and more surprising entries into the political talk genre is Dennis Miller, a former comedian best known for anchoring the satirical news segment "Weekend Update," on the NBC series, *Saturday Night Live*. With a background in stand-up comedy and friendships with Hollywood liberals, observers were surprised when Miller made a drastic career change in 2002 to enter the talk radio business as a "conservative libertarian."[25] In an interview with *USA Today*, Miller said, "I might be profane and opinionated, but underneath are some pretty conservative feelings. On most issues, between (Bill) Clinton and (Newt) Gingrich, I'd choose Newt in a second."[26]

When Miller joined the staff of New York City's WOR 710 in October 2007, media critics said it was part of the station's effort to gear up for the following year's election campaign.

Schnitt Happens

Todd Schnitt has a local morning program at WFLZ-FM in Tampa, Florida, where he works as "MJ Kelli," and a nationally syndicated afternoon show that originates from a studio in the same building. His signature line is "Schnitt Happens." Schnitt is a registered republican and fiscal conservative, but often finds his other political positions in alignment with other libertarian hosts. A publicist for Jones Radio Networks, which hold his syndication rights, identifies the program's target demographic as 25-44 and refers to Schnitt's style as "edgy talk radio with a rock radio edge."[27]

It Seemed Like a Good Idea at the Time

Prior to May 22, 2009, few people outside of Chicago had ever heard of radio shock-jock Eric "Mancow" Muller. That was the day Muller, a "conservative libertarian," staged an on-air demonstration in order to prove that waterboarding—the controversial interrogative technique which simulates drowning—is not as harmful as the media had been describing it. With a Chicago Fire Department paramedic and Marine Sergeant Klay South looking on, Muller was placed on a 7-foot long table, his legs were elevated, and his feet were tied. Muller thrashed on the table, and instantly threw the toy cow he was holding as his emergency tool to signify when he wanted the experiment to stop. The entire episode lasted less than ten seconds. "It is way worse than I thought it would be, and that's no joke," Mancow told the media after the demonstration. He later likened it to a time when he nearly drowned as a child. "It is such an odd feeling to have water poured down your nose with your head back. . . . It was instantaneous. . . . and I don't want to say this: absolutely torture."[28]

The waterboarding episode wasn't Muller's first stunt based on a controversial political issue. In 1993, after the national media reported that Air Force One had tied up a runway at Los Angeles International Airport for more than an hour to allow President Clinton to have his hair cut by a local stylist, Muller carried out his own parody of the incident. Instead of an airport runway, Muller chose the San Francisco-Oakland Bay Bridge, not far from his then-employer, KYLD in San Francisco. He used several vans to block the westbound lanes while his sidekick, Jesus Gomez, got a haircut.

The Best of the Rest

David Brudnoy, a gay activist stricken with AIDS late in his career, worked in the Boston talk radio market for nearly two decades. He was a libertarian who local media critics called "erudite and eclectic."

Brudnoy was a former film critic who earned a doctorate in east Asian studies from Brandeis University, then taught at several schools in the northeast, including Boston University. He began his talk radio career in 1976 at WHDH and immediately immersed himself in local political issues, the biggest of which was desegregation and busing plans for local schools. He later moved to WRKO and then WBZ, where he became the top-rated talk show host in New England.

After he admitted his homosexuality in 1994, he became involved in the gay-rights movement and established the David Brudnoy Fund for AIDS Research.

In 1997, Brudnoy received two of the industry's most prestigious honors: the National Association of Talk Show Host's Freedom of Speech Award and the Marconi Award for "Personality of the Year."

Due to his illness, he was forced to broadcast from his home for the last years of his life. Following his death in December 2004, he was eulogized by Massachusetts senator Edward Kennedy and then-Governor Mitt Romney.

Mark Davis is the host of *The Mark Davis Show*, which is based at WBAP-AM in the Dallas-Ft. Worth area and is heard on several stations across the state. Davis describes himself as a "libertarian conservative." He opposes religious influence in public schools, illegal immigration, and bans on public smoking. However, unlike many other libertarians, he opposes the legalization of drugs and supports the war in Iraq.

Davis was born in San Antonio, Texas, but raised in the Maryland suburbs of Washington, D.C., in the 1960s and 1970s. He graduated from the University of Maryland in 1979 with a degree in journalism. Davis began his broadcasting career as a reporter and anchor at a NBC television station in Charleston, West Virginia. His career took him in increasingly larger markets—Jacksonville, Florida; Memphis, Tennessee; and then Tampa, Florida—before landing in Dallas-Ft. Worth in 1994.

He has had two stints in national syndication: a three-hour Sunday afternoon broadcast from 1998 through 2003 and a two-hour weekday show, following his local program, from 2005 to 2007.

In addition to his radio show, Davis frequently does fill-in work for Rush Limbaugh and writes a weekly column in the *Dallas Morning News*, where he expresses libertarian views in a heavily conservative part of the country. In the summer of 2009, many of his columns dealt with President Obama's controversial appointment of Federal Appeals Court Judge Sonia Sotomoyer to fill a vacancy on the U.S. Supreme Court. After acknowledging the merit of the Sotomoyer's inspirational life story, Davis dismissed her appointment as one based solely on demographics rather than judicial qualifications. There was merit to nominating a qualified woman, and also nominating a qualified Latino, Davis admitted, but Sotomoyer was a candidate who belonged on neither list. "President Obama has, unfortunately, given us exactly what he promised, a nominee who allows feelings and personal agendas to color her judicial temperament," Davis wrote.[29]

Gene Burns is the host of a popular political talk show based at KGO-AM in San Francisco, where he has worked since 1994. He describes his style as "raw, rough and tumble, occasionally hostile, but basically honest and unfiltered."[30]

Burns was raised in Hornell, New York. As a child he dreamed of being a lawyer, but instead began a life-long career in broadcasting in 1962. He held various positions at radio stations in upstate New York, Pennsylvania, and Maryland, which included reporting assignments in Vietnam and the Middle East. He eventually returned to Hornell to become news director at WWHG-FM, where he also hosted a political talk show. He ran for president on the Libertarian Party ticket in 1984, then moved to Orlando, Florida, where he hosted a radio talk show and briefly ran a small retail candy business. In 1985, he moved to WRKO-AM in Boston, where he worked with local broadcasting icons Jerry Williams and David Brudnoy and saw his show became the top-rated midday show in the area.

In 1992, Burns was named one of the "25 Greatest Radio Talk Show Hosts of All Time" by *Talkers* magazine, and that same year moved to WOR in New York City, where his syndicated show was heard on more than 100 stations. After suffering a mild heart attack in 1994, he moved to KGO-AM, where he remains today. In addition to his nightly political talk show, Burns also does a weekly program on food and wine.

On his World Wide Web site, Burns laments the failure of libertarian candidates in the 2008 election and announced that until the libertarians establish themselves as a viable third party, he will align himself with the democrats. "The Libertarian Party has failed to gain meaningful traction for many reasons worth discussing at another time," he wrote. "For now, after a forty-year exile, I have re-registered as a democrat, allowing me the opportunity to participate in what I see as profound and fateful choices as we attempt political and policy course corrections desperately needed. I can't sit this one out secure in my libertarian bubble."[31]

Chapter 7

The Women

The Unfulfilled Dream

"Women in talk radio is an unfulfilled dream," declared an editorial in the June 2007 issue of *Talkers,* the industry's trade publication. "But the industry is tremendously interested—even to the point of obsession—with the relationship between females and the medium. As well it should be—both in terms of targeting female listeners and recruiting more females into on-air and management positions. If talk radio is to take its place on equal footing (and inevitably on superior footing) with music radio, then it must become a spectrum of distinctly different demographically targeted formats. Obviously, this includes females."[1] The editorial went on to express optimism stemming from the success of Randi Rhodes, Stephanie Miller, and other nationally syndicated women.

Georgia host Martha Zoller is one woman in the industry who shares the editorial's positive outlook. "I am optimistic," she says. "This is a third career for me and I love it. . . . it is not easy, especially being syndicated. There is a lot of product out there and you have to be competitive. . . . I just get up every day, put my armor on, and get out there again."[2]

The First "First Lady of Radio"

On March 6, 1933, Eleanor Roosevelt became the first first lady to hold a news conference, and she forever changed the role of how the president's spouse would be perceived by the public and the media. Many of her subsequent news conferences were exclusively for women reporters. In the early stages of World War II, she hosted a weekly radio program in which she interviewed prominent politicians of the day on issues such as the rising cost of living, freedom of speech, popular culture, and the duty of women to maintain family morale during the war. After her husband died and she moved out of the White House, she and her daughter, Anna, began fifteen-minute radio programs that ran three times per week on the ABC Radio Network.

The Second "First Lady of Radio"

As one of the pioneering women in television, Mary Margaret McBride is today referred to as the "Oprah Winfrey" of the early television era. While her television program of the early 1950s—consisting of recipe sharing, folk wisdom, and interviews with newsmakers—was popular, McBride would later make her mark in a different form of broadcasting, earning the title "First Lady of Radio" for her work in the late 1950s and early 1960s. In media interviews, McBride described her work as aimed at "young married women who had left their jobs to raise their children, but had not lost their interest in the outside world."[3] She continued working broadcasting part-time until her death in 1976.

The Third "First Lady of Radio"

Like many children growing up in the 1950s, Catherine Liggins-Hughes became fascinated with radio while listening to the Platters and the Everly Brothers in the privacy of her bedroom. Her first exposure to the world of broadcasting came at Howard University in Washington, D.C., where she worked for the dean of the university's communications school, famed broadcaster Tony Brown. She was eventually assigned to handle marketing and business affairs for the campus radio station, and within a year the station turned its first profit in its 100-year history. She later worked as general manager for a commercial station, then bought her first station, WOL-AM, in 1980.

As both owner and on-air talent, Hughes was successful in creating a talk station capable of serving the needs of Washington's African American population. In 1986 she purchased an FM station, WHUR in Washington, and her portfolio eventually grew to become the Radio One network. She prides herself on providing opportunities to female and African American talent. More than two-thirds of the company's employees are African American, and she has appointed several women as general managers of her stations.

Today, Radio One is a $2 billion enterprise that is the nation's largest black-owned radio network. She has received numerous awards inside and outside the radio industry, and her company was named "Black Business of the Year" by *Black Enterprise* magazine in 2000. She has turned over day-to-day operation-duties to her son, but she still handles the long-term planning responsibilities and occasionally still works behind the microphone.

According to radio historian Marc Fisher, Liggins-Hughes brought a level of sophistication to WHUR that station personnel had not seen before, including the first attempts to conduct and interpret audience research in a way that produced meaningful changes to the program schedule.[4] Prior to her taking that step in the mid-1970s, audience research was just beginning to gain the attention of station managers and sales representatives at white-oriented stations and was nonexistent at black stations.

Hannity in High Heels

As a student at Dartmouth University in 1983, Laura Ingraham wrote for the school newspaper, the *Dartmouth Review*, and while researching a story on controversial music Professor William Cole, audited his class. Cole was known for frequently sharing his Marxist-socialist views with his students, and when Ingraham's story reported those sentiments as well his lax grading policies, Cole sought her out in her residence hall. Cole demanded that she apologize to him in front of the class, and when she refused, he launched an obscenity-laden tirade in front of the class. Unknown to Cole, another *Dartmouth Review* reporter was present and wrote an article on the incident. Cole later sued both the newspaper and Ingraham for defamation and asked for $2.4 million in damages. The case was settled out of court, with the financial settlement not disclosed.

In addition to her one-woman campaign against Cole, Ingraham also crusaded against gay students, reportedly outing them by sending to their parents photographs of the students attending meetings of a campus gay support group. While at Dartmouth she dated fellow student newspaper reporter Dinesh D'Souza, who would later become a noted political author and commentator.

Ingraham's conservative credentials are beyond reproach—she's so far right that some critics call her "Hannity in High Heels"—a reference to ultraconservative host Sean Hannity. Her first foray into politics was working on the staff of Education Secretary Bill Bennett during the second term of President Ronald Reagan. When Bennett left that post, Ingraham became a clerk to Supreme Court Justice Clarence Thomas, an experience she drew upon in 2005 when she discussed and opposed President George W. Bush's nomination of Harriet Miers to the Court. Ingraham opposed Miers with the same fervor with which Rush Limbaugh had opposed Bill Clinton's appointment of Zoe Baird (to be attorney general) twelve years earlier.

In 2003, Ingraham assailed the liberal influence of the entertainment industry in a book titled *Shut Up and Sing*, the title of which was inspired by the controversy involving the Dixie Chicks' public denunciation of President Bush during a concert in London.

Ingraham (pronounced ING-ram) believes in traditional conservative values, writing about them in two books and allowing them to dominate her program. That includes being antitax increase, antiabortion, antipornography, antigay marriage, and antipublic school.

Ingraham can be tough on politicians she doesn't like (mostly liberal democrats), but her barbs are benign compared to those of fellow conservatives such as Limbaugh and Bill O'Reilly. During the 2004 presidential election campaign, for example, she played the theme song from the 1960s television program *Flipper* every time she talked at length about democratic candidate John Kerry, who earned a reputation for frequently reversing his positions on major issues.

Today, Ingraham has 5 million listeners per week. Her weekday morning program is nationally syndicated by Talk Radio Network. In 2005 she was treated for breast cancer, but has since made a complete recovery.

Apples Falling Far from the Trees

In the fall of 1964, Stephanie Miller was a three-year-old, growing up in the small town of Lockport, New York. Her life changed dramatically when her father, New York representative William E. Miller, was selected as Barry Goldwater's vice-presidential running mate. More than forty years later, Miller became friends with C. C. Goldwater, granddaughter of the late Arizona senator, and the two developed a World Wide Web site they titled "Goldwater-Miller 08" that mimicked the artwork of their ancestors' unsuccessful campaign. A disclaimer at the bottom of the home page clarifies that the campaign is fictional, and a closer examination of the site informs visitors its purpose is to draw attention to the downfalls of the current Republican Party (the younger Goldwater and Miller are both liberal democrats), which they believe has drifted far away from what the older Goldwater and Miller envisioned. The site also serves to promote C. C.'s documentary film about her grandfather that debuted on Home Box Office in 2007.

Miller was a one-time comedienne specializing in political satire. She moved into talk radio in 1993. Like many of her talk radio colleagues, she calls herself "progressive" rather than "liberal."

In July 2008, Miller was one of two American talk show hosts (libertarian Neal Boortz was the other) to participate in a panel discussion on political talk radio. Originating from the American Embassy in London as part of a larger meeting to examine the American political process, the session began with a brief discussion of talk radio and the presidential campaign, but soon reverted to the typical conservative talking points about the alleged liberal bias of the press. As they frequently do on their respective programs, Boortz insisted the bias is real, and Miller denied it. "Facts tend to have a liberal bias," Miller told the audience.[5] Later in the program the discussion turned to the role of Rush Limbaugh. "At one time, I was the only person listening to rush Limbaugh and asking, 'is this man on drugs?'" she quipped.[6]

High Stakes

Romain Morgan remembers her three-year-old daughter, Melanie, as a precocious child growing up in Missouri and once sitting on the lap of Harry S. Truman when the family visited the former president's home and library in Independence. The daughter of a liberal civil rights attorney and stay-at-home mom, Melanie had a conventional childhood. While attending a Catholic high school, she rebelled against the traditional student uniforms until school administrators made them optional—and a career as a political activist was born.

Melanie began her career in broadcasting while attending Lindenwood University, a Presbyterian school in nearby St. Charles. She didn't graduate, but did spend quite a bit of time at the school's radio station, where she learned both the technical and artistic sides of the business. Her first postcollege job was as a reporter for KGO, the ABC network affiliate in San Francisco. One of her early assignments was reporting on the 1983 bombing of Marine barracks in Beirut, Lebanon, which killed 241 Americans.

In the early 1990s Morgan's career almost ended when she became addicted to gambling, a problem chronicled in the 1997 made-for-television movie, *High Stakes: The Melanie Morgan Story*. Morgan has since served in leadership roles in a state-wide organization dealing with problem gambling and has told media interviewers she has not gambled since 1993.

In her fifteen years in political talk radio, Morgan has established herself as one of the leading conservative voices in the nation. From 1994 to 2008, Morgan was the cohost of one of San Francisco's top-rated drive time radio shows, *The Lee Rodgers and Melanie Morgan Show*, on KSFO 560 AM. One of her more significant accomplishments was a 2002-2003 interview with California Republican Party chairman Shawn Steel, during which the two discussed the potential for a recall vote for Governor Gray Davis. Several enthusiastic listener phone calls gave the idea momentum, and less than a year later Davis was out of office.

More recently, Morgan has established herself as a leader in the national pro-troop movement, rallying millions of Americans to support the U.S. military in general and war on terror in particular. *San Francisco Chronicle* media critic Joe Garofoli pointed out that Morgan's success in the liberal-dominated talk radio scene in San Francisco was based largely on KSFO's demographic profile, which reveals that 90 percent of its listeners live in the suburbs, an area he describes as "well-educated, largely well-heeled, predominantly male, overwhelmingly white—and starved for conservative chatter."[7]

In July 2005, Morgan led a delegation of talk radio hosts to Iraq to interview U.S. troops and allow them to tell their stories live to the American people. Morgan told her listeners that the goal of those interviews was to broadcast the voices of the troops live to the nation—"unedited and unfiltered by the liberal media." For her work in Iraq, Morgan won the Associated Press' Mark Twain Award for "Best Special Program."

In October 2006, Morgan coauthored a bestselling book, *American Mourning*, which told the story of two American heroes who had paid the ultimate sacrifice in the war on terror. Morgan said the goal of her book was to counter the media attention paid to anti-war activists, including Cindy Sheehan, the mother of a soldier killed in Iraq, who frequently protested outside the Bush ranch in Crawford, Texas.

Morgan created her own news headlines when she accompanied her fourteen-year-old son on his school field trip to a California mosque where John Walker Lindh, an American who sympathized with the Taliban, attended. During the trip she began to question mosque personnel about Lindh's attendance at the facility and whether they were aware of his radical leanings. "That pretty much haunted me ever since," the son told the *Chronicle* media critic. "Everybody said my Mom was crazy and teased me about it."[8]

In February 2007, Morgan and her cohost accused democratic activist George Soros of concealing his Jewish heritage and claimed that he was complicit with the Nazis in rounding up Jews for extermination during World War II. The next day KFSO Program Director Ken Berry issued an on-air apology to Soros and the station's listeners, and less than a year later, Morgan and Rodgers' show was off the air. KFSO's parent company, Citadel Broadcasting, claimed that move was unrelated to the show's tendency to generate controversy, but was instead related to the company's "across the board financial cost-cutting."[9]

Before leaving the airwaves, Morgan created controversy with personal attacks against democrats and media representatives. She said Speaker of the House Nancy Pelosi should be painted with a "bulls-eye against her wide laughing eyes" and that if *New York Times* Editor Bill Keller were to be tried and convicted for treason, she would "have no problem sending him to the gas chamber."[10]

Today, Morgan is chairwoman of Move America Forward, a nonprofit group that collects food, greeting cards, and small gift items for American troops serving overseas and provides counterprotests against antiwar efforts such as Michael Moore's documentary film, *Fahrenheit 9/11*. The organization supported many of the positions of the Bush administration, but the relationship is not reciprocal. Garofoli described the relationship as "toxic" and reported that Morgan and her supporters were so far right that she was often "stiff-armed" by the administration. Garofoli added that because of her blonde hair and telegenic appearance, she was often criticized as an "Ann Coulter wannabe," but Morgan doesn't shy away from the moniker. "I was a snotty bitch even before Ann made it fashionable," she said in a 2006 media interview.[11] Radio host Keith Olbermann twice named Morgan as "Worst Radio Host in America."[12]

Father Doesn't Always Know Best

As a child, Randi Rhodes was told by her father that because she "wasn't smart and wasn't pretty," her best career option was to go into the military.[13] She went to nearby Fort Hamilton and enlisted in the Air Force. After being honorably discharged in 1980, she began her career in radio at low-power country music stations in Texas. From there she moved to Mobile, Alabama, for her job in talk radio, and within a few years her career had taken her to the ultimate talk radio market—New York City. Throughout the 1990s she moved around the country, sometimes by her own choice but more often as a result of getting fired. In 2004 she joined the on-air talent pool at Air America, where she stayed until early 2009. In 2007, *Talkers* magazine named her "Woman of the Year."

Today, she hosts *The Randi Rhodes Show* on weekday afternoons. In many markets, Rhodes goes head-to-head against Limbaugh and often edges him in ratings points.

During the 2008 presidential primary season, Rhodes made profane remarks about New York Senator Hillary Clinton as well as 1984 vice-presidential candidate Geraldine Ferraro. She was suspended and eventually fired by Air America, prompting her to give numerous media interviews during which she questioned Air America's "commitment to free speech."[14] Within a month Rhodes was hired by Nova M Radio, and when that network filed for bankruptcy protection, she was hired by Premiere Radio Network, a subsidiary of Clear Channel Communications.

A Progressive Feminist, and More

Tammy Bruce hosts a nationally syndicated show across a variety of talk networks, including Clear Channel and Infinity. Her program generally reflects the content of her books: *The New Thought Police* (2003), *The Death of Right and Wrong* (2004), and *The New American Revolution* (2005). Similar in content and tone to Bill O'Reilly, Bruce rails against political correctness on college campuses and in the media and urges Americans to wake up from the "cultural coma" that has resulted in the "decline of the values and character that our nation was built on."[15]

Bruce is host of *The Tammy Bruce Show*, which in most markets airs weekdays in the early afternoon. Her World Wide Web site describes her as an "openly gay, pro-choice, gun-owning, pro-death penalty progressive feminist" who has voted for presidents as diverse as Ronald Reagan, Bill Clinton, and George W. Bush.[16] She is active in numerous social causes, mostly those related to AIDS and domestic violence prevention, and from 1990 through 1996 was president of the Los Angeles chapter of the National Organization for Women.

The Best of the Rest

Rachel Maddow is the host of a syndicated talk radio program, *The Rachel Maddow Show*, which airs on Air America Radio. Maddow also hosts a nightly television show of the same title on MSNBC.

Maddow is a native Californian who earned an undergraduate degree in public policy from Stanford University and PhD in political science from Oxford University, where she was the first openly gay American to be awarded a Rhodes Scholarship.

Maddow began her radio career at WRNX-FM in Massachusetts, where she earned the job as a result of a station contest. She worked at a number of stations throughout New England before earning her own national show on Air America in 2004.

Laura Flanders hosts a talk program that airs weekend evenings on Air America. She is one of the founders of a media watchdog group, Fairness and Accuracy in Reporting (FAIR).

Flanders says that talk radio has been a "old fashioned boys club" because men are better suited to its us-against-them style. "That's not the style that many women would choose," Flanders says. "It's safe to say that women are generally not so confrontational and provocative, but talk radio largely is, which is why I say the format itself is, basically, typically male."[17]

One advantage women find in radio, as opposed to television, is that they no longer have to be concerned about their looks. That's one of the factors that motivated Christine Craft, a veteran television news anchor who was fired, as she was told, for being "too old, too ugly, and not deferential to men."[18] She quickly landed at job at KFBK in San Francisco, the station that a decade earlier had given Rush Limbaugh his start. "Radio," she told author Peter Laufer for his 1995 book, *Inside Talk Radio*, "is far more satisfying than reading a teleprompter and looking perfect."[19]

Despite her preference for the field, Craft learned it was not without its own pitfalls—ratings. She was fired in 1993 when her ratings slumped and advertiser interest in sponsoring her program waned. She ended up enrolling in law school at the University of the Pacific, graduating in 1995. Today she practices law and does fill-in work for other talk radio hosts.

Diane Rehm began her broadcasting career as a volunteer at WAMU-FM in Washington, D.C., in the early 1970s. Within a few years she was chosen to take over the station's popular morning news and talk program, *Kaleidoscope*, which was eventually renamed *The Diane Rehm Show*. She recently celebrated her twentieth anniversary as host of the show, which is now nationally syndicated by National Public Radio. It is also available through Sirius XM Satellite Radio and on the Internet. Her trademark is her gravelly voice, but she rarely discusses its cause: a rare vocal condition called spasmodic dysphonia.

Over two decades she has interviewed presidents and presidential candidates, Supreme Court justices, other policy makers, and entertainers. In 2003, she recorded the last interview with children's television host Mister Rogers before his death.

Lynn Samuels began her broadcasting career as a fund-raising volunteer at public radio stations. When a host called in sick on short notice, she was chosen to fill-in, and that eventually turned into a full-time job. In 1992 she was hired as Barry Farber's cohost at WABC in New York, but she eventually earned her own show, and her liberal stances on most positions made her stand out against the station's otherwise conservative lineup of on-air talent. Also helping her standout was her thick "Noo Yawk" accent and habit of dropping the word "fuck" into her banter. She was fired in 2002, and after a brief stint at a crosstown station, she was hired at Sirius Satellite Radio.

Sandy Rios was the host of an afternoon drive time program on WYLL-AM in Chicago from 1993 to 2001, then left to be president of Concerned Women for America. During her six-year term she also hosted a nationally syndicated program titled *Concerned Women Today*. In 2007, she returned to the afternoon drive slot at WYLL. Today, she is president of a conservative political think tank, The Culture Campaign, as well as a Fox News contributor.

Martha Zoller is a 1979 graduate of the University of Georgia, where she earned a degree in broadcast journalism. She has spent her entire radio career serving that state. Her interest in talk radio began when she was listening to Gainesville's WDUN-AM in 1994 and heard a discussion of Hillary Clinton's comment that she didn't want to "stay home and bake cookies" like other women. She called the station to respond, and she eventually became a regular caller. Later that year, she began working at WDUN and has been at that station ever since. Her show, simply titled *The Martha Zoller Show*, is heard across the state, syndicated by Georgia News Network.

Zoller has a reputation for snagging big names for her show, including Senator Saxby Chambliss and former House Speaker Newt Gingrich. She is also a frequent guest on Cable News Network, Fox News, and MSNBC, commenting on southern politics as well as national issues. In 2005, Zoller was one of several American talk show hosts to visit Iraq as part of the "Voices of Soldiers" program organized by the Department of Defense.

Zoller says that while gender bias on the part of employers and listeners may have held back other women in political talk radio, she has embraced the challenge. "I do think that women in radio, especially in political talk, approach it differently," she says. "I haven't spent my life behind a microphone; I got into it a little late. I was in my thirties. I had run a business, been a mom and a stepmom, driven the car pool, helped out in my husband's office. So I brought to the table a 'regular person' approach. I'll be honest, it's much tougher for women in radio, but I am not deterred."[20]

Janet Parshall is the host of the ultraconservative, Christian-based radio talk show titled *Janet Parshall's America*, which airs daily on the Salem Radio Network. Parshall also hosts a daily television talk show for FamilyNet television. She is a graduate of Carroll College and serves on the board of directors of the National Religious Broadcasters. Parshall has hosted two television documentaries: *George W. Bush: Faith in the White House*, and *Speechless: Silencing the Christians*. Both aired on the Inspiration Network and other religious stations.

In 2005, she accepted President Bush's appointment to serve as the U.S. delegate at the 49th Session of the United Nations Commission on the Status of Women. She has also been named by *Talkers* magazine as one of the top 100 radio hosts in America and has received numerous other honors within the broadcasting industry and from Christian conservative groups. Parshall has coauthored seven books with her husband, Craig.

Chapter 8

The Haters and the Shockers

Cause and Effect, or Maybe Not

On January 27, 2008, a troubled Tennessee man named Jim Adkisson walked into a Knoxville church and began shooting, killing two people and wounding seven others. When police executed a search warrant for the man's home, they found a collection of books by talk show hosts associated with hate radio, including the modern-day king of hate, Michael Savage. Given Adkisson's known hatred of liberals and homosexuals—attitudes often reflected by Savage and other talk radio hosts—critics of the genre speculated that he was prompted to kill by what he heard on the radio. Rory O'Connor, a former newspaper reporter turned political blogger, suggested that talk show hosts who spread hate on the radio had "blood on their hands"[1] in the case, a charge similar to those leveled thirteen years earlier following the bombing of the federal building in Oklahoma City.

"Would Jim Adkisson have killed without prompting from extreme right-wing talkers?" O'Connor asked on his blog. "We'll never know—but isn't it time to step back and think about the effect this sort of debased dialogue is having on our democracy and our society? We all need to examine our accountability, as well as look for new strategies to contain the spread of hate speech in our media—before someone else gets killed."[2]

One respondent on O'Connor's blog responded with the following parable: "I knew a guy in college who would go into a bar, tell two other guys at different tables that each one had called the other an 'asshole,' then stand back and watch the idiots beat the crap out of each other," the person wrote. "I think that summarizes what talk radio shock jocks are doing—on the right and on the left—and then laughing all the way to the bank."[3]

A decade earlier, gun control advocates speculated that a Colorado man arrested for firing shots at the White House had been inspired by an on-air rant against President Clinton offered by Colorado Springs talk show host Don Bak-

Baker. A militant gun enthusiast and gun control opponent who occasionally broadcast from a local gun shop, Baker had suggested his callers "take the summer off" and go to Washington, D.C., to oppose Clinton's proposed ban on assault weapons. Upon hearing of the incident and speculation about the man's motivation, Baker denied his responsibility without backing away from his comments. He voluntarily took a thirty-day leave of absence, but before doing so called the suspect "a jerk, a wacko, and a creep. . . . if this man thinks that I or Rush Limbaugh are the reason he went out there, he needs psychiatric counseling."[4] When he returned to the airwaves, Baker reportedly agreed to "tone down" his remarks at the encouragement of station management.

That incident was not Baker's first brush with public criticism. He had previously said of Attorney General Janet Reno, "We ought to slap her across the face" and "send her back to Florida, where she can live with her relatives—the gators."[5]

In early 2009, three hate crimes generated national attention due to critics' belief that hate radio allegedly motivated the perpetrators to act. In Destin, Florida, a man killed two exchange students visiting from Chile because he believed them to be illegal aliens. A few weeks later and a few miles away in Fort Walton Beach, another troubled man killed two law enforcement officers because he heard on talk radio that President Obama was sending police to confiscate citizens' guns. In Pittsburgh, three police officers were killed by yet another mentally unbalanced talk radio listener.

Author and blogger David Neiwert coined the term "eliminationists" to refer to the radical conservative movement and its efforts to rid American society of every group outside of the mainstream: both legal and illegal aliens, feminists, abortion doctors, blacks, Latinos, Asians, gays, Jews, and Muslims—along with any liberal or moderates who defend them. Neiwert cites examples such as the near-extermination of native Americans in the 1800s, the rise of the Ku Klux Klan in the early 1900s, and the internment of Japanese-Americans during World War II.

The newest threats, Neiwert says, are the rise growth of hate groups spreading their messages across the Internet, as well as mentally unstable individuals who listen to talk radio and take the rhetoric seriously.

In his 2009 book, *The Eliminationists: How Hate Talk Radicalized the American* Right, Neiwert defined eliminationism as "the politics and a culture that shuns dialogue and the democratic exchange of ideas in favor of the pursuit of outright elimination of the opposing side, either through suppression, exile, and ejection, or extermination."[6] He compares some talk radio hosts and other provocateurs to the village idiot who is allowed to roam through a community poking anyone he dislikes in the eye with a sharp stick.

We Don't Discriminate; We Hate Everybody

Unlike conservative talk radio, which offends people unintentionally, "hate radio" does so on purpose. Media historians contend that hate radio was born in a backlash, with conservative white male hosts railing against the progressive movements for civil rights, gay rights, affirmative action, and women's liberation.

Gary Bledsoe, president of the Texas Conference of the National Association for the Advancement of Colored People (NAACP), places the blame for the increase in public expressions of hate on the growth of talk radio, which he believes makes such expressions more acceptable and even fashionable. "People drive around listening to it, hearing other people mocking, poking fun, and speaking in a black dialect trying to be funny," he said in a 2004 newspaper interview. "It's almost like inciting a riot. People who are already predisposed to be hostile toward minorities, people who hold racist views, are able to manipulate others into believing they shouldn't feel guilty about using derogatory and insensitive terms."[7]

Political scientist Murray Edelman claims that conservative talk radio—and more so those based on hate—have become instruments for denouncing all the groups that already suffer discrimination: homosexuals, women, racial minorities, and members of certain religions.

In an October 5, 2003, commentary on the CBS program *Sunday Morning*, contributor Nancy Giles chastised Limbaugh and other talk radio hosts for interjecting race in every issue, reminiscent of an early time in world history. "Hitler would have killed if he had been in talk radio," Giles said.[8]

Political journalist Randall Bloomquist claims that "while no responsible station would seek or condone racism or race-baiting from either callers or hosts, talk radio is nevertheless a reflection of society. . . . it reflects some of the racial hostility and bias that's out there."[9]

Media researcher Leigh Stephens Aldrich claims that hate radio represents a double standard for station owners, who routinely deny access to the airwaves to politicians and community activists they deem to be too offensive, while not applying such standards to their own on-air talent.[10]

The alleged connection between hate radio and violence can be traced back to 1995, when President Bill Clinton blamed the bombing of the Alfred P. Murrah Federal Building in Oklahoma City on the "promoters of paranoia" and "loud and angry voices" on talk radio. "It (talk radio) is too often used to keep some people as paranoid as possible and the rest of us all torn up and upset with each other," Clinton told a talk radio audience following the bombing. "They spread hate, they leave the impression by their very words that violence is acceptable. . . . I never want to look into the faces of another set of family members like I saw yesterday."[11]

While he didn't mention any hosts by name, media critics and fellow democrats inferred that he was talking about Rush Limbaugh. The next day, NBC newscaster Bryant Gumbel reported on Clinton's comments and extrapolated names such as Limbaugh, G. Gordon Liddy, Michael Reagan, Bob Grant, and Oliver North—talk show hosts who, in Gumbel's words, "cater to angry white men."[12] Gumbel clarified his comments by adding that talk show hosts "take to the air every day with the same basic format: detail a problem, blame the government or some other group, and invite invective from like-minded people."[13]

Reagan was one of several hosts assuming he was one of the talk radio hosts to whom Clinton referred, and the next day issued a news release demanding that the president clarify his remarks. One copy went directly to the White House press office. As he wrote in his book, Reagan claimed the statement said, "The president should either name me as one of the 'loud and angry voices' or say clearly, 'I wasn't talking about Michael Reagan.'"[14]

The *Los Angeles Times* joined the fray with a front-page editorial that claimed the bombing "alters the once-easy dynamic between charismatic talk show host and adoring audience. . . . Hosts who routinely espouse the same antigovernment themes as the militia movement must now walk a fine line between inspiring their audience and inciting the most radical among them."[15]

Nationally syndicated columnist Molly Ivins wrote in one of her columns, "Do I think the climate of hate speech, hate radio and hate politics contributed to the torn, tiny bodies in Oklahoma City? I know they did."[16] Another syndicated columnist, William Raspberry, added, "Talk show hosts need to understand that their words, no matter how innocent or rhetorical or satirical they may in fact be, have the power to push certain people over the edge and into violence."[17]

The Media Research Center, a conservative think tank based in Washington, D.C., called Clinton's bluff and offered a $100,000 reward to anyone who could prove the causal link between conservative talk radio and domestic terrorism or hate crimes.

O'Connor believes that ultraconservative hosts regularly employ and promote hate speech aimed against women, minorities, homosexuals, and foreigners over public airwaves, and in doing so, blur the lines between entertainment, opinion, and journalism. "Proclaiming that their antigay, antiwoman, and racially or ethnically charged remarks are merely meant as good-humored, inoffensive, and 'politically incorrect' fun, these highly paid, hugely powerful, mostly male and all-white 'shock jocks' deliver one-sided, highly politicized versions of the news, influence our national conversation, and affect legislation on important social issues ranging from immigration to abortion," he wrote in his 2008 book, *Shock Jocks: Hate Speech and Talk Radio*. "At the same time, they foster a climate of social acceptance of racist, homophobic, and xenophobic language and hate speech—one that inevitable leads to tolerance of hatred."[18]

The apparent willingness of some networks to defend their hosts against accusations of "hate speech" prompted conservative host John Ziegler to remark, "The more money you make your employer, the more free speech you get."[19]

The disdain of the extremist hosts for the administration of new President Barack Obama is not new. Some of them are so far right on the ideological spectrum that during the previous administration they held President George W. Bush in almost the same contempt—for not being conservative enough.

The World According to Charles Coughlin

Father Charles Coughlin began his broadcasting career in 1926 with a program for children, which was carried by telephone from his parish in Royal Oak, Michigan, to WJR in nearby Detroit. Within a few years, Coughlin was using the radio to preach to adults as well, broadcasting nationwide on Sunday afternoons on CBS Radio. *Fortune* magazine called him the "best thing to happen to radio."[20]

Coughlin (pronounced CAW-glen) was described as "silver-tongued" and "golden voiced" by some, and by others the "mad monk of Royal Oak" and the "Radio Messiah." Biographer Donald Warren describes Coughlin as "the first public figure to obliterate the distinction between politics, religion, and mass media entertainment."[21]

Coughlin was on the air decades before call-in shows became popular, yet he is known by media critics as the "father of hate radio." Modern-day hosts such as Limbaugh, Savage, Hannity, and O'Reilly are often compared to him, but except for Savage, few modern-day radio personalities reach the extremes that Coughlin did a half-century ago.

In the early years of the Great Depression, Coughlin believed that in both of his roles—preacher and radio host—his job was to motivate people to help others in the Catholic tradition.

Coughlin began his radio career by delivering messages with benign titles such as "The Importance of Religion in a Man's Life." But as America entered the Great Depression and a second world war loomed on the horizon, his rhetoric took an abrupt turn. He formed the Radio League of the Little Flower, which broadcast both benign religious content as well as inflammatory rhetoric that many critics labeled as racist, homophobic, anticommunist, and anti-Semitic. His topics included "The Red Menace" and other threats to society. That later expanded to the threat of "international business moguls" (code words for Jewish bankers). He referred to capitalism and communism as twin evils and denounced the press as demonstrating a liberal bias, with his favorite target being the *Detroit Free Press*. After a public disagreement with Notre Dame University president Theodore Hesburgh, Coughlin denounced the honorary degree he received from the university and accused the institution of teaching Marxist doctrine.

Not only was Coughlin the father of hate radio, but he may have also used his show for the first public opinion poll, as he asked his listeners to write to his studio indicating whether or not they wanted him to continue criticizing Roosevelt's New Deal.

When the CBS station in Philadelphia asked in an audience poll if listeners would prefer hearing Father Coughlin or the New York Philharmonic Orchestra on Sunday afternoons, Coughlin's program got 94 percent of the vote.

From 1926 to 1942, Coughlin was one of America's most persuasive orators and held considerable political power. His army of followers consisted mostly of misfits: elderly pensioners, farmers, rural and small-town merchants, and disillusioned middle-class men and women of many religious denominations. Many of those followers helped fund his political operation by mailing donations of one and two dollars each. Long before the Internal Revenue Service scrutinized churches that spent their money on political action, donations poured in to his church in Royal Oak. His church was housed in a huge octagon-shaped building that dwarfed neighboring buildings and featured a 150-foot cross on the front lawn. From that building he delivered his in-person sermons to local parishioners, offered weekly social and political commentaries on the radio, and published a weekly tabloid newspaper titled *Social Justice*. Across all three forms of communication, Coughlin's themes were consistent: the Roosevelt administration was corrupt, Jews and communists were taking over the country, and it was up to individuals to stand up for their rights, even if it meant challenging politicians and law enforcement. During the Great Depression of the 1930s, such ideas appealed to many middle-income Americans.

The groundswell of public support helped Coughlin form the National Union for Social Justice (NUSJ), a hybrid of a religious and political organization that was the forerunner of today's Moral Majority (founded by Reverend Jerry Falwell in the 1980s). Although they were not members of the NUSJ, Coughlin referred to as personal friends such influential persons as Joseph Kennedy Sr., Clare Booth Luce, Douglas MacArthur, Bing Crosby, Henry Ford, Eddie Rickenbacker, and CBS Radio Chairman Bill Paley.

His friendship with Paley was not enough, however, to save his network program in 1931. Paley and Coughlin disagreed over the content of his scripts, but out of friendship Paley helped Coughlin set up his own independent network, which the latter formed by purchasing time on more than two dozen local stations in the Midwest. Guarding against the loss of control that would come with selling advertising, Coughlin funded the operation entirely with donations that came in the mail. At the height of his popularity he was receiving more than 10,000 pieces of mail per week—more than anyone in the country, including President Roosevelt.

By the late 1930s, the National Association of Broadcasters (NAB) had established a code of ethics that prohibited criticism of individuals based on their race or ethnicity. Although the NAB denied that provision of the code was intended to curtail the broadcasts of any specific individuals, media historians speculate it was aimed at Coughlin and his Jehovah's Witness counterpart, Reverend Judge Rutherford. By the following year, both Coughlin and Rutherford were off the air, as one by one radio stations denied their requests to purchase air time.

In 1938, Coughlin organized a group known as the Christian Front, a paramilitary force that declared war against Jewish communists it believed to be undermining American society. The Christian Front's plans were to bomb public buildings and murder individuals they believed to be either communists or government officials thought to be sympathetic to communists. The plans never came to fruition, and in 1940 eighteen members of the Christian Front were indicted on conspiracy charges.

Coughlin died on October 27, 1979, six days after his eighty-eighth birthday. In 1992, an antiblack and anti-Semitic monthly magazine titled *The Truth at Last* devoted an entire edition to honoring Coughlin's memory and included excerpts from his sermons and radio addresses.

The World According to Billy James Hargis

Another notorious hater was the Reverend Billy James Hargis, who broadcast a nationally syndicated show on WGCB in Red Lion, Pennsylvania, in the 1960s. Unlike today's hosts, some of whom are paid millions of dollars per year for their work, Hargis paid the station for the air time—$7.50 for each fifteen-minute spot.

His favorite targets were Attorney General Robert F. Kennedy, civil rights leader Martin Luther King Jr., labor leader Walter Reuther, liberalism in general, and the United Nations. Hargis's rants were nothing worse than those of other haters on the radio airwaves of the early 1960s, but he earned national notoriety by providing the genesis for the U.S. Supreme Court case, *Red Lion Broadcasting v. FCC*, that was a test case for Fairness Doctrine (a more detailed account of the Red Lion case is found in the Epilogue).

WGCB was also the station that broadcast two other notorious hate radio stars of the 1960s: Dan Smoot and Dean Manion.

Smoot was a former FBI agent who compared the 1964 Democratic National Convention that nominated Lyndon Johnson to a "Munich beer hall coup."[22] Smoot had been a frequent critic of President Johnson because of his support for the Social Security system and civil rights. He even accused Johnson of escalating the Vietnam War prior to the 1964 election in order to secure his nomination and election. The Democratic National Committee and American Civil Liberties Union requested time to respond, citing the Fairness Doctrine, but those requests were routinely denied by WGCB.

In the 1950s and 1960s, Smoot's show could be heard on eighty-nine stations across thirty-one states. Sponsored by a Dallas pet food company, Smoot's show pushed for the impeachment of the Supreme Court that desegregated the nation's schools and claimed the civil rights movement was communist-inspired. Smoot claimed he had "inside sources" in the federal government that provided the material to back up his conspiracy theories, but it was later determined that much of it came from right-wing books and newsletters.

The World According to Joe Pyne

Joe Pyne was a World War II veteran who lost a leg while serving in the Marine Corps and spent the rest of his life struggling with a variety of prosthetics. He was also a chain smoker who referred to cigarettes as "coffin nails." After a long struggle against cancer, he succumbed to the disease at age forty-four, in 1970.

Media historians describe Pyne's style as a radio and television talk show host as acerbic, witty, controversial, sentimental, and bombastic—sometimes all in the same sentence.

Among Pyne's favorite insults were "go gargle with razor blades," "every time you open your mouth, garbage falls out," "take your false teeth out, put them in backwards, and bite yourself in the neck," and "get off the line, you creep."[23]

While no callers could out-do Pyne in the insult department (he would cut off any caller who threatened to do so), he occasionally met his match when verbally sparring against in-studio guests. His favorite technique was to throw off guests by opening the interview with an insult, but it occasionally backfired. One of those occasions was an interview with musician Frank Zappa, during which Pyne opened with, "I guess your long hair means that you are really a woman." Zappa replied, "So I guess your wooden leg makes you a table."[24]

On the afternoon of November 22, 1963, Pyne was a few hours away from going on the air when news crossed the wires that President John F. Kennedy had been assassinated. Station management knew of Pyne's dislike for the president and feared what he might say, so they made a last-minute switch to Bob Grant, the station's sports-talk director, who quickly made the switch to news-talk.

The World According to Michael Savage

Michael Savage, whose real name is Michael Alan Weiner, was born in 1942 to a Russian immigrant family in the Bronx, New York. He earned a doctoral degree in nutritional medicine from the University of California.

In the 1970s, Savage was a liberal whose first career was as a stand-up comedian, working in San Francisco and reportedly associating with counter-culturalists Allen Ginsburg and Timothy Leary. That career took him into the following decade, when he began a second career as an author of several books on nutrition and herbal medicine. It was the publisher of one of those early nutrition books who recommended he explore the potential for a third career—talk radio. That was in the early 1980s when there were only a handful of people in the business. The advantage of talk radio, the publisher told him, was that he would get immediate feedback, as opposed to the three or four years it takes to write a book, see it published, and then read the reviews. In talk radio, the publisher added, Savage could exchange ideas with people over the phone lines and airwaves and know immediately if there was a connection.

Savage made a demo tape, complete with fake phone calls, and sent it to 250 radio stations. Five of them offered him jobs immediately, and of those he chose KGO in San Francisco, where he got his start doing fill-ins, weekend shows, and graveyard shifts. He adopted the pseudonym to honor Charles Savage, a nineteenth-century pirate who plundered ships off the California coast.

After two years of part-time work, he moved to a sister station, KSFO, where he shared air time with a liberal host. He overshadowed the other man, however, and soon had his own show in the late afternoon. In 1999, he moved to KNEW-AM and his show, *The Savage Nation*, went into national syndication with the Talk Radio Network. Today his audience is estimated at 10 million listeners and is heard on 370 stations.

Although he calls himself a conservative and media critics call him a hater, Savage is not totally in the far-right camp. He champions the environment and animal rights and dispels the stereotype of talk show hosts "dumbing down" their commentaries by sprinkling his own with quotations from Plato's *Republic*, Ralph Waldo Emerson's *Self-Reliance*, and other works of classical philosophy. Savage once said in a media interview that his listeners are often treated to "bits of Plato, Henry Miller, Jack Kerouac, Moses, Jesus, and Frankenstein."[25]

For a brief time in 2007, Savage considered seeking the republican nomination for president in 2008. Under federal law, Savage would have been required to give up his radio show, but he admitted that the idea would not be to win, but rather to push the Republican Party back to its conservative roots. "I would think that somebody who's not a politician might be a viable candidate," he told *NewsMax* in an April 2007 interview.[26]

Savage analogizes the spending habits of the federal government to his own close call with death. When he was seventeen, he and a friend took a break from their restaurant jobs at a Catskills resort to take a ride in the friend's car. With his friend driving recklessly around and through the mountains of upstate New York and Savage in the passenger's seat, the car flipped over and stopped a few feet from falling down a ravine. With no seatbelts or airbags, both young men were seriously injured, and Savage nearly died. Four decades later, Savage claims the liberals in Washington, D.C., have "seized the wheel of government" and are driving the country dangerously close to the edge of the ravine. "They're speeding down the pathway of good intentions," Savage wrote in his 2003 book, *The Enemy Within*. "In their haste to push failed socialist ideals, the libs have placed us on a crash course of total destruction."[27]

Savage is best known for outrageous comments about public officials, celebrities, and groups of people in the news. His most frequent targets are liberals, feminists, homosexuals, pacifists, lawyers, and university professors. Although a conservative, he was critical of President George W. Bush as well as anyone who supported him. He called Rush Limbaugh and Ann Coulter "Bush-Bots"[28] for their unconditional support of the president. Among his other comments are that "the average prostitute is more honorable than most U.S. senators" and the thousands of Asians who died in the 2004 Indian Ocean tsunami "deserved their fate because they had harbored terrorists."[29] Speaking about the detention of suspected terrorists at Guantanamo Bay, Savage said he would "hang every lawyer who went down there to defend those murderers."[30] In 2007, he claimed that "90 percent of the people on the Nobel Prize Committee are into child pornography and molestation."[31]

Savage describes Limbaugh as "a swell-headed bullfrog, feeding primarily on his own ego," and O'Reilly "a real prick, a thousand times over, as only a porcupine could be."[32] Speaking of O'Reilly, Savage adds that "if Sean Hannity is the favorite son of the Republican Party—the one who makes mommy and daddy proud by dressing smartly and never saying a word about the family, O'Reilly is his cantankerous older brother."[33] Savage also rails against popular culture, referring to Britney Spears, Paris Hilton, and Jessica Simpson as "celebrity sluts."[34]

A 2003 on-air phone call, during which Savage once told a gay caller to "get AIDS and die, you pig,"[35] brought back memories of Pyne telling a caller to "gargle with razor blades." Shortly thereafter, MSNBC, which simulcast Savage's show, dropped him.

On January 2, 2007—his first program of the new year—Savage spent much of his program complaining about the media coverage following the death of former President Gerald R. Ford. Savage called Ford a "country club liberal" and criticized his work with Massachusetts Senator Edward Kennedy to draft the Foreign Intelligence Surveillance Act in the 1970s. Savage claimed that the act "gutted" the CIA's intelligence-gathering ability and left the agency unable to combat terrorism.

One industry expert calls Michael Savage "a creep. . . . but he's a talented creep who makes a lot of money for syndicators and stations. I pity people who believe what he says."[36]

Perhaps Savage's most outrageous comments to date were uttered on July 16, 2008, when he suggested that "99 percent" of autism cases were a result of lax parenting. He told his audience, "They don't have a father around to tell them to 'stop acting like a moron—you'll get nowhere in life.' They need to be told to 'straighten up and act like a man. Don't sit there crying and screaming, idiot.'"[37] After several days of public outrage—including a letter-writing campaign demanding that Savage be fired—he offered no apology, but instead said he wanted to "clarify his comments." He then blamed the increase in media coverage of autism on "greedy doctors and drug companies" that overdiagnosed the condition and created a "national panic."[38]

Organizations such as Autism United sprung into action and called for Savage's firing. "He characterizes children with autism who are very, very ill—disabled children—as essentially bad kids; the only thing wrong with them is they have parents who don't discipline them," said John Gilmore, executive director of Autism United and the father of an eight-year-old autistic child. "That completely misrepresents what is going on with children with autism."[39] Retired Philadelphia Eagles quarterback Rodney Peete and his wife, actress Holly Robinson Peete, had a ten-year-old autistic son and were among the many celebrities to publicly chastise Savage. "We find it shocking that the individuals who name-call and pass judgment on families like ours have zero experience with the disorder," the couple said in a statement.[40]

Ann Althouse, a University of Wisconsin law professor who blogs on issues involving family law, posed the question, "Is Savage's mother to blame for his idiocy? No, I think Savage himself is fully responsible."[41]

Protestors picketed outside of station WOR-AM in New York City—one of more than seventy stations airing Savage's program—and called for his firing. The station posted a response on its World Wide Web site that suggested the protest would be more effective it was directed at Talk Show Network, Savage's primary employer. "Unfortunately, it is impossible for WOR Radio to know the subject matter in advance of airing," the statement read. "WOR is in the business of serving the community in which we broadcast. That is our stated goal, and we will continue to do so. We regret any consternation that his remarks may have caused our listeners."[42]

Unlike the defection of advertisers that led to the firing of CBS Radio host Don Imus the previous year, in the Savage case only one advertiser—AFLAC—announced it would cancel its sponsorship of the program.

It wasn't Savage's first experience with public outrage. The previous year, more than a dozen advertisers withdrew their sponsorships after Savage's repeated comments about Islamic-Americans. In complaining about the public discussion of the need to "understand Islam," Savage fired back with, "I'm not gonna put my wife in a hijab or my daughter in a burqa. And I'm not getting on my all-fours and pray to Mecca. I don't want to hear any more about Islam. Take your religion and shove it up your behind."[43] The advertising boycott was organized by the Council on American-Islamic Relations (CAIR).

Savage responded to the CAIR complaints with a lawsuit, accusing the group of using material from his show in its own letter-writing campaign that targeted his advertisers. While Savage based the suit on federal copyright law, he claimed that CAIR's actions caused him to lose more than $1 million in cancelled ads. As of late 2009, the case had not been adjudicated.

The Savage Nation is the title of his second political book as well as his radio show, which is nationally syndicated out of WNEW in San Francisco. At last count he had written two dozen books, five under his radio name and nineteen (dealing with health issues) as Dr. Michael Alan Weiner. His other political books include *The Enemy Within: Saving America from the Liberal Assault on Our Schools, Faith, and Military* (2003) and *Liberalism Is a Mental Disorder* (2005). In his 2006 book, *The Political Zoo*, Savage blasted former House Speaker Newt Gingrich, republican presidential candidates John McCain and Rudy Giuliani, and fellow talk show hosts Limbaugh and O'Reilly as "fake conservatives" who have been given a "no confidence" vote by true conservatives.[44] But he saved the harshest criticisms for then-President George W. Bush, who he blamed for being too moderate on issues such as immigration, health care reform, and government spending. "Bush is the chief villain," he wrote. "He

(Bush) has destroyed the conservative movement and the Republican Party because of his constant waffling and weaknesses as a leader."[45]

In May 2009, Savage learned that across the Atlantic Ocean, English Home Secretary Jacqui Smith (the equivalent of the secretary of state in the United States) had included him on a list of sixteen international figures—many of the others were terrorists—who were banned from entering Great Britain. His show is not broadcast in that country, and it is unknown how many British subjects access the program via the Internet. Even though Savage had little interest in visiting that country, he instructed his attorney, Richard Thompson, to look into the matter. In a perfect example of politics making strange bedfellows, Thompson sought help from Secretary of State Hillary Clinton in asking Great Britain to rescind the ban. As of late 2009, the conflict had not been resolved.

Savage is founder of the Paul Revere Society, an organization he formed in 1996 to stand for "protection of our borders, our language, and our culture," according to its mission statement. On its Web site and other public documents, it rails against political correctness, multicultural education, and attempts by the American Civil Liberties Union and other liberal groups to remove religious references from public life.

Savage received the Freedom of Speech Award in 2007 for his courage in criticizing President Bush for conduct of the Iraq War.

The World According to Don Imus

Don Imus is a high school dropout and ex-Marine who received an honorable discharge and then worked as a miner, gas station attendant, railway brakeman, and rock musician. In 1968 he believed he had found his life's calling as a disc jockey for a small station in Palmdale, California. A year later he moved to a station in Stockton, but he was fired for saying "hell" on the air.

His next job was at KXOA in Sacramento, where he became famous for fraternity-level pranks such as calling local restaurants and ordering 1,200 hamburgers to go. He recorded a comedy album, *One Sacred Chicken to Go*, in 1970.

He later moved to WGAR-AM in Cleveland. His big break came in 1971 when he was hired at WNBC in New York. In 1977 he was fired after being unable to kick his addictions to alcohol and cocaine—missing more than 100 work days per year—but he was rehired in 1979. From 1982 to 1985, WNBC also employed shock-jock Howard Stern, and the two were featured together on the station's billboard advertising under the slogan, "If We Weren't So Bad, We Wouldn't Be That Good."

For his second stint at WNBC, he switched his act from playing records to providing listeners with commentary on politics and popular culture. Problems with cocaine and alcohol continued, however, but this time WNBC allowed him time off for lengthy stays in rehabilitation clinics. Imus claims he permanently kicked both addictions in 1988. In 1993, his radio show became nationally syndicated, and in 1996 it began being simulcast on cable television by MSNBC.

Imus and his wife founded the Imus Ranch, a working cattle ranch (ironic, considering both are vegetarians) in Ribera, New Mexico. The ranch is a charitable organization that hosts children with cancer and the siblings of children stricken by Sudden Infant Death Syndrome (SIDS). Each year between 1990 and 2008, Imus broadcasted his program from the ranch. Imus and his wife also championed the construction of a veteran's hospital in San Antonio, Texas, and today the continue to support numerous other charities.

At the height of his popularity, Imus's program was heard on sixty-one stations across the country, and according to Arbitron, drew an audience of 11.6 million listeners. *Time* magazine once named Imus one of the twenty-five most influential people in America, and in 1989 he was elected to the National Radio Hall of Fame.

Even before the show was simulcast on television, Imus wore his trademark cowboy hat and boots while on the air. *Time* media critic James Poniewozik described the Imus show as "half frat party, half political salon for the Beltway elite."[46]

Imus pushed the envelope with a sexist, homophobic, and racist act that earned the wrath of civil liberties groups as well as the Federal Communications Commission (FCC). He frequently mocked politicians who refused to come on his show, and those who did were treated only slightly better. Imus called himself "Howard Stern with a broader vocabulary."[47]

Many of his pet names for people in the news were sexually or racially offensive. Imus referred to Attorney General Janet Reno as a "big lesbian" and

New York Times journalist Gwen Ifill, one of the most prominent African American journalists in the country, as "the cleaning lady." He referred to professional basketball player Patrick Ewing as a "knuckle-dragging moron" and then-Senator Barack Obama as "that colored fellow."[49]

Imus often referred to Arabs in general "ragheads" and called the owners of the publishing house Simon & Schuster (owned by the same company that owned CBS Radio) as "thieving Jews." During a half-hearted apology offered later in the show, Imus said the term "thieving Jews" was redundant.[50] He called *Washington Post* media reporter Howard Kurtz, a frequent critic of his show, "that boner-nosed, beanie-wearing Jew boy." Imus called Vice President Dick Cheney "Pork Chop Butt."[51]

On April 4, 2007, Imus was reviewing current events on his early morning program when the subject turned to the NCAA Women's Basketball Championship tournament that had just concluded. Showing video clips of the final game as his show was simulcast by MSNBC, Imus commented on the appearance of the players representing Rutgers University, a team that was largely African American. "Those are some rough-looking women," Imus said. "Those are some nappy-headed hos."[52]

For the remainder of the show and later that day, nothing else was said about the matter. But the following day, an excerpt of the MSNBC show that included Imus's remark found new life on the Internet service YouTube. Several weeks of controversy followed, during which Reverend Jesse Jackson and about fifty protestors marched outside Chicago's NBC studios to protest Imus's comments, and the NAACP called for Imus to be fired. The National Association of Black Journalists echoed the NAACP statement and rejected Imus's repeated apologies.

Liberal groups such as Media Matters for America and the National Organization for Women used their massive email lists to urge people to contact CBS Radio and MSNBC and call for Imus's firing.

Imus responded with a series of apologies—at a news conference, on the radio show of civil rights leader Al Sharpton, and even in a face-to-face meeting with the Rutgers team and its coach. The apologies weren't enough, however. At first, Imus was suspended by the CBS Radio Network for two weeks, and MSNBC permanently dropped the simulcast of his show after Procter & Gamble and Staples cancelled their advertising. Under continued pressure from civil rights leaders, CBS radio eventually fired Imus.

While Imus did not defend his comments, preferring instead to simply apologize, his fans and other observers pointed out the double-standards applied to white and black speakers making racially insensitive and stereotypical remarks. Imus's comments were construed as racist because they focused on the physical appearance of the Rutgers women as thuggish, compared to the more graceful

graceful and feminine appearance of their opponents, the Lady Volunteers of the University of Tennessee.

At first, the controversy generated by Imus's remarks focused on the offense taken by the African American community. But as the controversy continued to grow, it also stirred debates over issues of prejudice, racial stereotypes, hypocrisy, and the roles played by talk radio and rap music in popular culture. Many critics claimed it was inappropriate for black leaders to criticize Imus while not criticizing rap music for using similar words. *Kansas City Star* sports columnist Jason Whitlock said that even the players themselves likely listened to rap music that included similar expressions.[53]

While not defending Imus or his comments, *New York Times* media critic Alessandra Stanley pointed out that the Imus show was intended to be satirical rather than informative and that "no one would confuse it with *Meet the Press*."[54]

A *USA Today* editorial chastised the hypocrisy implied in his public apology, pointing out that Imus himself often ridiculed politicians and other public figures who offered half-hearted excuses.

"It's really stunning that you can say these things and keep your job," added *USA Today* sports columnist and ABC News commentator Christine Brennan.[55]

In one of his many apologetic statements, Imus said, "Our agenda is to be funny, and sometimes we go too far. And this time, we went *way* too far."[56] In a later apology, Imus called himself "a good person who made a bad mistake."[57]

Bryan Monroe, president of the National Association of Black Journalists, said Imus's apologies were "too little, too late."[58]

Ironically, Imus was told of his firing during his annual Radiothon, a fundraiser that had generated more than $40 million for charity since its founding in 1990.

The following week, the Rutgers women and their coach met with Imus behind closed doors at the home of New Jersey governor Jon Corzine. The three-hour meeting was arranged by Buster Soaries, the pastor of Rutgers Coach Vivian Stringer and a former New Jersey Secretary of State. The governor was scheduled to be in the meeting, but was a no-show after being involved in an automobile accident en route.

Following the firing, Imus found support from a variety of points on the political spectrum. Liberals such as Massachusetts senator John Kerry, comedian Bill Maher, and *The View* cohost Rosie O'Donnell said that an apology should have been enough and that Imus should have kept his job on free-speech grounds. Even media critics with reputations for supporting free speech found that Imus had crossed the line one time too many, commenting that if it had been Imus's first offense they could find room to forgive him, but could not do so considering his long history of offensive commentary.

Imus hired First Amendment attorney Martin Garbus and threatened to sue CBS Radio for $120 million, but the case was settled out of court for considerably less. In early 2009, *Imus in the Morning* returned to the airwaves, this time syndicated by Citadel Media.

According to Jayne Pearl, special projects editor of *Talkers* magazine, the Imus affair "underscores the true nature of the contemporary media company with respect to its relationship with its talent. . . . it also demonstrates the precarious environment in which talk radio operates."[59] Pearl assigns partial blame for the Imus uproar and subsequent discussion of "hate" on talk radio on the Janet Jackson incident during the 2004 Super Bowl, which caused the FCC and general public to wonder if the rules about indecency on the airwaves had been relaxed a bit too much. The problem is not, Pearl and other industry experts say, that hosts are afraid of crossing the line—they're afraid of not knowing where the line has been moved to.

In an interview on CNN's Larry King Live, Imus defended himself by pointing out the double-standard being applied by his critics. "I've got black kids coming out to my ranch in New Mexico who don't think I'm a racist," he said. "And the people who are accusing me of being a racist haven't given a dime (to charity) in their lives."[60]

As the presidential primary season heated up the following spring, it was difficult for both republican and democratic candidates to ignore media requests to comment on the controversy. Republican candidates John McCain, Rudolph Giuliani, and Mike Huckabee all said they accepted Imus's apology and would consider appearing on any future shows he might host. Democratic candidates Barack Obama and Hillary Clinton were less forgiving. Obama said Imus's remarks were "hurtful, divisive, and offensive to Americans of all backgrounds,"[61] but he stopped short of saying he would not appear on a future Imus program if invited. Clinton, however, had never appeared on Imus's show before the incident (based on Imus's treatment of her husband as president) and said she had no intention of changing that stance.

The World According to Hal Turner

Hal Turner is a self-described white nationalist whose first exposure to talk radio was Bob Grant's controversial program in the 1980s, on which he was a frequent caller. His interest in politics motivated him to join the New Jersey campaign staff for republican candidate Pat Buchanan during the 1992 primary season. He went on to work on the campaigns of several unsuccessful libertarian candidates for statewide office in New Jersey in the 1990s. He continued to call in to national talk radio programs, including those of Grant (at WABC in New York), and his successor, Sean Hannity. He and several other talk radio fans pooled their resources to purchase air time on shortwave radio stations in rural New Jersey and developed talk programming that was conservative—sometimes bordering on extremist and racist. After seeing Mel Gibson's award-winning film, *The Passion of the Christ*, Turner cut his ties with one of the stations, claiming it was owned by Jews and he "no longer did business with Jews."[62]

In 2000, Turner was an unsuccessful candidate for the open seat representing New Jersey in Congress and was disillusioned with the lack of support he received from the New Jersey Republican Party. He formed his own countywide party and claimed it represented Hudson County, even though the official Hudson County Republican Party and National Republican Party did not recognize it.

Following that setback, Turner rejuvenated his radio career, this time broadcasting on the World Wide Web. The new program, which frequently consisted of racial epithets and references to overthrowing the federal government in order to restore segregation of the races, trashed African Americans, Jews, immigrants, and liberal public officials. On January 3, 2005, he published on his Web site the route of the inaugural parade scheduled for January 20. Without specifically advocating violence against President Bush or other government officials, Turner did mention on the site that lax security would not prevent an attack on the motorcade launched from outside the security perimeter. The following year, he used his radio program to publicly threaten the lives of justices on the New Jersey Supreme Court following its decisions in a series of civil rights cases.

The Southern Poverty Law Center frequently monitored Turner's broadcasts for evidence of specific threats against African Americans, and because of his public threats to presidents and other public figures, Turner was under constant scrutiny by the Federal Bureau of Investigation and U.S. Secret Service. Citing their rules about ongoing investigations, however, those government agencies seldom commented about Turner publicly.

Citing a lack of advertiser and listener support—what Turner described as "the free marketplace voting with its wallet"—he discontinued his Webcast on January 9, 2008. Today, he continues to spread hate on his daily blog.

The World According to Bill Cunningham

Bill Cunningham is host of *The Big Show*, a weekday afternoon program that airs on WLW-AM 700 in Cincinnati.

A former assistant attorney general for the state of Ohio, Cunningham was a mainstream conservative who won the Marconi Award as Broadcaster of the Year in 2001. But on September 11 of that year, Cunningham's demeanor changed dramatically, and ever since that day his tone has been hateful and demeaning toward blacks, immigrants, Muslims, and anything associated with potential terrorist threats. On his programs and in public appearances, he has compared Barack Obama to Adolf Hitler and asserted that his upbringing by a single mother supports the stereotype of black fathers being irresponsible. "Like most other black fathers, he left," Cunningham points out. "That's what most black fathers do—they leave."[63] He also rails against "welfare mothers," claiming they avoid using birth control so they can have more children and "get more checks from the government."[64]

Like many conservative hosts that followed Limbaugh's lead in the early 1990s, Cunningham was a profound Clinton hater, once commenting that Bill and Hillary "woke every morning in the White House and asked themselves, 'how can we screw the American people today?'"[65]

Cunningham routinely blasts liberal politicians, but his favorite targets are RINOs—republicans in name only—in Congress who vote too often in alignment with the democrats. Long before the 2008 incident in which he earned national publicity and embarrassed the McCain campaign with his rant against Obama, Cunningham earned the wrath of civil rights leaders and politicians in Cincinnati for ridiculing an obese African American who died in an altercation with local police in 2001. Many critics demanded that he be fired, to which Cunningham reportedly responded that he "could not see how this (the man's death) isn't funny."[66]

Prior to 2008 presidential election campaign, Cunningham was generally known as a local host, with little name-recognition outside the Cincinnati metropolitan area. That changed on February 26, 2008, when local Republican Party officials asked him to speak prior to a John McCain rally in downtown Cincinnati. During his lengthy tirade, Cunningham blasted Obama, Hillary Clinton, and democrats in general. He called Obama a "hack politician in the Chicago tradition"[67] and criticized the Illinois senator for meeting with middle-eastern leaders and warned that if elected, Obama would meet with the leaders of other foreign governments, to America's detriment. Cunningham also used Obama's middle name, "Hussein," three times.

McCain then incensed Cunningham by taking the stage and immediately apologized for the remarks. McCain later claimed that he didn't know who invited Cunningham to speak, but said he would make sure "something like that didn't happen again."[68] McCain repeated that apology in media interviews later in the day.

In a Cable News Network interview the following night, Cunningham said he "had it up to here" with McCain and complained the candidate should stop apologizing for him and get back to the business of attacking democrats. "They told me to fire up the crowd and give them some red meat, and that's what I did," Cunningham said. "But now McCain is throwing me under the bus—throwing me under the Straight Talk Express (a reference to McCain's campaign bus)."[69]

Despite the flap over his comments, Cunningham didn't let up on his criticisms of Obama after the election. On several occasions he said that Obama has "great verbal skills. . . . but so did Adolf Hitler, and he led his country to disaster."[70]

The World According to Bob Mohan

In 1997, Maricopa County (Arizona) Supervisor Mary Rose Wilcox was the victim of an assassination attempt. While in the hospital recovering from multiple gunshot wounds, she told local media that she suspected her attacker was motivated by "right-wing, conservative hate radio" in the Phoenix area.[71] She did not mention local broadcasting legend Bob Mohan, the conservative host at KFYI, by name, but many in the area speculated her comments were directed at him. Mohan had been one of Wilcox's most vocal critics, with much of his commentary centering on her support for the Arizona Diamondbacks, an issue that had divided the community for months. Wilcox's comments backfired, as a police investigation of the suspect turned up the fact that he was an avid listener of KTAR, the community's leading liberal talk station and chief competitor of KFYI.

Mohan was also criticized in 1994 for criticizing Sarah Brady, the wife of former White House Press Secretary James Brady, who was injured in a 1981 assassination attempt on President Ronald Reagan and had spent the previous thirteen years as a paraplegic. Sarah Brady had become an outspoken advocate for handgun control legislation, which endeared the couple to other gun control advocates but drew scorn from fellow republicans. Mohan said Ms. Brady "should be put down. . . . a humane shot at a veterinarian's office would be an easy way to do it. Because of all her barking and complaining, she really needs to be put down. I wish she would just keep wheeling her husband around to go to speaking engagements—wiping saliva off his mouth once in a while—and leave the rest of us damn well alone."[72]

The Best of the Rest

Jim Quinn and Rose Tennent are based in Pittsburgh and syndicated by Clear Channel Communications and Sirius XM satellite radio. Quinn described NOW as the "National Organization of Whores," told columnist Fatimah Ali of the *Philadelphia Daily News* to "get an American name,"[73] and suggested that voting rights be limited to Americans owning property. "In the past, that was the law, and there was good reason for it," Quinn says.[74] Any time a segment of the show is related to Hillary Clinton, Quinn introduces it by playing a snippet from Elton John's song, "The Bitch is Back."

In Des Moines, Iowa, radio host Jan Mickelson became enraged when he heard that a student group at a local high school had observed a "Day of Silence" in memory of victims of hate crimes based on sexual orientation, including Matthew Sheppard, the Wyoming college student who was the victim of a 1998 beating. Mickelson blasted the extracurricular student-run club as the "sodomy club" and said the only people who care about the feelings of gay people are "other perverts."[75] Within days, the school had to hire temporary workers to field the phone calls from both parents and the community, and both the principal and faculty advisor of the student group received threatening mail and phone calls.

Jay Diamond's hate-based program airs in the overnight time slot at WABC in New York. Like many other haters on the airwaves, Diamond promotes the idea of genetic inferiority—but instead of speaking of an alleged inferiority of blacks to whites, he speaks of an alleged inferiority of women to men. Sometimes he does both, as in the case of a 1994 exchange in which he referred to an African American female caller as a "black bitch."[76]

Chapter 9

The Locals

The Folly of the Trolley

For much of his thirty-seven years in radio, Rob Williams was a talk show host trapped inside the body of a hard-news journalist. Starting as a high school student at a small-town radio station in Texas, Williams enjoyed a career typical of those in his line of work—a succession of jobs in which he vacillated between news and sports, between large markets and small, and between the AM and FM dials.

He got his first taste of political talk radio in 1994 while working at WTKS in Orlando, Florida. With the local school system facing a multimillion dollar budget deficit, Williams became incensed when local public officials showed more concern for the tourism industry than the community's schools. When the city council began discussing a proposal for a $35 million trolley that would serve a one-mile loop and draw tourists to downtown, Williams pointed out to listeners the gap between that dollar amount and the $5 million shortfall in the county's school budget. Williams had heard about a town in South Dakota where a short stretch of public road was paved with gold, so he calculated how much it would cost, based on the price of gold and amount required, to pave that one-mile stretch the city council was looking at. The total came to $30 million, which would have left $5 million for public schools. When the station manager asked to see him when he went off the air, he feared his crossing of the line from news into satirical commentary had earned him a pink slip, but instead the station manager asked him to repeat the bit for the afternoon drive time. His proposal was facetious, of course, but it made the point. To this day, Orlando has no downtown trolley—a fact that Williams brags about when discussing the power of talk radio in local politics.

Mock Funeral

In late 2007, Clear Channel Communications, owner of WXXM-FM in Madison, Wisconsin, announced plans to convert the station from news-talk to sports-talk. Company spokespersons blamed declining advertising sales on the sponsors' reluctance to be associated with controversial programming. Citing the progressive slant of its programming, advertisers pushed the idea of the sports-talk format that would provide them with opportunities to sponsor safer alternatives, such as coverage of local high school sports as well as teams representing the University of Wisconsin. More than 5,500 listeners signed petitions opposing the switch, and many of them protested outside the company's executive offices on a cold winter day. When that effort failed, listeners organized a mock funeral procession through downtown, marching behind a black hearse rented from a local funeral home. In a compromise move, station owners agreed to retain syndicated programs hosted by Al Franken, Robert F. Kennedy Jr., Stephanie Miller, and Ed Schultz.

More Than News, Weather, and Traffic

The cases involving the Orlando trolley and WXXM illustrate the power of local radio hosts and their listeners to achieve what politicians oftentimes cannot.

For morning drive-time, typically defined as 6 a.m. to 9 a.m., many talk stations have abandoned the idea of call-in shows in favor of local news, weather, and traffic. And since most listeners during that time of day are in their cars on their way to work and may listen only for a short time, repetition is not a problem. "That time of day, we've found the order of importance for the listeners is local news, then state news, then national news, then world news," says Alan Caudle, programming manager at WCOA-AM in Pensacola, Florida. "They also want local sports, local time, local weather, and local traffic. Unless it's a breaking news story, they don't care about national news that early in the day."[1]

During the day, AM stations with signals of up to 25,000 watts can be heard for more than 100 miles. At night the signal travels much further, so Federal Communications Commission (FCC) rules require AM stations to limit their transmission strength to avoid overlapping signals. Without that rule, a listener in Tennessee might tune to a local station broadcasting at a certain frequency, but at the same time pick up stations in Florida and Pennsylvania that broadcast at the same frequency, producing little more than gibberish. As a result of the reduced signal, listeners loyal to certain stations listen on the Internet after sunset.

Robert Thompson, a Syracuse University professor who teaches courses in the history of television and radio, believes that local talk radio has done a good job of separating itself from the negative connotation of national talk radio with its angry hosts and us-against-them approach to debate. Thompson does thousands of interviews each year on topics related to the media, and many take place on local talk radio. "There's not a lot of ranting and raving, and most of the calls are good calls," he says. "In a four- or five-minute segment, we can do a good job of covering important issues."[2]

Morning Drive

Michael Smerconish is a local talk host in Philadelphia. His show is nationally syndicated, but the industry still considers him a local host for two reasons. First, his national reach is limited; and second, his political affiliation is difficult to categorize. He is conservative on some issues and liberal on others, which at first glance might earn him a libertarian label, but he rejects that description as well. He is hawkish on defense and national security but much more tolerant of racial and ethnic minorities and gays than conservative hosts. One issue dominating his radar screen is antipolitical correctness, which has provided the fodder for three of his first four books. He endorsed Barack Obama for president in 2008.

After graduating from the University of Pennsylvania Law School in 1987, Smerconish worked briefly in real estate, then for the Department of Housing and Urban Development (under HUD Secretary Jack Kemp) in the administration of President George H. W. Bush. When Bush left office, Smerconish joined a prestigious Philadelphia law firm and became influential in the city's social and political circles.

One Saturday night in May 1993, he was invited to the studios of WWDB-FM to discuss local politics on a call-in show. What was supposed to be a one-night stand turned into a frequent fill-in job for the station's regular talent. He still has his first radio paycheck—for $85.29.

By that fall, he was one of the station's full-time hosts while still practicing law and writing a newspaper column during the day. He liked the radio gig because it gave him an opportunity that the law practice and newspaper column could not—to provide an outlet for viewpoints that couldn't otherwise get access in traditional media. "Everybody and anybody gets their opportunity to speak their mind," Smerconish wrote in his 2009 book, *Morning Drive*. "I don't care if they're liberal or conservative, republican or democrat, socialist or communist; everybody gets the shot because that makes talk radio interesting—and that's what's most healthy for democracy."[3]

In 1997, Smerconish boycotted his own show for almost a month to protest the station's decision to cancel an interview he had scheduled with a journalist covering a high-profile murder trial. The interview was replaced with a paid infomercial for which Smerconish was told to conduct an interview which he called "an advertisement masquerading as news." Another station in town, WPHT, had just changed its format from sports to talk and was assembling a line-up of new talent, and Smerconish was quickly back on the air. He's reluctant to discuss, in media interviews and his books, how he got out of his contract at WWDB, but as a lawyer it's likely he could have negotiated his way out of any noncompete clause that may have been in his contract.

Despite being the most popular morning host in Philadelphia and at times beating Rush Limbaugh (broadcast on a competing station) in local ratings, Smerconish parted company with WPHT in the fall of 2001. The central issues in the departure were the station's refusal to allow him to broadcast from his home, despite him having financed the construction of a home studio, and the station's reluctance to support him in a defamation lawsuit against a local political agitator. By the following summer, WPHT's ratings had taken a nosedive, and local radio fans and media critics blamed it on Smerconish's departure. WPHT officials came to him groveling for his return, and within weeks he was back on the air.

While still doing his daily show, Smerconish was also a frequent fill-in host for Bill O'Reilly and today guest hosts for Chris Matthews on MSNBC's *Hardball*. He's also been a guest on television programs such as Bill Maher's *Politically Incorrect* and Cable News Network's *Larry King Live*.

Smerconish has written four books, including three dealing with political correctness. *Flying Blind: How Political Correctness Continues to Compromise Airline Safety* (2004) addresses the reluctance of the federal government to use ethnic profiling to spot potential terrorists, and *Muzzled: From T-Ball to Terrorism* (2007) criticizes the practice of giving trophies to participants in youth sports whether they win or not and teachers for grading papers in softer ink colors (instead of red) in order to avoid harming children's self-esteem.

In 2007, Smerconish teamed with Maureen Faulkner, the widow of a Philadelphia police officer Daniel Faulkner, to coauthor *Murdered by Mumia*. The book tells the story of how the officer was murdered in 1981 and how his killer escaped execution after he became a "poster boy" for political correctness and the anti-death penalty movement.

His fourth book, *Morning Drive* (2009), describes his career as well as his view of current issues affecting American politics.

Many observers have labeled Smerconish as a conservative, but he defies the stereotype of the angry conservative talk show host. "The perception of the hard-core group (talk radio listeners) is that we are all victims," Smerconish says. "But I am not among them. I favor stem-cell research and I'm OK with gays hooking up. Nevertheless I am painted with a broad brush as 'one of the wing nuts.'"[4]

Scratch Golfer and O. J. Expert

John Ziegler became famous as the conservative host of *Live and Local*, which aired late nights on southern California's KFI-AM from 2001 to 2007. A 2005 profile in *Atlantic Monthly* described Ziegler as a "Georgetown graduate, scratch golfer, and world-class authority on the O. J. Simpson trial. . . . the biggest part of Ziegler's on-air persona is that he doesn't have one."[5]

While the station's 50,000-watt transmitter limited the reach of his program to southern California, Ziegler earned national notoriety by making outrageous comments about high-profile criminal trials of O. J. Simpson, Kobe Bryant, and Scott Peterson and once briefly posted on his World Wide Web site the grizzly video showing American businessman Nicholas Berg being beheaded by al-Qaeda captors in Iraq. He describes his political philosophy as "more libertarian than conservative, more conservative than liberal, and more cynical and skeptical than anything else."[6]

Ziegler began his broadcasting career as a television sportscaster in Ohio in the early 1990s. He left the job to write a book about high school football, then returned to sportscasting at a Raleigh, North Carolina television station. He was fired in 1995 for editorializing on the air about the O. J. Simpson trial. Ziegler was so convinced of Simpson's guilt that the case haunted him for the next decade, and on his April 17, 2007 radio show he admitted that he wanted to kill Simpson himself. He also revealed on his show that he once dated Kim Goldman, the sister of Ron Goldman, who was also killed along with Simpson's wife, Nicole Brown Simpson.

After leaving the Raleigh station, he made a career change to talk radio, beginning at WWTN in Nashville, Tennessee. He lost that job in 1997 after using the word "nigger" during a discussion of race relations on his show, then hosted talk shows in Philadelphia and Louisville. He lost the Louisville job after describing in vivid detail the breasts and genitalia of former girlfriend Darcie Divita, a former Los Angeles Lakers cheerleader and local television news anchor. From there he moved to KFI in Los Angeles, where he stayed until 2007.

After being let go at KFI, Ziegler did fill-in work at other California talk stations for two years, then early in 2009 landed at KGIL in Los Angeles, where he took over the midafternoon time slot. In addition to his radio show, he also writes op-ed pieces for the *Los Angeles Times.*

In 2008, Ziegler and film producer David Bossie of Citizens United premiered a documentary titled *Blocking the Path to 9/11*, which examined the controversial American Broadcasting Corporation docudrama-miniseries, *The Path to 9/11*. The Ziegler-Bossie film accused ABC of slanting its report of the terrorist attacks in order to spare former President Clinton his share of the blame for intelligence failings that took place during his administration. It also accused ABC of deciding against releasing the documentary on DVD in order to avoid harming the presidential campaign of Clinton's wife, Hillary.

In May 2009, Ziegler was arrested on the campus of the University of Southern California for allegedly stalking CBS News anchor Katie Couric when she visited the campus to receive the Walter Cronkite Award for her 2008 interview of vice-presidential candidate Sarah Palin.

He may not hold the record for the most times being fired, but he if he doesn't, he's certainly close to the top of the list. He claims his liberal arts degree from Georgetown turned out to be a "great way to prepare for a life of being unemployed, which I've done quite a bit of."[7]

Apples and Oranges

In February 1993, Dallas talk show Ron Engelman became obsessed with the ongoing drama taking place a hundred miles away in Waco: the standoff between federal agents and cult leader David Koresh and his followers. Engelman used his show to broadcast advice to Koresh on how to deal with the situation. Agents from the Bureau of Alcohol, Tobacco, and Firearms first *asked* him to stay out of the situation, then *told* him to stay out. But Engelman persisted, calling Koresh and his followers "innocent victims" and the agents "predatory and Gestapo-like."[8] After being criticized by journalism ethicists for interjecting himself into a news story, Engelman responded that he felt no remorse for doing so, because expecting him to confirm to journalistic ethics was like "expecting apples to taste like oranges" and that he was "a talk show host—not a journalist."[9] He escalated the conflict with federal agents by setting up remote broadcasts outside the cult's compound.

After the standoff ended with agents storming the compound, the main building becoming engulfed in flames, and all eighty-two people inside dying, Engelman was not remorseful, even after law enforcement agencies and journalism ethicists continued their criticism. It was entertainment, not journalism, he insisted. But the Society of Professional Journalists disagreed, commenting that "the public often does not and cannot draw the distinction between a talk show host and a news reporter. . . . even if there are distinctions, all personnel who work in any capacity for a media organization have an obligation to uphold the highest ethical standards, particularly in cases of great risk to human life."[10]

Following the incident, the station moved him to the overnight shift, where he hosted a new show, titled *Engelman Overnight*, until his death from lung cancer in 2007.

Don't Hate Me Because I'm Dutiful

In 1957, twelve-year-old Mike Siegel paid $230 for a reel-to-reel tape recorder, and a career in broadcasting was born. With his brother Victor manning the turntable, the pair recorded shows that included popular music, weather reports, and advertisements. Material for the latter components was gleaned from that day's newspaper.

In 1960, Siegel became enamored with national politics as he watched the televised presidential debates between John F. Kennedy and Richard Nixon. The following year, he won an "Announcer of Tomorrow" contest hosted by a black radio station in Union, New Jersey. He credited the victory to an article about him in the local weekly newspaper—an article that resulted from Siegel's visit to the newspaper office. Through that experience, Siegel learned the value of self-promotion.

A Jewish political conservative, Siegel earned a degree in broadcasting from Paterson State College, despite failing in his first attempt at a public speaking class. Following college, he searched the Northeast for a job in radio. When that quest failed, he began a four-year teaching stint at an elementary school in Newark. He ran unsuccessfully for a seat on the town council in Glen Rock, a Newark suburb where he lived.

A number of radio jobs at low-power stations in New Jersey followed. Then Siegel got his big television break: a job at WNWS in Miami, Florida. The highlight of his stint there was an on-air interview with Bobby Sands, a political activist holding a hunger strike in a Northern Ireland prison. The job ended after Siegel got into a feud with fellow host Neil Rogers over Rogers's treatment of then-Florida Governor Bob Graham. Rogers called the governor "Graham Crackers," which Siegel thought to be a disrespectful remark about a public official.

Siegel then enrolled in law school, where he attended class during the day and worked a number of part-time radio jobs in the evening. Following graduation and further study that resulted in a doctorate in communications, Siegel failed at his second and last attempt at elected office—the mayor's race in Sunrise, Florida, a suburb of West Palm Beach.

Siegel briefly hosted the nationally syndicated late-night show *Coast to Coast*, which dealt mainly with supernatural phenomena, but he has since made more of a name for himself in the Pacific Northwest. In 1988, he moved to Seattle to take a job a KING, a powerful news/talk station that dominated the market in the Pacific Northwest. One of the highlights of his stint there was a series of reports about gang and drug violence in Seattle, and his editorial tone accused local law enforcement of ignoring the problem. Based partly on his visits to high-crime neighborhoods accompanied by the radio station's chief investigative reporter and a local private investigator, the series angered both the police department and city officials.

His other famous capers included the spearheading of a consumer revolt against Exxon in 1989, during which thousands of Exxon customers cut up their credit cards and mailed them back to the company following its oil spill off the coast of Alaska. He's also been known to organize his listeners for en masse trips to the state capitol building in Olympia to protest increases in state government spending.

In the early 1990s, Siegel turned his attention to national politics, taking aim at a proposed 51 percent pay raise for Congress. Part of the effort was the purchase of a million teabags to be sent to members of Congress. When Siegel was called in front of the Senate Government Operations Committee to testify, Senator John Glenn, chair of the committee, quipped, "So you're the guy who sent me a lifetime supply of teabags."[11]

While station management appreciated the publicity the stunt generated, local government leaders were still seething over Siegel's continuous criticism of the Seattle Police Department. Soon after the station changed general managers—with the new executive having social ties to local politicians—Siegel was fired. He quickly landed a job at rival station KVI. The highlight of his five-year stay there was the investigation of sexual molestation charges against sixty individuals in the central Washington town of Wenatchee. Applying his legal background to his radio work, Siegel was able to prove that most of the charges were either fabricated or exaggerated. As a result, all of the charges were dismissed, and several of the defendants filed multimillion-dollar civil rights suits against the local police. Siegel received national acclaim for his part in the story, but was fired a few years later after refusing to end his feud with Seattle Mayor Norm Rice.

Open Mouth, Insert Foot

With the exception of the firings of Bob Grant and Don Imus, national hosts have more job security than their local counterparts. Syndicated hosts may be subject for the occasional reprimand, but they are seldom fired. That degree of due process is seldom afforded to local hosts, who often find themselves out of work after the first offensive comment. In 1987, for example, Steven White of WKRI-AM in Providence, Rhode Island, was fired for calling local drug dealers "niggers" and "spics."

The following year, on Martin Luther King Day, host Frank Turck opened his program by telling his listeners in Pittsfield, Massachusetts, they should cel-

celebrate by eating watermelon and fried chicken. He was fired the next day. In 1990, Tim Lennox of WERC-AM in Birmingham, Alabama, was suspended after he banned black callers from his show.

While the syndicated hosts tackle topics such as the war in Iraq and illegal immigration, locals tackle issues such as local tax rates, school board decisions, and law enforcement issues. Local hosts tend to be more outrageous than their nationally syndicated counterparts and often draw more threatening reactions from listeners. In the 1980s, for example, Washington, D.C., host Gary Gilbert was assaulted in a restaurant and once found an explosive device planted in his car. Dave Dawson, a local host in San Diego, had to have round-the-clock security guards accompany him in public.

Talk Radio in the I-10 Corridor

Local journalists and demographers call it the I-10 Corridor; it's a collection of five moderately populated counties straddling Interstate 10 between Mobile, Alabama, and Fort Walton Beach, Florida. The region stretches for 100 miles east to west but only 30 miles north to south, and it includes the semi-metropolitan areas of Pensacola and Mobile and the smaller tourism communities of Fort Walton Beach, Gulf Breeze, and Orange Beach. The total population is about a half a million people. Unlike the region to the west (Louisiana and southern Mississippi), which is largely poor, and the region to the east (the Gulf beaches around Panama City), which is largely affluent, the I-10 Corridor is quite diverse in terms of demographics and cultures.

With numerous military bases and defense contractors, the region's primary employer is the Department of Defense. Tourist season—the region's other economic boon—begins April 1 and ends when the first tropical storm approaches. With no professional teams nearby, sports fans draw their inspiration from the football teams of Florida State, Auburn University, and the University of Alabama. It's a region that seldom makes the national news unless there's a hurricane.

Residents of the I-10 Corridor like their beachfront condominiums large and their government small. Despite the diversity in cultures and economic backgrounds, there is a high degree of political activism here, thus creating the perfect audience for talk radio.

Although there are more than a dozen all-talk stations serving the area, the genre is dominated by only five—two in Pensacola, and one each in Mobile, Milton, and Fort Walton Beach.

WNTM-AM, a Clear Channel station serving the panhandle of Alabama, broadcasts from the third floor of an office building in Mobile. Affiliated with Fox News, the station offers a conservative lineup of nationally syndicated programs—Rush Limbaugh, Glenn Beck, and Jason Lewis—throughout the late morning, afternoon, and evening. The only local host is Uncle Henry, a mid-forties radio veteran whose real name few people know. The persona, which includes a deeper voice and curmudgeonly demeanor, was one he invented at a previous job, where it was intended to mock his program's elderly callers. But now, the Uncle Henry act is meant to entertain rather than ridicule. "Some of our listeners know that Uncle Henry is not a real character, but most of them don't," he says. "And we get quite a bit of mail addressed to Uncle Henry from people who don't know."[12]

Uncle Henry's show gets more calls than the morning shows of competing stations, but the host can't explain why. In the last hour of his show, Uncle Henry is up against Neal Boortz and other nationally syndicated programs airing on other stations. "We know that's the time our listeners start to dial surf," he says. "If a host is not talking about something the listeners are interested in, they're quick to move on. Some days I'll hit the right topic and the calls will be wall to wall, but on most days it's a struggle."[13]

Overall, topics raised by callers tend to be evenly divided between local and national, except when current events dictate a change in the ratio. Examples of popular local issues include school-related issues and a county prosecutor's campaign against adult businesses. But throughout much of April 2009, national topics dominated, most of them related to President Obama's proposed stimulus package and bailout of the financial system. Uncle Henry fanned the flames by reminding his audience that it was Mobile congressman Jo Bonner who voted in favor of the stimulus package and Alabama governor Bob Riley who refused to accept his state's share of the money.

At one point he and his callers lamented the lack of challengers for Bonner's upcoming re-election bid and even challenged listeners to call in with their own nominations. One day he bantered with callers about the fate of a young Somali man who was captured off the east coast of Africa and accused of being a pirate. As news broke that the man was being arraigned in a federal courtroom in New York City, Uncle Henry joked that the pirate would soon have "his own book deal, reality TV program, and guest shot on Oprah."[14]

Even though there is a stool just a few feet behind him, on most days Uncle Henry does his four-hour show standing up. "I'm used to this being a lighthearted show, but recently people are just plain mad," he says. "It's a lot more grueling than it has been in the past. The callers are angry at the government, and they're angry at me because I don't sound angry enough. Most of them want me to be Rush Jr."[15]

Callers who are frustrated with Uncle Henry's reluctance to assert his conservative credentials—along with other callers who are just frustrated—often resort to profanity or other unacceptable comments in order to get the host's attention. But like most other stations, WNTM filters those out with the standard seven-second delay mechanism. "I don't worry as much about profanity as I do about the N-word," Uncle Henry says. "We have to do it. The potential for someone to sabotage the show is too real."[16]

A typical show includes Uncle Henry's commentary on the news of the day, lighthearted banter with call screener Trey Lane, five to ten calls per hour, and—typical for a morning show—frequent breaks for news, weather, traffic, and commercials. Coming out of each commercial break, he plays a brief voicemail message from a listener.

Following Rob Williams's time in Orlando, several more news jobs came and went, including a stint for CBS Radio during which he was twice imbedded with U.S. armed forces in Iraq. Most of the jobs were at local stations, where his purview was news, but he found himself constantly stepping over the line into opinion. "I got fired too many times for offering opinions and shooting off my mouth," Williams said. In 2009 Williams landed at WNRP-AM in Pensacola, where he finally got his first official opinion-based assignment.

While local hosts on competing stations spent the mornings scrutinizing the early days of the Obama administration, Williams stuck with his preference for local topics. Four months into his new job, in April 2009, that meant discussing the budget problems facing the local state university, the status of a controversial downtown development project called Community Maritime Park, and the debate over a Pentagon contract that would have awarded a multibillion-dollar project to build refueling aircraft in nearby Mobile.

But when the story broke that the Obama administration had decided to reverse the Pentagon's two-decade-old policy of barring news cameras from photographing the deplaning of caskets holding the remains of military personnel killed overseas at the Air Force base in Dover, Delaware, Williams couldn't resist attempting to provoke his listeners into calling. A conservative with an occasional libertarian bent, Williams surprised his listeners by supporting the decision and questioning the privacy argument of those who opposed the move. "Suppose there's a dozen or more caskets coming off the plane," Williams told his audience. "All of them are the same size and shape, none of them have names on them, and all of them are covered by American flags. I sympathize with the families, but I challenge them to point at one of the caskets and identify whose remains they are. There is no family privacy argument here."[17]

WNRP's studios are located in an abandoned steakhouse, where framed menus still adorn the walls and the kitchen was converted to an employee cafeteria. Plush carpeting provides the quiet interior conducive to radio broadcasts, while downstairs rooms were converted to studios and upstairs rooms converted to offices for the management and sales staffs.

Williams is fifty-four, with salt-and-pepper hair and a fondness for plaid shirts, blue jeans, and cowboy boots. During his three-hour morning drive program, he sips caffeinated soft drinks while waiting for listener calls with Paul Stadden, his twenty-five-year-old producer and on-air bantering partner, seated less than six feet away.

Like most morning shows, Williams's is fast-paced, with the three-way banter among him, Stadden, and callers frequently interrupted by news bulletins, weather reports, and traffic updates. Commercials alternated between prerecorded spots and those Williams reads live off a computer screen. Sprawled across his desk are dozens of news releases and that morning's *Pensacola News Journal*. During the five-minute news break at the top of one hour, Williams joked with traffic reporter Dave Maxwell about his habit of talking too fast. "Dave, two words, buddy," Williams told him off the air. "Just two words—less Starbucks."[18]

Williams doesn't fit the stereotype of talk show hosts as angry and distrustful of government. He believes it's more important for hosts to be skeptical rather than cynical. "We would rather provide the bully pulpit to the listeners rather than use it ourselves," he says.[19]

"I enjoy ruffling feathers, but Pensacola is the one hundred and twenty-fifth market in the country," Williams says. "There's a limit to how many feathers we can ruffle."[20] Taking a twelve-inch stepstool off the shelf, Williams says, "This is as big as my bully pulpit gets. I don't mind pissing people off; I just don't want to piss people off to the point at which I lose my job."[21]

On this particular day, Williams conducted phone interviews with local congressmen about the tanker project, the local university president about potential budget cuts and faculty layoffs, and the president of the Gulf Breeze Chamber of Commerce about a proposed city ordinance dealing with the opening and closing times for bars and restaurants serving alcohol. Shortly after that interview ended, Williams moved onto other local topics, but he was interrupted by a television news bulletin reporting that President Obama had made a surprise visit to American troops in Iraq during his return trip from a international conference in Turkey. "I knew it!" Williams said as he stood up behind the desk and pointed at the screen. Unbeknownst to his listeners, Williams had predicted such a surprise visit when discussing the Obama trip with other journalists.

Williams believes that local hosts are better suited than national hosts to identify with the concerns of listeners. "I see myself as an everyman, and I think our listeners do too," he says. "Rush (Limbaugh) and Sean (Hannity) have gone way beyond that. They're operating at a level at which they've lost touch, and their shows have become all about them. But local shows tend to be more issues-driven than personality-driven. There are enough local issues we can talk about that we don't have to focus on me."[22]

Producer Paul Stadden says that local talk provides a take on the news that the audience won't get from any other source. "Our listeners aren't just looking for the news; they're looking for the context," he says. "We can provide context and give them an opportunity to express their own opinions that they're not going to find in the newspaper, on television, or on the Internet."[23]

Williams usually likes to keep the focus on local issues, but on this day he spoke about the Dover issue as well as the tanker project. He expected his rant in support of Obama's policy change would cause the phone lines to light up, but today the lines were quiet. "It's hard enough just to get them to listen in the morning; it's even harder to get them to call," Williams says.[24]

After the show, Williams joined the advertising sales staff for a visit to a potential sponsor. Sales representative Dave Windsor had already pitched the station's advertising package to a local business, and he invited Williams to accompany him to the second meeting to seal the deal. Even though Williams had spent more than thirty years as a journalist, he didn't seem uncomfortable about ethical conflicts of blurring the lines between news and advertising. "The sales part of job is already done," Williams says. "This is just a meet and greet. The purpose of radio is to make money, and for advertisers in a small community such as ours, little things like that can make a big difference."[25]

Some local stations avoid political advocacy by hiring noncontroversial hosts and presenting fairly balanced looks at local political issues. Like Williams at WNRP, they explain their stance by claiming to be issues-driven rather than personality driven. One station recently switching to that approach is WCOA, a Cumulus Broadcasting station in Pensacola. In December 2008, conservative host Luke McCoy, a Vietnam veteran fond of telling stories of his days in the Marine Corps, retired after more than a decade on the air. His far-right agenda was popular among the station's older and conservative audience, but his tirades against government waste and bureaucracy angered the community's elected officials, many of whom refused to be interviewed on his program.

After he retired, station management decided that the morning drive program, *Pensacola Speaks,* would no longer take calls, but instead would present interviews with local newsmakers, without the partisanship. WCOA management says that listeners loyal to McCoy complained for several weeks about his absence as well as the lack of a conservative replacement, but by early March the calls subsided. Now, they contend, both the listeners and station management are pleased with the new noncontroversial approach to local news during the morning drive. After the local morning program ends, however, the station switches to an all-day lineup of nationally syndicated programming—Limbaugh, Hannity, Beck, Huckabee, and Savage—all far from noncontroversial.

WEBY 1330, an AM station serving northwest Florida, broadcasts from a 2,000-square foot building in the rural community of Milton, just east of Pensacola. Its signal reaches as far west as Mobile, Alabama, as far north as Montgomery, and to the east, about half-way to the state capital of Tallahassee. Despite the reach of its 25,000-watt signal, the operation is fairly lean. General Manager Mike Bates deals with FCC compliance and licensing issues, sells nearly all of the advertising, and hosts his own two-hour show on Tuesday afternoons. He also owns 51 percent of the stock and works 90 hours per week. He supervises a staff consisting of a secretary who doubles as a show producer, two engineers, and four part-time local hosts who take turns hosting an afternoon show called *Your Turn*.

Only six hours of each programming day is local; for the remainder of the day it carries nationally syndicated hosts Neal Boortz, Clark Howard, Greg Knapp, Bruce Williams, and Rusty Humphries.

Your Turn is the most popular afternoon call-in show in Florida's Panhandle. The four hosts include three attorneys and a small business owner, and their politics range from conservative to liberal. Bates describes his own political views as "conservative" and "constitutional libertarian," but says he respects all four of his hosts and considers them friends, even though he often disagrees with them on issues.

Unlike larger talk stations, where the names and hometowns of callers flash on computer screens in front of the hosts, the WEBY approach is comparatively low-tech. The call screener writes the names and line numbers for each caller on index cards and tapes them to the inside of the glass window that separates him or her from the host. And unlike other stations, WEBY programs don't use the standard seven-second delay technique that gives the call screener the opportunity to terminate callers whose commentary turns profane or libelous. "We know it's a risk, especially with FCC fines starting at $325,000 for a single incident," Bates says. "But we've been doing it this way a long time and it's never been a problem. The technology is not that expensive, so it's not a matter of not wanting to spend the money. It's more an issue of timing. When you're on a delay, it becomes harder to time coming in and out of commercial breaks and news breaks, and we end up either with dead air or we're talking over the commercials."[26]

WEBY host Kenneth E. Lamb often uses his once-a-week time slot to launch tirades against Congressman Jeff Miller, the Pensacola republican who voted in favor of the stimulus package and does little, in Lamb's opinion, to recognize and support the thousands of military veterans living in the area.

On WFTW 1260 in Fort Walton Beach, the only local programming is *Wake-up Call*, a three-hour show that airs weekdays and is hosted by Ken Walsh.

Walsh is a sixty-year-old former Air Force lawyer. His tiny studio is decorated with a six-foot by ten-foot American flag on one wall and memorabilia from his alma mater—Notre Dome—scattered around the other walls.

Walsh gives generously of his time to local charities, most of them involving children and families. But his favorite is "Honor Flight," a national program that raises money to send veterans to Washington, D.C., to visit the National World War II Memorial that was completed in 2004. Walsh organizes remote broadcasts from the locations of the events and lends his name recognition to the cause, which helps in recruiting sponsors. "Our station is big on keeping apples and oranges separate, so the sales department has to do the paperwork," Walsh says. "But I like getting involved and helping to seal the deal."[27]

Like most talk radio hosts, Walsh got his start as a listener. After retiring from the Air Force and living near Eglin Air Force Base, Walsh began listening to a low-power AM talk station in nearby Niceville. He called in so often that the station had to create a rule to limit his calls to one per week. Station owners became so frustrated at his persistence in circumventing the rule that they gave him his own show. "I had the two qualities they were looking for in a host," Walsh recalls. "A lot of opinions and a big mouth."[28]

One day in April 2009, Walsh tried to entice callers into discussing national issues such as the proposed stimulus package, the Obama tax plan, U.S. trade policies, and recent political positions taken on national issues by the Catholic Church in general and administrators at Notre Dame in particular. Walsh calls himself a loyal alumnus, but doesn't mind giving his old school the occasional barb.

But on this day, local issues prevailed. One was the ongoing lawsuit filed against the Air Force by the city of Valparaiso, a small municipality on the outskirts of Fort Walton Beach. The suit was aimed at blocking the Air Force plans to build a new facility at Eglin Air Force Base for maintaining its new F-35 strike fighter, an aircraft known for generating high decibel levels on takeoffs and landings. Walsh called the three council members voting in favor of the suit "The Three Stooges," which earned him the wrath of the council but accolades from his listeners. The other local story generating calls was the killing of two county sheriff's deputies in a shootout with a criminal suspect.

Walsh grew up in an Irish-Catholic democratic family in Clifton, New Jersey, a heavily unionized middle class suburb of East Rutherford. He commuted each day into downtown New York to attend a traditional Catholic school. In 1961, he stopped sharing with his family an admiration for the Democratic Party after the botched Bay of Pigs operation in Cuba. After law school and an eighteen-year stint as an Air Force lawyer, he briefly practiced law in civilian life before finding his next career in talk radio.

"I don't purport myself to be a disinterested party," Walsh says. "I don't want anyone to confuse me with a journalist. I'm a conservative and a big advocate of the military, and our listeners know that. Anyone who listens to the show knows exactly what they're getting."[29]

The Best of the Rest

In the New York City radio market, members of the Gambling family have hosted a show for more than eight decades. The family tradition began in 1925, when John Bradley Gambling began hosting *Rambling with Gambling*. The elder Gambling hosted the show until 1959, then handed it over to his son, John Alfred Gambling. In 1985, John took on a cohost with a familiar name: his son, John R. Gambling. The son took over as solo host in 1991 and kept the show until 2000, when he moved across town to WABC and changed the name of the program to *The John Gambling Show*. After WABC fired him due to budget cuts, he returned to WOR and was still there as of late 2009.

At one time, *Rambling with Gambling* was listed in the Guinness Book of World Records as "the world's longest-running radio show," but that record has since been eclipsed by *The Grand Ole Opry*.

Bill Handel hosts a morning show on KFI in Los Angeles, but is perhaps better known for his nationally syndicated weekend program focusing on the law. Following the 1994 Winter Olympics, he created controversy by commenting on American skaters Kristi Yamaguchi and Michelle Kwan, saying that "When I look at a box of Wheaties, I don't want to see eyes that are slanted and Oriental and almond shape. I want American eyes looking at me."[30] Handel apologized but claimed that he was actually mocking the bigoted callers on his show rather than being bigoted himself. Asian American leaders called for his firing, but KFI instead issued its own apology on top of Handel's personal contrition. A decade later he drew the ire of the Council on American-Islamic Relations for making repeated jokes about Muslims, but this time he refused to apologize, and his station ignored repeated demands that he be fired.

John Kobylt and Ken Chiampou, who conduct their weekday afternoon program as simply John and Ken, are veterans of the southern California radio market, drawing an audience of more than 1 million listeners.

They began their show in 1992 on KFI-AM in Los Angeles, replacing the short-lived talk show of former Los Angeles Police Chief Daryl Gates. Following a contract dispute in 1999, John and Ken moved across town to KABC, but the show lasted less than two years. In 2001 they returned to KFI, and in 2003 earned national recognition for their role in advocating the recall of Governor Gray Davis. They earned even more national recognition early in 2008 when they setup a remote broadcast outside the home of a convicted sex offender in order to draw attention to the ineffectiveness of the state's sex-offender registry system.

Roger Hedgecock is an avid surfer and part-time lawyer who first became interested in politics while working on Barry Goldwater's 1964 bid for the presidency. In 1983 he was elected mayor of San Diego, calling himself a "progressive republican."

He resigned midway through his term after being convicted of conspiracy and perjury in a scheme to funnel $350,000 into his campaign. The conviction was later overturned based on procedural errors, but he never forgot the role of the local newspaper in forcing him out of office. Four days after leaving office, he began his new career in talk radio and began using his microphone to denounce the paper for what he called biased reporting.

Today, he broadcasts weekday afternoons on KOGO-AM in San Diego. Early in 2009, show became nationally syndicated by Radio America Network.

Mark Belling, host of an afternoon show on WISN-AM in Milwaukee, Wisconsin, refers to his political philosophy as "principled conservatism." His show has been the top-rated program in the market for more than a decade.

In 2004 he was suspended for a week for using the term "wetback" to refer to illegal aliens attempting to vote in the presidential election. More than three hundred listeners protested outside the station, demanding Belling's return. Once back on the air, he apologized for the remark.

Like many of his national counterparts, Belling frequently chides the Republican Party for straying too far from its conservative principles, and included in that criticism was a rebuke of presidential candidate John McCain during the 2008 campaign.

Dan Caplis and Craig Silverman broadcast from KHOW in Denver, a Clear Channel station. Near their studio is the one from which Alan Berg once broadcast; a memorial plaque marks the door. Over the years, Caplis and Silverman have used their show to sound off—and allow their listeners to sound off—on a number of local issues, including the 1999 tragedy at Columbine High School and the 2003 rape investigation involving basketball player Kobe Bryant.

They approach their show from their respective legal backgrounds; Caplis is a personal injury lawyer and Silverman is a former deputy district attorney turned defense attorney. Caplis is a conservative and Silverman a liberal, and their political differences provide much of the fodder for the show. But when guests are involved, they bring out their nonpartisan blinders and give both conservative and liberal politicians equal time. Because of the size of the audience and their reputation for fairness, both local and state politicians are willing to be interviewed, either in-studio or by telephone. "It's like the city's own version of Punch and Judy," says Norman Provizer, professor of political science at Metropolitan State College of Denver. "It's a sign that you're a player when other players are more than happy to appear on your show."[31]

Bob "Gunny" Newman's show airs on KOA-AM radio in Denver on weeknights—the same time slot once held by Alan Berg. He is the author of a number of books outlining his far-right political views, most of them published by Paladin Press, a publishing house known mostly for publishing extreme far-right books. Newman has described Barack Obama as "a far-left terrorist-hugging politician" and suggested that every Muslim in America be required by law to wear a GPS tracking device. He has also asserted that the passage of state laws permitting gay marriage will eventually lead to legalized marriage between humans and animals.[32]

In the spring of 2007, when two Charlotte, North Carolina police officers were killed in the line of duty, local host Jeff Katz organized fund-raising events that generated more than $50,000 to help the families. After that, he generated listener support for a bill in the state legislature that increase penalties for those convicted of assaulting law enforcement officers.

Bob Ray Sanders, once a popular host at KLIF-AM in Dallas, was an African American host who enjoyed his role as a lightning rod for controversy, including those related to race. He preferred to attack bigotry head-on, and unlike his white counterparts, Sanders made no attempt to keep bigots off the air, believing that the best remedy against bigotry was to give it a public airing. One day in 1995 he did an entire show about the use of the word "nigger," and both black and white callers flooded the lines with a variety of viewpoints. "We got all types of calls," Sanders said. "We even got a call from an obese woman who said that 'people don't understand what it's like to be called fat.'"[33]

Howie Carr is the host of a weekday show airing on Boston's WRKO. Simply titled *The Howie Carr Show*, the program can be heard throughout much of New England, thanks to WRKO's powerful transmitter. Carr is also a columnist for the *Boston Herald*, and in 2006 published a biography of Billy and James Bulger, a pair of sibling criminals that terrorized Boston in the 1950s. Carr played himself in the 1998 John Travolta film, *A Civil Action*, a legal drama set in Boston.

Kirby Wilbur is a radio personality and conservative political activist. He currently hosts the morning drive show on KVI-AM in Seattle, Washington, and periodically guest-hosts for Sean Hannity on his nationally syndicated show. Like many others in the industry, Wilbur's interest in talk radio began as a listener and caller. After a brief career in real estate, Wilbur was invited to audition to be a substitute host at KVI-AM. That was 1993, and shortly after earning the part-time role, he became full-time, first in the evening, then in the morning. He began covering mainly the entertainment industry and popular culture, but today covers local, regional, and national politics.

Doug McIntyre is the morning host on KABC in Los Angeles, California. He is married to actress Penny Peyser and has also tried his hand at writing and directing, working on situational comedies such as *Married. . . . With Children* and *WKRP in Cincinnati*.

After four years of hosting an overnight show titled *Red Eye Radio*, McIntyre moved to the morning drive position in 2004. His describes his political positions as "moderately conservative," as he endorses much of the republican platform—especially those issues related to illegal immigration—while still being critical of President George W. Bush, who he calls "the worst two-term president in history."[34] He also supports gay rights and the legalization of marijuana. He is a contributor to *American Heritage* magazine and writes a weekly column for the *Los Angeles Daily News*.

Chapter 10

In Theory: Talk Radio and American Politics

Phone Booth Politics

In 1938, Thomas Dewey was a crusading district attorney in New York City and a republican candidate for governor of New York. His opponent was Herbert Lehman, the popular democratic incumbent who was heavily favored to win. On the final day before New Yorkers went to the polls, Dewey worked an eighteen-hour shift at a local radio station, inviting prospective voters to call in and ask him questions. What the listeners did not know was that most of the calls were from one of Dewey's assistants, who spent the day in a phone booth across the street, armed with a stack of coins.

Lehman won the next day, but by a margin much slimmer than was predicted. Seven decades later, political scientists cite the Dewey-Lehman campaign as the first example of radio playing a part in the electoral process.

Neutral and Unbiased, or Maybe Not

For much of the last twenty years, conservatives have complained about an alleged "liberal bias of the media." Although academic studies typically find that no such bias exists—claiming that the liberal orientation of working journalists is counterbalanced by the conservative ownership of newspaper chains and television networks—the charge continues to be made by talk radio hosts, conservative watchdog groups, and individual authors who use dubious sampling techniques and anecdotal evidence to support their point.

Many talk radio hosts believe their programs can help remedy that (perceived) liberal bias by offering conservative or libertarian perspectives on politics and current events. Many media critics and watchdog groups, however, say that talk radio has overcompensated for a problem that doesn't exist, especially in cases in which hosts align their views too closely with those of the Republican Party.

Former Vice President Al Gore called talk radio the "Limbaugh-Hannity-Drudge Axis" and wrote that the "fifth column of the fourth estate is made up of propagandists pretending to be journalists. . . . through multiple overlapping outlets covering radio, television, and the Internet, they relentlessly force-feed the American people right-wing talking points and ultra-conservative dogma disguised as news and infotainment."[1]

Jim Bohannon, a conservative host syndicated by Westwood One, says that while it is acceptable for hosts to align themselves with ideologies such as conservative or liberal, it was dangerous for them to align themselves with political parties. "If you consider yourself an arm of a political party, it cuts into the positions you take, and the extent to which you can be entertaining," he says.[2]

John Dean, a former White House lawyer in the Nixon administration and political commentator, wrote in his 2007 book that the Republican Party is not well-served by having talk radio hosts endorse its messages. "One of the best ways to keep republicans out of power is to encourage their cheerleaders—pundits like Rush Limbaugh, Sean Hannity, and Ann Coulter—to continue serving as spokespeople and catalysts for authoritarian conservatism," he wrote. "Few want to go where they would take the country, as republican losses in the 2006 election were solid signs that Americans are not interested in GOP authoritarianism."[3]

Former California governor Jerry Brown, who enjoyed a brief career as a progressive talk show host after leaving office, believes that conservative ownership of talk radio stations is problematic because it results in a near blackout of liberal voices. Jim Hightower believes the problem lies more with the Democratic Party leadership, which has been reluctant to challenge the ownership rules that have allowed the imbalance to occur in the first place. "Progressives tend to ignore a very little democratic box, the radio, which better than 170 million people a day are plugged into," Hightower said in an interview with *Mother Jones* magazine.[4]

A Times-Mirror survey found that slightly more than half of talk radio hosts believe their callers are representative of the larger public in their listening area. And most listeners and callers—about 60 percent—said the programs they listen to offer a diversity of viewpoints rather than being dominated by one perspective, either liberal or conservative.

Political journalists and bloggers Ross Douthat and Reihan Salam contend that conservative radio hosts often take advantage of republicans' alleged abandonment of traditional conservative values. "The more the party elite kept patriotism at arm's length and treated national pride with a sophisticate's tolerance, the more the breach was filled by Sean Hannity-style jingoists," they wrote in their 2008 book, *Grand New Party*.[5]

Michael J. West, who writes frequently about political talk radio on his blog dealing with politics and popular culture, disputes the claim of conservative talkers that they seek out opposing voices and invite them on the air for constructive debate. "They may ask for the other guy to call in and explain some point, but they don't actually want the other guys to call into the show and take part in any kind of real discussion," West wrote in a 2006 blog entry. "Sure, if you've listened to any of those people, you've heard the opposition call, but when was the last time you heard them get in a word edgewise? The hosts cut them off, do their best to make them look like fools, and move on. Why? Not because they're political hacks who don't want to allow the other guys to have any influence. They do it because that's what their fans want to hear: they want to hear the other side be made to shut up and look like idiots."[6]

Many media theorists and critics believe there is room across the media spectrum, and on talk radio specifically, for some type of "unbiased" news. While stopping short of advocating a return to the Fairness Doctrine or similar regulatory edict creating ideological balance, they believe that democracy is best served by having three sources of information: a large core of media outlets striving for neutrality and objectivity, flanked by smaller factions free to admit their place on the political extremes. "It is tempting to say that, since perfect objectivity is unobtainable, we should just say 'to hell with it' and go back to the days of nakedly partisan media," writes John Hinderaker, a contributor to the popular conservative political blog, PowerLine. "I don't agree with that at all. It is important that there be media outlets that are reasonably unbiased and that are consumed equally by liberals and conservatives. Alongside them should be other news sources that are tilted in one direction or another."[7]

The Fourth Branch of Government

Through the 1970s and 1980s, talk radio had been dismissed as having only a minor role in political campaigns, as the genre was considered as too loud, too cranky, and too dominated by rabble-rousers—some of them being hosts and some being callers. The landscape changed in 1992, when Arkansas Governor

Bill Clinton and Tennessee senator Al Gore challenged incumbents George H. W. Bush and Dan Quayle for the presidency and vice-presidency. It was two baby-boomer democrats with a typical liberal agenda going up against republican blue-bloods seen as out of touch with everyday America. Early in the campaign, Quayle and Clinton both spoke at a talk radio industry conference, then the two campaigns set out on separate tracks to woo the talk radio audience.

Clinton later swapped on-air jokes with Don Imus. Fellow democrat Jerry Brown won the 1992 Connecticut democratic primary based largely on his appearance on radio talk shows in that state. Bush invited Rush Limbaugh to spend the night at the White House, an experience which provided weeks of on-air material for the host.

On a cool, foggy morning early in 1993, dozens of talk radio hosts gathered on the White House lawn at the invitation of President Bill Clinton. The day before, the new chief executive had introduced his health care plan, and he wanted the help of the talk radio industry in selling it to the American people and Congress. A cadre of Clinton aides was available for interviews, each armed with democratic talking points to support the plan. The experiment generated mixed results, but that was just the beginning of the Clinton administration's love-hate relationship with talk radio. Realizing the power that the new Limbaugh-led industry could wield, Clinton's aides began referring to talk radio as the "fourth branch of government."[8]

Two years later, newly elected House Speaker Newt Gingrich executed his own outreach program, inviting radio talk show hosts to cover close-up his proposed Contract with America, a package of legislative initiatives covering areas such as taxes, health care, and welfare reform. Congressional rules prohibited media personnel from setting up their equipment or work stations anywhere in the Capitol building except designated press areas, and the television news personnel claimed the radio hosts were not true journalists and therefore refused to give up any of their working space in the press room to accommodate them. Gingrich helped the talk show hosts circumvent the rules by providing them their own work space in the basement of the building. Although hosts of both political persuasions accepted invitations, conservatives far outnumbered the liberals, and most expressed their support for the Contract.

For the first 100 days of the congressional session, talk radio hosts broadcast live from the Capitol building and captured live and taped interviews of congressional representatives and senators passing in the hallway. When the talk radio throng outgrew the working spaces available, Gingrich allowed some hosts to work in the extra space in his office.

The Contract with America was defeated, but Gingrich and many of his republican colleagues enjoyed the experiment and the opportunity to connect with the talk radio audience. "They brought an undisciplined, inquisitive, back-home kind of curiosity to what's going on," he wrote in his 1995 book, *To Renew America*. "Talk shows are not simply more conservative than the elite media; they are a lot less cynical. Talk-show hosts are usually pleased to have someone drop by and actually engage in interesting conversation. They may have a streak of skepticism, but they are not infected with the corrosive contempt and cynicism of the regular press corps."[9]

Deborah Parenti, vice president and general manager for the industry publication *Radio Ink*, believes that while talk radio provides a forum for debate, it is not the major factor in most voter's decisions. "I think talk radio certainly opens the door to discussion and debate, exposing audiences to contrasting views and philosophies, but at the end of the day, when voters entered that booth, they made choices based on their own beliefs and especially this year, their pocket books," she says. "At the same time, people tend to listen more to those with whom they agree. In that case, what they hear on a particular show and how it is framed might be considered influential by some while others would argue that it only validates the already held opinion of the listener."[10]

Many talk radio hosts insist their job is to entertain and not to stir political passions, yet congressional leaders report that much of their issue-related mail indicates the correspondence was prompted by talk radio programming. David Keene, a political consultant and chairman of the American Conservative Union, credits talk radio with "revitalizing and refueling the conservatives and republicans at the grass roots level."[11]

During the mid-1990s debate on health care reform, a survey of representatives and senators indicated that nearly half believed that talk radio was the most influential form of media in terms of public awareness of the issue, while only 15 percent identified the *New York Times*.

"Talk radio listeners alone don't make policy, of course, but the talk show mike does provide a forum for public opinion that no one in the administration, Congress, or the news media can miss," says National Public Radio host Diane Rehm. "When events get them riled, concerned people call radio shows like mine, and many further express their unhappiness by calling and writing the White House and congressional offices. Then, when listeners hear others voice their opinions, they feel justified in voicing their own. Sometimes the vox populi chorus becomes too loud for the wise to ignore, ultimately rising above the din of conventional wisdom."[12]

Boston Globe media critics Steve Elman and Alan Tolz contend that despite its claims to the contrary, political talk radio can no longer be a true town square because it long ago gave up its appearance of neutrality. "American listeners no longer expect talk-radio hosts to be reasonable, or even rational," they wrote in an analysis of the 2008 presidential election. "Talk radio no longer even pretends to be a 'town meeting of the air.' Hosts ordinarily do not perceive callers' contributions as valuable uses of airtime."[13]

In recent presidential campaigns, the influence of talk radio can be found even on television. To cover the campaigns, for example, television interview programs are turning to two-way talk formats, allowing callers to ask direct questions of the candidates—essentially imitating talk radio.

Most media critics and observers, including bloggers who frequently write about the industry, believe that talk radio has little impact on voting patterns because most hosts are preaching to those already converted rather than the undecideds in the congregation. "Post-Limbaugh talk radio is not about convincing people to vote one way or the other," wrote Michael J. West on his politics and popular culture blog. "The people who listen to any given radio host have already made up their minds. Anybody who listens to Rush Limbaugh is already going to vote republican. Anybody who listens to Air America is already going to vote democratic. They are not there to change minds—they're there to reassure their constituencies. People like to hear their own opinions repeated back to them, and they absolutely hate to hear opinions on the radio that they disagree with."[14]

In a 1999 study, media researcher Barry Hollander found that the audience for talk radio is subject to constant turnover, meaning that at any one time there may be a large number of people listening, but over the long-term the effect of the programming they listen to is minimal.

Kathleen Hall Jamieson, dean of the Annenberg School for Communication at the University of Pennsylvania, says that call-in programs produce only a "voyeuristic sense of participation." Jamieson minimizes the claims of some talk show hosts that their programs provide an exchange of views between different segments of the public or between the public and the government. On radio in particular, she says, most talk programs "tend to have just one side ideologically" and merely "reinforce the existing views of their audiences."[15]

Communication researcher David C. Barker contends that the expanding popularity of talk radio means more negatives than positives for the political process because it is based on entertainment and persuasion—as opposed to broadcast news and print journalism, that are based on objectivity. "As more Americans receive from sources whose primary objectives are to entertain and persuade, democratic dialogue may become more misinformed, contentious, and polarized—resulting in legislative gridlock and/or restricted policy alternatives," Barker wrote in his 2002 book, *Rushed to Judgment.*[16]

Ain't Over 'Til It's Over

When Bill Bradley vacated his U.S. Senate seat in 1996, New Jersey representatives Richard Zimmer and Robert Torricelli both coveted the job. Their campaign was one of the dirtiest in the state's history, and political journalists across the state labeled it "a Jersey street fight."[17] They accepted invitations to appear together on the national radio show of Howard Stern, whose programming focused more on popular culture than politics. But more specifically, Stern trafficked in shock. His program featured crude humor, double entendres, and language that came close to and occasionally crossed the regulatory lines drawn by the Federal Communications Commission.

Always reluctant to reveal his political leanings or endorse candidates, Stern brought both candidates to his studio with no preconceived notions as to what would happen and which, if either, of the men he would eventually endorse. But after nearly an hour of trash talk, half-truths, and personal insults exchanged by the two candidates, Stern announced that he was so impressed he would endorse both of them.

The Bradley-Zimmer-Stern anecdote is an excellent illustration of *agenda-setting*, a theoretical term used in the study of how individuals process information in the news and apply it to current events. The agenda-setting concept was developed by communication researchers Max McCombs and Donald Shaw in the 1970s. It has been applied to nearly every form of media—from the earliest newspapers to television news to cyberspace—with numerous experiments providing consistent results: when individuals in a given community were asked to list and rank-order the most serious issues facing that community, their rankings were consistent with the degree of attention paid to those issues by local media. In an ideal situation, McCombs and Shaw contend, the media does not tell members of the audience *what to think*, but it tells them *what to think about*.[18]

The application of agenda setting theory to talk radio has been minimal. But within the industry, talk radio hosts and broadcasting executives generally agree on the industry's ability to influence the public agenda, even without empirical data to back up their perceptions.

Phil Boyce, vice president for the news/talk division at Citadel Broadcasting, denies that programs within his control set the agenda for what is discussed in those communities and insists that the opposite is truer—that the banter heard on talk radio reflects what is being said in the community rather than influences it. "If I have to tell our hosts what to talk about, then I've got the wrong hosts," Boyce says. "The impression that there is someone up there (in upper management) pulling the strings, setting the agenda—is just not the way it is."[19]

In many communities, public officials complain about "government by talk show" that results when radio hosts give out their mailing addresses, phone numbers, and fax numbers over the air. Despite their complaints, however, many admit that communication from their constituents that are motivated by their radio listening habits does play a role in their decision-making.

In 1990, station WKXW in Trenton, New Jersey, switched formats from adult contemporary music to talk. Governor Jim Florio had just pushed a sizable tax hike through the state legislature, and that was one of the first topics dealt with on a morning drive-time show hosted by Jim Gearhart. In a moment of levity, he suggested not a "period of mourning," but rather a "period of mooning."[20] While there were no reported incidents of "mooning" at the state capitol, the public uproar generated by the broadcast prompted Florio to roll back parts of the tax-increasing legislation. Taking full credit for the governor's change of heart, WKXW saw a increase in its audience from 400,000 to 500,000 listeners per day and leapfrogged from eighth place to first in the local market.

That same year, Bob Grant of WABC in New York said he and his show got involved in a New Jersey tax protest in order to "throw the bastards out" in the upcoming election.[21]

In San Diego, host Roger Hedgecock initiated a crusade to get the government to police the U.S.-Mexican border more vigorously to stop illegal immigrants. He urged motorists to drive to the border and shine their headlights across it to draw attention to its porous nature.

Although Hedgecock's program is known for its "Hold Their Feet to the Fire" campaign that takes partial credit for the 2003 recall of California governor Gray Davis as well as other legislative wins and defeats, the host himself downplays his role. "To translate the talk to action, most hosts don't do that," he says. "They prefer infotainment and letting listeners do what they want to do."[22] While Hedgecock may have been the biggest name in the Davis recall effort, he may not have been the first. Nationally syndicated host Melanie Morgan claims to have started the effort, after which Hedgecock and other hosts around the state joined in.

In the Pacific Northwest, Seattle talk show host Mike Siegel has been setting the agenda for decades. In one case in the 1970s, Siegel rallied his listeners and together they derailed a plan to building a million-dollar daycare center for state employees. In 1990, Siegel generated enough opposition to a proposed taxpayer bailout of the state's savings and loan industry that the legislature reversed its support for the idea. He takes his show to the capitol building in Olympia once a year to protest waste in state government spending.

When Connecticut governor Lowell Weicker wanted to generate public support for a proposed tax increase in 1991, he took the campaign to talk radio. While opponents of the plan were not moved to change their minds, they did respect Weicker for putting himself "on the line" by taking calls from both sides of the debate.

The following year, Boston host Jerry Williams led a fight to repeal Massachusetts' mandatory seatbelt law. Williams also claims to have single-handedly defeated Mayor Ray Flynn by throwing his endorsement behind Flynn's opponent.

Tom Leykis has been known for setting the agenda for listeners in southern California for decades. When singer Cat Stevens expressed support for the Ayatollah Khomeini's death threat against controversial author Salman Rushdie in 1993, Leykis announced plans to stage a public burning of Stevens's records. When the local fire department expressed concerns for public safety, he instead donned a hard hat and publicly crushed the records with a steamroller. In 2003, local talk show hosts around the country (and some deejays at country music stations) mimicked the Leykis stunt by staging ceremonies in which they steamrolled compact disks of the Dixie Chicks after their controversial remarks about President Bush and the war in Iraq.

In 2005, Seattle radio personalities John Carlson and Kirby Wilbur supported a local political group's campaign to repeal a gasoline tax passed by the Washington legislature. The movement failed, but several municipalities sued the group, claiming its campaign violated state election laws as they pertain to referenda. The suit included a claim that Carlson's and Wilbur's support for the repeal constituted an in-kind contribution. A trial court agreed, but the Washington Supreme Court eventually overturned that decision, ruling 9-0 that the group was exercising its First Amendment rights and the municipalities' suit was an "abusive attempt to silence political opposition."[23]

Media researchers C. Richard Hofstetter and Christopher L. Gianos contend that political candidates find talk radio shows appealing because they serve as opportunities to "get their messages out" with being seriously challenged on their positions by the media, as they would be in the case of news conferences or one-on-one interviews with journalists. Although talk radio hosts often claim they and their listeners will play the role of skeptical questioners, that is seldom the case. Regardless of party affiliation, candidates are usually treated to "softball" questions by hosts who are either intimidated by the candidate's presence or simply reluctant to treat the candidate in a manner that might discourage other politicians from appearing on the show.

Democratic media strategist Tony Schwartz urges candidates for local offices to take advantage of talk radio as an inexpensive medium, but gives them three ground rules: (1) insist on being live rather than on tape, so comments cannot be edited or juxtaposed with different questions; (2) avoid sharing the microphone with an opponent; insist on a separate time slot; and (3) instead of insisting on a host who agrees with your position, insist only on one who knows the issues. Schwartz believes that a knowledgeable host will typically be fair, even if he or she does not agree with the guest; whereas a host without a command of the facts will often compensate with bluster and even hostility.[24]

While anecdotal evidence indicates the talk radio strategy can be successful for local political candidates, similar evidence indicates it can backfire for candidates on the national political stage. During recent presidential primary seasons, candidates and their spokespersons took advantage of friendly hosts and their reluctance to press them on the issues, but experienced political journalists criticized the candidates for ducking the tough questions from trained journalists in favor of "softball" questions from talk radio hosts and their audiences.

The Leader of the Opposition

In their 1955 book titled *Personal Influence,* researchers Elihu Katz and Paul Lazarsfeld coined the term "opinion leaders" to describe individuals who possess the ability to influence others by either position of authority or personal characteristics such as charisma and assertiveness. Talk radio hosts are not authority figures in the sense that Lazarsfeld specified, but many certainly are charismatic and assertive enough to be opinion leaders for their listeners.[25]

Closely related to the agenda-setting theory is a question that communication researchers often pose about political talk radio: do audience members listen to talk radio in search of new and objective information to help them make voting decisions, or do they merely seek out hosts and programs that validate beliefs they already hold? The latter theory is known as "cognitive consistency," and in the early days of radio talk that was surely the case, as the angry and disenfranchised listeners tuned in to hear radio hosts who shared their pessimism about society and distrust of government. That was the dominant listener motivation throughout the 1980s and 1990s, but in the new century, the audience expanded to include the more optimistic, open-minded listeners seeking out both entertainment and information. Joseph Klapper, the communications theorist who developed the cognitive consistency theory, wrote that, "By and large, people tend to expose themselves to those mass communications that are in accord with their existing attitudes and interests. Consciously or unconsciously, they avoid communications of the opposite hue. In the event of their being nevertheless exposed to unsympathetic material, they often seem not to perceive it, or to recast and interpret it to fit their existing views, or to forget it more readily than they forget sympathetic material."[26]

Two other closely related theoretical concepts applicable here are "cognitive dissonance" and "selective exposure." Cognitive dissonance refers to the tendency of individuals to "explain away" new ideas that are inconsistent with previously held beliefs. In the case of talk radio, a liberal individual listening to Rush Limbaugh would likely react to one of his conservative pronouncements by saying "That's just Rush being Rush," or words to that effect. Likewise, one of Limbaugh's loyal conservative listeners, surprised to find Limbaugh's show being taken over by a liberal guest host, would likely react to the host's comments with "that's just liberal hogwash," or similar response.

Selective exposure refers to individuals' tendency to expose themselves to sources of information that are consistent with their beliefs while avoiding those sources that are inconsistent. "Democrats may watch every minute of their party's national convention on television," Lazarsfeld wrote. "But when the Republican Convention comes on the following week, they go bowling."[27] Uncle Henry, host of a local morning show in Mobile, Alabama, is among the many hosts who believe in cognitive consistency—that the majority of his listeners typically seek out hosts and programs that confirm beliefs they already hold. "People like to hear their own opinions reflected back to them," he says. "Quite often they're listening for someone who can articulate their opinions better than they can do it themselves."[28]

Many who agree with that line of thinking will analogize talk radio programming to the newspaper editorial page. "The editorial page is a gathering place for people who had already made up their minds on an issue could speak to each other; no one undecided about an issue goes there for information to help them make decisions," says one former governor. "No one picks up the newspaper editorial page expecting to learn anything new."[29] Many media critics believe the same principle could be applied to talk radio—people go there to find others who will agree with them and reinforce what they already believe. Conservatives will listen to conservative talk radio to confirm what they already believe, while liberals will listen to liberal talk radio for the same reason. The talk radio forum is not a place where the undecided will learn anything new.

Shortly after Bill Clinton was sworn into office in 1993, the conservative *National Review* anointed Limbaugh as the "leader of the opposition" and put a caricature of him on its cover. Limbaugh and other conservative hosts may have spoken of Clinton's election in anathematic terms at the time of his inauguration, but during the eight years that followed many secretly acknowledged that the president was the perfect foil to generate fodder for themselves and their callers. During the eight-year reign of George W. Bush that followed, hosts turned their wrath toward Senator Hillary Clinton of New York, the former first lady, who had her own presidential aspirations. Shortly after Barack Obama was elected, many hosts believed his administration would be a good thing for talk radio. "I cherish the notion that the last time a young democrat took over the White House with gauzy visions of change, it produced a 'Golden Age' for right-wing talk," wrote conservative host Michael Medved in a December 2008 op-ed in *USA Today*.[30]

Media critic Sharon Crowley agrees. "When dittoheads listen to Rush Limbaugh articulate positions that confirm beliefs they already hold, they must experience satisfaction and pleasure, which in turn must reinforce their belief in the accuracy of assessments made within Limbaugh's (and their own) ideologics," Crowley in her 2006 book, *Toward a Civil Discourse*. "They may in fact derive additional pleasure from the knowledge that an extended community of listeners shares in that satisfaction as well. I suspect that Limbaugh's audience also enjoys knowing that his rants irk people who don't share their positions on issues. The joy of resistance is enhanced by a feeling of solidarity."[31]

Barker's study of the 1996 and 2000 presidential campaigns indicated that many listeners reported their voting decisions were influenced by talk radio—mostly by Limbaugh. In the 1996 race, third-party candidate Ross Perot was doing well until Limbaugh ridiculed his candidacy on the air, causing his poll numbers to drop dramatically. Barker's study is cited in David Brock's 2004 book, *The Republican Noise Machine*. Barker claimed that Limbaugh's lukewarm endorsement of republican nominee Bob Dole in 1996 hindered his chances against incumbent Bill Clinton, and a similar half-hearted support for John McCain caused him to lose the republican nomination to George W. Bush in 2000.[32]

In 2005, the Annenberg Public Policy Center at the University of Pennsylvania conducted an in-depth study of American media and their influence in the political process. One of the startling findings of the study was that almost as many Americans (27 percent) labeled Limbaugh as a "journalist" as they did *Washington Post* Associate Editor Bob Woodward (30 percent).[33]

"Good talk show hosts can get their listeners so lathered up that they truly can change public policy," says Dan Shelley, a former news director at WTMJ, a news/talk station in Milwaukee, Wisconsin. "They can inspire like-minded folks to flood the phone lines and email inboxes of aldermen, county supervisors, state legislators, and federal lawmakers. They can inspire their followers to vote for candidates the hosts prefer. How? By pounding away on an issue or candidate, or more likely, exploit whatever Achilles heel the other candidate may have. Influencing elections is more likely to occur at the local rather than national level, but that still gives talk radio power."[34]

The idea of political commentators using the radio airwaves to encourage their listeners to contact congressional representatives is not a new one. As far back as the 1930s, Father Charles Coughlin used his national radio show to urge his audience to write letters on a variety of issues. In 1935, for example, Congress was poised to approve the United States' joining of the World Court until legislators were deluged with more than 20,000 telegrams from Coughlin's listeners who objected to the plan.

In the late 1980s, academic studies of talk radio found it a venue for blowing off steam in a variety of forms—some constructive and some not. While researchers were encouraged by positive examples of tax revolts and generating support for local charities and other worthy causes, they also documented numerous cases of hate speech and other forms of vitriol. According to Wayne Munson, who documented many such cases in a 1993 book, content analyses of white- and black-oriented call-in shows in New York, Philadelphia, and Chicago revealed "far more examples of racial divisiveness than of ethnic affirmation."[35]

Russ Hill, program director at a talk station in Phoenix, believes that hosts should seek to activate their listeners, pointing to the immigration debate as a positive example. "Politicians are used to having an apathetic base," he says. "People don't call or write Congress that much unless they want a tour of the Capitol." He adds that when hosts can get their callers to make their voices heard, "it's a good wake-up call for politicians of both parties."[36]

Audience research indicates that most listeners believe they are getting unbiased information, yet most hosts readily admit they are biased in their approach. The more assertive the host in expressing his or her opinion, the less-likely callers are to express a contrary opinion; in most cases they defer to the opinion of the host. In those rare cases that hosts are neutral on an issue, callers are slightly more likely to assert their own opinions.

Yasmin Alibhai-Brown, a European newspaper columnist who writes about American media and politics, says she finds the humility of American talk radio hosts a bit perplexing. At a July 2008 conference in London, Alibhai-Brown posed the question, "How can they (radio talk show hosts) have those great radio voices and make all that money, then say they have no influence?"[37]

Talkers magazine publisher Michael Harrison believes that the role of Limbaugh and other talk radio hosts is largely exaggerated. "Rush is first and foremost a radio performer," he told Associated Press in a January 2009 interview. "He's not a political leader. He's doesn't make money by turning elections. He only exists to gather large audiences and raise more advertising revenue, and he does it terrifically."[38]

Harrison downplays the impact of talk radio endorsements on the outcome of elections and denied that their accuracy—or lack of it—in predicting the outcome reflects on their job performance. "Talk show hosts aren't judged on whom they pick as a candidate, any more than the jobs of football announcers are on the line with their Super Bowl predictions," he told Associated Press.[39]

At a 2008 conference in London, Neal Boortz expressed concern about the role of talk radio in the political process. "I'm sometimes troubled by the influence that talk radio can have on elections," Boortz told the audience. "I warn listeners to never believe anything I say on the radio unless it is consistent with what they already know to be true or they go out and do their own research. I have a somewhat odd view of talk radio. Our job is not to influence opinion or to change minds but to attract listeners to our radio stations and hold them long enough to play commercials for them. Then, when the commercials are over and it comes back to us, our job is to hold them for another ten minutes so we can play more commercials. The way we do that is to be entertaining. We don't do that by trying to change their political opinions or tell them who to vote for."[40]

Some station managers are not comfortable with the discussion of how talk radio programming affects elections. "If you're doing what you're supposed to be doing, you're not supposed to be affecting the outcome," says Alan Caudle, programming manager at WCOA-AM in Pensacola, Florida.[41]

Despite the denials of Harrison and others in the industry, there is anecdotal evidence to the contrary. In 1988, for example, House Speaker Jim Wright tried to push through a congressional pay raise without a floor vote, and the issue quickly came to the attention of talk show hosts across the country. Local hosts gave out the mailing addresses and fax numbers for the Washington offices of their local congressional delegations, and those lines were flooded for several days. The pay raise was put on hold. The following congressional session, the raise that congress voted itself was much smaller than the one originally opposed, and the legislation included several ethical provisions not previously considered. In the early 1990s, congress and the American people passed the Twenty-seventh Amendment to the Constitution, which prohibited congressional representatives from accepting pay raises until after the following election.

President Bill Clinton fell victim to talk show democracy twice in his first month in the White House. He abandoned his first choice for attorney general after talk show hosts and their audiences heavily criticized it, and opposition to health care reform—fueled largely by talk radio hosts and their listeners—caused Clinton to back away from his own proposal.

The attorney general drama began on Christmas Eve 1992, when the president-elect announced his choice for attorney general. At first, Zoe Baird, a forty-year-old corporate lawyer with no previous government experience, was seen as a slam-dunk for Senate confirmation and would have become the first woman to hold the post. Although she was a relative unknown in national legal circles and had no ties with the National Organization for Women or other women's advocacy groups, her nomination had their support, even though several groups had already expressed support for another woman candidate: attorney and feminist scholar Brooksley Born.

Except for her advocacy for reducing product liability judgments (while representing several insurance companies), there was little not to like about Baird. But a week before Clinton's inauguration and before confirmation hearings could be scheduled, the *New York Times* broke the story that Baird had employed two illegal immigrants as her nanny and part-time driver and failed to pay Social Security taxes on them. Both the employment of the illegal immigrants and failure to pay taxes were violations of federal law, and the irony of blatant law-breaking by a nominee to be the nation's highest-ranking law enforcement officer was too much for the mainstream media and talk radio to resist.

While print and broadcast journalists scrutinized the failure of Clinton's transition team to uncover Baird's legal problems during the vetting process—as well as his stubbornness in not withdrawing the nomination right away—talk radio hosts and callers were vehement. Clinton's honeymoon with the media was over even before he took the oath of office.

Across the FM and AM radio dials, it was impossible to find any support from talk radio hosts—even those labeling themselves as progressives who had supported Clinton during the campaign. Many hosts reported opposition to the Baird nomination running at 70 to 90 percent among their callers. When the televised confirmation hearings began, opposition grew stronger as viewers learned about Baird's income from her corporate job and her husband's income as a professor at Yale Law School. With two healthy incomes, callers mused, why couldn't the couple afford to hire legal workers and pay their Social Security taxes?

Unfortunately for Baird, the talk radio listeners who called the hosts to express their opposition were not her only problem. A substantially higher number called their senators to oppose her, and many senatorial staffers reported calls were running 20 to 1 against her confirmation.

When those staffers asked callers where they got their information on her candidacy and why they were so motivated to call, the majority identified talk radio as the culprit. A few hours before the Senate Judiciary Committee was scheduled to vote, Clinton withdrew the Baird nomination. Talk radio hosts around the country celebrated their role in her demise.

The failure of the Zoe Baird nomination and failure of his health care reform proposals were not the last defeats the Clinton administration would face at the hands of talk radio. When the president announced his intention to reverse the Pentagon's long-standing policy of banning gay men and women from serving openly in the military, talk radio phone lines lit up again, and in turn calls poured into congressional offices as well as the White House. "This isn't government by talk show,"[42] complained one White House staffer, perhaps unaware that his boss had done more than any other politician to make it just that.

Other talk show hosts followed suit, and within weeks, the proposal was dead. Had talk radio scored another victory, just as it had in the cases of Zoe Baird, the congressional pay raise, and health care reform? Media critics believed that that was plenty of credit to go around, and that talk radio deserved its share.

In February 1994, Congress debated legislation that would have limited parents' ability to home-school their children. A nonprofit organization calling itself the Home School Legal Defense Association sprung into action but found its usual methods of writing op-ed pieces and faxing position statements to the media weren't working, and its recently discovered tactic of stirring up discussion on computer bulletin boards (this was the early days of the Internet) was not generating any traction, either. Then the group decided to take its case to talk radio. A half dozen staff members were interviewed on more than fifty talk shows across the country without leaving their offices in Purcellville, Virginia. They asked listeners to call their congressional representatives to express their opposition to the proposed law, and within days, House and Senate offices were flooded with an estimated 1 million phone calls. "We got a lot of calls on the North American Free Trade Agreement and gays in the military," Texas representative Dick Armey told the media. "But I've never seen anything like this—going from no calls on one day to the switchboards shutting down the next."[43]

Later that year, Limbaugh was given so much credit for the republican landslide in congressional mid-term elections that the party made him an honorary member of the freshman class. Political observers say he not only moved the voters, but also the party itself. "Rush talked about the Contract with America before there was a Contract with America," said Karl Rove, advisor to President George W. Bush. "Rush helped set the agenda."[44] Limbaugh takes credit for chasing fifty-four democratic incumbents from the House of Representatives, eight from the Senate, and Mario Cuomo from the governor's mansion in New York. Some political observers believe the "Gingrich Revolution" could be more accurately called the "Gingrich-Limbaugh Revolution."

Tony Blankenship, press secretary for House Speaker Newt Gingrich, credits Limbaugh for generating much of the public support for republican legislative successes during Clinton's first term. "Rush doesn't give out congressional phone numbers, but when he talks about an issue, the switchboards light up," he told media critic Howard Kurtz.[45]

In addition to rallying their listeners to support or oppose legislation, talk show hosts have a strong track record in generating support for and opposition to presidential appointments of cabinet members and Supreme Court justices. In addition to opposing Clinton's nomination of Baird, talk radio hosts also led the opposition to President George W. Bush's 2005 appointment of Harriet Miers to fill a vacancy on the Supreme Court. Miers had the conservative credentials the party wanted, but her lack of experience caused talk show hosts and callers to worry that if she took a seat surrounded by liberal justices, she might be too easily drawn toward the center. After twenty-four days of being pilloried on talk radio and on newspaper editorial pages, Miers withdrew, and the seat eventually went to Samuel Alito.

In February 2006, Michael Savage was trolling the news wires for tidbits for his radio show, *The Savage Nation*, when he came across a brief but curious item about the federal government's plans to outsource the operation of six major American ports to a company owned by the government of Dubai in the United Arab Emirates. Displaying his usual level of angst, Savage introduced the issue to his radio audience, claiming the United States was turning over the security of its ports to "potential Muslim terrorists." Despite Savage's hyperbole, the gist of the story was true, and the proposal generated opposition—expressed on the floor of Congress and on television and radio talk shows—that was bipartisan and immediate. Republicans viewed it as a potential risk to national security, and democrats saw it as more evidence of the incompetence of the Bush administration. Even New York senator Chuck Schumer, who Savage has once called "that ambulance chaser from Brooklyn,"[46] went on Savage's show twice to oppose the deal.

Barker used the Dubai ports deal to illustrate his belief that talk radio in general, and Limbaugh in particular, is more effective at generating opposition than support.

Talk radio is also widely credited with rallying public sentiment against a bipartisan 2007 immigration bill sponsored by Republican senator John McCain of Arizona and Democratic senator Edward Kennedy of Massachusetts. The bill would have granted amnesty for 12,000 to 20,000 illegal immigrants already in the country while funding new enforcement techniques. The bill also included the Dream Act, a law designed to give children of illegal immigrants the opportunity to remain in the country by either enrolling in college or joining the military. The bill already had the tacit support of President Bush.

As expected, conservative talk show hosts such as Limbaugh, Hannity, O'Reilly, Ingraham, and Savage led the assault against the bill. While they applauded provisions of the bill that would have tightened the borders and increased enforcement of workplace violations, their larger objections were based on their belief that illegal immigrants were criminals who deserved deportation.

Prompted by talk radio, conservative listeners called their federal legislators, who reported that 95 percent of constituents who said they learned about the details of the bill from talk radio had called to state their opposition to it. Even though Republican Senator Arlen Specter of Pennsylvania supported the bill, he told reporters that Congress would not be influenced by "a small number who object and an even smaller number who make the effort to call."[47]

Some listeners may have done more than that: although none could provide proof, many congressional leaders—including Senators Mel Martinez of Florida, Lindsey Graham of South Carolina, and Richard Burr of North Carolina—claimed to have received threatening mail and phone calls at their offices and homes that were prompted by talk radio.

The proposed legislation died on the Senate floor, and talk radio hosts gloated for weeks. Harrison claimed that "talk radio should be credited with possibly saving the American people from George W. Bush's immigration bill."[48]

Jamieson agreed. "Talk radio and talk TV are most effective when there's an immediate action pending," she said in a 2007 interview.[49] Senator Trent Lott blamed the loss on talk radio, stating, "Talk radio is running America. . . . we have to deal with the problem."[50]

Even though the bill was dead before the official kickoff of the 2008 presidential election campaign, McCain was forced to defend his association with the bill almost from the start. Also tainted was fellow republican candidate Rudy Giuliani, who had no official connection to it, but was asked about it because of his reputation for being reluctant to have New York City police enforce immigration laws when he was that city's mayor.

While the Truth Is Still Putting on Its Shoes

Artemus Ward, a ninteenth-century English educator and humorist, once said that, "It ain't the things we don't know that hurts us. . . . what hurts us are the things we think we know that ain't so."[51] Bad grammar aside, Ward's point is directly related to callers (and sometimes the hosts) on talk radio. More than a century later, Barker found that the central problem of talk radio is that instead of callers being uninformed, the majority are instead misinformed. Compounding the problem is that the misinformed hold their false beliefs with a high degree of confidence. That observation seems to paraphrase a Bertrand Russell quote about the origin of myths: "If a man is offered a fact which goes against his instincts, he will scrutinize it closely, and unless the evidence is overwhelming, he will refuse to believe it. If, on the other hand, he is offered something which affords a reason for acting in accordance to his instincts, he will accept it even on the slightest evidence."[52] One cynical blogger wrote in 2008 that "talk radio is for the conservative listener what the lamppost is for the drunk—used not for illumination but for support."[53]

Barker found that Limbaugh and other conservative talk show hosts present their listeners with a great deal of new information, but much of it is wrong. Examples included listeners believing (based on information from the host) that the administration of President Bill Clinton spent more money on welfare than on national defense, when the opposite was true; and that the national deficit increased during the Clinton's presidency, while it actually was eliminated. Barker found that audiences that listened to liberal talk show hosts not only retained more information they heard, but also had a more accurate picture of national affairs.[54]

Critics say that many hosts are more concerned with their Arbitron ratings then than they are in making sure that they and their callers have their facts straight.

The tendency of talk radio to spread falsehoods based on callers' outrageous comments was proven early in the Clinton administration. A caller to a Washington, D.C. program, for example, claimed the administration had banned military aides from wearing their uniforms when working in or conducting business at the White House. Host Brian Wilson did little to challenge the caller's allegations, and within days conservative hosts across the country were citing the story as evidence of the Clinton administration's contempt for the military. Washington journalists attempted to verify the story but could find no evidence to support it, and in fact found just the opposite was true: military protocol *required* members of the armed forces to wear their uniforms when conducting business at the White House or on Capitol Hill, and the administration had made no attempts to change the policy. Despite numerous White House news releases and media stories to the contrary, many radio hosts continued to repeat the fabrication for weeks, reminding observers of the Mark Twain quip that "a falsehood can travel half-way around the world while the truth is still putting on its shoes."[55] By the time the story had been discredited, the damage was already done.

Later in the Clinton presidency, a caller to G. Gordon Liddy's show provided stories of the president's "dalliances with Hollywood starlets" and claimed the president had an underground tunnel constructed to connect the White House with the Treasury building so that Clinton mistresses who worked in that cabinet department could secretly move back and forth between the two buildings. As usual, Liddy allowed the caller's allegations to go unchallenged, and the White House found the report so preposterous that it refused to respond.

"One of the right's strategies for getting so much time on television and radio talk shows is to shout louder than anyone else, and to make more ruder, obnoxious, and inflammatory remarks," wrote feminist Gloria Feldt in her 2004 book, *The War on Choice*. "There's a wide civility gap between us (pro-choice) and our anti-choice opponents."[56]

Progressive host Bill Press made a similar point in his 2001 book, *Spin This: All the Ways We Don't Tell the Truth*. "More so than television news, talk radio is spin heaven," Press wrote. "The talk show host begins with an opening spin on the topic of the hour. Then listeners call to spin the host. It's great fun, and it's the most democratic forum that exists for the debate and discussion of ideas. Talk radio is the home of equal opportunity spinning."[57]

David Brudnoy, the late host at WBZ in Boston, modestly downplayed the influence of talk show hosts and believes that listeners put far more belief in the opinions of their on-air heroes than is deserved. "A lot of talk show hosts are opportunistic twits," he said. "They and their listeners believe that they (the hosts) are the only ones with answers. No one says, 'I don't believe in doctors any more, so I'm going to take out my own appendix.' But with politics, somehow we don't need any experts."[58]

Propaganda Models

During World War II, Columbia University Professor Clyde R. Miller founded the Institute for Propaganda Analysis (IPA). At first, the emphasis was to study the use of propaganda in the war in Europe, but he quickly expanded its scope to include the study of propaganda from all sources, including the Ku Klux Klan, other extremist groups, and the American advertising industry. The Institute is still in operation today and identifies—in its publications and on its World Wide Web site—nine common propaganda devices:

Name-calling is the use of emotional labels that are offered in the place of logic or evidence. Examples of labels applied to individuals include "extremist," "radical," "liberal," "fundamentalist," and "racist." Examples of labels applied to ideas include "social engineering," "radical," "legislating morality," and "counter-culture."

Glittering generalities represent the opposite of name-calling. Instead of asking the audience to reject an idea without examining the evidence, a communicator resorting to glittering generalities wants the audience to accept an idea without requiring evidence. What results are generalizations so extreme that receivers disregard the lack of substance behind those appeals. Examples are claims that begin with "everyone knows that. . . . " and "it goes without saying that. . . . "

Transfer is a device by which the communicator wants the audience to take the authority, sanction, prestige, or negativity of one idea and apply it to another idea that the communicator wants the audience to accept or reject. Transfer is often used as a tactic in political races. In the 2008 presidential primary campaign, for example, opponents of Senator Hillary Clinton reminded voters of the policy decisions and scandals associated with her husband, former President Bill Clinton, hoping that voters would transfer their distrust of Bill to Hillary. Later, during the general election campaign, opponents of Senator John McCain attempted to link him with the policies of President George W. Bush, hoping voters would transfer their dislike of Bush to McCain.

The *bandwagon* approach is one in which audiences are encouraged to adopt a certain idea or behavior because "everyone else is doing it" and they "do not want to be left behind."

The *plain folks* approach suggests that audiences should adopt an idea because it comes from people similar to them or reject an idea because it comes from someone unlike them.

Testimonials are appeals from influential celebrities or other authority figures whose expertise may be irrelevant to the product being sold or idea being promoted. A common example is the use of professional athletes to endorse companies or products, including those that are unrelated to the sport for which the athletes are known.

Card-stacking is a method in which the communicator stacks the cards in favor of the desired result, presenting one-side evidence or half-truths. For example, critics of a university's athletic program may point out the graduation rate for the school's athletes is only 45 percent (and therefore the athletic program should be eliminated), but not mentioning (or perhaps not knowing) that the graduation rate for nonathletes is only 42 percent.

Scare tactics are devices intended to influence behavior and are common in advertising and political campaigns. A communicator using this tactic typically pairs a negative result with the desired behavior required to avoid it. Examples include television commercials showing an accident scene followed by the suggestion of wearing seat belts, or the scene of a house fire followed by a pitch for smoke detectors.

Euphemisms are terms intended to obscure or soften the true meaning of behaviors or concepts. Examples include a company referring to employee layoffs as "early retirement opportunities" or the government referring to a tax increase as a "revenue adjustment."

Although not officially part of the IPA list, there are two other argumentative techniques used in political communication, including talk radio: the *false dichotomy* and the *straw man argument*. Both are basically extensions of the "scare tactics" method described above in that they are based on warning decision-makers (usually voters) of the perceived negative consequences associated with choices to which the persuader is opposed. They are often used in desperation because the persuader has already found more legitimate persuasive techniques ineffective.

The false dichotomy is an oversimplified or artificial division of a political issue in a way that tells voters or other decision-makers that they must choose between the two opposing ideas, with no alternatives possible. Political clichés that represent this idea include "us against them" and "you're either for us or against us." In each presidential election, the false dichotomy is reflected in constant references to "red states" and "blue states."

The straw man argument (sometimes called the "straw man fallacy") is a technique used to persuade the audience to oppose an idea based on a premise that is likely false or exaggerated, but also easier to understand. The metaphor is based on the fact that a straw man (a falsehood) is easier to attack and defeat than a real man (a truth).

The IPA employed communication researchers Alfred McClung Lee and Elizabeth Briant to analyze Charles Coughlin's speeches and radio broadcasts. Their results, published in a 1939 book, indicated that Coughlin used all seven of the propaganda devices to some extent.[59] Sixty-six years later, three communication researchers at the University of Indiana conducted a similar analysis of Bill O'Reilly's radio and television broadcasts. They reported that O'Reilly used one of the nine propaganda devices on an average of twelve times per minute, with the most common device being name-calling and scare tactics.

The Indiana University study compared O'Reilly to Coughlin, who often praised dictators such as Adolf Hitler and Benito Mussolini, and found that O'Reilly was three times as likely to be a name-caller as Coughlin and that he used age-old propaganda techniques such as "glittering generalities" and "card-stacking" far more than Coughlin—an average of thirteen times per minute. The same study showed that 96.3 percent of O'Reilly's references to democratic politicians cast them as villains.

"It's obvious he's very big into calling people names, and he's very big into glittering generalities," wrote Mike Conway, the coauthor of the study. "He's not very subtle. He's going to call people names, or he's going to paint something in a positive way, often without any real evidence to support that viewpoint."[60] The Indiana study found that on both his radio and television programs, O'Reilly paints certain people and groups as villains and others as victims to present the world, as he sees it, through political rhetoric.

Name-calling has long been a staple of political talk radio, and none is better at it than O'Reilly. O'Reilly often referred to liberal politicians as the "Kool-Aid Left." The term "left," while often used in a derogatory sense, is not by itself to be true name-calling. But when combined with the adjective "Kool-Aid," it be comes name-calling because it refers to the cliché "drink the Kool-Aid," an allusion to cult members who committed mass suicide in 1978 by drinking a concoction of fruit juice and strychnine; ever since the term "drinking the Kool-Aid" is used satirically to refer to anyone showing blind allegiance to a cause. He also referred to war protestors as "anti-American voices" and "traitors."[61]

In the year that followed Bush's declaration of "Mission Accomplished," the antiwar sentiment around the country was epitomized by a number of Americans who had lost family members in either 9/11 or the subsequent wars. Among them was a group of 9/11 widows calling themselves the "Jersey Girls" as they made the rounds of Sunday morning television talk shows, and Cindy

Sheehan, a California woman who lost her son, Casey, in Iraq in 2004. The Jersey Girls were instrumental in getting the Bush administration to cooperate—albeit reluctantly—with the 9/11 Commission. Limbaugh labeled Kristen Breitweiser, the most outspoken of the four, a "democratic operative" (even though she had voted for Bush in 2000) and said the women were not grieving widows, but instead were "obsessed with rage and hatred."[62]

While all talk show hosts use glittering generalities, Limbaugh might be the best exemplar. He often uses terms such as "democratic values" and "American traditions," but seldom defines those terms or provides examples. Sean Hannity is fond of terms such as "true hero," "upstanding citizen," and "great American," and O'Reilly used terms such as "the greater good" and referred to the Mexican border as "the birth of all American ills."

In the 2000 presidential election, no one worked harder than Limbaugh to employ the transfer technique and encourage Clinton haters to transfer their loathing of the president to Al Gore, the democratic presidential candidate who hoped to succeed him.

O'Reilly frequently used the bandwagon technique in his attempt to generate support for antiterrorism causes with comments such as "we live in dangerous times, as you know."[63] Speaking on government entitlement programs, he often said that "no fair person could object to the privatizing the Social Security system."[64]

O'Reilly also employed the plain folks technique by referring to himself as "your humble correspondent."[65]

Hannity and O'Reilly, as well as other hosts, employed the testimonial approach during the early stages of the 2008 election campaign by interviewing former Clinton advisor Dick Morris, who had turned against the former first couple and was one of Hillary Clinton's fiercest critics.

Once the presidential campaign was in full swing, many hosts employed the card-stacking technique in describing Barack Obama's ideas for sex education. "Obama wants to teach sex-education to first-graders," the hosts often said.[66] But that overgeneralization misrepresented what Obama said. Official campaign statements clarified that Obama's platform called for "age-appropriate" content. For first graders, he was not advocating that they be taught specific sexual information; his idea of age-appropriate for first graders was just basic safeguards about avoiding sexual predators.

Throughout much of the 1990s, Limbaugh and other talk radio hosts used the card-stacking technique by focusing their attention on what they viewed as Clinton's misguided agenda in addressing the national debt, while ignoring the fact that it was military spending by the Reagan administration in the previous decade that was responsible for much of the debt in the first place.

"Generally speaking, the facts cited on talk radio have been selectively chosen because they support the host's preconceived opinion, or can be interpreted to seem as if they do," says Dan Shelley, a former news director at WTMJ, a news/ talk station in Milwaukee, Wisconsin.[67]

Many talk show hosts employ scare tactics in their description of the American Civil Liberties Union. O'Reilly often did so during his show-opening commentaries, referring to ACLU as "flat-out dangerous" and an organization that "gives aid and comfort to our enemies."[68]

The most common example of a euphemism employed by talk show hosts is referring to the estate tax the "death tax," a euphemism also employed by politicians in speaking against it.

The Indiana study found that talk show hosts in general, and O'Reilly specifically, are masters of the false dichotomy, as they typically divide politicians, celebrities, and even everyday Americans (including listeners) into two camps—good and evil—with no one in between.

When used to label individuals, the false dichotomy is sometimes known as the "angel-devil" interpretation. In discussing the Iraq War, for example, Limbaugh, O'Reilly, and Hannity employ this technique by referring to American soldiers as universally good (even in light of the abuse of prisoners at Abu Ghraib) and all Muslims—not just the extremists—as evil. Coughlin used a similar technique in the 1930s when referring to public officials as either good or evil, and O'Reilly used the same two simplistic characteristics on his radio show.

"Much of national talk radio today serves the same purpose as Big Brother's Ministry of Truth," wrote *Salt Lake City News* columnist Bryan Hyde in 2006, alluding to George Orwell's bleak look at the future of free speech in his novel, *1984*. "It spins coverage of the issues in a light favorable to the chosen party line. Narrowly constructed arguments attempt to define issues with the false choices of liberal vs. conservative, Republican vs. Democrat, etc. Airwaves bristle with constant agitation for war and the demonizing of those who are designated as enemies."[69]

One example of the straw man argument was seen in the early stages of the 2008 presidential campaign. Opponents of democratic candidate Barack Obama focused public attention on his former pastor, Reverend Jeremiah Wright, who was known for inflammatory comments he made about race relations and other controversial issues. Even after Obama denounced Wright's comments and resigned from his church, talk radio hosts continued to publicize and play excerpts of those comments in order to make them a campaign issue—because the relationship between Obama and Wright was easier to criticize than other aspects of Obama's campaign.

The most recent application of the straw man argument can be heard in discussions of the Fairness Doctrine. Many observers believe that conservative talk radio's insistence on warning listeners about the possible return of the doctrine—which legal experts say is highly unlikely—is based on how easy it is to get listeners to rail against it, compared to how hard it is to get them interested in opposing other democratic programs that are more complex and difficult to understand. "It's something to get the audience excited and scared of the new administration—something with which they can paint Obama, (Nancy) Pelosi, and (Harry) Reid," says Bob Beckel, a *USA Today* columnist and Fox News contributor.[70]

Habermas and the Public Sphere

In the 1950s, German sociologist Jurgen Habermas developed the concept of the "public sphere" based on the phenomena of eighteenth century French intellectuals who would gather in public venues to debate the issues of the day. The result was an exponential growth in the number of salons, social clubs, and coffee houses. He described the "public sphere" as a place where the public collectively decides such issues as taxation, foreign relations, and other matters of government or social policy, and distinguished it from the "private sphere" in which families or other groups of individuals privately discuss matters affecting them personally.

His concept of the public sphere was based on his belief that rational argumentation and critical discussion of issues were the best way to study conflicts, and that the strength of one's argument was more important than one's identity or credentials. According to Habermas, the goal of such public discussion and debate was not to reach consensus, but to provide the boldest new ideas a fair hearing. These venues were autonomous in two respects: first, that participation in them was voluntary; and second, that they were independent of economic and political systems. His book, *The Structural Transformation of the Public Sphere*,[71] charts the growth of such places, their gradual decline, and disintegration—at least in the form in which he described them. Many media theorists contend that the public sphere concept is found today on the newspaper editorial page and on political talk radio, and those two conditions still apply.

Habermas's central contention was that the "public sphere" was a place in which both new and existing ideas could be debated and evaluated in a constructive atmosphere. His work did not limit the definition of the public sphere as a physical place such as a coffee shop or other gathering place, although that was his focus at the time. Habermas's theory could easily be applied to metaphysical gathering places as well, such as the newspaper editorial page, Internet chat room, or talk radio—and today media researchers and theorists are doing just that.

Although Habermas never specifically mentioned talk radio in his published research on the public sphere, he did issue a warning about public discourse in general that definitely applies to that genre. In particular, he worried that the contemporary public sphere has been overtaken by publicity and those striving to maintain a positive image in the public eye.

Whether it is called a form of "participatory democracy," "citizen journalism" (although journalism purists cringe at the term), or simply "new media," talk radio has emerged along with its cousin, the blogosphere, as a force to be recognized, even if it cannot be controlled. The comparison to Habermas's public sphere was not lost on former Vice President Al Gore. In his 2007 book, *The Assault on Reason,* he cited Habermas and his concern over the "refeudalization of the public sphere."[72] Gore paraphrased Habermas in describing feudalism as "a system in which wealth and power were intertwined, with knowledge playing no mediating role."[73] Gore specifically pointed to the consolidation of radio ownership—more and more stations being owned by fewer and fewer companies—as a potential threat to free speech. Gore advocates diversity ownership as a way to provide audiences with a broader range of viewpoints and believes that as a component of the public sphere, radio should do a better job of providing multiple sides of controversial issues—but he stopped short of advocating the return of the Fairness Doctrine.

The Toulmin Model

The Toulmin Model was developed by British logician Stephen Toulmin in the 1950s. The model is a method of analyzing argumentation in a variety of forms, including face-to-face communication, as in candidate debates; or written, as in newspaper columns and editorials. Toulmin described the typical argument as being constructed using six elements: claim, grounds, warrant, backing, qualifiers, and rebuttal.

According to Toulmin, *claims* typically fall into one of four categories: (1) factual claims, which are those that state something did or did not occur; (2) definitional claims, which argue how a concept can be labeled or categorized; (3) value claims, which assign opposing labels such "good" and "bad" to concepts; and (4) policy claims, which argue for or against government action. Of the four, factual claims are the only ones that could be proven true or false, as the latter three are mostly matters of opinion (as the U.S. Supreme Court has ruled, there is no such thing as a false opinion).

It is not difficult to apply Toulmin's model, especially his description of claims, to discourse heard on political talk radio. In two thirty-day samplings of national talk radio programming—one conducted during the 2008 election season and another in early 2009—there was little difference between the conservative and liberal programs in terms of the types of claims made. Approximately

50 percent of the claims made by both hosts and callers were value claims. Examples include "conservatism is good" and "liberalism is bad" on the conservative programs and the opposite on the liberal program. The other half of the claims were fairly evenly split between the other three categories. Examples of factual claims included those related to Obama's heritage and religious beliefs. Policy claims heard prior to the election dealt with support and opposition for the Obama's campaign promise to end the war in Iraq, while in March 2009 the policy claims dealt more with the national economy and proposed bailouts for the automobile, banking, and insurance industries. During the primary season, the most common definitional claims dealt with labeling the campaign platforms of Hillary Clinton and Obama as "socialist" in nature. Following Obama's inauguration, that same label was applied to the proposed multibillion-dollar stimulus package.

In a similar sampling of local talk radio programming, the proportion and nature of the categories were nearly identical to the national sampling.

The second component of the Toulmin model is *grounds*, or put more simply, evidence to support the claim. In his original explanation of his model, Toulmin himself stated that "the claim under discussion can be no stronger than the grounds that provide its foundation."[74] While Toulmin and scholars familiar with his work warn against basing an argument on grounds which amount to little more than "because I said so," that is often the basis for many of the arguments heard on political talk radio.

Those same scholars point out that arguments, as well as the claims and grounds used to support them, are best made with information that is current and forward-looking rather than outdated and backward-looking. But the converse is often true on talk radio, and one frequent example is the tendency of talk radio hosts to blame a president's current problems on the previous presidential administration. When discussing problems facing the Reagan administration in the 1980s, for example, conservative hosts and callers were quick to blame them on the presidency of Jimmy Carter. When discussing problems facing the Clinton administration in the 1990s, liberal hosts were quick to blame them on Reagan and his successor, George H. W. Bush. During the administration of George W. Bush, conservative hosts blamed the problems on Clinton, and once Obama was in office, liberal hosts blamed problems faced by his administration on the younger Bush. By extension, it's not difficult to imagine that if the next president is a republican, conservative hosts will blame Obama for the problems faced by the new president.

The third element of the Toulmin model is *warrant*, a device meant to tie the grounds to the claim. Put simply, it means that if a listener accepts the grounds, he or she is obligated to accept the associated claim. In talk radio, phrases such as "everyone knows that" (also a "glittering generality" on the list of propaganda models) is a frequently heard example of a warrant. "Everyone knows that the media wants President Bush to fail" is a warrant that supports many hosts' claim that the media exhibits a liberal bias. Another common type of warrant is the consequence of *not* acting. One example frequently heard on talk radio during the debate over the Iraq War was that if "we don't support the Iraqi people, the country will become a safe haven for terrorists."

Toulmin refers to the first three steps of his model as the preliminary triad. Once through the first three steps of the Toulmin model, many arguments made on talk radio stall, as either hosts or callers abandon them to either stand or fall on their merits. It is rare for any argument to proceed through the last three steps, which Toulmin calls the secondary triad. Once through first three steps, the host or caller either drops the argument or returns to the original claim and starts over again through the preliminary triad.

The fourth element of the model is *backing*, which is supporting information behind the warrant. Unlike the warrant, which may or may not conclusively prove the claim, the purpose of backing is to offer detailed information to support the claim or "seal the deal." The fifth element is the *qualifier*, which shows the degree of force behind the claim.

Qualifiers sometimes heard in talk radio include phrases such as "in all probability" and "in certain cases." The final step in the process is *rebuttal*, which involves the speaker admitting potential weaknesses in the argument and addressing them up front, such as "my opponent says my plan is too expensive, but the harm caused by not taking action will be even more expensive to deal with."

Talk Radio and the Town Square Metaphor

In the summer of 1967, media researchers at Indiana State University studied the role of talk radio in local politics. Researchers studied transcripts from the station's talk shows, interviews with hosts and frequent callers, and the results of questionnaires administered to the community's opinion leaders as well as ordinary citizens. As one of the first studies of the talk radio genre, the project provided results that appear obvious today, but they were considered groundbreaking at the time. Among those findings:

- A disproportionate number of calls came from a small number of listeners, a phenomenon still very true today.

- The majority of callers were conservatives who considered themselves well-informed and interested in civic duty.

- The majority of listeners viewed both local and national government with a high degree of skepticism and distrust.

- The majority of listeners believed the hosts of the programs they listened to were looking out for their interests and championing the same causes in which they believed.[75]

Many hosts have research staffs that peruse national and local newspapers looking for brief off-beat items buried in the back. Rather than simply rehashing what other hosts are talking about, they attempt to lure listeners by explaining how all of their problems can easily be blamed on other parties: greedy employers, illegal aliens, and corrupt public officials. And they're not shy in claiming that continuing to listen to the program will provide all the answers they need to respond to life's challenges.

Reporter Gwen Ifill, then of NBC but later of PBS, echoed that sentiment when she described talk radio as one of those forums that "caters to people who used to sit on bar stools and complain to each other. . . . now they call a 1-800 number and complain for free."[76]

Marvin Kalb, a former CBS television reporter now teaching broadcast journalism at George Washington University, believes that talk radio now fills a void created by the loss of the cordial "town meetings" that once defined public discourse. "If we still gathered at town meetings, and if our churches were still-community centers, we wouldn't need talk radio," Kalb said. "People feel increasingly disconnected, and talk radio gives them a sense of connection."[77]

Media researcher Ian Hutchby says one of the intriguing aspects of talk radio is its spontaneity. "Talk radio is unlike many other institutional settings for dispute, such as a courtroom," he explained in his 1996 book, *Confrontation Talk*. "In such settings, participants from both sides have a good idea beforehand what their argument will be about and may have well prepared their case in detail. On talk radio, on the other hand, arguments emerge locally out of improvised opening statements that callers make at the beginning of calls."[78]

Talk show host Diane Rehm, whose syndicated program is based in Washington, D.C., analogizes talk radio to the discussion of community issues over the backyard fence. "Today, talk radio has expanded the backyard," she wrote in a 1993 article. "In many ways, in both presidential campaigns and in day-to-day life, the importance of talk radio has been both underestimated and exaggerated."[79]

Rehm adds that "listener safety" is critical for talk radio to work. "Callers can remain anonymous and use fictitious 'handles,'" she says. "They impart their very personal stories to strangers out in the ether, weep over their losses, and express their hopes and their fears. They scream at what they perceive to be injustice. For them, when they're talking with me over the phone and over the airwaves, I am their friend and confidante, someone with whom they can risk a new idea or an unguarded emotion."[80]

Media researcher Andrew Tolson compared talk radio to public oratory, analogizing the exchanges between hosts and callers to the discourse heard in the public square of the 1700s. But he warns that much like the orators of that the colonial era, the talk radio hosts are often guilty of doing their jobs too well—sometimes oversimplifying complex issues. "One of talk radio's functions is to mediate between the world of public affairs, carried out by public figures, and the private, domestic sphere—by translating the former into terms intelligible by the latter," he wrote in his 2006 book, *Media Talk*. "But there is much concern, particularly at election times, that public issues are being oversimplified to sustain audience ratings. By speaking through its 'simulacrum of conversational give and take,' it may be that broadcast talk is guilty of trivializing and/or dumbing down."[81]

Religious leaders contend that the goal of religious talk radio was not to promote spirituality by proselytizing on the radio. But media historians cite the examples of Father Charles Coughlin in the 1930s and modern-day radio personalities such as Reverend Jerry Falwell and Dr. James Dobson as individuals capable of doing both at the same time.

Talk Radio and the Hutchins Commission

In the late 1940s, with radio and television growing rapidly and newspapers and magazines still popular as well, executives at *Time* magazine and the University of Chicago School of Journalism created the Hutchins Commission. The Commission was charged with examining the role of the media in American society and developing a list of ideals they should aspire to. The Commission established five obligations for the mass media: (1) provide a comprehensive, truthful, and intelligent account of the day's events in a context that gives them meaning; (2) serve as a forum for the exchange of comment and criticism; (3) provide a representative picture of the constituent groups in society; (4) be responsible for the presentation and clarification of the goals and values of society; and (5) provide full access to the day's intelligence (i.e., information about governmental activity and public affairs).[82]

Which of these apply to talk radio? It would depend on who you ask. In terms of the first goal—providing a "truthful, comprehensive, and intelligent account of the day's events"—certainly many hosts believe that they do. Their critics, however, claim that like any form of opinion-based media content, the first casualty is likely the truth. Similar true and false claims could be made about the third and fifth goals.

The second and fourth goals, however, are the most appropriate ones to apply to talk radio. "Serving as a forum for the exchange of comment and criticism" is an obvious purpose of talk radio, and perhaps its most important function—although some do it better than others. "Presenting and clarifying the goals and values of society" is something that most talk show hosts aspire to do, although most admit they do so from a specific point of view—conservative, progressive, or libertarian.

The overarching principle associated with all five goals is that of the "watchdog function." Convinced that the "liberally biased mainstream media" does a poor job of performing the watchdog function—especially when a democrat is in the White House—many talk radio hosts claim to have assumed that role. In other cases, they prefer to motivate their listeners to do it for them through letter-writing campaigns and attendance at local government meetings.

Old Habits Are Hard to Break

A thirty-day sampling of both local and national talk radio programming revealed that nearly every call begins with the host and caller exchanging pleasantries, followed by the host either asking the caller "What's on your mind?" or repeating some variation of what the call screener has told him or her through the headset. "(Name of call screener) says you agree (or disagree) with me about X," is a typical approach. If the caller agrees with the opinion already stated by the host, the host will often ask the caller to expand on areas of agreement, or agree with other opinions—usually any comments glorifying the host or massaging his or her ego will suffice. When callers disagree with the host, most will react in one of three ways:

The yes-but response. The host will agree with the overall premise of what the caller is saying, but then shift the focus to an area of disagreement so he or she can find some weaknesses in the caller's position. "Yes, I agree that the war in Iraq is not going well, but what are the alternatives—pull out and allow the country to be overrun by terrorists?" is the general approach taken by many conservative hosts. Communication theorists who study debating styles call this the "You say X, but what about Y?" approach.

The non-starter response. The host disputes the entire premise of the caller's comments, often interrupting him or her in midsentence. Both conservative and liberal hosts do so with comments such as, "You haven't been listening" or "It's obvious you don't know the first thing about X." Neal Boortz's standard nonstarter response is "You're an idiot, sir," usually delivered in a belligerent tone that is followed by a comment about the caller's education level, such as "It's obvious you went to a public school." During the 2008 election campaign, when callers professed a liking for the policy proposals of democratic candidate Barack Obama, Boortz, and other hosts, accused them of "drowning themselves in the Obama Kool-Aid."

The change-the-subject response. This is sometimes called the "straw man argument" (discussed earlier in this chapter). The metaphor is based on the fact that a straw man (a falsehood or perceived weakness) is easier to attack and defeat than a real man (a truth). Nearly every conservative talk show host used a variation of the straw man technique in diverting attention away from the strengths of Obama and the weaknesses of John McCain. By focusing public attention on Obama's former pastor, Reverend Jeremiah Wright (known for inflammatory comments he made about race relations and other controversial issues), hosts were able to avoid giving credence to callers' references to other aspects of the campaigns for which the hosts did not have a simple response.

Chapter 11

In Practice: Talk Radio and the 2008 Presidential Election

The Best and the Brightest, and Some Other People

In the fall of 2007, more than two dozen candidates were seeking to succeed George W. Bush and become the forty-fourth president of the United States. By the following February, the field had been trimmed to six serious contenders and a handful of fringe candidates.

On the democratic side were senators Barack Obama of Illinois and Hillary Clinton of New York. For much of the previous year, Clinton had been considered the frontrunner, but by February, Obama had closed the gap and was even running ahead of Clinton in some polls.

On the republican side, the frontrunner had been former New York City Mayor Rudy Giuliani, the hero of the city's post-September 11 recovery effort who had earned the title of "America's Mayor." He was polling well among independents and most republicans, but his moderate positions on gay rights and abortion were concerns for the party's hardliners. By February he had lost ground to former Massachusetts governor Mitt Romney and Arizona senator John McCain, a former prisoner of war during the Vietnam War and unsuccessful presidential candidate in 2000. The wild card in the race was former Arkansas governor Mike Huckabee, a populist who had earned support from Christian conservatives.

In early 2008, the conservative *Washington Times* reported that Romney had emerged as the favorite of talk radio hosts and audiences and was benefiting greatly from the industry's disdain for McCain. Conservative host Hugh Hewitt seemed to be speaking on behalf of his fellow hosts when he told the *Times* that

McCain's voting record in the Senate indicated he advocated nearly everything that "true conservatives" opposed, while opposing nearly everything that constituency advocated. "The hostility (of conservatives) toward the McCain voting record shouldn't surprise anyone," Hewitt said. "Senator McCain is a great American, a lousy senator, and a terrible republican."[1]

By early spring, McCain had a considerable lead over Giuliani, Romney, and Huckabee, but still lacked the necessary number of delegates to secure the nomination. A latecomer to the race was former Tennessee senator Fred Thompson, who was better known for his acting roles, including that of the gruff district attorney on television's *Law & Order*. His campaign was short-lived.

Media critics commented that conservative talk radio hosts found themselves in the midst of sports metaphor—after eight years of playing defense for the Bush administration, they now found themselves on offense, trying to decide who to support from among the four remaining republicans—Romney, McCain, Giuliani, and Huckabee.

By early summer, McCain had a substantial lead in the delegate count, prompting Romney and Giuliani to drop out. Remaining in the race were Huckabee and one of the fringe candidates: Texas congressman Ron Paul. Paul was a republican with libertarian leanings who held no delusions of being the nominee—he just seemed to be enjoying the race, especially the televised debates. Huckabee insisted he still had a shot at the nomination, even though the math did not work in his favor. Political pundits believed he was remaining in the race to either position himself for the vice-presidential slot or a cabinet position, or perhaps lay the groundwork for another presidential run in 2012.

While conservative talk show hosts resisted the shifting of Republican support away from Giuliani and Romney and toward McCain, the biggest name in progressive talk—Ed Schultz—had to deny he was endorsing Obama. Despite interviewing numerous representatives of Clinton campaign during the primary season, callers to his show accused Schultz of having already made up his mind to support her opponent. Schultz deflected the criticism by repeating his pledge to provide access to all democratic candidates and then endorse whoever the party's nominee turned out to be.

Early in the primary season, Rush Limbaugh launched Operation Chaos, which was his plan to encourage republican voters to temporarily switch parties to vote for Hillary Clinton in the democratic primaries. Not only would that prolong the in-fighting in the opposing party, but if she was able to overtake Obama to win the democratic nomination, it would make her easier to defeat in the general election.

Unlike her husband—the former president who frequently sparred with Limbaugh and often lost his composure when discussing the talk show host in public—Hillary Clinton playfully deflected his on-air criticisms, claiming that Limbaugh had a "secret crush" on her.[2]

Sean Hannity joined the fray by introducing his new project: the "Stop Hillary Express," a daily assault on the reputation of Clinton and her husband, the former president. As the primary season wore on and Clinton's candidacy became less certain, Hannity hedged his bets and introduced the "Stop Obama Express."

Limbaugh and his producers composed a song, "Barack the Magic Negro," a parody of the song, "Puff the Magic Dragon." Limbaugh insisted that the song was not meant as a direct affront to Obama, but instead was meant to ridicule his supporters and the media for what he labeled as unearned adulation.

Putting the Toothpaste Back in the Tube

Bill Cunningham, host of WLW-AM in Cincinnati, was asked by local Republican Party officials to speak prior to McCain at a February 26 rally in downtown Cincinnati. During his lengthy tirade, Cunningham blasted Obama, Hillary Clinton, and democrats in general. He called Obama a "hack politician in the Chicago tradition" and criticized the Illinois senator for meeting with middle-eastern leaders and warned that if elected, Obama would meet with the leaders of foreign governments, to America's detriment. Cunningham also used Obama's middle name, Hussein, three times.[3]

McCain then incensed Cunningham by taking the stage and immediately apologizing for the remarks. "I regret any comments that may have been made about these two individuals (Obama and Clinton), who are honorable Americans," McCain told the crowd. "We have strong philosophical differences, and so I want to disassociate myself from any disparaging remarks that may have been made about them." McCain later claimed that he didn't know who invited Cunningham to speak, but said he would make sure "something like that didn't happen again." McCain repeated that apology in media interviews later in the day.[4]

In a CNN interview the following night, Cunningham said he "had it up to here" with McCain and complained that the candidate should stop apologizing for him and get back to the business of attacking democrats. "They told me to fire up the crowd and give them some red meat, and that's what I did," Cunningham said. "But now McCain is throwing me under the bus—throwing me under the Straight Talk Express (a reference to McCain's campaign bus)."[5]

The dust-up between Cunningham and McCain would not be the only example of a relationship with a radio host reflecting poorly on the Arizona republican. Later in the campaign, opponents admonished McCain for his friendship with right-wing conservative host G. Gordon Liddy, a convicted felon as a result of his role in the Watergate scandal. The criticism focused on the hypocrisy of McCain's demand that Obama explain his past association with former domestic terrorist William Ayers, contrasted with McCain's refusal to explain or apologize for his past association with Liddy. In addition to providing McCain with softball interview questions when the candidate was a guest on his radio show, Liddy hosted a fund-raiser in his home during McCain's 1998 re-election bid and two years later spoke at McCain rally during his first presidential campaign.

Lamenting that the field of candidates in the republican primaries lacked a candidate in the mold of his hero, Ronald Reagan, Limbaugh did not endorse any of them, telling his listeners the election might come down to "Which guy do we dislike the least." He said that if McCain or Huckabee were nominated, it would "destroy the Republican Party."[6]

Limbaugh, Hannity, Hewitt, and other conservative hosts seemed frustrated that their efforts to derail the McCain and Huckabee campaigns were ineffective, as they were the two top vote-getters in the primaries. In the general election, they reluctantly supported McCain while scrutinizing his vice presidential running mate, Alaska governor Sarah Palin. Despite the lukewarm support, the McCain-Palin ticket got the support of 90 percent of republican voters on November 4.

Michael Medved chastised his fellow conservative hosts for what he called "demonizing" McCain and Huckabee for not being "real conservatives." Medved pointed out that while talk radio favorites Romney and Thompson might have met the criteria to be considered "true conservatives," they lacked the one quality that republicans should have focused on more—realistic chances of getting elected. Medved added that despite the best efforts of Limbaugh, Hannity, Savage, and other conservative hosts, McCain and Huckabee finished first and second in the South Carolina primary and left Romney and Thompson a distant third and fourth. But the biggest loser in that primary, Medved claimed, was talk radio itself. "South Carolina demonstrates the utter ineffectiveness of concerted efforts by the conservative media elite to derail the campaigns of two popular candidates," Medved wrote on TownHall.com. "Continued efforts in that direction will prove no more effective, and will hurt both our industry and the Republican Party."[7]

According to his critics, McCain began shedding his conservative credentials in 2001 and 2003, when he opposed the first two rounds of Bush tax cuts. He also cosponsored the Bipartisan Campaign Reform Act of 2002 with Wisconsin Senator Russ Feingold. The McCain-Feingold bill was followed three years later by the McCain-Kennedy bill, an immigration reform act he cosponsored with Massachusetts senator Edward Kennedy. And if cosponsoring controversial legislation with two of the Senate's most liberal members wasn't enough, McCain sealed his fate by joining the "Gang of 14," a group of mostly democratic senators who blocked many of President Bush's more conservative judicial appointments.

At one point, McCain complained that he had to campaign not only against his republican primary opponents, but also against conservative talk show hosts. His campaign staff was unfazed, however, with one spokesperson pointing out that the more opposition McCain received from conservative hosts, the higher his poll numbers went. When asked directly about the "talk radio factor," McCain replied, "I don't listen to them and haven't even met them. I don't even listen to Rush. . . . I'm not a masochist."[8]

Despite the polling data, there was concern that dissatisfaction with McCain might generate interest in a third-party run by an independent, with most of the conversation centering on New York mayor Michael Bloomberg. Like Romney, Bloomberg had a large personal fortune and could have financed a presidential campaign using his own checkbook. Some political pundits even speculated that his ideal running mate would be Iowa senator Chuck Hagel.

James Dobson, on his Christian conservative program *Focus on the Family,* said that if McCain won the republican nomination, the general election campaign between him and either Clinton or Obama would offer "the worst choices for president in my lifetime. . . . if these are the choices, I will not cast a ballot for president for the first time in my life."[9]

Early in the primary season, Limbaugh bristled at supporters of McCain, claiming the candidate's positions were basically warmed-over versions of democratic ideas. "If you republicans don't mind McCain's positions—what is it about Hillary Clinton's positions that you dislike?" he rhetorically asked listeners to explain. "They're the same!"[10]

During the primaries, Limbaugh called McCain a "phony conservative and apostate Reaganite."[11] Between the later primaries—during which McCain wrestled the nomination away from Huckabee—and the Republican National Convention, there was speculation in the media that Limbaugh would not support him and might seek a third-party candidate to endorse. But as the convention drew near, Limbaugh came out with a lukewarm backing of the candidate. "It's like the Super Bowl," Limbaugh told the *New York Times Magazine.* "If your team isn't in it, you root for the team you hate less. For me, that's McCain."[12]

Although Limbaugh let his disdain for McCain known to his audience, he downplayed the impact of his nonendorsement and said McCain should not change to meet his expectations. "He's got to be who he is," Limbaugh told *Time* magazine in a February 25, 2008 interview. "His job is not to be acceptable to a single person. I'm not sitting here demanding that. I don't have that sense of power."[13] In the same interview, Limbaugh clarified his role was that of businessman and not political powerbroker. "I treat this (talk radio) as a business," he said. "My definitions for success have nothing to do with who wins the election, but rather, is the program growing audience-wise and are we attracting new sponsors. In terms of content, I just come here and try to have fun every day. I don't say outrageous things I don't believe just to get people in a tizzy. I have the benefit of not having anybody telling me what I can't say."[14] On his February 5 show, Limbaugh told his listeners that "McCain has stabbed his own party in the back, I can't tell you how many times."[15]

Later in the primary season, Limbaugh even delivered a mock McCain concession speech on his show.

Limbaugh wasn't the only host attempting to block McCain's nomination. Hannity told his listeners that McCain might claim to be a conservative but was not one according to Hannity's definition—Reagan conservative. Laura Ingraham told her listeners, "There is no way in hell I could pull the lever for John McCain,"[16] and libertarian Glenn Beck claimed that "John McCain is more dangerous even than Hillary Clinton."[17]

New Yorker writer Ryan Lizza wrote that the hosts' opposition to McCain was based on the candidate's reluctance to court them. "He (McCain) never sucked up to them like Romney did," Lizza wrote.[18]

From the beginning, McCain found populist support from moderate republicans, independents, and even some democrats who were not happy with the liberal proposals of Clinton and Obama. He also had the backing of those in his party who supported the war. The republican base, however, was troubled by his moderate-to-liberal views on issues such as abortion, gay marriage, immigration, and campaign finance reform.

And even though he promised in his early television spots to "make the Bush tax cuts permanent," critics pointed to the fact that he opposed them on the Senate floor many years earlier. He defended those votes by claiming he opposed the cuts only because they were not accompanied by a reduction in spending, but many in the party were still skeptical.

Not seeing Huckabee as a viable alternative, many in the republican base continued to reject McCain, even after it was inevitable he would be the nominee. No one worried about conservatives voting for Clinton or Obama; the fear was that they might stay home on Election Day. Limbaugh and Hannity (and their callers) spent much more airtime discussing their disappointment with the likely republican nominee than their much larger disdain for the two democratic frontrunners.

Hannity even began using the phrase "conservatism in exile" to describe the possibility that conservatives might already be preparing to surrender the election to the democrats and begin to retool the party platform for their yet-to-be-found candidate in 2012.

The dichotomy of the two approaches—"conservatism in exile" or accepting McCain under the "half a loaf is better than none" approach—provided considerable fodder for Limbaugh, Hannity, O'Reilly, and other conservative hosts for much of the spring and summer. Many callers chastised the hosts for appearing to encourage voters to stay home, suggesting that McCain was the man to vote for—especially if the alternative was Hillary Clinton. Limbaugh and Hannity, while sticking to their philosophy of not overtly endorsing any candidate, nonetheless repeated their intention to vote for McCain but then continue to scrutinize the parts of his platform with which they disagreed.

Half a Loaf Is Better Than None

Once McCain secured the nomination, conservative radio hosts started to drift slowly in his direction, realizing the alternative would be Barack Obama. But such support was difficult to find during the primary season, as hosts rallied around Romney and Huckabee. Among the few conservative hosts to come to McCain's defense during the primary season were Medved, the former movie critic turned talk show host, and Bill Bennett, the former education secretary and drug czar. Both had syndicated shows on Salem Radio Networks.

Bennett called McCain a "war hero" with whom he disagreed on many serious matters, but pointed out to listeners that McCain was pro-life and anti-government spending—two positions that warranted conservative support. But Bennett admitted that anti-McCain sentiment was running high on his radio show and questioned why callers were more interested in bashing McCain than they were bashing Hillary Clinton, who was the democratic front-runner at the time.

On his show and in op-ed columns in *USA Today,* Medved continued to admonish his fellow conservative hosts for attempting to derail McCain. Like Bennett, Medved believed the energy of his callers as well as influential individuals within the Republican Party could be better spent criticizing the democratic candidates.

Dobson had backed Huckabee over McCain early in the primary season, but when McCain secured the republican nomination, Dobson was at first skeptical but quickly warmed up to him after he selected Palin, a pro-life conservative, as his running mate. Once Obama won, Dobson declared he was "in mourning for the country" and accused Obama of "distorting the traditional understanding of the Bible to fit his own world view."[19] In his radio show and on his World Wide Web site, Dobson predicted that if Obama were to serve two terms, by the time he leaves office in 2016, America would be a country in which "homosexuality was taught in the schools, pornography was free on daytime and prime-time television, and the government enforced bans on firearms, home schooling, Christian school groups, and talk radio."[20]

Immediately after McCain's vice-presidential announcement, conservative hosts were nearly unanimous in their support for Palin, although a few still held out for Romney to be the pick. "I don't even think Obama is half the man Sarah Palin is, in terms of achievement, toughness, grit and down in the trenches," Limbaugh told his listeners.[21]

Many conservative hosts were quick to criticize the treatment of Palin by the national media and label it as sexist, even though they had no problems with similar treatment afforded former democratic candidate Hillary Clinton. The double standard was the subject of a *Saturday Night Live* parody featuring co-mediennes Tina Fey as Palin and Amy Poehler as Clinton.

When the McCain-Palin campaign revealed that Palin's seventeen-year-old daughter was pregnant, liberal hosts were quick to take the high road, limiting their criticisms to Palin's policy positions while avoiding references to family issues. Chicago-based host Roland S. Martin found a way to cover both bases in one comment, telling his audience, "It's legitimate to criticize her on public policy, because she believed in funding for abstinence-only programs, but she did not believe in funding for sex education. . . . Abstinence-only did not work in her own household."[22]

The Obama campaign produced a Spanish-language ad showing a photo of Limbaugh with his quotes in subtitles: "Mexicans are stupid and unqualified" and "Shut your mouth or get out."[23] When questioned about the ad by *Washington Post* media critic Ed O'Keefe, Limbaugh accused Obama of "race-baiting" and produced the original transcripts of the shows from which those comments were excerpted in an attempt to argue that they were taken out of context.[24]

When Colin Powell, a moderate republican, former chairman of the Joint Chiefs of Staff and one of the most respected African Americans in the country, crossed party lines to endorse Obama, Limbaugh declared it "an act of racial loyalty."[25] Powell, appearing the following Sunday on *Meet the Press*, denied the charge, saying that "if that was the only factor I had in mind, I could have done this six, eight, ten months ago."[26]

In effect, Limbaugh was 0-for-2 in his efforts to influence the 2008 presidential election. He railed against McCain in the primaries and predicted the Arizona republican could never win the nomination. Once McCain was nominated, Limbaugh softened his tone and said that McCain was not his first choice but was better than the democratic alternative. The general election found Limbaugh on the wrong side again.

G. Gordon Liddy accused Obama of strategizing to win Pennsylvania's electoral votes by relying on that state's low-income demographics. Liddy described Pennsylvania as "Pittsburgh and Philadelphia, with Alabama in the middle.... Obama is counting on urban elites and the welfare class to win the state for him. But he's putting on a show for the rest of the state."[27] Michael Savage added that an Obama win would produce the "first affirmative action presidency."[28]

Many hosts and callers kept insisting that Obama was a Muslim, despite his lifelong membership in Christian churches in Hawaii and Illinois. Many based their belief on Obama's middle name, Hussein, which despite being the last name of a late Iraqi dictator, is also a common middle name for people of African descent. Michael Savage asked, "How could he not be a Muslim if he has a Muslim name?"[29]

With less than two weeks to go in the campaign, libertarian Neal Boortz published on his Web site an open letter titled "To the Undecided Voter," a lengthy and complex document he would refer to numerous times during his show. He covered a number of policy areas, including race, economics, and national security, but scarcely mentioned the political positions of republican candidate John McCain. Instead, Boortz's letter dealt only with what he saw as the faulty positions taken on those same issues by Obama. He also blamed the Bush administration and republicans in general for making the mistakes—bad decision-making in Iraq and failing to follow-through on 2000 and 2004 campaign promises to shrink the size of the federal government—that allowed Obama's popularity to be a factor in the first place. "The republicans deserve exactly what is happening to them in this election," Boortz wrote. "They got drunk with power, and the hangover affects all of us."[30]

On the air and elsewhere on his Web site, Boortz warned listeners that if elected, Obama would pander to labor unions, limit individual freedom (in areas such as free speech and gun ownership), and would burden small businesses with overwhelming tax increases.

In July, Boortz and liberal Stephanie Miller represented the talk radio industry in a panel discussion that was part of a two-day conference on American politics and the press, held at the American Embassy in London. Much like he had already done on his show, Boortz downplayed the role of talk radio in the political process and claimed his role was to generate advertising revenue for his employers—not to influence the electoral process. Miller generally agreed, but also used the opportunity to ridicule talk show hosts of both political extremes for their dichotomous portrayals of Obama. "If you listen to progressive talk radio, you hear that Obama is an inspirational figure that's a cross between Martin Luther King and John F. Kennedy," she told the audience. "If you listen to conservative talk radio, you find out that he and his wife are Muslim radicals and terrorist-loving black militants who want to enslave white people. I heard a right-wing host say that Obama has a lot of crazy European ideas like health care and world peace. Like Neal, I don't believe that we're there to change opinion and influence elections. We're there to get ratings and sell stuff."[31]

On the night following the election, comedian and political commentator Bill Maher appeared on CNN's *Larry King Live* and warned viewers that Obama will be a favorite target of talk radio criticism. "The second he takes the oath of office, we'll see the same thing we saw with Bill Clinton," Maher said. "Sean Hannity and his ilk will try to make something out of nothing and delegitimize the guy before he even gets started by casting him as some type of a demon."[32] Maher added that Hannity and Limbaugh bear some of the blame for McCain's defeat because of how they treated Obama during the campaign. "By characterizing him (Obama) the way they did, their 'Who is Barack Obama campaign?' backfired," Maher said. "Here's a guy who had already been on the public figure on a national stage for two years, on the front page of the newspaper and every night on television. And they're still asking the question, 'Who is Barack Obama?' as though he was a black man driving an old Chevy through a white neighborhood late at night."[33]

Turning Water into Whine

Faiz Shakir, research director for for the Center for American Progress, believes that talk radio played a major role in McCain's loss. "I think John McCain suffered from the fact that far right activists—embodied by talk radio—never viewed him as one of them," Shakir said. "McCain was never a culture warrior; he rarely demagogued on social policy issues; and his record had been one of seeking compromise on major legislation in the Senate. These qualities meant that he had a lot of catching up to do with the far right activists when his campaign got started, and he never quite did it. I'm still surprised that the far right activists didn't embrace McCain's policy agenda. On almost everything—from tax cuts to health care to foreign policy—McCain was even more Bush than Bush in terms of conservative orthodoxy. But the far right seemed upset that he never embraced their hot rhetoric. While talk radio was fuming over conspiracy theories—such as speculating about Obama's 'socialist takeover,' questioning whether he was a covert Muslim extremist, or asserting he was going to take away your guns—McCain to his credit largely eschewed this rhetoric."[34]

Dan Shelley, a former talk radio station executive now working in television, says that the lack of support from talk radio was only partially to blame. "Conservative talk show hosts will always carry water for GOP presidential candidates," Shelley says. "But they must be very careful not to waste the credibility capital they have with their followers on candidates or causes that are weak. My personal opinion is that McCain lost because he and Sarah Palin were clearly inferior candidates. Talk show hosts may have contributed to the margin of loss because, by and large, they didn't voice their support for them enthusiastically enough to motivate large numbers of voters in their base to get out and vote. Again, that's because the hosts can't afford to spend their credibility capital on candidates or causes they don't think can win."[35]

Lynn Woolley, a local conservative host in Memphis, Tennessee, agrees. He believes that talk radio is only partially responsible for the election results. "Talk radio may very well have contributed to the McCain loss, but who's to say that it was simply radio hosts that fanned the flame of McCain's own weaknesses within his own party?" Woolley asks. "For example, many hosts lambasted him about his liberal views on immigration—his support of amnesty. I think the conclusion can be made that talk radio reflected the view from those who tend to vote Republican, rather than the other way around. McCain, as a self-styled maverick, loved to go against the grain. So essentially, McCain alone is responsible for McCain's loss."[36]

Two days after the election, Media Matters for America issued a report claiming that the damage done to democratic candidates was not inflicted just by the usual suspects—Rush Limbaugh and Sean Hannity. They placed much of the blame for the partisan vitriol on local and regional hosts, which are just as conservative as the bigger names, but capable of spreading equal amounts of falsehoods, innuendo, and hate.

"Beyond the echelon of widely know conservative hosts with national audiences lies a vast network of lesser-known regional hosts who have become key components of an echo chamber for conservative talking points and falsehoods," the report concluded. "Like their better-known counterparts, these syndicated and regional hosts have played active roles this election season in promoting falsehoods and smears in an all-out effort to foment hate and distrust among their listeners for the president-elect."[37]

The report cited dozens of examples in which these hosts attempted to exploit misconceptions and ignorance about Obama's heritage, either by spreading falsehoods themselves, or giving airtime on their programs to authors and conspiracy theorists. Many hosts and their guests compared Obama to Hitler, Mao Tse Tung, and the anti-Christ.

Many of the falsehoods about Obama's heritage were based on photos from a 2006 trip he took to Kenya, the birthplace of his father. The photos showing Obama wearing traditional African attire provided new material for Obama haters on the Internet, and oral descriptions of them provided plenty of fodder for talk radio hosts and their callers. Denver host Dan Caplis, syndicated by Clear Channel Communications, noted the similarity between the garb seen in the photos and that worn by Osama bin Laden. Caplis questioned why Obama would wear "clothing similar to that worn by the man who personally ordered thousands of Americans, including women and kids, to be burned to death," he told his listeners. "It would be as if John Kennedy had gone out and thrown on the fatigues and funny baseball hat that Castro wore."[38] Curtis Silwa, the ABC Radio host occupying the time slot once held by Bob Grant, compared Obama rallies to appearances by Adolph Hitler during World War II. "Those rallies remind me of Hitler, Olympic Stadium, 1938," Silwa told listeners.[39]

Late in the campaign and even after Election Day, one of the hottest topics on conservative talk radio was the allegation that Obama's Hawaiian birth certificate was a forgery, implying that he was actually born in Kenya. If true, that would have made Obama constitutionally ineligible to serve as president. Despite denials from the state officials in Hawaii, denials from the Obama campaign and even posting of the certificate on the campaign's Web site, the rumors persisted. Few hosts overtly made the allegations themselves, instead airing the comments from authors and conspiracy theorists claiming to have inside information about the alleged forgery and subsequent cover-up. One of those conspiracy theorists was Philip J. Berg, an attorney who filed suit in federal court challenging the authenticity of the birth certificate and by extension, Obama's eligibility to serve as president. Berg made the rounds on a number of talk shows, but he found his warmest reception on *The War Room*, a satellite radio program hosted by conservatives Jim Quinn and Rose Tennent. One of the few hosts to make the charges himself, instead of allowing Berg and others to spread the falsehoods, was conservative Bob "Gunny" Newman. He continued to air the allegations even after Hawaii officials verified the authenticity of the certificate and nonpartisan watchdog groups such as FactCheck.org declared the matter as settled. Like the photos showing Obama wearing African garb, rumors and falsehoods about the birth certificate had been circulating on the Internet for weeks, and callers repeated the allegations to their favorite hosts, many of whom made no effort to dissuade them.

Conservatism in Exile

During the eleven weeks that elapsed between Election Day and Inauguration Day, nearly every conservative talk show host in the country expressed some degree of concern over Obama's cabinet choices and proposed economic policies. Limbaugh did more than lead the pack; on some days he was so far out in front he was leaving other hosts behind. "I hope he fails,"[40] Limbaugh said repeatedly on his program, referencing a variety of Obama proposals. Moderate and liberal talk show hosts were quick to say Limbaugh's remarks were inappropriate, and even some conservative hosts, including Bennett, said he was "out of line."[41]

During the transition period, while many republican officeholders referred to the president-elect in language that foreshadowed a bipartisan approach, Limbaugh's tone was the opposite. "His mission is to restructure and reform this country so that capitalism and individual liberty are no longer its foundation," Limbaugh continued. "Why would I want that to succeed?"[42]

In reaction to those comments, Obama's team, including White House Chief of Staff Rahm Emanuel, seemed to like the idea that Limbaugh was the new de facto spokesperson for the opposition party. But Limbaugh pointed out he is a conservative first and a republican second. Michael Steele, newly elected chairman of the Republican National Committee and the first African American to hold that post, fueled the controversy by saying publicly that Limbaugh was "just an entertainer"[43] and downplaying his quasi-leadership role. Criticism from party leaders caused Steele to apologize the following day.

In December, former Secretary of State Colin Powell told CNN that Limbaugh "appeals to America's worst instincts" and that association with the talk show host was not in the best interests of the Republican Party. On his show the next day, Limbaugh responded by accusing Powell of being a "career Washingtonian"[44] who would say anything to be back in the limelight. Addressing the criticism of the Republican Party as being too aligned with Limbaugh, the host said the opposite was actually true—that the party had harmed itself by not following him—and identified the party's choice of McCain as evidence to support that point.

Media critic Michael Wolff believes that the back-and-forth between Obama and Limbaugh may have been orchestrated by the White House in order to set-up Limbaugh as a foil for the new president—a poster boy for conservative opposition that would sway undecided moderates to the president's side.[45]

Boston Globe media critics Steve Elman and Alan Tolz believe the influence of talk radio in the outcome of the 2008 presidential election is largely overstated. "It (2008 election) may have been the first in more than thirty years on which talk radio had no major impact," they wrote less than a week after the election. "Perhaps the Ford-Carter contest in 1976 (pre-Limbaugh) was the last in which talk radio was so irrelevant to public opinion on candidates and issues."[46]

Elman and Tolz cited the success of John McCain in securing the republican nomination despite opposition from nearly every conservative talk show host (except Michael Medved), coupled with his loss in the general election (despite the late conversions of those same hosts), as evidence that talk radio didn't matter nearly as much as democrats feared it might.

Elman and Tolz contrast the presidential election of 2008 with the two that proceeded it, in which conservative hosts were nearly unanimous in their support for George W. Bush. They blamed the shift in the emergence of alternative venues for political information, including satellite television and radio and of course, the Internet.

Shortly before his inauguration, Obama hosted a dinner party for conservative newspaper columnists but declined to extend the guest list to include talk radio hosts, a move that many saw as not a slap at the genre in general, but as a slap at Limbaugh specifically.

After the inauguration, Limbaugh continued his criticisms of Obama, his cabinet appointments, and economic proposals. During his first week in office, Obama fired back from behind the presidential seal. "There are things that unify republicans and democrats," Obama said. "We shouldn't let partisan politics derail what are very important things we need to get done."[47]

In the aftermath of the inauguration and debate over the stimulus package, Obama learned that the toughest opposition to the bill might not be the republicans in Congress, but rather his critics on talk radio. Limbaugh, Boortz, and Hannity were among the toughest critics, identifying Obama's economic proposals as examples of "socialist" models put forth by Obama, Senate Majority Leader Harry Reid, and House Speaker Nancy Pelosi. Boortz called the proposed stimulus package the "government growth bill." Congressional democrats and White House staffers publicly commended the new president for his patience in dealing with the exaggerations and half-truths about the proposed legislation being spread by talk radio, but by late January the new president was out of patience. He reportedly told prominent republicans, including House Minority Leader John Boehner and Senate Minority Leader Mitch McConnell, "You can't just listen to Rush Limbaugh and get things done."[48]

Advocates of the stimulus package, however, believed that Limbaugh's opposition to the proposal may have reinforced the previously held beliefs of legislators and talk radio callers but did not help in persuading any of the previously undecided to join the opposition camp. Some went as far as suggesting that it might have helped steer some undecided legislators to vote for it so as to avoid being seen on the same side as Limbaugh. Media critic Michael Wolff suggested that Limbaugh was "being played."[49]

In early March, Limbaugh was a featured speaker at the Conservative Political Action Conference. Speaking to more than 2,000 in the auditorium and overflow crowds in adjoining rooms, as well as audiences watching on the Cable

News Network, FOX News, and C-Span, Limbaugh repeated his desire to see Obama and his administration fail. "The dirty little secret is that every Republican in the country wants Obama to fail," Limbaugh said. "But none of them have the guts to say so. I do."[50]

It was Limbaugh's first speaking engagement in months, and one observer described his appearance as one resembling Tony Soprano of the fictional television series, *The Sopranos*. "There he was—black silk shirt opened at the chest, black sport coat, gold chains, the whole deal," Air America host Mike Papantonio wrote in a newspaper column. "There are some viewers no longer laughing *with* Rush. They're laughing *at* him."[51]

In exchange for donations of $10 or more, Media Matters for America offered a bumper sticker reading "Rush Doesn't Speak for Me." Although the organization expected customers to be mostly liberals, a spokesperson confirmed that many customers ordering the sticker by telephone and through the Web site identified themselves as conservatives.

Meanwhile, Hannity continued his "conservatism in exile" theme on his show, along with other conservative and libertarian hosts. On April 15, the due date for federal income tax returns, angry citizens across the country staged hundreds of "tea parties" at shopping malls and other public venues to draw attention to their opposition to the government's bailout of the banks and automobile manufacturers.

During the preceding month, many radio hosts were skeptical about the events when their callers tried to promote them, but as the day drew closer nearly all of them were on board, and many were converted to the cause as participants and speakers. The day after those events, they criticized local and national media for downplaying the scope and impact of the events and used the perceived slight as further evidence to support their "liberal bias of the media" argument.

Looking ahead to 2012, talk show hosts have already begun talking about their candidates for the republican presidential nomination. Limbaugh is leaning toward Louisiana governor Bobby Jindal, a young conservative that Limbaugh likens to his political hero, Ronald Reagan. Jindal will be only forty-one in 2012. Hannity has hinted at supporting former House Speaker Newt Gingrich, a frequent guest on his show. A handful of other hosts are already aligned with three unsuccessful candidates from the 2008 primaries: Romney, Giuliani, and Huckabee. Few if any are mentioning either republican from the party's 2008 ticket: McCain, who will be seventy-six in 2012, or Palin, who may have detracted from the ticket far more than she added.

Epilogue

Talk Radio, the First Amendment, and the Fairness Doctrine

Sound and Fury, Signifying Nothing

Among all of the apprehension and hand-wringing over the election of Barack Obama and the strengthening of the democratic hold on Congress, the most unfounded concern involves the future of talk radio. In the summer of 2008, when it became likely that either Hillary Clinton or Obama would become the next president, conservatives began tossing around unsubstantiated rumors that high on the agenda of a new democratic administration would be reinstating the Fairness Doctrine, a once relevant but now arcane federal regulation that required broadcasters to provide equal opportunities for all political viewpoints to be expressed across the airwaves.

Talk radio hosts Rush Limbaugh, Sean Hannity, Mark Levin, Michael Savage, and Neal Boortz were the first to begin spreading the idea, and they escalated the alarm in the days immediately following the election. Joining them in their concern were local hosts across the nation.

Most media experts, however, agree that hosts and their listeners have little to worry about. Even if Obama did have the power to reinstate the Fairness Doctrine, he won't. And he shouldn't. If he or the democratic Congress did, the rumbling sound heard underneath the ground in southeastern Virginia would be that of James Madison rolling over in his grave.

Madison was the author of the First Amendment to the U.S. Constitution, which includes a free speech provision that he believed would protect everyone's right to participate in the public debate without requiring the media to provide the space or time. The latter idea did not come along until 1949, when Congress passed the Fairness Doctrine and charged the Federal Communications Commission (FCC) with enforcing it.

There was no test case for the regulation until 1969, when the U.S. Supreme Court ruled in favor of the FCC in a Fairness Doctrine case. The Court upheld the authority of the FCC to regulate the airwaves, ruled that the Fairness Doctrine did not violate the First Amendment, and stated that the rights of the viewers and listeners were more important than the rights of broadcasters. For the next eighteen years, many broadcasters avoided Fairness Doctrine woes by simply avoiding controversy in their programming.

Under President Ronald Reagan in the 1980s, FCC enforcement of the Fairness Doctrine slowed down dramatically, then came to a full stop. One by-product of that move was the exponential growth of talk radio, and today the industry worries that a return of the doctrine would mean the end of free expression on the airwaves. But any politician who believes the rule is as important now as it might have been a half century ago doesn't understand how political communication works today.

When the Fairness Doctrine was passed, part of the rationale was that targets of public criticism had few avenues by which they could respond. With the growth of the Internet, personal and organizational World Wide Web sites, blogs, and social media venues, that rationale doesn't apply. Targets of criticism have a variety of avenues through which they can be heard, and neither the FCC nor the courts should require broadcasters to provide additional avenues. Madison did not live long enough to see the First Amendment applied to broadcasting and the Internet, but if asked he would—unlike the Supreme Court in 1969—say that the Fairness Doctrine is inconsistent with what he envisioned.

The idea of not forcing the media to carry opposing viewpoints is not a new one. As far back as the 1700s, publisher Benjamin Franklin quipped that his newspaper was "not a stagecoach with seats on it for everyone."[1] More than two centuries later, industry experts contend that talk radio should not be required to provide those seats, either.

The Fairness Doctrine is often confused with equal time provision, a Federal Elections Commission rule that requires broadcasters to offer advertising time to all candidates at the same price and in the same quantity. While the equal time provision deals with advertising—a form of communication the Supreme Court acknowledges deserves less First Amendment protection than other forms—the Fairness Doctrine deals with news and opinion.

Two clarifications: First, to be legally accurate, it is important to point out that the Fairness Doctrine was never actually repealed, as many Americans believe; there was simply a directive from the Reagan administration that the FCC should not enforce it. Numerous rulings from federal district courts and the U.S. Supreme Court supported that policy change. The FCC did, however, keep in place the Personal Attack Rule, a corollary to the doctrine that required broadcasters to provide targets of on-air criticism the opportunity to respond; it was in effect until 2000.

Second, the original Fairness Doctrine never required a mathematically precise fifty-fifty mix of conservative and liberal viewpoints, and it is unlikely that any new version would do so, either. Instead, the original doctrine merely suggested that broadcast licensees "afford reasonable opportunity for discussion of conflicting views on matters of public importance."[2] Christian broadcasters, for example, unnecessarily fear that the return of the Fairness Doctrine would mean that each time they spoke out against abortion or gay marriage, they would have to provide opportunity for a spokesperson from the opposition.

Pioneer talk show producer Ed McLaughlin, who has worked with Limbaugh and several other conservatives, says the current imbalance in talk radio is the opposite of what he saw producing talk radio programs in the 1960s. "I had more liberals on the air than I had conservatives or even moderates for that matter," McLaughlin says. "And I had a hell of a time finding other voices."[3]

Clarence Manion, a conservative radio host who worked from 1954 through 1979, was one of the first broadcasters to feel the sting of the Fairness Doctrine. In 1957, Manion taped an interview with plumbing magnate Herbert Kohler about union issues at his manufacturing plant in Wisconsin. The network carrying Manion's program refused to air it, worrying (incorrectly) that the network would then have to provide the union with time to respond.

Historians examining the papers of President John F. Kennedy have uncovered numerous references to his administration threatening to use—but never actually using—the Fairness Doctrine to inhibit conservative broadcasters by threatening to revoke their licenses. A decade later, the Nixon administration allegedly used the doctrine to threaten the licenses of television and radio stations in order to intimate their parent company—the *Washington Post*. Under both the Kennedy and Nixon administrations, the idea was not to go so far as to revoke broadcasting licenses; it was to make the legal defense so expensive that it would produce a chilling effect that would result in less controversy, less risky programming, and less editorial outspokenness.

The test case for the Fairness Doctrine began on the afternoon of November 25, 1964, at WGCB in Red Lion, Pennsylvania. The Reverend Billy James Hargis, one of several far-right conservative voices on the station, used part of one of his daily spots to attack investigative reporter Fred J. Cook. Cook had taken on a number of controversial topics and targets, including former Vice President Richard Nixon, Federal Bureau of Investigation Director J. Edgar Hoover, and Vietnam policy in general. In the fall of 1964, Cook had just published *Goldwater: An Extremist on the Right*, a book critical of former presidential candidate Barry Goldwater, who Hargis had vigorously supported. Earlier that year, Cook had published in *The Nation* a 4,500-word investigative piece that labeled right-wing political radio as the "hate clubs of the air."[4]

Hargis's rant against the book and its author lasted less than two minutes. His spot for that day cost him the usual $7.50 for the air time and the not-so-usual legal costs that eventually exceeded $1 million during the five-year legal battle.

Cook began by writing a letter to WGCB, citing the Personal Attack Rule and demanding the opportunity to respond on-air. The station offered him that opportunity but said it would charge him the same rate ($7.50 for fifteen minutes) it charged Hargis and other commentators. Despite the nominal cost, Cook insisted on getting the air time for free, but in his letter he misquoted the law by using the term "equal time." The FCC regulations do not use that term, but instead use the phrase, "an opportunity to respond." Cook sent copies of the letter to the 200 stations that carried the Hargis broadcast. Most responded but rejected his request for free air time, suggesting instead that he pay the same rate as their advertisers. Some denied the request altogether, whether paid or not. For the fifty or so stations that granted him free air time, he provided a three-minute audio tape he recorded with support from the Democratic National Committee. On the tape, he referred to Hargis as a "demagogue," and while Hargis had every right to criticize his work, the personal tirade against him was "a vicious attack. . . . it was smear, innuendo, and the discrediting of a man by libel."[5]

Meanwhile, Cook continued his pursuit of free air time on WGCB. After the station repeatedly denied his request, Cook turned to the FCC, which decided to make it a test case for the Fairness Doctrine. The FCC filed suit on Cook's behalf against Red Lion Broadcasting, the parent company of WGCB. When the case reached the U.S. Supreme Court, Red Lion attorney Roger Robb warned that if the Court supported the FCC's enforcement of the Fairness Doctrine, Red Lion (and by extension, broadcasters in general), would "tread more cautiously" in the future. The result, he argued, would amount to censorship, "nonetheless virulent for being self-imposed."[6]

The Supreme Court ruled in the favor of the FCC, and Cook got his free air time. Until his death in 2004, Hargis remained bitter about the ruling, claiming it "set back free speech two hundred years."[7]

The case of *Red Lion Broadcasting v. FCC* served as the test case that upheld the Fairness Doctrine, and more than two decades after the law became irrelevant in 1987, "Red Lion" is still used as a code word to refer to government interference in freedom of speech.

Following the Red Lion case, the Fairness Doctrine and Personal Attack Rule were seldom enforced and seldom even mentioned for nearly two decades.

In 1986, however, a local television station in Syracuse, New York aired a series of paid advertisements in favor of a nuclear power plant in the vicinity. An anti-nuclear group demanded time to air its own ads in response, and when the station refused, it took the matter to the FCC, which ruled in its favor and required the station to air the ads. The station appealed the decision in federal court, which gave the FCC permission to drop the Fairness Doctrine if it felt it was "contrary to the public interest." The anti-nuclear group that filed the original complaint then sued the FCC, but the court once again gave the FCC the authority to disregard the Fairness Doctrine.

Launching a Thousand Lips

Depending on one's ideological perspective, either the credit or blame for the massive deregulation of the broadcasting industry in the 1980s is assigned to Reagan. During one of his State of the Union addresses, he pointed to a tower of paper on the rostrum that represented the old and cumbersome regulations under which broadcasters were operating at the time. He then held up a much thinner volume—the thickness of a high school term paper is how one media critic described it—which would be his proposal to Congress. The biggest changes Congress passed involved the relaxation of ownership rules. As a result, broadcast ownership became concentrated in the hand of fewer and fewer licensees, giving them more control for programming content and editorial slant.

One by-product of that deregulation was a directive from the White House that the FCC no longer enforce the Fairness Doctrine. It was an easy directive to follow, as FCC Chairman Mark Fowler was already on record as saying that he wanted his agency "out of the content regulation business."[8]

The official FCC statement said that, "If we must choose between whether editorial decisions are to be made in the free judgment of individual broadcasters or imposed by bureaucratic fiat, the choice must be for freedom."[9]

One of the few areas of agreement between liberals and conservatives is their belief that the FCC's decision to stop enforcing the Fairness Doctrine is the explosion of talk radio. A *Los Angeles Times* media critic called the elimination of the doctrine "the decision that launched a thousand lips."[10]

There have been several attempts to bring back the Fairness Doctrine—in one form or another—in the last two decades.

The first debate over possible return of the doctrine began with a June 1994 appearance by President Clinton on a radio program in St. Louis. "After I finish this interview and get back on the plane, Rush Limbaugh will have three hours to say whatever he wants," Clinton told the host and audience. "And I won't have any opportunity to respond."[11]

When Congress began discussing bringing back the Fairness Doctrine in its original form, Clinton hinted he would sign such a law if it came to his desk. Conservative publications such as the *Wall Street Journal* and the *Washington Times* editorialized against it, agreeing with the critics who speculated that Limbaugh and conservative talk radio were the targets of the law. The proposal never made it out of either of the two congressional committees that oversee FCC operations.

Even though the Fairness Doctrine was effectively moot, the FCC did not eliminate its appendage, the Personal Attack Rule, until early in 2000. The U.S. Court of Appeals in Washington, D.C., was reviewing a challenge to the rule and requested from the FCC a formal written justification for keeping it. Instead of responding immediately, the FCC suspended the rule for sixty days and indicated it wanted time to study how permanent elimination of the rule might affect the industry and how the broadcasters would "handle their new found freedom."[12] Another rationale for the moratorium was that it would prevent generating an avalanche of cases related to discussions of the presidential election campaign of that fall.

The sixty-day moratorium came and went, but the court had not forgotten about its original request. After the FCC dragged its feet for months beyond the original time period, the court tired of the delay and granted the petitioner's request and invalidated the rule, claiming that the rule "interferes with journalists' editorial judgment, entangles the government in media operations, and therefore raised First Amendment concerns."[13]

In 2005, a group of twenty-four members of the House of Representatives introduced the Fairness and Accountability in Broadcasting Act, which would have shortened the term of a broadcasting licenses from eight years to four and require that broadcasters "cover public issues fairly"—language even fuzzier than that found in the original Fairness Doctrine. The proposal never made it to the floor for discussion. Later in the same session, a proposal to bring back the doctrine—similar to its original form but renamed the Media Ownership Reform Act—also failed.

Some conservative media critics believe that the 2007 controversy involving Don Imus and the Rutgers University women's basketball team was the opening salvo in a long-term campaign to rid the airwaves of conservative talk. The effort began with the firing of Imus, they speculated, and would end with the silencing of Limbaugh and other talk radio hosts by a new version of the Fairness Doctrine.

That same year, Senator John Kerry of Massachusetts indicated he was interested in a "discussion" of the Fairness Doctrine but had no intention of introducing legislation. Senator John Edwards, in the early stages of his second run for the White House, went much further and said he would make the Fairness Doctrine part of his campaign platform (but never did).

A 2008 survey by Pew Research Center indicated that 66 percent of Americans would favor a law requiring broadcasters to provide equal time to conservative and liberal viewpoints, and 62 percent favor a law requiring newspapers to do so—even though, unlike broadcasting and the Fairness Doctrine—there is no precedent for doing so.

When All Is Said and Done, Far More Will Be Said Than Done

Senator Debbie Stabenow, a democrat from Michigan, is one of the many liberal voices in Congress calling for a discussion of a new form of the Fairness Doctrine. "I think it's absolutely time to pass a standard," she told Politico.com in a February 5, 2009 interview. "Now, whether it's called the Fairness Standard, whether it's called something else—I absolutely think it's time to be bringing accountability to the airwaves. Our new president has talked rightly about accountability and transparency. . . . that we all have to step up and be responsible. And I think in this case, there needs to be some accountability and standards put in place."[14] To some observers, opposition to Stabenow's plan is tempered by the fact that she is married to Tom Athans, the cofounder of TalkUSA, a liberal radio network.

In addition to Kerry and Stabenow, other politicians showing support for resurrecting the Fairness Doctrine (or similar legislation) include House Speaker Nancy Pelosi; Representatives Dennis Kucinich of Ohio, Bernie Sanders of Vermont, and Maurice Hinchey and Louise Slaughter of New York; and Senators Richard Durbin of Illinois, Jeff Bingaman of New Mexico, Charles Schumer of New York, and Tom Harkin of Iowa. Except for Sanders (the only socialist member of Congress), all are democrats.

As rumors of the possible return of the Fairness Doctrine surfaced during his second term, President George W. Bush pledged to veto any law regardless of its new name. At a Washington, D.C., event in 2007, Bingaman suggested to a radio station general manager from his state that he consider striving for more "ideological balance" on his station in order to pre-empt legislative action.[15]

Those opposing its return include representatives Mike Pence of Indiana, John Boehner of Ohio, and Greg Walden of Oregon. All are republicans. Support and opposition is generally along party lines: almost all politicians in favor of it are democrats; nearly all against it are republicans.

In 2005, Hinchey introduced a bill titled the Media Ownership Reform Act (MORA) that would have reinstated the Fairness Doctrine and required the FCC to monitor the political content of all radio and television programs. Hinchey said the MORA was aimed at providing "ideological balance and diversity" to the broadcasting industry; it was seen by most observers as a softer version of the Fairness Doctrine. Later that year, Slaughter introduced the Fairness in Broadcasting Act. One supporter of the bill, Reverend Jesse Jackson, conceded the partisan nature of the bill when he told reporters that it would help democrats because the key to winning elections is "having access to the media."[16]

Gigi B. Sohn, director of the Media Access Project, a liberal Washington public interest lobbying group, claims that a new Fairness Doctrine would not violate the First Amendment, but instead would enhance free speech on the radio. "It would bring more voices into the marketplace of ideas, thereby maximizing the discussion of issues in our democracy," she wrote in a January 1994 editorial in *World & I*.[17] Added Andrew Jay Schwartzman, director of the Media Access Project: "We've been trying to restore the Fairness Doctrine since Rush Limbaugh was spinning records in Sacramento."[18]

Critics of the Fairness Doctrine contend that it is no longer necessary because the original "scarcity" principle no longer applies and the return of the doctrine would provide the president or members of Congress the opportunity to abuse it for partisan political purposes.

The original Fairness Doctrine was based on the principle of "scarcity," a once-true principle that because of the limited number of avenues through which one could express political views, the government had the obligation to make sure every credible voice had the opportunity to be heard.

Another rationale for the Fairness Doctrine and many other broadcasting regulations (including the licensing procedure) is that broadcasters use the "publicly owned airwaves"—a concept that many radio talk show hosts dispute. The expansion of the cable television spectrum has reduced the validity of the "scarcity" argument, and the proliferation of advocacy venues on the Internet has lessened the criticisms that broadcasters hold a monopoly. As a result, many in the broadcasting industry contend that not only should the Fairness Doctrine not return, but existing broadcast regulations should be loosened. "The press that uses air and electrons should be and must be as free from government control as the press that uses paper and ink," said talk show host Mark Levin on his show in February 2009.[19]

Not a Part-Time Job

Media attorney Steven J. Weisman believes the Fairness Doctrine had the opposite effect than the one intended: instead of creating more opportunities for the expression of opinion, it actually created fewer, as broadcasters simply shied away from controversial topics and guests in order to avoid having to walk the tightrope between two sides of an issue. Weisman analogizes the Fairness Doctrine to laws such as the Clean Water Act and the Patriot Act—laws that sound great in theory but do little to accomplish the goals implied in their names.

"Ultimately, the Fairness Doctrine is an attempt to solve a problem that does not exist," Weisman wrote in a 2007 column in *Talkers*. "Information from every viewpoint can be found in a multitude of media sources. There is no longer a scarcity of media or viewpoints. However, the battle over the Fairness Doctrine is not likely to fade away soon. Defense of the First Amendment is not a part-time job."[20]

Part of the argument against the Fairness Doctrine or similar regulation is that individuals or groups wishing to provide contrary points of view or respond to criticism have more alternative methods than they did when the doctrine was enacted in 1949. Most opponents of new regulations cite the Internet as the most practical alternative. Media critic Brian Jennings made that point in his 2009 book, *Censorship: The Threat to Silence Talk Radio*. Jennings cited a 2008 Pew Research Survey that found that 46 percent of Americans get the majority of their political news from the Internet, while earlier studies found the percentage for talk radio between 15 and 17.[21] The majority of experts tend to go along with the "conservatives have talk radio, liberals have the internet" theory of ideological balance.

Political commentator George Will adds that the term "Fairness Doctrine" is "Orwellian" because it disguises the law's true purpose: an attempt on the part of liberal politicians to stifle competition on the airwaves.[22]

Representative John Boehner of Ohio said the return of the doctrine would be "nothing less than a sweeping takeover by Washington bureaucrats of broadcast media, and it is designed to squelch conservative speech on the airwaves."[23]

Talk radio hosts, both conservative and liberal, use their own programs (and in some cases, their books) as bully pulpits to oppose the return of the doctrine.

In her 2007 book, *Power to the People*, Laura Ingraham railed against the possible return of the doctrine. "For years now, the liberal elite have been trying to shoot down talk radio—the only major media outlet they don't control," she wrote. "Rather than let listeners and the free market decide who should be on the air, the liberal elites would have the federal government demand that for every hour that Rush is on the air, Rosie O'Donnell (liberal television personality) would have to be on the air. Every hour of the Laura Ingraham Show would have to be 'balanced' by an hour of the Hillary Rodham Clinton Show."[24] Ingraham finds it ironic that advocates of the Fairness Doctrine, who "claim that 'diverse viewpoints' are being shut out," repeatedly refuse invitations to appear on her show to discuss the issue.[25]

Hannity frequently refers to the Fairness Doctrine as "the Censorship Doctrine" and Limbaugh facetiously calls it the "Hush Rush Law."

Mike Rosen, a conservative at KOA in Denver, says that "in 1987, President Reagan put the Fairness Doctrine out of its misery. . . . it made very little sense then and makes absolutely none today. In the modern world of communications, there are an infinite number of broadcast outlets, from cable to satellite TV and radio to the Internet. No one can hope to dictate public opinion."[26]

Lynn Woolley, host at KTEM in Temple, Tennessee, adds that the government should not be put in the position of arbitrating what gets on the air and what does not. "I remember when political talk on-air was little more than public affairs, broadcast simply to fulfill FCC service commitments," Woolley wrote in a November 2007 editorial in *Talkers*. "I remember when talk show hosts acted as 'traffic cops' directing calls, but advancing no opinions of their own. And I revel in the current days of free, unlimited speech that we all enjoy on the radio today. I want to keep it that way."[27]

Like many conservative hosts, Woolley believes the recent discussion about "fairness" on the radio can be traced back to the success of one man. "The fact that Rush Limbaugh has been so successful is also the reason that the medium he largely created is in constant danger," he wrote. "It would actually be advantageous, in a way, to on-air conservatives if a liberal Limbaugh were to emerge. Ed Schultz has perhaps come the closest, but his audience is negligible in comparison to Limbaugh's, just as the total audience for 'progressive' talk is virtually non-existent when compared to the conservative audience. If Air America or another liberal network could succeed, then maybe the clamor on the left for the return of the Fairness Doctrine would subside."[28]

In a 2007 book, *The Death of Talk Radio*, coauthored with Accuracy in Media founder Cliff Kincaid, Woolley provided a satirical glimpse at how talk radio might sound following a return of the Fairness Doctrine: the host simply alternates calls in favor of and opposed to the topic of the day, while not offering any opinions of his or her own for fear of violating the doctrine. "That's not too far off from what political talk radio would be under the (new) Fairness Doctrine," Woolley added in a postscript. "That's *if* you could find political talk anywhere on the dial. Under the Fairness Doctrine, the talk show host would once again become the 'traffic cop,' directing calls while rarely if ever putting forth an opinion of his own. It would be 'what do you think?' followed by the next caller and the same question, 'what do you think.'"[29]

Although he does not use the term "marketplace of ideas" that Supreme Court Justice Oliver Wendell Holmes coined in a 1919 free speech case, Limbaugh believes that talk radio should be an open forum. In his 1993 book, *See, I Told You So*, he wrote, "I say let a thousand flowers bloom. . . . if someone wants to state a view, radical or moderate, let free speech reign and let the people decide who succeeds. Since I brought it up, there have been dozens of news articles and opinion pieces all across the fruited plain. And virtually every television story and published piece discussing the Fairness Doctrine have put my name in the lead."[30]

Syndicated host Lars Larson says the doctrine is not only unconstitutional, but also unnecessary. "The Fairness Doctrine violates the First Amendment by putting the government in the position of dictating the content of speech," Larson says. "I could point out that voices like Ed Schultz are out there successfully drawing an audience to progressive points of view without the government forcing it on stations."[31]

Michael Harrison, publisher of *Talkers* magazine, added that even if the Fairness Doctrine does not return, any possibility of government intervention in the industry must be opposed. "It is important for us to continue a never-ending discussion of the First Amendment," Harrison wrote in a 2007 editorial. "It is important to understand that it primarily means freedom from government repression of the expression of ideas and opinions while not guaranteeing each citizen a soapbox. Furthermore, this is a concept with abstract nuances that cannot be over-stated."[32]

Harrison adds that not only should the government not infringe on free speech *primarily* by telling a person what he may or may not say, but should not infringe on free speech *secondarily* by forcing someone with a soapbox to make time on that soapbox available to opposing viewpoints. He concluded the editorial by stating the Fairness Doctrine should be "permanently locked in the trash box of ugly ideas."[33]

Congressman Mike Pence is a former talk radio host and an opponent of the Fairness Doctrine each time it is discussed on Capitol Hill. He points to the 1950s, a decade in which controversial talk radio could not exist, as evidence of what the future of the genre might be like under a future incarnation of the Fairness Doctrine. "To avoid administrative costs and hours of paperwork and legal fees, broadcasters opted to offer non-controversial programming," Pence wrote in the foreword to Woolley and Kincaid's book. "As a result, talk radio, as we know it today, did not exist. . . . Bringing back the Fairness Doctrine would amount to government control over political reviews expressed on the public airwaves. It is dangerous to suggest that the government should be in the business of rationing free speech."[34]

In mid-2007, Pence proposed (and Congress passed) a bill that established a one-year moratorium on funding FCC re-imposition of the doctrine. Many democrats in Congress, including Representative David Obey of Wisconsin, suggested in media interviews the law was addressing a threat that didn't exist and was a deliberate attempt to provide republicans and conservatives the opportunity to talk about their support for the First Amendment in media interviews. Obey quoted Shakespeare in calling the discussion "much ado about nothing. . . . sound and fury, signifying nothing."[35]

"If the goal is really to improve public discourse," says one observer, "then we should also get rid of *Entertainment Tonight, American Idol,* and all of those reality television shows."[36]

In her 2004 book, *The War on Choice,* feminist Gloria Feldt stopped short of advocating government reinstatement of the Fairness Doctrine, but did hint that talk radio hosts should do a better job of presenting viewpoints contrary to their own, and used the abortion issue as an example. "Democracy can't survive unless we embrace controversy," she wrote. "We need to air our differing perspectives and clarify the issues. But we need real fairness. When right-wing extremists are given air time but the pro-choice position is deemed 'too controversial'. . . . true debate is frozen in fear. The more bullies and screamers are allowed to corrupt the truth and to frame the issues, the more ordinary Americans feel excluded from the debate, or choose to exclude themselves. And truth is relegated to the cutting room floor."[37]

A 2007 study by the Center for American Progress (CAP) found that progressive content on talk radio is more often found on stations that are owned by women, minorities, or local interests. In contrast, stations operated by non-minority owners—especially larger broadcasting companies with multiple stations in the same cities—were more likely to include mostly conservative content. The study did not advocate a return of the Fairness Doctrine, but recommended instead that FCC rules reflect the need for more diversity in media ownership, which would in turn produce more diversity in content and viewpoint. "Simply reinstating the Fairness Doctrine will do little to address the gap between conservative and progressive talk unless the underlying elements of the public trustee doctrine are enforced, in particular, the requirements of local accountability and the reasonable airing of important matters," the report concluded. "The key principle here is not shutting down one perspective or another—it is making sure that communities are informed about a range of local and national public affairs."[38]

Bob Beckel, a *USA Today* columnist and frequent Fox News contributor, appeared on Hannity's television program in February 2009 to talk about a variety of issues, but spent much of his allotted time trying to assure Hannity and his fans that a return of the Fairness Doctrine—which the host called the Censorship Doctrine—was not a realistic possibility. "It gets your audience excited and gets Rush's audience excited, but it's not going to happen," Beckel told Hannity and other panelists. "It might have made sense when there were only a limited number of outlets, but now the number of outlets for political speech has increased exponentially. It's a free-speech issue—something that the marketplace is fully capable of taking care of."[39]

Russ Hill, program director at KTAR-FM in Phoenix, stops short of advocating a return to the Fairness Doctrine or even a similar policy in a voluntary form. "I have no problem with on-air personalities endorsing a candidate," Hill says. "But I do have a problem when hosts don't look at anyone from a particular party. Some conservatives won't have a democrat on their show. They call themselves news/talk stations and position themselves not only as talk but as covering the news of the day—the election campaign—and yet they never have a democrat on. I do think that is crossing the line."[40]

A 2007 CAP position statement supports alternatives to the Fairness Doctrine, such possibly rolling back broadcasting ownership rules and thus increasing opportunities for minority ownership. "Few would argue that markets such as Philadelphia and Houston are well served with 100 percent conservative talk, but that doesn't mean the answer to this pervasive imbalance is the Fairness Doctrine," the statement read.[41]

Both during the campaign and after his election, Obama denied rumors that he would seek to reinstate the Fairness Doctrine in its original form—or any other form. During the campaign, however, spokesperson Michael Ortiz said the candidate supported "media ownership caps, network neutrality, (more support for) public broadcasting, as well as increased minority ownership of broadcasting and print outlets."[42]

In July 2009, the House Appropriations Committee defeated the Walden-Pence Broadcaster Freedom Amendment. Sponsored by republicans Greg Walden of Oregon and Mike Pence from Indiana, the amendment sought to block any return of the Fairness Doctrine, whether in its original form or under the cover of other initiatives proposed by the FCC as new "localism" regulations. "If given an up-or-down vote on the House floor, I truly believe the Walden-Pence Broadcaster Freedom Amendment would have passed easily," Walden said in a statement issued by his office. "Unfortunately, the majority party never gave us an explanation for why they're afraid to allow our amendment to have that chance."[43]

Notes

Chapter 1

1. Murray Levin, *Talk Radio and the American Dream* (Lexington, MA: D. C. Heath and Company, 1987), 13.
2. Carol Nashe, interview by the author, May 15, 2009.
3. Mike Stern, interview by the author, May 18, 2009.
4. Lloyd Rohler, interview by the author, May 10, 2009.
5. Wayne Munson, interview by the author, May 8, 2009.
6. Robert Thompson, interview by the author, May 14, 2009.
7. Thompson.
8. Michelle Williams, interview by the author, May 18, 2009.
9. Nicole Hemmer, interview by the author, May 14, 2009.
10. Michael Reagan, *Making Waves* (Nashville, TN: Thomas Nelson Publishers, 1996), 56.
11. Reagan, *Making Waves*, 48.
12. L. Brent Bozell, *Weapons of Mass Distortion: The Coming Meltdown of the Liberal Media* (New York: Crown Forum, 2004), 5.
13. Michael C. Keith, *Sounds in the Dark: All-Night Radio in American Life* (Ames: Iowa State University Press, 2001), 38.
14. Tim Rutten, "Are Americans Talked Out on Talk Radio?," syndicated newspaper column, September 4, 2005.
15. Kathleen Hall Jamieson and Paul Waldman, *The Press Effect: Politicians, Journalists, and the Stories that Shape the Political World* (New York: Oxford University Press, 2003), 169.
16. Gloria Feldt, *The War on Choice: The Right-Wing Attack on Women's Rights and How to Fight Back* (New York: Bantam Books, 2004), 173.
17. David Ward, "Radio Emerges as a Tech, Personality Topic," *PR Week*, November 3, 2008, 11.
18. Murray Edelman, *The Politics of Misinformation* (New York: Cambridge University Press, 2001), 8.
19. Mike Hoyt, "Talk Radio: Turning Up the Volume," *Columbia Journalism Review*, November/December 1992, 45-50.
20. Peter Laufer, *Inside Talk Radio: America's Voice or Just Hot Air?* (New York: Carol Publishing Group, 1995), 247.
21. Ann Coulter, *How to Talk to a Liberal (If You Must)* (New York: Three Rivers Press, 2004), 233.
22. Arianna Huffington, *Right Is Wrong* (New York: Alfred A. Knopf, 2008), 20.

23. Jack Rice, "Is This All Talk Radio Has Become?," *Talkers*, April 2007, 34.
24. "Politics and Pundits: The Effect of The Media on Elections and Democracy." Panel discussion at the United States Embassy, London, July 16, 2008.
25. Rory O'Connor, *Shock Jocks: Hate Speech and Talk Radio* (San Francisco: AlterNet Books, 2008), 4.
26. Michael Smerconish, interview on *Larry King Live*, Cable News Network, April 29, 2009.
27. Michael Harrison, "Freedom of Speech," *Talkers*, July/August 2007, 52.
28. Jay Leno frequently made this joke as host of *The Tonight Show*.
29. From the back cover of the DVD version of the film.

Chapter 2

1. Ken Walsh, interview by the author, April 28, 2009.
2. Mike Bates, interview by the author, April 7, 2009.
3. Bates.
4. Bates.
5. Michael Mendelssohn, interview by the author, April 17, 2009.
6. Diane Rehm, "Talking Over America's Backyard Fence," in *Radio: The Forgotten Medium*, eds. Edward C. Pease and Everett Dennis (New York: Columbia University Press, 1993), 63-69.
7. Tom Lewis, "Triumph of the Idol—Rush Limbaugh and a Hot Medium," *Media Studies Journal* 7, no. 3 (Summer 1993), 51-61.
8. Murray Edelman, *The Politics of Misinformation* (New York: Cambridge University Press, 2001), 65.
9. Morgan Stewart, "Pump Up the Volume," *Campaigns & Elections*, October/November 1993, 22-26.
10. Dan Shelley, "Secrets of Talk Radio," *Milwaukee Magazine*, November 13, 2008.
11. C. Richard Hofstetter, Mark C. Donovan, Melville R. Klauber, Alexandra Cole, Carolyn J. Huie, and Toshiyuki Yuasa, "Political Talk Radio: A Stereotype Reconsidered," *Political Research Quarterly* 47, no. 2 (June 1994), 467-79.
12. Thom Hartmann, "Let Liberal Talk Radio Be Political," *Talkers*, March 2007, 24.
13. Rehm, "Talking Over America's Backyard Fence."
14. William McGowan, *Coloring the News: How Crusading for Diversity Has Corrupted American Journalism* (San Francisco: Encounter Books, 2001), 246.
15. Ken Walsh, interview by the author, April 28, 2009.
16. Ian Hutchby, "The Pursuit of Controversy: Routine Skepticism on Talk Radio," *Sociology*, Vol. 26 (1992), 673-94.
17. Kenneth Jost, "Talk Show Democracy: Are Call-in Programs Good for the Political System?," *CQ Researcher*, April 29, 1994, 361-84.
18. Neal Boortz makes the comment and similar comments on a regular basis.
19. Stewart, "Pump Up the Volume."
20. Stewart, "Pump Up the Volume."
21. Peter Laufer, *Inside Talk Radio: America's Voice or Just Hot Air?* (New York: Carol Publishing Group, 1995), 203.
22. "Politics and Pundits: The Influence of the Media on Elections and Democracy." Panel discussion at United States Embassy, London, July 16, 2009.

23. Peter Laufer, *Inside Talk Radio: America's Voice or Just Hot Air?* (New York: Carol Publishing Group, 1995), 185.
24. Laufer, *Inside Talk Radio*, 190-91.
25. Uncle Henry, interview by the author, April 21, 2009.
26. Uncle Henry.
27. Bates.
28. David Wallace, "Host," *Atlantic Monthly*, April 2005, 51-72.
29. Randy Bobbitt, *Decisions, Decisions: Case Studies and Discussion Problems in Communication Ethics* (Dubuque, IA: Kendall-Hunt, 2009), 29.
30. Uncle Henry.
31. Robert Thompson, interview by the author, May 14, 2009.
32. Thompson.

Chapter 3

1. Maria Aspan, "Some Advertisers Shun Air America, a Lonely Voice from Talk Radio's Left," *New York Times*, November 6, 2006, 4
2. *The Media Circus*. Cable News Network documentary, 1998.
3. Brenda Franco, interview by the author, April 28, 2009.
4. Dave Windsor, interview by the author, April 7, 2009.
5. Michael Mendelssohn, interview by the author, April 17, 2009.
6. Mendelssohn.
7. Mendelssohn.
8. Bill Press, *Spin This: All the Ways We Don't Tell the Truth* (New York: Pocket Books, 2001), 197.
9. Andrew Hampp, "Imus Mess Makes Arbiters Out of Advertisers," *Advertising Age*, April 16, 2007, 43.
10. Hampp, "Imus Mess Makes Arbiters Out of Advertisers."
11. Hampp, "Imus Mess Makes Arbiters Out of Advertisers."
12. Peter Laufer, *Inside Talk Radio: America's Voice or Just Hot Air?* (New York: Carol Publishing Group, 1995), 210.
13. Media Matters for America, "Michael Savage Is at It Again," September 18, 2008.
14. Mendelssohn.
15. Mendelssohn.
16. Marc Fisher, *Something in the Air: Radio, Rock, and the Revolution That Shaped a Nation* (New York: Random House, 2007), 209.
17. Alan Caudle, interview by the author, April 17, 2009.
18. Douglas Rushkoff, *Coercion: Why We Listen to What "They" Say* (New York: Riverhead Books, 1994), 147.

Chapter 4

1. James Fallows, *Breaking the News: How the Media Undermine American Democracy* (New York: Pantheon Books, 1996), 48.
2. Ann Coulter, *How to Talk to a Liberal (If You Must)* (New York: Three Rivers Press, 2004), 233.

3. L. Brent Bozell, *Weapons of Mass Distortion: The Coming Meltdown of Liberal Media* (New York: Crown Books, 2004), 256.

4. *The Air America Playbook* (New York: Rodale Books, 2006), 9.

5. Tim Rutten, "Are Americans Talked Out on Talk Radio?," syndicated newspaper column, September 4, 2005.

6. Anonymous post to *Milwaukee Magazine* blog, November 13, 2008.

7. Newt Gingrich, *To Renew America* (New York: HarperCollins Publishers, 1995), 211.

8. Dan Shelley, "Secrets of Talk Radio," *Milwaukee Magazine*, November 13, 2008.

9. Eric Boehlert, *Bloggers on the Bus: How the Internet Has Changed American Politics* (New York: Free Press, 2009), 77.

10. Bob Grant, *Let's Be Heard* (New York: Pocket Books, 1996), 6.

11. Grant, *Let's Be Heard*, 7.

12. Grant, *Let's Be Heard*, 7.

13. Fairness and Accuracy in Reporting, "Bob Grant's Success," June 1996.

14. Fairness and Accuracy in Reporting, "Bob Grant's Success."

15. Fairness and Accuracy in Reporting, "Bob Grant's Success."

16. Fairness and Accuracy in Reporting, "Bob Grant's Success."

17. Fairness and Accuracy in Reporting, "Bob Grant's Success."

18. Fairness and Accuracy in Reporting, "Bob Grant's Success."

19. Chuck Raasch, "Twenty Years of Rush," Gannett News Service column, August 8, 2008.

20. Steven B. Roberts, "What a Rush!," *U.S. News & World Report*, August 16, 1993, 27-35.

21. Margaret Carlson, "My Dinner with Rush," *Time*, June 24, 2001.

22. "The 25 Greatest Radio Talk Show Hosts of All Time," *Talkers*, September 2002.

23. Richard Corliss, "Conservative Provocateur or Big Blowhard?," *Time*, October 26, 1992, 76-79.

24. "Here's Where Limbaugh Stands on Some Points," *St. Louis Post-Dispatch*, September 27, 1992, 9-C.

25. Roberts, "What a Rush!"

26. Stuart A. Kallen, *Media Bias* (San Diego, CA: Greenhaven Press, 2004), 43.

27. John C. Stauber and Sheldon Rampton, *Toxic Sludge Is Good for You: Lies, Damn Lies, and the Public Relations Industry* (Monroe, ME: Common Courage Press, 1995), 97.

28. Sara Diamond, *Not By Politics Alone: The Enduring Influence of the Christian Right* (New York: Guilford Press, 1998), 98.

29. Bill Clinton, *My Life* (New York: Random House, 2004), 587.

30. George Stephanopoulos, *All Too Human: A Political Education* (Boston: Little, Brown and Company, 1999), 119.

31. Stephanopoulos, *All Too Human*, 224.

32. David Brock, *The Republican Noise Machine* (New York: Crown Books, 2004), 277.

33. Brock, *The Republican Noise Machine*, 277.

34. Andrea Stone, "Limbaugh Says Actor Fox Exaggerated His Disease as Stem Cell Issue Churns," *USA Today*, October 25, 2006.

35. Craig Unger, *The Fall of the House of Rush* (New York: Scribner, 2007), 319.

36. Frank Rich, *The Greatest Story Ever Sold: The Decline and Fall of Truth in Bush's America* (New York: Penguin Books, 2006), 127.

37. Unger, *The Fall of the House of Rush*, 330.
38. Kallen, *Media Bias*, 43.
39. Howard Kurtz, *Hot Air: All Talk All the Time* (New York: Bantam Books, 1996), 232.
40. Kurtz, *Hot Air*, 232.
41. Carlson, "My Dinner with Rush."
42. Roberts, "What a Rush!"
43. Unger, *The Fall of the House of Rush*, 291.
44. Roberts, "What a Rush!"
45. Arianna Huffington, *Right is Wrong* (New York: Alfred A. Knopf, 2008), 108.
46. Paul D. Colford, *The Rush Limbaugh Story: Talent on Loan from God* (New York: St. Martin's Press, 1993), 52.
47. Examples are from a number of articles and Limbaugh biographies.
48. William Dorman, "Press Theory and Journalistic Practice: The Case of the Gulf War," in *Do the Media Govern?*, eds. Shanto Iyengar and Richard Reeves (Thousand Oaks, CA: Sage Publications, 1997), 118-25.
49. Tom Lewis, "Triumph of the Idol—Rush Limbaugh and a Hot Medium," *Media Studies Journal* 7, no. 3 (Summer 1993), 51-61.
50. Jeff Land, "Sitting in Limbaugh: Bombast in Broadcasting," in *Media, Culture, and the Religious Right*, eds. Linda Kintz and Julia Lesage (Minneapolis: Minnesota University Press, 1998), 227-28.
51. Keith Olbermann, *The Worst Person in the World* (Hoboken, NJ: John Wiley & Sons, 2006), 34.
52. Bozell, *Weapons of Mass Distortion*, 258.
53. Richard Corliss, "Conservative Provocateur or Big Blowhard?," *Time*, October 26, 1992, 76-79.
54. James Bowman, "The Leader of the Opposition," *National Review*, September 6, 1993, 50-56.
55. Stephen Talbot, "The Wizard of Ooze," *Mother Jones*, May/June 1995, 41-43.
56. Bozell, *Weapons of Mass Distortion*, 256.
57. Michael Savage, *The Political Zoo* (Nashville, TN: Thomas Nelson Publishers, 2006), 205.
58. Zev Chafets, "Late-Period Limbaugh," *New York Times Magazine*, July 6, 2008.
59. Chafets, "Late-Period Limbaugh."
60. Chafets, "Late-Period Limbaugh."
61. Dan Weil, "Limbaugh's New Radio Contract Worth $285 Million," *Palm Beach Post*, July 20, 2001, 1-D.
62. Rush Limbaugh, *See, I Told You So* (New York: Pocket Books, 1993), 338.
63. Michael Reagan, *Making Waves* (Nashville, TN: Thomas Nelson Publishers, 1996), 207.
64. Reagan, *Making Waves*, 82.
65. Rich, *The Greatest Story Ever Sold*, 122.
66. Sean Hannity, *Let Freedom Ring* (New York: Harper Publishing, 2002), 264.
67. Hannity, *Let Freedom Ring*, 264.
68. Rich, *The Greatest Story Ever Sold*, 122.
69. Rory O'Connor, *Shock Jocks: Hate Speech and Talk Radio* (San Francisco: AlterNet Books, 2008), 60.
70. Hannity makes this claim on a regular basis.
71. Sharon Crowley, *Toward a Civil Discourse: Rhetoric and Fundamentalism* (Pittsburgh: University of Pittsburgh Press, 2006), 15.

72. Julie Hollar and Jim Naureckas, eds. *Smearcasting: How Islamophobes Spread Fear, Bigotry, and Misinformation* (New York: Fairness and Accuracy in Reporting, 2008), 11.
73. David Bauder, "As Bush's Approval Rating Sinks, Hannity Stays True," Associated Press report, April 21, 2006.
74. *Fresh Air*, National Public Radio, October 8, 2003.
75. Fairness and Accuracy in Reporting, "O'Reilly Ambushes His Latest Critic," March 25, 2009.
76. Olbermann, *The Worst Person in the World*, 97.
77. *Fresh Air*.
78. *Fresh Air*.
79. Bill O'Reilly, *Culture Warrior* (New York: Broadway Books, 2006), 95.
80. O'Reilly, *Culture Warrior*, 100.
81. O'Reilly, *Culture Warrior*, 102.
82. O'Reilly, *Culture Warrior*, 95.
83. Al Franken, *Rush Limbaugh Is a Big Fat Idiot* (New York: Dell Publishing, 1999), 44.
84. Media Matters for America, "O'Reilly Surprised There Was No Difference Between Harlem Restaurant and Other New York Restaurants," September 21, 2007.
85. O'Connor, *Shock Jocks*, 74.
86. O'Connor, *Shock Jocks*, 78.
87. O'Connor, *Shock Jocks*, 79.
88. "10 Questions for Bill O'Reilly," *Time*, September 22, 2008, 8.
89. Marvin Kitman, *The Man Who Would Not Shut Up* (New York: St. Martin's Griffin, 2008), 113.
90. Bob Allen, "Dobson Claims Obama Election Sets Pro-Lifers Back Severely," Associated Baptist Press, November 6, 2008.
91. Allen, "Dobson Claims Obama Election Sets Pro-Lifers Back Severely."
92. Mark Levin, *Men in Black: How the Supreme Court Is Destroying America* (Washington, D. C.: Regnery Publishing, 2005), 77.
93. Levin, *Men in Black*, 79.
94. Dahlia Lithwick, "The Limbaugh Code," Slate.com, April 1, 2005.
95. Levin, *Liberty and Tyranny: A Conservative Manifesto* (New York: Simon and Schuster, 2009), 97.
96. Media Matters for America, "It's Not Just Limbaugh and Hannity," November 6, 2008.
97. Roy L. Moore, *Mass Communication Law and Ethics* (Mahwah, NJ: Lawrence Erlbaum Associates, 1999), 289.
98. *Call-In Political Talk Radio: Background, Content, Audiences, and Portrayal in Mainstream Media* (Philadelphia: Annenberg Public Policy Center, 1996), 45.
99. Reagan, *Making Waves*, 55.
100. Peter Laufer, *Inside Talk Radio: America's Voice or Just Hot Air?* (New York: Carol Publishing Group, 1995), 211.
101. Greg Toppo, "Education Department Paid Commentator to Promote Law," *USA Today*, January 7, 2005.
102. Toppo, "Education Department Paid Commentator to Promote Law."
103. Stuart Elliot, "Paid Endorsement Ignites a Debate in the Public Relations Industry," *New York Times*, January 12, 2005.
104. Ben Ferguson, *It's My America Too* (New York: Harper Collins, 2002), 5.

105. Jack Huberman, *The GOP Haters Handbook* (New York: Nation Books, 2007), 36.
106. "FCC May Look Into Hamblin Case," *Denver Post*, December 4, 1993, 1.
107. Megan Chuchmach, "Inside the Mind of Mark Foley," ABCNews.com, September 9, 2009.

Chapter 5

1. Stuart A. Kallen, *Media Bias* (San Diego, CA: Greenhaven Press, 2004), 127.
2. Rory O'Connor, *Shock Jocks: Hate Speech and Talk Radio* (San Francisco: AlterNet Books, 2008), 176.
3. David Brock, *The Republican Noise Machine* (New York: Crown Books, 2004), 310.
4. Cliff Kincaid and Lynn Woolley, *The Death of Talk Radio?* (Washington, DC: Accuracy in Media, 2007), 4.
5. O'Connor, *Shock Jocks*, 155.
6. Robert Thompson, interview by the author, May 14, 2009.
7. Sheldon Rampton, "Talking Back to Talk Radio," Alternet.org, December 11, 2002.
8. L. Brent Bozell, *Weapons of Mass Distortion: The Coming Meltdown of the Liberal Media* (New York: Crown Forum 2004), 262.
9. Faiz Shakir, interview by the author, July 16, 2009.
10. Marc Fisher, "Air America, in the Throes of Victory?," *Washington Post*, December 10, 2006.
11. "Attention Talkers on the Left," *Free Library*, October 6, 2006.
12. Susan Douglas, *Listening In: Radio and the American Imagination* (Minneapolis: University of Minnesota Press, 1999), 285.
13. Ronald Bush, "Liberal Talk Can't Compete," *Pensacola News Journal*, September 5, 2008, 7-A.
14. Dan Mason, interview by the author, April 21, 2009.
15. Stephen Singular, *Talked to Death: The Life and Murder of Alan Berg* (New York: Beech Tree Books, 1987), 70.
16. Singular, *Talked to Death*, 98.
17. Singular, *Talked to Death*, 11.
18. Stephen Singular, interview by the author, February 26, 2009.
19. Center for American Progress biography of Jim Hightower.
20. *Free Speech for Sale*, Corporation for Public Broadcasting documentary, 1999.
21. *Free Speech for Sale*.
22. Center for American Progress biography of Jim Hightower.
23. Thom Hartmann, "Let Liberal Talk Radio Be Political," *Talkers*, March 2007, 24.
24. Hartmann, "Let Liberal Talk Radio Be Political."
25. Brock, *The Republican Noise Machine*, 327.
26. Brock, *The Republican Noise Machine*, 327.
27. Joshua Green, "The Air American Plan," *Atlantic Monthly*, April 2005, 32-34.
28. Green, "The Air America Plan."
29. Susan Saulny, "In Courtroom, Laughter at Fox and a Victory for Al Franken," *New York Times*, August 23, 2003.
30. Saulney, "In Courtroom, Laughter at Fox and a Victory for Al Franken."

234 Notes

31. Al Franken, *Lies and the Lying Liars Who Tell Them* (New York: Penguin Books, 2004), 365.
32. Bill O'Reilly, *Culture Warrior* (New York: Broadway Books, 2006), 95.
33. Kenneth Jost, "Talk Show Democracy: Are Call-in Programs Good for the Political System?," *CQ Researcher*, April 29, 1994, 361-84.
34. Jeffrey L. Katz, "The Power of Talk," *Governing*, March 1991, 38-42.
35. Jost, "Talk Show Democracy."

Chapter 6

1. Keith Olbermann, *The Worst Person in the World* (Hoboken, NJ: John Wiley & Sons, 2006), 213.
2. Boortz made this comment numerous times early in 2009.
3. Boortz made this comment in September 2006.
4. "Politics and Pundits: The Influence of the Media on Elections and Democracy." Teleconference, London, July 16, 2009.
5. Donald R. Gallerani. *Everything Worth Knowing. . . . I Heard on Talk Radio* (North Charleston, SC: Booksurge Publishing, 2007), 271.
6. Boortz made this comment on his radio program several times during the week following the Virginia Tech tragedy.
7. *The Media Circus*, Cable News Network documentary, 1998.
8. "Politics and Pundits: The Influence of the Media on Elections and Democracy."
9. Nealz Nuze, http://www.boortz.com, 2008 (accessed October 23, 2008).
10. Nealz Nuze.
11. "Politics and Pundits: the Influence of The Media on Elections and Democracy."
12. Boortz made this comment in January 2009.
13. Biography on World Wide Web site, http://www.boortz.com (accessed July 20, 2008).
14. Larry Elder, *Showdown: Confronting Bias, Lies, and the Special Interests That Divide America* (New York: St. Martin's-Griffin, 2003), 332.
15. Elder frequently makes this comment on his program.
16. Elder, *Showdown*, 320.
17. Elder, *Stupid Black Men: How to Place the Race Card and Lose* (New York: St. Martin's Press, 2008), 98.
18. Elder frequently makes this comment on his radio program.
19. Media Matters for America, "Beck Says to Be Consistent," January 28, 2008.
20. Rory O'Connor, *Shock Jocks: Hate Speech and Talk Radio* (San Francisco: AlterNet Books, 2008), 88.
21. Jack Huberman, *The GOP Haters Handbook* (New York: Nation Books, 2007), 35.
22. David Von Drehle, "The Agitator," *Time*, September 28, 2009, 30-36.
23. Von Drehle, "The Agitator."
24. Von Drehle, "The Agitator."
25. David Brock, *The Republican Noise Machine* (New York: Crown Books, 2004), 260.
26. Duncan Currie, "Dennis the Right-Wing Menace," *National Review Online*, June 27, 2003.
27. Jones Radio Network World Wide Web site, http://www.jonesradio.com (accessed January 14, 2009).

28. Ryan Pollyea, "Mancow Waterboarded, Admits That It's Torture," NBCChicago.com, May 22, 2009 (accessed June 10, 2009).
29. Mark Davis, "The Case against Sotomoyor's Confirmation," *Dallas Morning News*, May 26, 2009.
30. Kenneth Jost, "Talk Show Democracy: Are Call in Programs Good for the Political System?," *CQ Researcher*, April 29, 1994, 361-84.
31. Jost.

Chapter 7

1. "Women and Talk Radio," *Talkers*, January 2007, 14.
2. Martha Zoller, interview by the author, July 25, 2009.
3. Jacci Duncan, *Making Waves: The 50 Greatest Women in Radio and Television* (Kansas City, MO: Andrews McMeel Publishing 2001), 179.
4. Marc Fisher, *Something in the Air: Radio, Rock, and the Revolution That Shaped a Nation* (New York: Random House, 2007), 208.
5. "Politics and Pundits: The Influence of the Media on Elections and Democracy." Teleconference, London, England, July 16, 2009.
6. "Politics and Pundits: The Influence of the Media on Elections and Democracy."
7. Joe Garofoli, "Fanning the Flames," *San Francisco Chronicle*, October 8, 2006.
8. Garofoli, "Fanning the Flames."
9. Garofoli, "Fanning the Flames."
10. Garolofi, "New Chapter in the Battle of Words," *San Francisco Chronicle*, June 29, 2006.
11. Garofoli, "Fanning the Flames."
12. *The Keith Olbermann Show*, March 1, 2007.
13. Elinor J. Brecher, "Left-Leaning Radio Hostess Carves Out an Audience," *Miami Herald*, November 9, 2004.
14. "Rhodes Says Air America Breached Her Contract," *Huffington Post*, April 3, 2008.
15. "Listen Up, America, Tammy Bruce Is Talking," *Talk Radio News*, January 2007.
16. "Listen Up, America, Tammy Bruce Is Talking."
17. O'Connor, *Shock Jocks: Hate Speech and Talk Radio* (San Francisco: AlterNet Books, 2008), 206.
18. Peter Laufer, *Inside Talk Radio: America's Voice or Just Hot Air?* (New York: Carol Publishing Group, 1995), 201.
19. Laufer, *Inside Talk Radio*, 201.
20. Zoller.

Chapter 8

1. Rory O'Connor, "Talk Radio and the Conspiracy to Kill," AlterNet, August 1, 2008.
2. O'Connor, "Talk Radio and the Conspiracy to Kill."
3. O'Connor, "Talk Radio and the Conspiracy to Kill."
4. Timothy Egan, "Talk Radio or Hate Radio? Critics Assail Some Hosts," *New York Times*, January 1, 1995, 22.

5. Egan, "Talk Radio or Hate Radio?"

6. David Niewart, *The Eliminationists: How Hate Talk Radicalized the American Right* (Sausalito, CA: PoliPoint Press, 2009), 11.

7. Selwyn Crawford and Tiara Ellis, "Tolerance for Intolerance Fuels Fears of Cultural Rift," *Dallas Morning News*, April 18, 2004.

8. Nancy Giles, *Sunday Morning*, CBS News, October 5, 2003.

9. Kenneth Jost, "Talk Show Democracy: Are Call-in Programs Good for the Political Process?," *CQ Researcher*, April 29, 1994, 361-84.

10. Leigh Stephens Aldrich, *Covering the Community: A Diversity Handbook for the Media* (Thousand Oaks, CA: Pine Forge Press, 1999), 96.

11. Michael Reagan, *Making Waves* (Nashville, TN: Thomas Nelson Publishers, 1996), 44.

12. Reagan, *Making Waves*, 45.

13. Reagan, *Making Waves*, 45.

14. Reagan, *Making Waves*, 45-46.

15. L. Brent Bozell, *Weapons of Mass Distortion: The Coming Meltdown of the Liberal Media* (New York: Crown Forum, 2004), 24.

16. Reagan, *Making Waves*, 48.

17. Reagan, *Making Waves*, 42.

18. O'Connor, *Shock Jocks: Hate Speech and Talk Radio* (San Francisco: AlterNet Books, 2008), 1-2.

19. O'Connor, *Shock Jocks*, 15.

20. Donald Warren, *Radio Priest: Charles Coughlin, the Father of Hate Radio* (New York: Free Press, 1996), 16.

21. Warren, *Radio Priest*, 6.

22. Fred Friendly, *The Good Guys, the Bad Guys, and the First Amendment: Free Speech vs. Fairness in Broadcasting* (New York: Random House, 1976), 44.

23. "Acid-Tongued Joe Pyne Dies," *Delaware County Times*, March 25, 1970.

24. "Acid-Tongued Joe Pyne Dies."

25. O'Connor, *Shock Jocks*, 17.

26. Phil Brennan, "Michael Savage Mulls Presidential Run," *NewsMax*, February 2007, 17.

27. Michael Savage, *The Enemy Within* (Nashville, TN: WND Books, 2003), 2-3.

28. O'Connor, *Shock Jocks*, 73.

29. O'Connor, *Shock Jocks*, 73.

30. Media Matters for America, "Michael Savage Is at It Again," September 18, 2008.

31. Center for American Progress, "Five More Advertisers Abandon Michael Savage's Hate-Filled Radio Show," February 11, 2008.

32. Savage, *The Political Zoo* (Nashville, TN: Thomas Nelson, Inc., 2006), 205.

33. Savage, *The Political Zoo*, 237.

34. Savage made this comment and similar comments numerous times on his radio show throughout December 2007 and January 2008.

35. Gloria Feldt, *The War on Choice: The Right-Wing Attack on Women's Rights and How to Fight Back* (New York: Bantam Books, 2004), 197.

36. O'Connor, *Shock Jocks*, 197.

37. Center for American Progress, "Five More Advertisers Abandon Michael Savage's Hate-Filled Radio Show."

38. Center for American Progress, "Five More Advertisers Abandon Michael Savage's Hate-Filled Radio Show."

39. Jacques Steinberg, "Savage Stands by Autism Remarks," *New York Times*, July 22, 2008.
40. *Access Hollywood*, July 22, 2008.
41. "Savage Autism," www.althouse.com (accessed July 30, 2008).
42. Statement on WOR World Wide Web site, July 21, 2008.
43. Julie Hollar and Jim Naureckas, eds. *Smearcasting: How Islamophobes Spread Fear, Bigotry, and Misinformation* (New York: Fairness and Accuracy in Reporting, 2008), 11.
44. Michael Savage, *The Political Zoo* (Nashville, TN: Thomas Nelson Publishers, 2006), 33.
45. Savage, *The Political Zoo*, 27.
46. James Poniewozik, "Who Can Say What?," *Time*, April 23, 2007, 32-37.
47. Weston Kosova, "The Power That Was," *Newsweek*, April 23, 2007, 24-31.
48. O'Connor, *Shock Jocks*, 88.
49. Peter Johnson, "Critics Demand That Imus Be Fired for Rutgers Remark," *USA Today*, April 10, 2007, 3-D.
50. Johnson, "Critics Demand That Imus Be Fired for Rutgers Remark."
51. Weston Kosova, "The Power That Was."
52. *Imus in the Morning*, April 4, 2007.
53. Jason Whitlock, "Imus Isn't the Real Bad Guy," *Kansas City Star*, April 11, 2007.
54. Alessandra Stanley, "Don Imus, Suspended, Still Talking," *New York Times*, April 11, 2007, 1-B.
55. "Critics Demand Imus Be Fired Over Remarks," ABCNews.com, April 9, 2007.
56. "Imus, Sharpton Spar Over Racial Comment," MSNBC.com, April 9, 2007.
57. "Imus, Sharpton Spar Over Racial Comment."
58. Johnson, "Critics Demand Imus Be Fired for Rutgers Remark."
59. Jayne Pearl, "The Swift Execution of Don Imus," *Talkers*, April 2007, 1+.
60. O'Connor, *Shock Jocks*, 18.
61. Peter Johnson, "There's a Close Eye on Imus," *USA Today*, April 10, 2007, 3-A.
62. "Hannity's Soul-Mate of Hate," *Nation*, June 20, 2005.
63. Media Matters for America, "Cunningham on Obama, Sr.," October 30, 2008.
64. Media Matters for America, "It's Not Just Limbaugh and Hannity," November 6, 2008.
65. Howard Kurtz, *Hot Air: All Talk All the Time* (New York: Bantam Books, 1996), 294.
66. "Protestors Call for Resignation of WLW Host," WCPO.com, December 5, 2003.
67. "McCain Apology Angers Conservative Host," CNN.com, February 26, 2008.
68. "McCain Apology Angers Conservative Host."
69. "McCain Apology Angers Conservative Host."
70. Media Matters for America, "It's Not Just Limbaugh and Hannity."
71. Kenneth S. Stern, *Hate on Talk Radio* (New York: American Jewish Committee, 1995), 20.
72. Egan, "Talk Radio or Hate Radio?"
73. Media Matters for America, "It's Not Just Limbaugh and Hannity."
74. Media Matters for America, "It's Not Just Limbaugh and Hannity."
75. David Brock, *The Republican Noise Machine* (New York: Crown Publishers, 2004), 289.
76. Aldrich, *Covering the Community*, 96.

Chapter 9

1. Alan Caudle, interview by the author, April 17, 2009.
2. Robert Thompson, interview by the author, May 14, 2009.
3. Michael Smerconish, *Morning Drive: Things I Wish I Knew Before I Started Talking* (Guilford, CT: Lyons Press, 2009), 39.
4. Rory O'Connor, *Shock Jocks: Hate Speech and Talk Radio* (San Francisco: AlterNet Books, 2008), 173.
5. David Foster Wallace, "Host," *Atlantic Monthly*, April 2005, 51-74.
6. Wallace, "Host."
7. Wallace, "Host."
8. Peter Laufer, *Inside Talk Radio: America's Voice or Just Hot Air?* (New York: Carol Publishing Group, 1995), 232.
9. Laufer, *Inside Talk Radio*, 232.
10. Laufer, *Inside Talk Radio*, 234.
11. Michael A. Siegel, *Power Talk!* (Seattle: Ebbetts Publishing, 2004), 77.
12. Uncle Henry, interview by the author, April 21, 2009.
13. Uncle Henry interview.
14. Uncle Henry, on-air comment, April 21, 2009.
15. Uncle Henry interview.
16. Uncle Henry interview.
17. Rob Williams, interview by the author, April 7, 2009.
18. Williams, off-air comment, April 7, 2009.
19. Williams interview.
20. Williams interview.
21. Williams interview.
22. Williams interview.
23. Paul Stadden, interview by the author, April 7, 2009.
24. Williams interview.
25. Dave Windsor, interview by the author, April 7, 2009.
26. Ken Walsh, interview by the author, April 28, 2009.
27. Walsh.
28. Walsh.
29. Walsh.
30. "Asian-Americans Protest Radio Satire," *On-Line Library*, 2006.
31. Dan Frosch, "Politically Divided Talk Radio Team Has Denver Firmly in Its Grip," *New York Times*, August 8, 2008, 15.
32. Media Matters for America, "Fox News Hosts 'Terror Expert' Bob Newman," June 10, 2009.
33. Kenneth S. Stern, *Hate on Talk Radio* (New York: American Jewish Committee, 1995), 14.
34. *McIntyre in the Morning*, May 6, 2006.

Chapter 10

1. Al Gore, *The Assault on Reason* (New York: Penguin Books, 2007), 66.
2. Jayne Pearl, "Talk Radio Activism," *Talkers*, September 2007, 1.
3. John Dean, *Broken Government* (New York: Penguin Group, 2008), 189.
4. "Take Back the Airwaves," *Mother Jones*, January/February 1995, 41-43.

5. Russ Douthart and Reihan Salam, *Grand New Party: How Republicans Can Win Back the Working Class and Save the American Dream* (New York: Doubleday, 2008), 61.

6. Michael J. West, blog entry, 2006.

7. Mike France and Tom Lowry, "Is There a Market for Nonpartisan News?," *BusinessWeek*, November 29, 2004.

8. George Stephanopoulos, *All Too Human: A Political Education* (Boston: Little, Brown and Company, 1999), 327.

9. Newt Gingrich, *To Renew America* (New York: HarperCollins Publishers, 1995), 211.

10. Deborah Parenti, interview by the author, July 18, 2009.

11. Kenneth Jost, "Talk Show Democracy: Are Call-in Programs Good for the Political System?," *CQ Researcher*, April 29, 1994, 361-84.

12. Diane Rehm, "Talking Over America's Backyard Fence." In *Radio: The Forgotten Medium*, eds. Edward C. Pease and Everette Dennis (New York: Columbia University Press, 1993), 63-69.

13. Steve Elman and Alan Tolz, "The Rising Irrelevance of Talk Radio," *Boston Globe*, November 8, 2008, 13-A.

14. West, blog entry.

15. Jost, "Talk Show Democracy."

16. David C. Barker, *Rushed to Judgment: Talk Radio, Persuasion, and American Political Behavior* (New York: Columbia University Press, 2002), 1.

17. Kerwin Swint, *Mudslingers: The Twenty-Five Dirtiest Political Campaigns of All Time* (New York: Union Square Press, 2008), 95-102.

18. Max McCombs and Donald Shaw, "The Agenda-Setting Function of Mass Media," *Public Opinion Quarterly* 36 (1972), 176-87.

19. Jayne Pearl, "Talk Radio Activism," *Talkers*, September 2007, 1.

20. "Anti-Tax Station Turns FM into Florio Mashing," *New York Times*, July 17, 1990.

21. Wayne King, "Tax Protest, Fueled by Talk Shows, Is Getting Steamed Voters Organized," *New York Times*, October 26, 1990.

22. Pearl, "Talk Radio Activism."

23. Brian Jennings, *Censorship: The Threat to Silence Talk Radio* (New York: Simon and Schuster, 2009), 64-65.

24. Morgan Stewart, "Pump Up the Volume," *Campaigns & Elections*, October/November 1993, 22-26.

25. Elihu Katz and Paul F. Lazarsfeld, *Personal Influence* (Glencoe, IL: Free Press), 1955.

26. Stanley J. Baran and Dennis K. Davis, *Mass Communication Theory: Foundations, Ferment, and Future* (Belmont, CA: Wadsworth Publishing, 2000), 139.

27. Baran and Davis, *Mass Communication Theory*, 139.

28. Uncle Henry, interview by the author, April 21, 2009.

29. Randy Bobbitt, *Lottery Wars: Case Studies in Bible-Belt Politics* (Lanham, MD: Lexington Books, 2007), 137.

30. Michael Medved, "Will Talk Radio Get a Wake-Up Call?," *USA Today*, December 4, 2008, 11-A.

31. Sharon Crowley, *Toward a Civil Discourse: Rhetoric and Fundamentalism* (Pittsburgh: University of Pittsburgh Press, 2006), 86.

32. David Brock, *The Republican Noise Machine* (New York: Crown Books, 2004), 281.

33. News release from Annenberg Public Policy Center, June 13, 2005.
34. Dan Shelley, "Secrets of Talk Radio," *Milwaukee Magazine*, November 13, 2008.
35. Wayne Munson, *All Talk: The Talkshow in Media Culture* (Philadelphia: Temple University Press, 1993), 4.
36. Pearl, "Talk Radio Activism."
37. "Politics and Pundits: The Effect of the Media on Elections and Democracy." Panel discussion at the United States Embassy, London, July 16, 2008.
38. David Bauder, "Limbaugh Challenges Notion of New Politics," Associated Press report, January 31, 2009.
39. Tim Graham, "McCain May Prove Talk Radio Having Little Effect," NewsBusters.com, January 28, 2008.
40. "Politics and Pundits: The Effect of the Media on Elections and Democracy."
41. Alan Caudle, interview by the author, April 17, 2009.
42. Tom Lewis, "Triumph of the Idol—Rush Limbaugh and a Hot Medium," *Media Studies Journal* 7, no. 3 (Summer 1993), 51-61.
43. Jost, "Talk Show Democracy."
44. Zev Chafets, "Late-Period Limbaugh," *New York Times Magazine*, July 6, 2008.
45. Howard Kurtz, *Hot Air: All Talk All the Time* (New York: Times Books, 1996), 291.
46. Lowell Ponte, "Talk about Power," *NewsMax*, November 2006.
47. Laura Ingraham, *Power to the People* (Washington, DC: Regnery Publishing, 2007), 250.
48. O'Connor, *Shock Jocks*, 43.
49. James Poniewozik, "Who Can Say What?," *Time*, April 23, 2007, 32-37.
50. Pearl, "Talk Radio Activism."
51. Randy Bobbitt and Ruth Sullivan, *Developing the Public Relations Campaign* (Boston: Allyn & Bacon, 2009), 45.
52. Bertrand Russell, *An Analysis of the Mind* (London: Routledge, 1995), 175.
53. Anonymous post to *Milwaukee Magazine* blog, November 13, 2008.
54. Barker, *Rushed to Judgment*, 282.
55. Randy Bobbitt, *Exploring Communication Law* (Boston: Allyn & Bacon, 2007), 106.
56. Gloria Feldt, *The War on Choice: The Right-Wing Attack on Women's Rights and How to Fight Back* (New York: Bantam Books, 2004), 196.
57. Bill Press, *Spin This: All the Ways We Don't Tell the Truth* (New York: Pocket Books, 2001), xiii.
58. Richard Corliss, "Look Who's Talking," *Time*, January 23, 1995, 22-25.
59. Alfred McClung Lee and Elizabeth Briant, *The Fine Art of Propaganda: A Study of Father Coughlin's Speeches* (New York: Harcourt Brace, 1939).
60. Mike Conway, Maria Elizabeth Grabe, and Kevin Grieves, "Villains, Victims, and the Virtuous in Bill O'Reilly's No-Spin Zone: Revisiting World War II Propaganda Techniques," *Journalism Studies* 8, no. 2 (2007), 197-225.
61. Conway, "Villains, Victims, and the Virtuous."
62. *The Rush Limbaugh Show*, March 9, 2004.
63. Conway, "Villains, Victims, and the Virtuous."
64. Conway, "Villains, Victims, and the Virtuous."
65. Conway, "Villains, Victims, and the Virtuous."
66. Limbaugh, Hannity, and other conservative talk show hosts made this observation throughout the campaign.

67. Shelley, "Secrets of Talk Radio."
68. Conway, "Villains, Victims, and the Virtuous."
69. Bryan Hyde, "Talk Radio Has Become the Mouthpiece of Big Brother," *Salt Lake City Tribune*, August 25, 2006.
70. Media Matters for America, "It's Not Just Limbaugh and Hannity," November 6, 2008.
71. Jurgen Habermas, *The Structural Transformation of the Public Sphere* (Cambridge, MA: MIT Press, 1989).
72. Al Gore, *The Assault on Reason* (New York: Penguin Books, 2007), 18.
73. Gore, *The Assault on Reason*, 18.
74. Stephen E. Toulmin, *The Uses of Argument* (New York: Cambridge University Press, 2003), 77.
75. John Crittenden, "Democratic Functions of the Open Mike Radio Forum," *Public Opinion Quarterly* 33 (Spring 1971), 200-210.
76. Jesse Walker, *Rebels on the Air: An Alternative History of Radio in America* (New York: New York University Press, 2001), 283.
77. Corliss, "Look Who's Talking."
78. Ian Hutchby, *Confrontation Talk: Arguments, Asymmetries, and Power on Talk Radio* (Mahwah, NJ: Lawrence Erlbaum Associates, 1996), 59.
79. Rehm, "Talking Over America's Backyard Fence."
80. Rehm, "Talking Over America's Backyard Fence."
81. Andrew Tolson, *Media Talk: Spoken Discourse on TV and Radio* (Edinburgh: Edinburgh University Press, 2006), 16.
82. Randy Bobbitt, *Decisions, Decisions: Case Studies and Discussion Problems in Communication Ethics* (Dubuque, IA: Kendall-Hunt, 2009), 46.

Chapter 11

1. Tim Graham, "McCain May Prove Talk Radio Having Little Effect," NewsBusters.com, January 28, 2008.
2. "Clinton Claims Limbaugh Has 'Secret Crush' on Her," NewsBusters.com, May 4, 2008.
3. "McCain Apology Angers Conservative Host," CNN.com, February 27, 2008.
4. "McCain Apology Angers Conservative Host."
5. "McCain Apology Angers Conservative Host."
6. Susan Page, "Which Hopeful Is the New Face of the GOP?," *USA Today*, January 24, 2008, 1-A.
7. Michael Medved, "South Carolina's Big Loser: Talk Radio," TownHall.com, January 19, 2008.
8. Eve Conant, Holly Bailey, and Michael Hirsh, "So Much for a Warm Welcome," *Newsweek*, February 18, 2008, 27-32.
9. Eric Gosky, "Dobson Accuses Obama of Distorting Bible," Associated Press report, June 24, 2008.
10. Gosky, "Dobson Accuses Obama of Distorting Bible."
11. Gosky, "Dobson Accuses Obama of Distorting Bible."
12. Zev Chafets, "Late-Period Limbaugh," *New York Times Magazine*, July 6, 2008.
13. Chafets, "Late-Period Limbaugh."
14. Chafets, "Late-Period Limbaugh."
15. Chafets, "Late-Period Limbaugh."

16. Conant, Holly Bailey, and Michael Hirsh, "So Much for a Warm Welcome."
17. Conant, Holly Bailey, and Michael Hirsh, "So Much for a Warm Welcome."
18. Chafets, "Late-Period Limbaugh."
19. Dana Milbank, "The Mouths That Run against McCain," *Washington Post*, February 5, 2008, 2-A.
20. "Obama Dismisses Dobson Criticism about Bible," MSNBC.com, June 25, 2008.
21. Howard Kurtz, "From the Radio Right Comes an Amen Chorus for Palin." *Washington Post*, September 4, 2008, 25-A.
22. Kurtz, "From the Radio Right Comes an Amen Chorus for Palin."
23. "Limbaugh Strikes Back against Obama Ad," Associated Press report, September 15, 2008.
24. "Limbaugh Strikes Back against Obama Ad."
25. Gwen Ifill, *The Breakthrough: Politics and Race in the Age of Obama* (New York: Doubleday, 2009), 164.
26. Ifill, *The Breakthrough*, 164.
27. Ifill, *The Breakthrough*, 164.
28. Media Matters for America, "It's Not Just Limbaugh and Hannity," November 6, 2008.
29. Media Matters for America, "It's Not Just Limbaugh and Hannity."
30. Neal Boortz, "To the Undecided Voter," Boortz.com, October 23, 2008.
31. "Politics and Pundits: The Effect of the Media on Elections and Democracy." Panel discussion at the United States Embassy, London, July 16, 2008.
32. Bill Maher, interview on *Larry King Live*, Cable News Network, November 5, 2008.
33. Maher, *Larry King Live*.
34. Faiz Shakir, interview by the author, July 16, 2009.
35. Dan Shelley, interview by the author, July 19, 2009.
36. Lynn Woolley, interview by the author, August 4, 2009.
37. Media Matters for America, "It's Not Just Limbaugh and Hannity," November 6, 2008.
38. Media Matters for America, "It's Not Just Limbaugh and Hannity."
39. Media Matters for America, "It's Not Just Limbaugh and Hannity."
40. David Bauder, "Limbaugh Challenges Notion of New Politics," Associated Press report, January 31, 2009.
41. Bauder, "Limbaugh Challenges Notion of New Politics."
42. Bauder, "Limbaugh Challenges Notion of New Politics."
43. Clarence Page, "Limbaugh Profits at His Party's Expense," syndicated newspaper column, March 5, 2009.
44. Bauder, "Limbaugh Challenges Notion of New Politics."
45. Bauder, "Limbaugh Challenges Notion of New Politics."
46. Steve Elman and Alan Tulz, "The Rising Irrelevance of Talk Radio," *Boston Globe*, November 8, 2008, 13-A.
47. Bauder, "Limbaugh Challenges Notion of New Politics."
48. Page, "Limbaugh is Giving Obama the Bum's Rush," syndicated newspaper column, January 29, 2009.
49. David Bauder, "Limbaugh Challenging Notion of New Politics."
50. Steve Holland, "Talk Show Host Fills 'Demon' Role for White House," Reuters News Service, March 6, 2009.

51. Mike Papantonio, "The GOP Should Turn Its Back on Limbaugh," *Pensacola News Journal*, March 11, 2009, 11-A.

Epilogue

1. Frank Luther Mott, *American Journalism* (New York: Macmillan, 1950), 55.
2. Roger L. Sadler, *Electronic Media Law* (Thousand Oaks, CA: Sage Publications, 2005), 67.
3. David Foster Wallace, "Host," *Atlantic Monthly*, April 2005, 51-72.
4. Fred Cook, "Hate Clubs of the Air," *Nation*, May 25, 1964, 523-27.
5. Fred Friendly, *The Good Guys, the Bad Guys, and the First Amendment: Free Speech vs. Fairness in Broadcasting* (New York: Random House, 1976), 43.
6. Friendly, *The Good Guys, the Bad Guys, and the First Amendment*, 62.
7. Friendly, *The Good Guys, the Bad Guys, and the First Amendment*, 76.
8. Susan J. Douglas, *Listening In: Radio and the American Imagination* (Minneapolis: University of Minnesota Press, 1999), 299.
9. Michael C. Keith, *Sounds in the Dark: All-Night Radio in American Life* (Ames: Iowa State University Press, 2001), 146.
10. Rory O'Connor, *Shock Jocks: Hate Speech and Talk Radio* (San Francisco: AlterNet Books, 2008), 143.
11. L. Brent Bozell, *Weapons of Mass Distortion: The Coming Meltdown of the Liberal Media* (New York: Crown Forum, 2004), 256.
12. Keith, *Sounds in the Dark*, 196.
13. Peter Gutmann, "The Repeal of Political Editorial and Personal Attack Rules," www.wcsr.com (accessed October 23, 2006).
14. Politico.com, February 5, 2009.
15. Brian Jennings, *Censorship: The Threat to Silence Talk Radio* (New York: Simon and Schuster, 2009), 33.
16. Jennings, *Censorship*, 33.
17. Gigi B. Sohn, "Is a Fairness Doctrine Needed Today?," *World & I*, January 1994.
18. Kenneth Jost, "Talk Show Democracy: Are Call-in Programs Good for the Political System?," *CQ Researcher*, April 29, 1994, 361-84.
19. *The Mark Levin Show*, February 10, 2009.
20. Steven J. Weisman, "Fair Is Foul," *Talkers*, November 2007, 34.
21. Jennings, *Censorship*, 183.
22. George Will, "In the Interest of 'Fairness,' Leave Well Enough Alone," syndicated newspaper column, December 7, 2008.
23. John Eggerton, "Obama Does Not Support Return of Fairness Doctrine," *Broadcasting & Cable*, June 25, 2008.
24. Laura Ingraham, *Power to the People* (Washington, DC: Regnery Publishing, 2007), 4-5.
25. Ingraham, *Power to the People*, 4-5.
26. Mike Rosen, "The Unfairness Doctrine," *Talkers*, July-August 2007, 38.
27. Lynn Woolley, "Fair and Balanced?," *Talkers*, November 2007, 30.
28. Woolley, "Fair and Balanced?"
29. Woolley, "Fair and Balanced?"
30. Rush Limbaugh, *See, I Told You So* (New York: Pocket Books, 1993), 338.
31. Lars Larson, "Fair(ness) Warning," *Talkers*, November 2007, 32.
32. Michael Harrison, "Freedom of Speech," *Talkers*, July/August 2007, 52.

33. Harrison, "Freedom of Speech."
34. Mike Pence, forward to *The Death of Talk Radio?* by Cliff Kincaid and Lynn Woolley (Washington, DC: Accuracy in Media, 2007), ix-xii.
35. Eggerton, "Obama Does Not Support Return of Fairness Doctrine."
36. Anonymous post to blog, FairnessDoctrine.com, July 10, 2005.
37. Gloria Feldt, *The War on Choice: The Right-Wing Attack on Women's Rights and How to Fight Back* (New York: Bantam Books, 2004), 197.
38. *The Structural Imbalance of Political Talk Radio* (Washington, DC: Center for American Progress, 2007), 7.
39. *The Sean Hannity Show*, February 13, 2009.
40. Jayne Pearl, "Talk Radio Activism," *Talkers*, September 2007, 1.
41. Center for American Progress, "Forget the Fairness Doctrine," 2007.
42. Eggerton, "Obama Does Not Support Return of Fairness Doctrine."
43. Eggerton, "Obama Does Not Support Return of Fairness Doctrine."

Sources

Books and Book Chapters

The Air America Playbook. New York: Rodale Books, 2006.
Aldrich, Leigh Stephens. *Covering the Community: A Diversity Handbook for the Media.* Thousand Oaks, CA: Pine Forge Press, 1999.
Baran, Stanley J., and Dennis K. Davis. *Mass Communication Theory: Foundations, Ferment, and Future.* Belmont, CA: Wadsworth Publishing, 2000.
Barker, David C. *Rushed to Judgment: Talk Radio, Persuasion, and American Political Behavior.* New York: Columbia University Press, 2002.
Beck, Glenn. *The Real America.* New York: Simon and Schuster, 2003.
———. *An Inconvenient Book.* New York: Simon and Schuster, 2007.
Bobbitt, Randy. *Exploring Communication Law.* Boston: Allyn & Bacon, 2007.
———. *Lottery Wars: Case Studies in Bible-Belt Politics.* Lanham, MD: Lexington Books, 2007.
———. *Decisions, Decisions: Case Studies and Discussion Problems in Communication Ethics.* Dubuque, IA: Kendall-Hunt, 2009.
Boehlert, Eric. *Bloggers on the Bus: How the Internet Has Changed Politics and the Press.* New York: Free Press, 2009.
Boortz, Neal. *Somebody's Gotta Say It.* New York: William Morrow, 2007.
Bozell, L. Brent. *Weapons of Mass Distortion: The Coming Meltdown of the Liberal Media.* New York: Crown Forum, 2004.
Brock, David. *The Republican Noise Machine.* New York: Crown Publishers, 2004.
———. *Blinded by the Right: the Conscience of an Ex-Conservative.* New York: Crown Publishers, 2002.
Clinton, Bill. *My Life.* New York: Random House, 2004.
Colford, Paul D. *The Rush Limbaugh Story: Talent on Loan from God.* New York: St. Martin's Press, 1993.
Coulter, Ann. *How to Talk to a Liberal (If You Must).* New York: Three Rivers Press, 2004.
Crossley, Nick, and John Michael Roberts, eds. *After Habermas: New Perspectives on the Public Sphere.* New York: Blackwell Publishing, 2004.
Crowley, Sharon. *Toward a Civil Discourse: Rhetoric and Fundamentalism.* Pittsburgh: University of Pittsburgh Press, 2006.
Dean, John W. *Broken Government.* New York: Penguin Group, 2007.
Denton, Robert E. *Political Communication in America.* New York: Praeger, 1990.
Diamond, Sara. *Not by Politics Alone: The Enduring Influence of the Christian Right.* New York: Guilford Press, 1998.

D'Sousa, Dinesh. *The Enemy at Home: The Cultural Left and Its Responsibility for 9/11.* New York: Doubleday, 2007.
Dorman, William. "Press Theory and Journalistic Practice: The Case of the Gulf War." Pp. 118-25 in *Do the Media Govern?*, edited by Shanto Iyengar and Richard Reeves. Thousand Oaks, CA: Sage Publications, 1997.
Douglas, Susan J. *Listening In: Radio and the American Imagination.* Minneapolis: University of Minnesota Press, 1999.
Douthart, Ross, and Reihan Salam. *Grand New Party: How Republicans Can Win the Working Class and Save the American Dream.* New York: Doubleday, 2008.
Duncan, Jacci, ed. *Making Waves: The 50 Greatest Women in Radio and Television.* Kansas City, MO: Andrews McMeel Publishing, 2001.
Edelman, Murray. *The Politics of Misinformation.* New York: Cambridge University Press, 2001.
Elder, Larry. *Showdown: Confronting Bias, Lies, and the Special Interests That Divide America.* New York: St. Martin's-Griffin, 2003.
———. *Stupid Black Men: How to Play the Race Card and Lose.* New York: St. Martin's Press, 2008.
———. *Ten Things You Can't Say in America.* New York: St. Martin's-Griffin, 2000.
Feldt, Gloria. *The War on Choice:The Right-Wing Attack on Women's Rights and How to Fight Back.* New York: Bantam Books, 2004.
Ferguson, Ben. *It's My America Too.* New York: HarperCollins, 2002.
Finlayson, James Gordon. *Habermas: A Very Short Introduction.* New York: Oxford University Press, 2005.
Fisher, Marc. *Something in the Air: Radio, Rock, and the Revolution That Shaped a Generation.* New York: Random House, 2007.
Friendly, Fred. *The Good Guys, the Bad Guys, and the First Amendment: Free Speech vs. Fairness in Broadcasting.* New York: Random House, 1976.
Gallerani, Donald R. *Everything Worth Knowing . . . I Heard on Talk Radio.* North Charleston, SC: BookSurge Publishing, 2007.
Gerth, Jeff, and Don Van Natta Jr. *Her Way: The Hopes and Ambitions of Hillary Rodham Clinton.* New York: Back Nine Books, 2007.
Gingrich, Newt. *To Renew America.* New York: HarperCollins Publishers, 1995.
Glassner, Barry. *The Culture of Fear.* New York: Basic Books, 1999.
Gore, Al. *The Assault on Reason.* New York: Penguin Books, 2007.
Grant, Bob. *Let's Be Heard.* New York: Pocket Books, 1996.
Habermas, Jurgen. *Structural Transformation of the Public Sphere.* Cambridge, MA: MIT Press, 1989.
Hangen, Tona K. *Redeeming the Dial: Radio, Religion, and Popular Culture in America.* Chapel Hill, NC: University of North Carolina Press, 2002.
Hannity, Sean. *Let Freedom Ring.* New York: Harper Publishing, 2002.
Hart, Roderick. *Campaign Talk: Why Elections are Good for Us.* Princeton, NJ: Princeton University Press, 2000.
Hilliard, Robert L., and Michael C. Keith. *Waves of Rancor: Tuning in the Radical Right.* Amonk, NY: M. E. Sharpe, 1999.
Huberman, Jack. *The GOP Haters Handbook.* New York: Nation Books, 2007.
Huffington, Arianna. *Right Is Wrong.* New York: Alfred A. Knopf, 2008.
Hutchby, Ian. *Confrontation Talk: Arguments, Asymmetries, and Power on Talk Radio.* Mahwah, NJ: Lawrence Erlbaum Associates, 1996.
Ifill, Gwen. *The Breakthrough: Politics and Race in the Age of Obama.* New York: Doubleday, 2009.

Ingraham, Laura. *Shut Up and Sing*. Washington, DC: Regnery Publishing, 2003.
———. *Power to the People*. Washington, DC: Regnery Publishing, 2007.
Iyengar, Shanto, and Richard Reeves, eds. *Do the Media Govern? Politicians, Voters, and Reporters in America*. Thousand Oaks, CA: Sage Publications, 1997.
Jackson, Brooks, and Kathleen Hall Jamieson. *Un-Spun: Finding Facts in a World of Disinformation*. New York: Random House, 2007.
Jamieson, Kathleen Hall, and Paul Waldman. *The Press Effect: Politicians, Journalists, and the Stories That Shape the Political World*. New York: Oxford University Press, 2003.
Jennings, Brian. *Censorship: The Threat to Silence Talk Radio*. New York: Simon & Schuster, 2009.
Kallen, Stuart A. *Media Bias*. San Diego: Greenhaven Press, 2004.
Keith, Michael C. *Sounds in the Dark: All-Night Radio in American Life*. Ames: Iowa State University Press, 2001.
Kellner, Douglas. *Media Spectacle and the Crisis of Democracy: Terrorism, War, and Election Battles*. Boulder, CO: Paradigm Publishers, 2005.
Kincaid, Cliff, and Lynn Woolley. *The Death of Talk Radio?* Washington, DC: Accuracy in Media, 2007.
Kitman, Marvin. *The Man Who Would Not Shut Up: The Rise of Bill O'Reilly*. New York: St. Martin's Griffin, 2008.
Klapper, Joseph. *The Effects of Mass Communication*. New York: Free Press, 1960.
Krasny, Michael. *Off Mike: A Memoir of Talk Radio and Literary Life*. Stanford, CA: Stanford University Press, 2008.
Kurtz, Howard. *Hot Air: All Talk, All the Time*. New York: Times Books, 1996.
———. *Spin Cycle: Inside the Clinton Propaganda Machine*. New York: Free Press, 1998.
Lakoff, George. *Moral Politics: How Liberals and Conservatives Think*. Chicago: University of Chicago Press, 2002.
Laufer, Peter. *Inside Talk Radio: America's Voice or Just Hot Air?* New York: Carol Publishing Group, 1995.
Lazarsfeld, Paul F., Bernard Berelson, and Helen Gaudet. *The People's Choice: How the Voter Makes Up His Mind in a Presidential Campaign*. New York: Duell, Sloan & Pearce, 1944.
Levin, Mark R. *Men in Black: How the Supreme Court Is Destroying America*. Washington, DC: Regnery Publishing, 2005.
———. *Liberty and Tyranny: A Conservative Manifesto*. New York: Simon & Schuster, 2009.
Levin, Murray B. *Talk Radio and the American Dream*. Lexington, MA: D. C. Heath and Company, 1987.
Limbaugh, Rush. *The Way Things Ought to Be*. New York: Pocket Books, 1992.
———. *See, I Told You So*. New York: Pocket Books, 1993.
Locke, John L. *Why We Don't Listen to Each Other Anymore*. New York: Simon & Schuster, 1998.
McGowan, William. *Coloring the News: How Crusading for Diversity Has Corrupted American Journalism*. San Francisco: Encounter Books, 2001.
Mindich, David T. *Just the Facts: How "Objectivity" Came to Define American Journalism*. New York: New York University Press, 1998.
Moore, Roy L. *Mass Communication Law and Ethics*. Mahwah, NJ.: Lawrence Erlbaum Associates, 1999.

Munson, Wayne. *All Talk: The Talkshow in Media Culture.* Philadelphia: Temple University Press, 1993.
Mutz, Diana C. *Hearing the Other Side: Deliberative versus Participatory Democracy.* New York: Cambridge University Press, 2006.
Neiwert, David. *The Eliminationists: How Hate Talk Radicalized the American Right.* Sausalito, CA: PoliPoint Press, 2009.
O'Connor, Rory. *Shock Jocks: Hate Speech and Talk Radio.* San Francisco: AlterNet Books, 2008.
Olbermann, Keith. *The Worst Person in the World.* Hoboken, NJ: John Wiley & Sons, 2006.
O'Reilly, Bill. *Culture Warrior.* New York: Broadway Books, 2006.
———. *The No Spin Zone: Confrontations with the Powerful and Famous in America.* New York: Broadway Books, 2001.
Owen, Diana. "Who's Talking? Who's Listening? The New Politics of Radio Talk Shows." Pp. 127-146 in *Broken Contract: Changing Relationships between Americans and Their Government,* edited by Steven Craig. Boulder, CO: Westview Press, 1996.
Page, Benjamin I. *Who Deliberates? Mass Media in Modern Democracy.* Chicago: University of Chicago Press, 1996.
Potter, W. James. *Media Literacy.* Thousand Oaks, CA: Sage Publications, 2005.
Press, Bill. *Spin This! All The Ways We Don't Tell the Truth.* New York: Pocket Books, 2001.
Reagan, Michael. *Making Waves.* Nashville, TN: Thomas Nelson Publishers, 1996.
Rehm, Diane. "Talking Over America's Backyard Fence." Pp. 63-69 in *Radio: The Forgotten Medium,* edited by Edward C. Pease and Everette Dennis. New York: Columbia University Press, 1993.
Rich, Frank. *The Greatest Story Ever Sold: The Decline and Fall of Truth in Bush's America.* New York: Penguin Books, 2006.
———. *The Wrecking Crew: How Conservatives Rule.* New York: Metropolitan Books, 2008.
Rushkoff, Douglas. *Coercion: Why We Listen to What "They" Say.* New York: Riverhead Books, 1994.
Rybacki, Karyn Charles, and Donald Jay Rybacki. *Advocacy and Opposition.* Boston: Pearson Education, 2004.
Sadler, Roger L. *Electronic Media Law.* Thousand Oaks, CA: Sage Publications, 2005.
Savage, Michael. *The Enemy Within.* Nashville, TN: WND Books, 2003.
———. *The Political Zoo.* Nashville, TN: Thomas Nelson, Inc., 2006.
———. *The Savage Nation.* New York: Penguin Group, 2002.
Shrum, Robert. *No Excuses: Confessions of a Serial Campaigner.* New York: Simon & Schuster, 2007.
Siegel, Michael A., and Stan Emert. *Power Talk! The Influence of Talk Radio.* Seattle: Ebbetts Publishing, 2004.
Singular, Stephen. *Talked to Death: The Life and Murder of Alan Berg.* New York: Beech Tree Books, 1987.
Smerconish, Michael A. *Morning Drive: Things I Wish I Knew Before I Started Talking.* Guilford, CT: Lyons Press, 2009.
Squier, Susan Merrill, ed. *Communities of the Air: Radio Century, Radio Culture.* Durham, NC: Duke University Press, 2003.
Stauber, John C. and Sheldon Rampton. *Toxic Sludge Is Good For You: Lies, Damn*

Lies, and the Public Relations Industry. Monroe, ME: Common Courage Press, 1995.
Stephanopoulos, George. *All Too Human: A Political Education.* Boston: Little, Brown and Company, 1999.
Swint, Kerwin. *Mudslingers: The Twenty-five Dirtiest Political Campaigns of All Time.* New York: Union Square Press, 2008.
Thomas, Frank. *What's the Matter with Kansas? How Conservatives Won the Heart of America.* New York: Metropolitan Books, 2004.
Tolson, Andrew. *Media Talk: Spoken Discourse on TV and Radio.* Edinburgh: Edinburgh University Press, 2006.
Unger, Craig. *The Fall of the House of Bush.* New York: Scribner, 2007.
Walker, Jesse. *Rebels on the Air: An Alternative History of Radio in America.* New York: New York University Press, 2001.
Warren, Donald. *Radio Priest: Charles Coughlin, the Father of Hate Radio.* New York: Free Press, 1996.

Academic Studies and Unpublished Papers

Call-In Political Talk Radio: Background, Content, Audiences, and Portrayal in Mainstream Media. Philadelphia: Annenberg Public Policy Center, 1996.
The Structural Imbalance of Political Talk Radio. Washington, DC: Center for American Progress, 2007.

News Releases, Position Papers, and Special Reports

"Government Mandated Political Balance on TV and Radio." Rasmussen Reports news release, August 13, 2008.
Hollar, Julie, and Jim Naureckas, eds. *Smearcasting: How Islamophobes Spread Fear, Bigotry, and Misinformation.* New York: Fairness and Accuracy in Reporting, 2008.
Lloyd, Mark. "Forget the Fairness Doctrine." Position statement from the Center for American Progress, July 24, 2007.
Stern, Kenneth S. *Hate on Talk Radio.* New York: American Jewish Committee, 1995.

Newspaper, Magazine, and Journal Articles

Albiniak, Paige. "Court Scraps Reply Rules." *Broadcasting & Cable*, October 16, 2000, 6-7.
Armstrong, Cameron B., and Alan M. Rubin. "Talk Radio as Interpersonal Communication." *Journal of Communication* 34 (1989), 84-94.
Aspan, Maria. "Some Advertisers Shun Air America, a Lonely Voice from Talk Radio's Left." *New York Times*, November 6, 2006, 4.
"Audiences Love to Hate Them." *Time*, July 9, 1984, 80.
Avery, Robert K., Donald G. Ellis, and Thomas W. Glover. "Patterns of Communication on Talk Radio." *Journal of Broadcasting* 22, no. 1 (Winter 1978), 5-17.

Barone, Michael, and Joannie M. Scrof. "The Changing Voice of Talk Radio." *U.S. News & World Report*, January 15, 1990, 51-53.
Bauder, David. "As Bush's Approval Rating Sinks, Hannity Stays True." Associated Press report, April 21, 2006.
———. "Limbaugh Challenging Notion of New Politics." Associated Press report, January 31, 2009.
Bennett, Stephen Earl. "Americans' Exposure to Political Talk Radio and Their Knowledge of Public Affairs." *Journal of Broadcasting and Electronic Media* 45, no. 4 (2001), 72-78
Bloomquist, Randall. "Female Talkers Making Slow Progress." *Radio & Records*, February 18, 1994, 37.
Bobbitt, Randy. "The Fairness Doctrine and Talk Radio." *Pensacola News Journal*, March 4, 2009, 11-A.
Boortz, Neal. "To the Undecided Voter," October 23, 2008.
Bowman, James. "The Leader of the Opposition." *National Review*, September 6, 1993, 50.
Bumiller, Elisabeth. "McCain Gathers Support and Donations." *New York Times*, February 23, 2008, 13.
Bush, Michael. "Conservative Talk Radio Won't Lose Its Bluster." *Advertising Age*, February 11, 2008, 8.
Bush, Ronald. "Liberal Talk Can't Compete." *Pensacola News Journal*, September 5, 2008, 7-A.
Calhoun, Craig J. "Populist Politics, Communication Media, and Large Scale Social Integration." *Sociological Theory* 6, no. 3 (1988), 219-41.
"Campaign Insider: A Conservative Icon and Agitator Explains Why McCain Isn't Right." *Time*, February 25, 2008, 14.
Carlson, Margaret. "My Dinner with Rush." *Time*, June 24, 2001.
Chafets, Zev. "Late-Period Limbaugh." *New York Times Magazine*, July 6, 2008.
"The Changing Voice of Talk Radio." *U.S. News & World Report*, January 15, 1990, 51-52.
Chapman, Stephen. "McCain is Scared to Talk about His Extremist Pal Liddy." Syndicated newspaper column, October 28, 2008.
Chuchmach, Megan. "Inside the Mind of Mark Foley: Disgraced Congressman Turned Talk Radio Host." ABC News On-Line, September 9, 2009.
Cillizza, Chris, and Shailagh Murray. "Radio Host Denies Broadcasting His Support for Obama." *Washington Post*, February 3, 2008, 2-A.
Conant, Eve, Holly Bailey, and Michael Hirsh. "So Much for a Warm Welcome." *Newsweek*, February 18, 2008, 27-32.
Conway, Mike, Maria Elizabeth Grabe, and Kevin Grieves. "Villains, Victims, and the Virtuous in Bill O'Reilly's No-Spin Zone: Revisiting World War Propaganda Techniques." *Journalism Studies* 8, no. 2 (2007), 197-225.
Corliss, Richard. "Conservative Provocateur or Big Blowhard?" *Time*, October 26, 1992, 76-79.
———. "Look Who's Talking." *Time*, January 23, 1995, 22-25.
Crawford, Selwyn, and Tiara M. Ellis. "Tolerance for Intolerance Fuels Fears of Cultural Rift." *Dallas Morning News*, April 18, 2004.
Crittenden, John. "Democratic Functions of the Open Mike Radio Forum." *Public Opinion Quarterly* 33 (Spring 1971), 200-210.
Cuprisin, Tom. "In Madison, Liberal Talk Radio Dodges a Bullet." *Milwaukee Journal-Sentinel*, December 26, 2006, 8.

D'Alessio, Dave, and Mike Allen. "Media Bias in Presidential Elections." *Journal of Communication* 50 (2000), 133-56.
De Lafuente, Della. "Look Who's Talking: Putting a Face on Hispanic Radio." *AdWeek*, September 17, 2007.
Doherty, Thomas. "Fairness Doctrine Fog." *Washington Times*, February 24, 2008, 16-A.
Egan, Timothy. "Talk Radio or Hate Radio? Critics Assail Some Hosts." *New York Times*, January 1, 1995, 22.
Eggerton, John. "Obama Does Not Support Return of Fairness Doctrine." *Broadcasting & Cable*, June 25, 2008.
Eisler, Peter. "Hot-Tongued Talk Show Hosts Do Little to Cool Rhetoric." Gannett News Service, April 25, 1995.
Ellis, Donald G., Leonard C. Hawes, and Robert K. Avery. "Some Pragmatics of Talking on Talk Radio." *Urban Life* 10, no. 2 (July 1981), 155-77.
Elman, Steve, and Alan Tolz. "The Rising Irrelevance of Talk Radio." *Boston Globe*, November 8, 2008, 13-A.
"Fairness and a Free Press." *Washington Post*, February 15, 2009, 8-B.
Fischer, Raymond. "Hate Fills the Airwaves." *USA Today Magazine*, May 1996.
Fisher, Marc. "Air America, in the Throes of Victory?" *Washington Post*, December 10, 2006.
Flamm, Matthew. "Liberal Media's Voice Grows Stronger." *Crain's New York Business*, October 13, 2008, 8.
France, Mike, and Tom Lowry. "Is There a Market for Nonpartisan News?" *Business Week*, November 29, 2004.
Freier, Peter, and William J. Middleton. "How Talk Radio Helped the GOP's Resurgence." *Chicago Tribune*, December 21, 1994.
Frosch, Dan. "Politically Divided Talk Radio Team Has Denver Firmly in Its Grip." *New York Times*, August 8, 2008, 15.
Gallagher, Robert S. "The Radio Priest." *American Heritage*, October 1972, 38-41 and 100-109.
Green, Joshua. "The Air America Plan." *Atlantic Monthly*, April 2005, 32-34.
Hallow, Ralph Z. "Limbaugh Steals CPAC Spotlight." *Washington Times*, March 1, 2009, 2-A.
Hampp, Andrew. "Imus Mess Makes Arbiters of Advertisers." *Advertising Age*, April 16, 2007, 43.
Hanson, Victor Davis. "All's Fair in Love and Talk Radio." *National Review*, July 19, 2007.
Harrison, Michael. "Freedom of Speech." *Talkers*, July/August 2007, 52.
Hartmann, Thom. "Let Liberal Talk Radio Be Political." *Talkers*, March 2007, 24.
Hemmer, Nicole. "Liberals, Too, Should Reject the Fairness Doctrine." *Christian Science Monitor*, November 15, 2008, 9.
"Here's Where Limbaugh Stands on Some Points." *St. Louis Post Dispatch*, September 27, 1992, 9-C.
Herndon, John. "Campaigns against Distorted Talk Radio Continue." *Austin American-Statesman*, January 25, 1996, 25.
Hinckley, David. "Talk Radio: Election Means Banner Year." *New York Daily News*, September 11, 2008, 86.
———. "Righties Mighty Whiney; Talk Radio Ranters Rage as McCain Trails." *New York Daily News*, October 31, 2008, 29.
———. "Liberal Talk Network Back on the Air." *New York Daily News*, May 22, 2007, 76.

———. "2007 Brought Many Happy Returns in New York Radio." *New York Daily News*, December 28, 2007, 120.
———. "Dennis Miller to WOR; Imus Return Looming." *New York Daily News*, October 8, 2007, 88.
———. "It's a McCain Mutiny among WABC Hosts." *New York Daily News*, February 6, 2008, 86.
Hofstetter, C. Richard, Mark C. Donovan, Melville R. Klauber, Alexandra Cole, Carolyn J. Huie, and Toshiyuki Yuasa. "Political Talk Radio: A Stereotype Reconsidered." *Political Research Quarterly* 47, no. 2 (June 1994), 467-79.
Hofstetter, C. Richard, and Christopher L. Gianos. "Political Talk Radio: Actions Speak Louder Than Words." *Journal of Broadcasting and Electronic Media* 41 (1997), 501-15.
Holland, Steve. "Talk Show Host Fills 'Demon' Role for White House." Reuters News Service, March 6, 2009.
Hornaday, Ann, and Ziba Kashef. "Talk Radio! Why Women Are Tuning Into America's Biggest Baddest Boy's Club." *McCall's*, June 1995, 82-84.
Hoyt, Mike. "Talk Radio: Turning Up the Volume." *Columbia Journalism Review*, November/December 1992, 45-50.
Hutchby, Ian. "The Pursuit of Controversy: Routine Skepticism in Talk on Talk Radio." *Sociology* 26, no. 4 (November 1992), 673-95.
Hyde, Bryan. "Talk Radio Has Become the Mouthpiece of Big Brother." *Salt Lake City Tribune*, August 25, 2006.
"Imus Over the Edge." *USA Today*, April 10, 2007, 10-A.
"Imus Settles With CBS, Takes Steps to Resume Broadcasting." Associated Press report, August 15, 2007.
Jackson, Janine. "Talk Radio: Who Gets to Talk?" *St. Louis Journalism Review*, July 1993, 8-9.
Johnson, Peter. "Critics Demand Imus be Fired for Rutgers Remark." *USA Today*, April 9, 2007, 1-D.
Johnson, Peter. "There's a Close Eye on Imus." *USA Today*, April 10, 2007, 3-D.
Jost, Kenneth. "Talk Show Democracy: Are Call-in Programs Good for the Political System?" *CQ Researcher*, April 29, 1994, 361-84.
———. "Talk Radio Brings Politicking into America's Living Rooms." *Minneapolis Star-Tribune*, May 31, 1994, 1-E.
Katz, Jeffrey. "The Power of Talk." *Governing*, March 1991, 38-42.
Kolbert, Elizabeth. "The People Are Heard, at Least Those Who Call Talk Radio." *New York Times*, January 29, 1993, 12-A.
Kosova, Weston. "The Power That Was." *Newsweek*, April 23, 2007, 24-31.
Krane, Stuart. "Making Progressive Talk Work." *Talkers*, February 2007, 1+.
Kurtz, Howard. "From The Radio Right Comes an Amen Chorus for Palin." *Washington Post*, September 5, 2008, 25-A.
———. "Look Who's Talking Too: Ex-Pols Find a New Home Behind the Mike." *Washington Post*, February 1, 1994, 1-C.
———. "Who Is a Journalist? It Depends." *Washington Post*, June 14, 2005, 4-C.
Lacayo, Richard. "Audiences Love to Hate Them." *Time*, July 9, 1984.
Larson, Lars. "Fair(ness) Warning." *Talkers*, November 2007, 32.
Lewis, Tom. "Triumph of the Idol—Rush Limbaugh and a Hot Medium." *Media Studies Journal* 7, no. 3 (Summer 1993), 51-61.
Lieberman, David, Laura Petrecca, and Gary Straus. "Imus Flap a Matter of Black, White, and Green." *USA Today*, April 11, 2007, 1-A.

"Listen Up, America, Tammy Bruce Is Talking," *Talk Radio News*, January 2007.
Marquez, Miriam. "There Are the Facts, and Then There's Limbaugh." *Baltimore Sun*, July 13, 1994, 13-A.
"McCain Apologizes for Bill Cunningham's Obama Comments." *Business Courier of Cincinnati*, February 26, 2008.
McCombs, Max, and Donald Shaw. "The Agenda-Setting Function of Mass Media," *Public Opinion Quarterly* 36 (1972), 176-87.
Meadows, Donella H. "Talk Shows Don't Democracy." *Houston Chronicle*, February 21, 1993, 1-F.
Medved, Michael. "It Wasn't Supposed to Go Like This." *USA Today*, February 5, 2008, 13-A.
———. "South Carolina's Big Loser: Talk Radio." Townhall.com, January 19, 2008.
———. "Will Talk Radio Get a Wake-Up Call?" *USA Today*, December 4, 2008, 11-A.
Milbank, Dana. "The Mouths That Run against McCain." *Washington Post*, February 5, 2008, 2-A.
Mondello, Bob. "Talk to Me: The Mouth That Roared in 60's D.C." *National Public Radio Online*, July 13, 2007.
O'Connor, Rory. "Talk Radio and the Conspiracy to Kill." AlterNet, August 1, 2008.
O'Sullivan, Sara. "The Illusion of Participation: The Case of Talk Radio." *Media Culture Reviews*, October 25, 2001.
Page, Benjamin I., and Jason Tannenbaum. "Populist Deliberation and Talk Radio." *Journal of Communication* 46, no. 2 (Spring 1996), 33-54.
Page, Clarence. "Limbaugh is Giving Obama the Bum's Rush." Syndicated newspaper column, January 29, 2009.
———. "Limbaugh Profits at His Party's Expense." Syndicated newspaper column, March 5, 2009.
Page, Susan. "Which Hopeful Is the New Face of the GOP?" *USA Today*, January 24, 2008, 1-A.
Papantonio, Mike. "Hate Crimes Fanned by Flames of Talk Radio." *Pensacola News Journal*, July 1, 2009.
———. "Let Rush Talk to a Laid-Off Worker." *Pensacola News Journal*, January 28, 2009, 12-A.
Pearl, Jayne. "The Swift Execution of Don Imus." *Talkers*, April 2007, 1+.
———. "Talk Radio Activism." *Talkers*, September 2007, 1.
Pierce, Greg. "The Gloves Are Off." *The Washington Times*, December 4, 2007, 6-A.
———. "The Talk of the Town." *The Washington Times*, February 5, 2008, 10-A.
Pitts, Leonard. "Limbaugh is What's Wrong With GOP." Syndicated newspaper column, March 7, 2009.
———. "Limbaugh Legions Are Playing a Child's Game." Syndicated newspaper column, January 31, 2009.
Poniewozik, James. "Who Can Say What?" *Time*, April 23, 2007, 32-7.
Ponte, Lowell. "Glenn Beck: Multimedia Talk Machine Refuses to be Categorized." *NewsMax*, September 2007, 55-56.
———. "The Opinion Leaders." *NewsMax*, July 2008, 47-57.
———. "Talk About Power." *NewsMax*, October 2006, 54-71.
Raasch, Chuck. "Twenty Years of Rush." Gannett News Service column, August 8, 2008.
Rehm, Diane. "A Tower of Babel: Talk Shows and Politics." *Harvard International Journal of Press and Politics* 1, no. 1 (1996), 138-42.
———. "Voices of America: The Talk-Show Campaign Isn't Showbiz, Angry Voters Really Want to be Heard." *Washington Post*, October 25, 1992, 1-C.

Rendall, Steve. "Rough Road to Liberal Talk Success." *Fairness and Accuracy in Reporting*, January/February 2007.
Rice, Jack. "Is This All Talk Radio Has Become?" *Talkers*, April 2007, 24.
Roberts, James C. "The Power of Talk Radio." *American Enterprise*, May/June 1991, 56-61.
Roberts, Steven B. "What a Rush!" *U.S. News & World Report*, August 16, 1993, 27-35.
Rosen, Mike. "The Unfairness Doctrine." *Talkers*, July/August 2007, 38.
Rutenberg, Jim. "Black Radio's Zeal for Obama Is Left's Answer to Limbaugh." *New York Times*, July 27, 2008, 1-A.
Rutten, Tim. "Are Americans Talked Out on Talk Radio?" Syndicated newspaper column, September 4, 2005.
Shelley, Dan. "Secrets of Talk Radio." *Milwaukee Magazine*, November 13, 2008.
"Silencing Free Speech." *Washington Times*, June 27, 2008, 24-A.
Sohn, Gigi B., and Andrew Schwartzman. "Fairness—Not Silence." *Washington Post*, January 31, 1994, 21-A.
Stanley, Alessandra. "Don Imus, Suspended, Still Talking." *New York Times*, April 11, 2007, 1-B.
Stein, Loren. "Hot Talk Radio Stirs San Francisco Airwaves." *Christian Science Monitor*, May 3, 1995, 3.
Stelter, Brian. "For Conservative Radio, It's a New Dawn, Too." *New York Times*, December 22, 2008, 1-B.
Stewart, Morgan. "Pump up the Volume." *Campaigns & Elections*, October/November 1993, 22-26.
"Survey: Women Are Talk Radio Fans." *Atlanta Journal and Constitution*, September 25, 1995, 4-A.
"Take Back the Airwaves." *Mother Jones*, January/February 1995, 18.
Talbot, Stephen. "The Wizard of Ooze." *Mother Jones*, May/June 1995, 41-43.
"Talk Radio Goes After McCain." *Atlanta Journal-Constitution*, February 5, 2008.
"Talk Radio Impugns McCain's Liberal Record." *Washington Times*, January 30, 2008.
Thomas, Evan. "I Am Addicted to Prescription Medication." *Newsweek*, October 20, 2003, 43-47.
Verhovek, Sam H. "Out of Politics but Still Talking, Radio Style." *New York Times*, March 13, 1995.
Verne, Gay. "What's Hate Got to Do with It? *Newsday*, October 18, 2005.
Viles, Peter. "Talk Radio a Player in Presidential Campaign." *Broadcasting* 122, no. 25 (June 15, 1992), 14.
———. "Talk Radio Riding High; Both Ratings and Influence Are on the Rise; Can Respect Be Far Behind?" *Broadcasting* 122, no. 25 (June 15, 1992), 24.
Von Drehle, David. "The Agitator." *Time*, September 28, 2009, 30-36.
Wallace, David Foster. "Host." *Atlantic Monthly*, April 2005, 51-72.
Ward, David. "Radio Emerges as a Tech, Personality Topic." *PR Week*, November 3, 2008, 11.
"Why AM Radio Stations Are Talking Up." *BusinessWeek*, June 15, 1981, 99-100.
Weisman, Steven J. "Fair is Foul." *Talkers*, November 2007, 34.
White, Bill. "Live and Local at Night." *Talkers*, March 2007, 26.
"Why AM Radio Stations Are Talking Up." *Media & Advertising*, June 15, 1981, 99-100.
Will, George. "In the Interest of Fairness, Leave Well Enough Alone." Syndicated newspaper column, December 7, 2008.
Williams, Walter. "Leftists Fuss at Rush, But the Real Target Is Talk Radio." Syndicated newspaper column, October 12, 2007.

"Women and Talk Radio." *Talkers*, June 2007, 14.
Woolley, Lynn. "Fair and Balanced? Who Decides?" *Talkers*, November 2007, 30+.
Zarecki, Tom. "Political Radio Spots Mirror Election Results." *Talkers*, November 2006, 32.
Zoglin, Richard. "Bugle Boys of the Airwaves." *Time*, May 15, 1989, 88-89.

Videos and Documentary Films

The Media Circus. Cable News Network documentary, 1998.
The History of Talk Radio. White Star Productions, 2000.
Left of the Dial. Home Box Office, 2006.
Talk Radio. Universal City Studios, 2000.

Interviews

Bates, Mike. General manager, WEBY-AM, Milton, FL. Interview by the author, April 7, 2009.
Caudle, Alan. Program director, WCOA-AM, Pensacola, FL. Interview by the author, April 17, 2009.
Franco, Brenda. Sales executive, WTFW-AM, Fort Walton Beach, FL. Interview by the author, April 28, 2009.
Hemmer, Nicole. Fellow Miller Center for Public Affairs, University of Virginia, Charlottesville, VA. Interview by the author, May 14, 2009.
Henry, Uncle. Morning host, WPMI-AM, Mobile, AL. Interview by the author, April 21, 2009.
Mason, Dan. Program director, WPMI-AM, Mobile, AL. Interview by the author, April 21, 2009.
McBride, Dave. Program director, WNRP-AM, Pensacola, FL. Interview by the author, April 7, 2009.
Mendelssohn, Michael. Sales director, WCOA-AM, Pensacola, FL. Interview by the author, April 17, 2009.
Munson, Wayne. Professor of Communication, Fitchburg State College, Fitchburg, MA. Interview by the author, May 8, 2009.
Nashe, Carol. Executive director, National Association of Radio Talk Show Hosts, Las Vegas, NV. Interview by the author, May 15, 2009.
Parenti, Deborah. Vice president and general manager, *Radio Ink*. Interview by the author, July 18, 2009.
Rohler, Lloyd. Professor of Communication Studies, University of North Carolina at Wilmington, Wilmington, NC. Interview by the author, May 10, 2009.
Shakir, Faiz. Research director, Center for American Progress, Washington, DC. Interview by the author, July 16, 2009.
Shelley, Dan. Former radio industry executive. Interview by the author, July 19, 2009.
Singular, Stephen. Author and investigative reporter, Denver, CO. Interview by the author, February 26, 2009.
Stadden, Paul. Studio engineer, WNRP-AM, Pensacola, FL. Interview by the author, April 7, 2009.

Stern, Mike. Associate editor, *Radio & Records*. Interview by the author, May 18, 2009.
Thompson, Robert. Director, Bleier Center for Television and Popular Culture, Syracuse University, Syracuse, NY. Interview by the author, May 14, 2009.
Walsh, Ken. Morning host, WTFW-AM, Fort Walton Beach, FL. Interview by the author, April 28, 2009.
Williams, Michelle. Associate professor of political science, University of West Florida, Pensacola, FL. Interview by the author, May 18, 2009.
Williams, Rob. Morning host, WNRP-AM, Pensacola, FL. Interview by the author, April 7, 2009.
Windsor, Dave. Sales director, WNRP-AM, Pensacola, FL. Interview by the author, April 7, 2009.
Woolley, Lynn. Talk radio host and author, Memphis, TN, Interview by the author, August 4, 2009.

Index

ABC Television News, 61, 85, 138
ABC Radio Network, 3, 47, 85, 95, 112, 115, 208
Abortion debate, 51, 65, 114, 124, 203
Abstinence-only, 204
Abu Ghraib, 50, 188
Abzug, Bella, 42
Accuracy in Media, 222
Adkisson, Jim, 123
Advertisers, 29-37, 100
Advertising Age, 34
Affirmative action, 47
AFLAC, 35
African Americans: as radio listeners, 92, 112-13; as targets of hate, 137-39, 140
Agenda-setting theory, 171
Agnos, Art, 92
AIDS and AIDS activists, 44, 51, 52
Ailes, Roger, 52
Air America Network, 5, 16, 29, 75, 76-77, 86-88, 93, 94, 117, 118
Air Force, 117
Air Force One, 108
Albany Hotel, 81
Alcohol, Tobacco, and Firearms, Bureau of, 68-69
Aldrich, Leigh Stephens, 125
Alexander, Lamar, 71
Alibhai-Brown, Yasmin, 177
Alito, Samuel, 181
All I Did Was Ask, 63
All Too Human, 49
al-Qaeda, 50, 149
Althouse, Ann, 134
AM radio signals, 146
America Abroad, 91

American Broadcasting Corporation, 150
American Civil Liberties Union, 58, 62, 130, 188
American Conservative Union, 169
American Embassy (London), 115
American Express, 34
American Federation of Television and Radio Artists, 79
American Heritage, 163
American Idol, 77, 224
American Mourning, 116
American Red Cross, 79
American Society for the Prevention of Cruelty to Animals, 100
Americans with Disabilities Act, 43-44
Amos 'n' Andy, 47
Animal rights, 43
Annenberg Public Policy Center, 11, 13, 176
Annenberg School for Communication, 170
Answering the Critics, 102
Arbitron ratings, 17-18, 45, 136
Arctic National Wildlife Refuge, 51
Arguing with Idiots, 106
Arizona Diamondbacks, 142
Arkansas Development Finance Authority, 56
Arlington National Cemetery, 39
Armed Forces Radio Network, 86
Armey, Dick, 180
Armstrong, Cameron B., 20-21
Aryan Nation, 84
Asians, 124
"Ask the Experts" segments, 44
Assault on Reason, The, 190

Associated Press, 60, 116, 177-78
Athans, Tom, 219
Atlantic Monthly, 26, 88, 149
Attention deficit disorder, 101
Attention deficit hyperactivity disorder, 87, 106
Auburn University, 153
Audience demographics, 17-27
Autism, 133-34
Autism United, 133
Ayers, William, 200

Baird, Zoe, 49, 113, 179-80
Baisden, Michael, 92
Baker, Don, 124
Baldwin, Alec, 61
Ballentine, Warren, 91-92
Bandwagon, 185
Barber, Rick, 83
Barker, David C., 20, 170-71, 176, 182-83
Barry Farber's Open Mike, 42
Bates, Mike, 18, 26, 158
Baxter, Ted, 54
Bay of Pigs, 159
Beck, Glenn, 64, 99, 105-7, 154, 157, 202
Beckel, Bob, 189, 224
Belling, Mark, 161
Benatar, Pat, 102-3
Benchmark Company, 11
Bennett, Bill, 5, 73, 203, 209
Bennett, Buck, 16
Berg, Alan, 3, 9, 15, 80-84, 162
Berg, Nicholas, 149
Berg, Philip J., 208
Berry, Ken, 116
Bible, 204
bin Laden, Osama, 208
Bingaman, Jeff, 219
Bipartisan Campaign Reform Act, 201
Black audiences for talk radio, 19
Black Enterprise, 112
Black, Hugo, 67
Bledsoe, Gary, 125
Blocking the Path to 9/11, 150
Bloggers on the Bus, 41
Bloomberg, Michael, 88, 201
Bloomquist, Randall, 23-24, 125
Boehlert, Eric, 41

Boehner, John, 210, 219-20, 221
Bogosian, Eric, 16
Bohannon, Jim, 166
Bonner, Jo, 154
Boortz, Neal: on 2008 election, 115, 195, 205; on abortion issue, 26; advertising on show, 33; attitude toward liberal talk radio, 29; books by, 102; career of, 58, 100-104; competitors of, 154; criticism of, 65; on Fairness Doctrine, 213; and Bob Grant, 37; on influence of talk radio, 178, 206; libertarian philosophy, 99; and Al Sharpton, 95; on stimulus package, 210; treatment of callers, 24; and Virginia Tech shooting, 102-03; and WEBY, 158
Born, Brooksley, 179
Bossie, David, 150
Boston Globe, 170, 209-10
Boston Herald, 163
Boston University, 3, 108
Boxer, Barbara, 92
Boyce, Phil, 171-72
Bozell, L. Brent, 8-9, 76
Bradley, Bill, 43, 171
Brady, James, 56, 142
Brady, Sarah, 142
Branch, Arthur, 71
Brandeis University, 108
Brantridge College, 86
Breaking the News, 39-40
Brennan, Christine, 138
Briant, Elizabeth, 186
Briem, Ray, 72
Brock, David, 87, 176
Brown, Jerry, 90, 94, 166, 168
Brown, Ron, 44
Bruce, Lenny, 80
Bruce, Tammy, 117
Brudnoy, David, 9-10, 108, 110
Bryant, Kobe, 149, 161
Buchanan, Pat, 59, 140
Buckley, William F., 45
Bulger, Billy and James, 163
Bureau of Alcohol, Tobacco, and Firearms, 68-69, 150
Burns, Gene, 109
Burr, Richard, 182

Bush Must Go, 94
Bush, George H. W., 4, 48, 56, 58, 168, 191
Bush, George W.: and 9/11 Commission, 187; and 2008 election, 197; and Tammy Bruce, 118; and Crawford, Texas, ranch, 116; criticized by talk radio callers, 24; criticized by talk radio hosts, 93, 127; defended by Sean Hannity, 60; defended by talk radio hosts, 11, 89, 175, 192, 210; on Fairness Doctrine, 10, 219; first term, 5, 191; and immigration, 182; and John McCain, 176, 185, 202-8; and Doug McIntyre, 163; and Harriet Miers nomination, 113, 181; and Move America Forward, 117; and Janet Parshall, 120, 121; and Michael Savage, 132, 134-35; second term, 103; support from Christian conservatives, 63; and Hal Turner, 140; and Armstrong Williams controversy, 70
Bush, Ronald, 77

Cable News Network, 13, 93, 94, 95, 97, 105, 120, 139, 142, 148, 199, 206, 209, 211
California Republican Party, 115
Call screeners, 195
Callers, characteristics of, 23-24
Campbell, Norm, 89
Canadian Football League, 86
Cantor, Eric, 90-91
Cape Girardeau Central High School, 48
Capitol, U.S., 168-69, 177
Caplis, Dan, 161-62, 209
Card-stacking, 185, 187-88
Carlson, John, 173
Carlson, Margaret, 46
Carr, Howie, 163
Carroll College, 120
Carson, Rachel, 60
Carter, Jimmy, 191, 209
Casale, Jim, 77
Castro, Fidel, 208
Cat-chasing hoax, 100-101
Caudle, Alan, 146, 178

CBS Television News, 125, 150
CBS Radio Network, 15, 31, 34, 79, 95, 127, 128, 137, 139, 155
Censorship: The Threat to Silence Talk Radio, 221
Center for American Progress, 11, 76-77, 206, 224, 225
Chambliss, Saxby, 120
Champlain, Barry, 16
Cheadle, Don, 80
Cheney, Dick, 137
Chiampou, Ken, 160-61
Chicago Fire Department, 107-8
Chick-fil-A, 35
Christian broadcasters, 215
Christian conservatives, 197
Christian Front, 129
Christie, Jeff, 38
Cingular, 29
Citadel Broadcasting, 116, 171-72
Citizens United, 150
Civil Action, A, 163
Clean Water Act, 221
Clear Channel Communications, 77, 105, 117, 143, 146, 208
Clinton, Bill: 1996 election, 176; 2008 election, 185; and Zoe Baird, 113, 178-79, 181; and Don Baker, 124; and Neal Boortz, 101, 102; and Tammy Bruce, 118; criticism by talk radio hosts, 4, 47, 48, 49, 59, 68, 175, 178, 183, 187, 191; criticism of hate radio, 125-26; and Fairness Doctrine, 217-18; and Vince Foster, 39; and founding of Air America, 87; and Sean Hannity, 59; and health care reform, 36-37, 168; and Ben Jones, 90; and G. Gordon Liddy, 68; and Rush Limbaugh, 48, 49, 113, 175, 198; and Dick Morris, 59; and "Mancow" Muller, 108; and Michael Reagan, 56-57, 126; and September 11 terrorist attacks, 150
Clinton, Chelsea, 48
Clinton, Hillary: and 2008 election, 103, 117, 150, 185, 187, 197, 198-209; and Air America, 88; and Glenn Beck, 106; and Neal

Boortz, 101; and Bill Cunningham, 141; and Fairness Doctrine, 213, 222; as first lady, 48, 56, 57, 120; and Vince Foster, 57; and Sean Hannity, 59, 187; and Don Imus, 139; and G. Gordon Liddy, 68; and Rush Limbaugh, 49; and Dick Morris, 59, 187; and Bill O'Reilly, 187; and Randi Rhodes, 117; and Michael Savage, 135; as U.S. senator, 175; and Whitewater, 56; and Martha Zoller, 120
Coalition for Health Insurance Choices, 48
Coast to Coast, 151
Cognitive consistency, 174-75
Cognitive dissonance, 175
Cohen, Evan, 5, 88
Colbert, Stephen, 60
Cold War, 42
Cole, Gary, 15
Cole, William, 113
Collins, Peter, 25
Colmes, Alan, 87
Columbia University, 188
Columbine High School, 161
Comedy Central, 53, 60
Commencement Speech You Need to Hear, The, 102
Communists, 2, 128
Community Maritime Park, 155
Computer dating, 30, 106
Concerned Women for America, 120
Confederate flag controversy, 26, 101
Congress, U.S., 5, 14, 140, 152, 168, 169, 177, 178, 180, 213, 220, 223-24
Conservative Political Action Conference, 211
Conservative slant of talk radio, 11, 40
Conservatives and conservatism, 1, 19, 23, 166, 188, 191
Constitution, U.S., 58, 67, 87, 213
Contract with America, 168-69, 180
Conway, Mike, 186
Cook, Fred J., 215-16
Corliss, Richard, 53
Corzine, Jon, 138
Coughlin, Charles, 106, 127-28, 177, 186, 188, 194

Coulter, Ann, 13, 40, 59, 104, 117, 132, 166
Council on American-Islamic Relations, 35, 134, 160
Couric, Katie, 150
Court of Appeals, U.S., 218
Cox Media, 100
Craft, Christine, 24, 119
Crosby, Bing, 128
Crossfire, 94
Crowley, Sharon, 59, 176
C-Span, 53, 211
Culture Campaign, The, 120
Culture Warrior, 63
Cunningham, Bill: and 2008 election, 141-42, 199-200; career of, 140-42; comments at Cincinnati rally, 141-42
Cuomo, Mario, 44, 50, 90, 180-81

Dallas Morning News, 109
Dannemeyer, Bill, 49
Dartmouth Review, 113
Dartmouth University, 113
Daschle, Tom, 66, 101
Davenport, "Crazy Cooter," 90
David Brudnoy Fund for AIDS Research, 108
Davis, Gray, 115-16, 160, 171
Davis, Mark, 108
Dawson, Dave, 153
Dean, John, 166
Death of Right and Wrong, The, 117-18
Death of Talk Radio, The, 75, 222
Death penalty debate, 118, 148
Dees, Morris, 84
Defense, Department of, 120
Deliver Us from Evil, 59
Democratic National Committee, 130, 216
Democratic National Convention: in general, 175; 1964 event, 130; 1984 event, 83
Democratic Party, 4, 110, 159, 166
Democratic politicians, 99
Demographics of talk radio listeners, 17-27
Denver Broncos, 80, 81
Denver Nuggets, 80
Denver Post, 84

Department of Defense, 153
Department of Education, U.S., 69-70
DePaul University Law School, 80
DePaulo, Lisa, 34
Detroit Free Press, 128
Devane, William, 79
Dewey, Thomas, 165
Diamond, Jay, 143
Diane Rehm Show, The, 119
Diddley, Bo, 52
Dinkins, David, 44
Dionne, E.J., 53
Divita, Darcie, 149
Dixie Chicks, The, 114, 173
Dobson, James, 65-66, 194, 201, 204
Dole, Bob, 68, 71, 176
Donahue, Phil, 58
Dorman, William, 52
Douglas, William O., 67
Douthat, Ross, 167
Dover Air Force Base, 155, 156
Dream Act, 181-82
Drobny, Anita, 5, 87-88
Drobny, Sheldon, 5, 87-88
Drudge, Matt, 7, 166
Drugs, legalization of, 163
Dubai ports controversy, 181
Dukakis, Michael, 91
Dukes of Hazzard, 90
Durbin, Richard, 219
Dvorkin, Jeffrey, 63

Early Show, The, 92
Edelman, Murray, 13, 20, 125
Edwards, John, 106, 219
Eglin Air Force Base, 159
Eisenhower, Dwight D., 85
Elan, Steve, 170, 209-10
Elder, Larry, 99, 104, 105
Elders, Joycelyn, 49
Eliminationists, The, 124
Elliman, Herb, 100
Ellison, Keith, 59
Emanuel, Rahm, 209
Emerson, Ralph Waldo, 132
Enemy Within, The, 132
Engelman Overnight, 151
Engelman, Ron, 150
Entertainment Tonight, 224
ESPN, 50

Euphemisms, 185
Everly Brothers, 112
Ewing, Patrick, 137
Exxon Mobil, 29
Exxon-Valdez, 152

Facebook, 6
Fahrenheit 9/11, 117
Fair Tax Book, The, 102
Fairness and Accountability in Broadcasting Act, 218
Fairness and Accuracy in Reporting, 40
Fairness Doctrine: elimination of, 4; history of enforcement, 130, 214-17; possible return of, 5, 10, 55, 103, 130, 167, 189, 190, 213-25; and Supreme Court case, 130, 215-16
Fairness in Broadcasting Act, 220
Fallows, James, 39-40
False dichotomy, 186
Falwell, Jerry, 66, 128, 194
FamilyNet Television, 120
Family Research Council, 65
Farber, Barry, 3, 41-42, 44, 49
Faulk, John Henry, 78-79
Faulkner, Daniel, 148
Faulkner, Maureen, 148
Fear on Trial, 79
Federal Bureau of Investigation, 68, 140
Federal Communications Commission, 4, 10, 32, 73, 83, 100, 103, 158, 171, 214, 216, 217, 218, 222, 224
Federal Elections Commission, 32, 214
Feingold, Russ, 201
Feldt, Gloria, 11, 184, 224
Feminists, 50, 124
Ferguson, Ben, 4, 5, 70-71
Ferraro, Geraldine, 117
Fey, Tina, 204
Field, Stephen J., 67
Fifth Dimenson, 52
First Amendment, 10, 51, 59, 83, 139, 173, 213-25, 221, 223
Fisher, March, 1113
Fitchburg State College, 7
Fitzgerald, Marta, 54
Flanders, Laura, 118
Flipper, 114

Florida Citrus Commission, 35
Florida State University, 153
Florio, Jim, 43, 172
Flying Blind, 148
Flynn, Ray, 173
Focus on the Family (organization), 65-66
Focus on the Family (radio show), 65-66, 201
Foley, Mark, 74
Ford, Gerald R., 133, 209
Ford, Henry, 128
Foreign Intelligence Surveillance Act, 133
Fort Hamilton, 117
Fortune, 127
Foster, Vince, 4, 49, 56-57
Fowler, Mark, 217
Fox Business News, 92
Fox News, 13, 39-40, 73, 87, 89, 95, 105, 120, 189, 211, 224
Fox Radio, 87
Fox, Michael J., 15, 50
Franco, Brenda, 31
Franken, Al, 5, 40, 62, 75, 87, 88, 89, 146
Frankenstein, 132
Frankfurter, Frank, 67
Franklin, Benjamin, 214
Frasier, 16
Freedom of Speech Award, 135
Fresh Air, 62,
Fusion, 106-7

Gallagher, Mike, 14, 58
Gallup Poll, 13
Gambling, John Alfred, 160
Gambling, John Bradley, 160
Gambling, John R., 67, 160
"Gang of 14," 201
Garbus, Martin, 139
Garofalo, Janeane, 88
Garofoli, Joe, 106, 107
Gartner, Michael, 53
Gay marriage, 114
Gays and gay rights, 47, 65-66, 67, 99, 114, 132, 163, 180
Gays in the military, 180
Gearhart, Jim, 171
Geico, 34

Gelbart, Mark, 16
General Motors, 34
George W. Bush: Faith in the White House, 120
George, Wally, 2
Georgetown University, 149, 150
Georgia News Network, 120
Gephardt, Richard, 71
Gianos, Christopher L., 22, 173
Gibson, Mel, 140
Gigante, Robert, 42
Gilbert, Gary, 153
Giles, Nancy, 125
Gillett Amendment, 70
Gingrich, Newt, 40, 71, 90, 120, 134, 168-69, 181, 211
Ginsburg, Allen, 40, 131
Giuliani, 134, 139, 182, 197, 211
GlaxoSmithKline, 34
Glenn, John, 152
Glittering generalities, 184
Global warming, 51, 101
Goldman, Kim, 149
Goldman, Ron, 149
Goldwater, Barry, 43, 83, 114, 161, 216
Goldwater, C. C., 114
Goldwater: Extremist on the Right, 216
Gomez, Jesus, 108
Gore, Al, 47, 50-51, 68, 71, 87, 106, 166, 168, 190
Graham, Bob, 151
Graham, Lindsey, 181
Graham-Williams Group, 70
Grammer, Kelsey, 16
Grand New Party, 167
Grand Ole Opry, The, 160
Grant, Bob, 2, 3, 42-45, 57, 58, 72, 26, 139, 152, 172, 208
Gray, Barry, 1-2
Great Britain, 135
Great Depression, 127, 128
Green Family Media, 5, 88
Green Party, 93
Green, George, 56
Green, Joshua, 88
Greene, Ralph Waldo "Petey," 79-80
Gross, Laurence, 81
Gross, Terry, 62-63
Guantanamo Bay, 132
Guinness Book of World Records, 160

Gulf Breeze (Florida) Chamber of Commerce, 156
Gumbel, Bryant, 126

Habermas, Jurgen, 1, 189-90
Haitian refugees, 44
Hamblin, Ken, 4, 71, 73, 83
Hampp, Andew, 34
Handel, Bill, 160
Hannity and Colmes, 87
Hannity, Sean: and 2008 election, 199, 200, 203, 207; advertising on show, 33, 35; books by, 57; career of, 44, 57-60; and Alan Colmes, 87; comparison to Rush Limbaugh, 54; criticism of, 156, 167, 188; criticism of Obama administration, 210, 211; and Fairness Doctrine, 213, 224-25; and false dichotomy, 188; and Al Gore, 166; popularity of, 9, 14, 78, 156; and Laura Ingraham, 113; and Michael Savage, 132-33; and Hal Turner, 140; and Kirby Wilbur, 163
Hardball, 148
Hargis, Billy James, 129-30, 215-16
Harkin, Tom, 85, 219
Harper's, 62
Harris, Fred, 85
Harrison, Michael, 177-78, 182, 223
Hart, Gary, 90
Hart, Peter, 65
Hartmann, Thom, 5, 21-22, 76, 86-87
Hartsfield-Atlanta International Airport, 101
Hartz Mountain, 35
Harvard University Kennedy School of Government, 89
Harvard University, 61
Hate crimes, 124
Hate radio, 123-43
Hate speech, 126-27
Health care debate (early 1990s), 36-37, 178
Health care debate (2009-2010), 207
Hedgecock, Roger, 161, 176
Hee Haw, 79
Hemmer, Nicole, 7
Herman, Woody, 1-2

Hesburgh, Theodore, 128
Hess, Bill, 72
Hewitt, Hugh, 72, 198, 200
Hewlitt-Packard, 29
High Stakes, 115
High-definition radio, 13
Hightower, Jim, 85, 166
Hill, Russ, 177, 225
Hilton, Paris, 133
Hinchey, Maurice, 219-20
Hinderaker, John, 167
Historically black colleges and universities, 96
"Hit Me with Your Best Shot," 102
Hitler, Adolph, 59, 125, 141, 142, 186, 208
Hofstetter, C. Richard, 21, 22
Hollander, Barry, 19-20, 170
Holmes, Oliver Wendell, 215
Home Box Office, 16, 88, 114
Home Depot, 100
Home School Legal Defense Fund, 180
Home schooling, 204
Homelessness, 86
Honor Flight, 158-59
Hoover, J. Edgar, 215-16
Hot talk, 10
House of Representatives, U.S., 90, 180-81, 218, 225
Housing and Urban Development, Department of, 147
How to Conceal Stupidity, 42
How to Not Make the Same Mistake Once, 42
How to Talk to a Liberal (If You Must), 13
Howard, Clark, 158
Howard University, 112
Howie Carr Show, The, 163
Huckabee, Mike: as presidential candidate, 9, 139, 197, 198, 203, 204, 211; as talk show host, 9, 157
Hudson County Republican Party, 140
Hughes, Catherine Liggins, 80, 112-13
Hughes, Dewey, 80
Humphries, Rusty, 158
Hurricane Katrina, 62
Hutchby, Ian, 23
Hutchins Commission, 194
Hyde, Brian, 188

Hydrocodone, 54

I'm Just a DJ, But It Makes Sense to Me, 96
If the Gods Had Meant Us to Vote They Would Have Given Us Candidates, 85
Ifill, Gwen, 137
Immigration, 67, 106, 109, 124, 172, 181-82, 187
Imus, Don: career of, 135-39, 152, 168; and Fairness Doctrine, 218; firing of, 134, 138-39; and Rutgers basketball controversy, 15, 34, 43, 95, 137-39
Imus in the Morning, 139
Imus Ranch, 136, 139
Inconvenient Book, An, 106
Inconvenient Truth, An, 106
Indiana State University, 192
Indiana University, 96, 186
Infinity Broadcasting, 117
Ingraham, Laura, 9, 64, 113-14, 182, 221-22
Inside Edition, 61
Inside Talk Radio, 25
Inspiration Network, 120
Institute for Propaganda Analysis, 184-89
Internal Revenue Service, 95, 102, 128
Internet, 7, 221
Interstate 10 Corridor, 153-59
Investor's Business Daily, 104
Iran-Contra hearings, 57
Iran-Contra scandal, 3, 57
Iraq War, 5, 24, 60, 89, 116, 135, 188
Islam, 35, 59
It's My America, Too, 70
It's Your Nickel, 2
Ivins, Molly, 85, 126

Jackson, Jesse, 50, 101, 220
Jackson, Michael, 2-3, 93
Jamieson, Kathleen Hall, 11, 170, 182
Janet Parshall's America, 120
Jesus, 132
Jews, 124, 128, 140
Jindal, Bobby, 211
Joe Pyne Show, The, 2

John F. Kennedy School of Government, 61, 89
John Gambling Show, The, 160
John Marshall Law School, 100
John, Elton, 143
Johnny Appleseed, 86
Johnson, Lyndon, 91, 130
Johnson, Magic, 44
Jones Radio Networks, 77, 107
Jones, Ben, 90
Jones, Candy, 78
Joyner, Tom, 95
Justice, William Wayne, 84

KABC, 42, 56, 72, 104, 163
Kaleidoscope, 119
Kansas City Royals, 3, 47, 54
Kansas City Star, 138
Katz, Elihu, 174
Katz, Jeff, 162
Keene, David, 169
Keepin' It Real, 95
Keller, Bill, 116
Kemp, Jack, 147
Kennedy, Edward, 50, 51, 108, 133, 181-82, 201
Kennedy, John F., 3, 42, 56, 91, 94, 131, 151, 206, 215
Kennedy, Joseph, Sr. 128
Kennedy, Robert F., Jr., 5, 94, 146
Kennedy, Robert F., Sr., 61, 94, 129
Kerouac, Jack, 132
Kerry, John, 114, 138, 218
Ketchum Public Relations, 70
KEWB, 93
KFI, 149, 150, 160
KFBK, 3, 47, 119
KFSO, 116
KFYI, 142
KGIL, 93
KGMC, 81, 82
KGO, 33, 92, 109, 115, 131
KHOW, 81
Kilmeade, Brian, 73-74
Kincaid, Cliff, 222
KING, 151
King, Larry, 206
King, Martin Luther, Jr., 129, 152-53, 206

King, Stephen, 106
Kitman, Marvin, 64
KKDA, 95
Klapper, Joseph, 174
KLIF, 162
Knapp, Greg, 158
KNEW, 92
KNUS, 83
KOA, 82, 83, 162, 222
Kobylt, John, 160-61
Koch, Ed, 42, 90
Koernke, Mark, 10
KOGO, 161
Kohler, Herbert, 215
Koresh, David, 150
KSDO, 56
KSFO, 115, 131
KTAR, 142, 225
KTEM, 222
Ku Klux Klan, 82, 124, 184
Kucinich, Dennis, 106, 219
Kurtz, Howard, 137
KVI Radio, 152, 163
Kwan, Michelle, 160
KWBZ, 82
KXL, 71-72
KXOA Radio, 135
KYLD, 108

Lamb, Kenneth E., 158
Land, Jeff, 53
Landmark Legal Foundation, 67
Lane, Trey, 155
Lanier, Bob, 48
Larry King Live, 139, 148
Larson, Lars, 71-72
Latinos, 124
Laufer, Peter, 13, 25
Laugh If You Like, Ain't a Damn Thing Funny, 80
Law & Order, 71, 197
Lazarsfeld, Paul, 174
Lear, Norman, 84
Leary, Timothy, 131
Lebron, Michael, 10
Lee Rodgers and Melanie Morgan Show, The, 115
Lee, Alfred McClung, 186
Left of the Dial, 16, 88
Lehman, Herbert, 165

Let Freedom Ring, 57, 58
Let's Be Heard, 43
Levin, Mark, 5, 9, 45, 66-67, 213, 221
Levin, Murray, 3
Lewinsky, Monica, 4
Lewis, Jason, 154
Lewis, Tom, 20, 52
Lexis-Nexis, 45
Leykis, Tom, 173
Liberal talk radio, failure of, 14
Liberal talk show hosts, 29, 75-97
Liberals and liberalism, 1, 14, 19, 23, 51, 67, 129, 132, 141, 166, 175, 188, 191
Liberalism Is a Mental Disorder, 134
Libertarian Party, 110
Libertarian talk show hosts, 99-110
Libertarians and libertarianism, 24, 99, 147
Library of Congress, 39
Liddy, G. Gordon, 4, 5, 39, 45, 68-69, 126, 183-84, 200, 205
Liebermann, Joe, 105
Lies and the Lying Liars Who Tell Them, 62, 89
Limbaugh, Millie, 46
Limbaugh, Rush: and 1992 election, 168; and 1994 election, 180; and 2008 election, 200, 201-2, 204, 205, 207; advertising on show, 32, 33, 35, and Zoe Baird, 113; and Don Baker, 123; books about, 39; books by, 39, 46; and George H. W. Bush, 168; callers to show, 23, 24; and card-stacking, 188; career of, 3-4, 45-55, 47-48, 119; connection to hate radio, 126; conservative views, 175; criticism of, 15, 39-40, 41, 53, 89, 115, 123, 132, 134, 183, 187, 188; criticism of liberal talk radio, 75; criticism of Obama administration, 198, 199, 209, 210; and Bill Cunningham, 141; drug addiction, 54-55; and Fairness Doctrine, 213, 222, 223; and Michael J. Fox, 15; and glittering generalities, 187; and Al Gore, 166; and Sean Hannity, 59; hearing loss, 54-55; and immigration, 182; and inaccuracies, 183;

and Laura Ingraham, 112; and Mark Levin, 67; and Mike Malloy, 93; and Donovan McNabb controversy, 49-50; and Stephanie Miller, 115; as opinion leader, 13, 170; personal appearance and health, 15, 54; personal life, 54; popularity of, 14, 59, 78, 141, 156, 176; program on WNRP, 157; program on WNTM, 154; and Republican Party, 166; role in popularity of talk radio, 3; and Michael Smerconish, 148; West Palm Beach estate, 55; and Armstrong Williams, 69
Limbaugh, Rush, Jr., 46
Limbaugh, Rush, Sr., 46
Limbaugh, Stephen N., Jr., 46
Limbaugh, Stephen N., Sr., 46
Limon, Emiliano, 26
Lindenwood University, 115
Linder, John, 102
Lindh, John Walker, 116
Listener demographics, 17-27
Listening habits, 8, 166
Lizza, Ryan, 202
Los Angeles City Council, 96
Los Angeles Daily News, 163
Los Angeles Lakers cheerleaders, 149
Los Angeles Times, 126, 150, 217
Lott, Trent, 182
Louisiana Baptist University, 97
Luce, Clare Booth, 128

MacArthur, Douglas, 128
Maddow, Rachel, 118
Maddox, Lester, 100
Madison, James, 213, 214
Madonna, 50
Maher, Bill, 138, 148, 206
Making People Talk, 42
Making Waves, 8, 69
Malloy, Mike, 87, 93
Man Who Would Not Shut Up, The, 64
Manion, Clarence, 130, 215
Marconi Award, 96, 108, 141
Marcy Park, 49
Marine Corps, 130
Marist College, 60
Mark Davis Show, The, 108

Mark Twain Award, 116
Married . . . With Children, 163
Marshall, Thurgood, 67
Martha Zoller Show, The, 120
Martha's Vineyard, 51
Martin Luther King Day, 152-53
Martin, Roland, 97, 204
Martinez, Mel, 182
Mary Tyler Moore Show, The, 54
Mason, Dan, 78
Mason, Jackie, 81
Matthews, Chris, 148
Maxwell, Dave, 156
McBride, Mary Margaret, 112
McCain, John, 14, 134, 139, 141-42, 161, 176, 181, 185, 195-96, 197, 198, 199, 200, 201, 202, 204, 205, 206-7, 212
McCarthy, Joseph, 79
McCaskill, Claire, 50
McCombs, Max, 171
McConnell, Mitch, 210
McCoy, Luke, 157
McDonalds, 29
McGowan, William, 22
McIntyre, Doug, 163
McKinney, Cynthia, 101
McLaughlin, Ed, 47, 215
Media Access Project, 220
Media Matters for America, 40, 77, 137, 207, 211
Media Ownership Reform Act, 218, 220
Media Research Center, 126
Media Talk, 193
Medicaid, 99
Medicare, 99, 102
Medved, Michael, 176, 200, 203, 210
Meese, Edwin, 66
Meet the Press, 205
Mein Kampf, 59
Men in Black, 67
Mendelssohn, Michael, 19, 31, 32, 35
Merchant Marines, 79
Metropolitan State College of Denver, 162
Michigan State University, 86
Mickelson, Jan, 143
Microsoft, 29
Midnight Caller, 15

Miers, Harriet, 113, 181
Miller Center for Public Affairs, 7
Miller, Clyde R., 184
Miller, Dennis, 99, 107
Miller, Henry, 132
Miller, Jeff, 158
Miller, Stephanie, 5, 14, 111, 114-15, 146, 206
Miller, William E., 112
Mohan, Bob, 142
Mondale, Walter, 91
Mondiacs, Chris, 13
Monroe, Bryan, 138
Moore, Michael, 72, 117
Moorhead State University, 86
Moral Majority, 128
Morgan, Melanie, 115-16, 172
Morgan, Romain, 115
Mormon Church, 105
Mormon in the White House, A, 72
Morning Drive, 14, 147, 148
Morning in America, 73
Morris, Dick, 59, 187
Moses, 132
Mother Jones, 53, 166
Move America Forward, 116-17
Moveon.org, 77
MSNBC, 13, 15, 34, 53, 64, 94, 95, 120, 133, 148
Muller, Eric "Mancow," 10, 107-8
Multicultural Radio Network, 88
Munson, Wayne, 7
Murdered by Mumia, 148
Murtha, John, 60
Muslims, 124
Mussolini, Benito, 186
Mutual Radio Network, 78
Muzzled: From T-Ball to Terrorism, 148
My Dinner with Andre, 16
MySpace, 6

1984 (novel), 188
Name-calling, 184
Napolitano, Andrew, 73-74
Nashe, Carol, 6
National Association for the Advancement of Colored People, 125, 137
National Association of Black Journalists, 138

National Association of Broadcasters, 13, 96, 128
National Association of Radio Talk Show Hosts, 6, 12, 108
National Broadcasting Company, 107
National Economic Blackout, 92
National Endowment for the Arts, 50
National Football League, 49-50, 55
National Organization for Women, 35, 67, 118, 137, 143, 178
National Public Radio, 1, 60, 62-63, 77, 89, 91, 119, 169
National Radio Hall of Fame, 46, 96, 136
National Religious Broadcasters, 120
National Review, 175
National Union for Social Justice, 128
National World War II Memorial, 159
Navy, U.S., 29
Nazism, 59
NBC News, 53
NBC Television, 15, 16
Nebel, Long John, 78-79
Neiwart, David, 124
New American Revolution, The, 118
New Jersey Republican Party, 140
New Jersey Supreme Court, 140
New Media Conference, 12
New Thought Police, The, 117
New York City Police Department, 182
New York Philharmonic Orchestra, 128
New York Times Magazine, 202
New York Times, 1, 49, 52, 62, 116, 137, 169, 179
New York, 44
New Yorker, 202
Newman, Bob "Gunny," 162, 208
Newman, Paul, 88
NewsMax, 132
Nichols Arena, 80
Nichols, Larry, 56
Nielsen Media Research, 17-18
Nike, 85
Nixon, Richard M., 46, 151, 166, 215
No Child Left Behind Act, 69-70
Nobel Prize Committee, 132
North American Free Trade Agreement, 106, 180

North, Oliver, 57, 59, 126

No-Spin Zone, The, 61
Nostalgia Network, 53
Notre Dame University, 128, 158-59
Nova M Radio Network, 117
Nuclear power debate, 51

O'Connor, Rory, 59, 123, 126
O'Donnell, Rosie, 61, 106, 138-39, 222
O'Franken Factor, The, 89
O'Keefe, Ed, 204
O'Reilly Factor, The, 61
O'Reilly, Bill: and 2008 election, 203; advertising on show, 35; books about, 39, 65; books by, 62; and Tammy Bruce, 118; career of, 60-61; childhood, 60-61, 63; criticism of, 14, 40, 89, 132, 134, 186-88, 188; ending of show, 9, 71; and false dichotomy, 188; and Al Franken, 88; and Arianna Huffington, 14; on immigration, 187; and Laura Ingraham, 114; sexual harassment case, 63-64; and Rush Limbaugh, 54; and name-calling, 186-87; and Al Sharpton, 95; and Fred Thompson, 71
Obama, Barack: and Air America, 88; birth certificate controversy, 208; criticism of, 206, 208; on Fairness Doctrine, 213; first year in office, 9, 55, 60, 109, 124, 127, 154, 155, 159, 175-76, 209-11; and Don Imus, 137; and Rush Limbaugh, 50-51, 52; popularity of, 206; presidential campaign, 14, 66, 97, 147, 162, 187-88, 189, 195, 197-208, 201, 203; and "socialist" label, 191, 207; trip to Kenya, 208
Obey, David, 224
Office of National Drug Control Policy, 73
Oh Really Factor, The, 65
Oklahoma City bombing, 123, 125-26
Olbermann, Keith, 53, 63, 117
Oliver, Audrey, 81
One Sacred Chicken to Go, 135
Order, The, 84
Origin of myths, 182-83

Ortiz, Michael, 225
Orwell, George, 188
Oxford University, 118
OxyContin, 54

Pacifica Radio Network, 90
Paladin Press, 162
Paley, Bill, 128-29
Palin, Sarah, 200, 204, 212
Papantonio, Mike, 94, 211
Parenti, Deborah, 169
Parkinson's Disease, 50
Parshall, Craig, 121
Parshall, Janet, 120-21
Passion of the Christ, The, 140
Paterson State College, 151
Path to 9/11, The, 150
Patriot Act, 221
Paul Revere Society, 135
Paul, Ron, 198
Pearl, Jayne, 139
Peete, Holly Robinson, 133
Peete, Rodney, 133
Pelosi, Nancy, 101, 115, 210, 219
Pence, Mike, 219-20, 223
Penn, Sean, 51, 61
Pensacola News Journal, 77-78
Pentagon, 180
Penthouse, 52
People for the Ethical Treatment of Animals, 100
Perot, Ross, 176
Perry, Rick, 85
Personal Attack Rule, 214-16, 218
Personal Influence, 174
Peters, Pete, 10
Peterson, Scott, 149
PetMeds, 34
Pew Research, 8, 18-19, 219, 221
Peyser, Penny, 163
Philadelphia Eagles, 49-50
Plain folks, 185
Planned Parenthood, 11-12, 58
Plato, 132
Platters, The, 112
Poehler, Amy, 204
Political bloggers, 7-8, 40, 140, 167, 183
Political correctness, 43, 51, 102
Political journalists, 167

Political Zoo, The, 134
Politically Incorrect, 148
Politico.com, 7, 219
Politics of Misinformation, The, 13
Poniewozik, James, 136
Pornography, 114
Powell, Colin, 205, 209
Power to the People, 221-22
Pozner, Vladimir, 72
Premiere Radio Network, 9, 55, 117
Presidential election (1992), 48, 168
Presidential election (1996), 68, 176
Presidential election (2000), 4-5
Presidential election (2008), 9, 14, 170, 185, 187-88, 195, 197-212
Presidential election (2012), 211-12
Presley, Elvis, 45
Press, Bill, 5, 33, 94, 184
Procter & Gamble, 34, 137
Professors, 51, 132
Progressive talk show hosts, 75-97
Progressive, The, 40
Propaganda models, 184-89
Provizer, Norman, 162
Public Broadcasting Service, 96
Public schools, 101
Public sphere, 1, 189-200
Pyne, Joe, 2, 42, 130-31, 133

Quayle, Dan, 168
Quinn, Jim, 143, 208
Quran, 59

Race relations, 104
Rachel Maddow Show, The, 118
Radio & Records, 6, 45
Radio America Network, 68, 161
Radio League of the Little Flower, 127-28
Radio One Network, 92, 95, 112-13
Radiothon, 138
Rambling with Gambling, 160
Rampton, Sheldon, 37
Ramsey, Jon Benet, 84
Randi Rhodes Show, The, 117
Rap music, 138
Rapping with Petey Greene, 80
Raspberry, William, 126
Reagan, Michael: career of, 56-57; and Bill Clinton, 56-57, 126; connection to hate radio, 126; criticism of liberal talk radio, 75; and G. Gordon Liddy, 69; and late-night talk, 9; on popularity of talk radio, 8; program on WEBY, 19; relationship with father, 56; and satellite radio, 5
Reagan, Nancy, 57
Reagan, Ronald: assassination attempt, 142; and Bill Bennett, 73, 113; and James Brady, 142; and broadcasting deregulation, 4; and Tammy Bruce, 118; and Jimmy Carter, 191; and Fairness Doctrine, 4, 214, 222; and Sean Hannity, 58; and Laura Ingraham, 113; and Mark Levin, 66; and Rush Limbaugh, 54, 200, 211; presidency of, 4, 12, 56, 66, 73, 75, 113, 142, 191; relationship with Michael, 56, 75
Real America, The, 106
Red Eye Radio, 163
Red Lion Broadcasting v. FCC, 216
Reeves, Dan, 80
Rehm, Diane, 119, 169
Reid, Harry, 101, 210
Religious talk radio, 194
Reno, Janet, 124, 136-37
Repeat callers, 25-26
Republic, The, 132
Republican National Committee, 209
Republican National Convention: in general, 175; 1992 event, 48; 2008 event, 201-2
Republican Noise Machine, The, 87, 176
Republican Party, 11, 40, 105, 132, 133, 140, 161, 166, 200, 203-4, 207
Republican politicians, 99, 141
Reuther, Walter, 129
Rhodes Scholarship, 118
Rhodes, Randi, 5, 111, 117
Rice, Jack, 14
Rice, Norm, 152
Richie, Lionel, 95
Rickenbacker, Eddie, 128
Riley, Bob, 154
Ring of Fire, 94

Rios, Sandy, 120
Riverkeepers, 94
Robertson, Pat, 66
Rogers, Neil, 151
Rogers, Will, 85
Rohler, Lloyd, 6
Romney, Mitt, 72, 108, 197, 201, 211
Roosevelt, Anna, 112
Roosevelt, Eleanor, 111
Roosevelt, Franklin D., 67, 91, 128, 129
Rosen, Mike, 222
Rove, Karl, 85, 89, 180
Rubin, Alan M., 20-21
Rush Limbaugh Is a Big Fat Idiot, 89
Rushdie, Salman, 173
Rushed to Judgment, 170-71
Russell, Bertrand, 182-83
Rutgers University women's basketball team, 15, 34, 95, 137-39, 218
Rutherford, Judge, 129
Rutten, Tim, 11

Safire, William, 49
Sajak, Pat, 52
Salam, Reihan, 167
Salem Radio Networks, 72, 73, 130
Salt Lake City News, 188
Salvation Army, 86
Same-sex marriage, 65
Samuels, Lynn, 119
San Diego State University, 21, 22
San Francisco Chronicle, 92, 116
San Francisco-Oakland Bay Bridge, 108
Sanders, Bernie, 219
Sanders, Bob Ray, 162
Sands, Bobby, 151
Saturday Night Live, 89, 107, 204
Savage Nation, The, 131, 134, 181
Savage, Michael: on 2008 election, 205; advertising on program, 35; autism controversy, 133-34; books by, 131, 132, 134-35; career of, 131-35; connection to "hate radio," 123; controversial nature, 157; criticism of, 123, 133; criticism of other radio hosts, 132-33; and Dubai Ports controversy, 181; on Fairness Doctrine, 213; on immigration, 184; popularity of, 9; and Rush Limbaugh, 53, 54
Savage, Charles, 131
Scare tactics, 185
Schmitt, Richard, 16
Schnitt, Todd, 99, 107
Schroeder, Patricia, 83
Schultz, Ed, 5, 23, 77, 85, 87, 146, 198, 222
Schumer, Charles, 181, 219
Schwartz, Tony, 174
Sean Hannity Show, The, 31, 58
Second Amendment, 99
Secret Service, U.S., 140
See, I Told You So, 46, 55, 223
Selective exposure, 175
Self-Reliance, 132
Senate Government Operations Committee, 152
Senate Judiciary Committee, 66, 179
Senate, U.S., 89, 132, 171, 179, 180-81, 202-3
September 11 terrorist attacks, 5, 50, 58, 74, 141, 187, 197, 208
Seven-second delay, 158
Sex education, 187-88, 204
Shakespeare, William, 224
Shakir, Faiz, 76-77, 206
Sharpe, Rusty, 46
Sharpton, Al, 50, 64, 92, 94-95, 101, 137
Shaw, Donald, 171
Sheehan, Cindy, 115, 187
Sheen, Martin, 51, 71
Shelley, Dan, 21, 41, 176, 188, 207
Sheppard, Matthew, 143
Shock Jocks, 126
Showdown, 104
Shut Up and Sing, 114
Siegel, Mike, 151-52, 172-73
Siegel, Victor, 151
Silent Spring, 60
Silverman, Craig, 161-62
Silwa, Curtis, 208
Simon & Schuster, 137
Simpson, Jessica, 61, 133
Simpson, Nicole Brown, 149
Simpson, O. J., 149
Singular, Stephen, 82, 84
Sirius XM Radio, 5, 9, 91, 94, 119, 143

Sixta, Michelle, 54
Slaughter, Louise, 219
Smerconish, Michael, 14, 34, 147, 148-49
Smiley Report, The, 96
Smiley, Tavis, 96
Smith, Jacqui, 135
Smoking, bans on, 109
Smoot, Dan, 130
Soaries, Buster, 138
Social Justice, 128
Social networking, 6-7, 214
Social Security, 102, 130
Society of Professional Journalists, 150-51
Sohn, Gigi B., 220
Somali pirates, 154
Somebody's Gotta Say It, 102
Sopranos, The, 211
Soros, George, 116
Sotomoyer, Sonia, 109
South, Klay, 107-08
Southern Poverty Law Center, 140
Spasmodic dysphonia, 119
Spears, Britney, 50, 61-62, 133
Spears, Jamie Lynn, 61-62
Specter, Arlen, 66, 182
Speechless: Silencing the Christians, 120
Spellings, Margaret, 70
Spin City, 105
Spin Room, The, 94
Spin This!, 33, 94, 184
Spitzer, Eliot, 88
Sprint, 34
St. Jude Children's Hospital, 69
St. Louis Rams, 55
Stabenow, Debbie, 219
Stadden, Paul, 155-56
Stanford University, 118
Stanley, Alessandra, 138
Staples, 34, 137
Starbucks, 156
State Department, U.S., 85
State of the Union address, 217
Stauber, John, 37
Steel, Shawn, 115
Steele, Michael, 209
Stem-cell research, 50
Stephanopoulos, George, 49

Stern, Howard, 10, 136, 171
Stern, Mike, 6
Stevens, Cat, 173
Straight Talk from the Heartland, 86
Straight Talk Express, 142, 198
Straw man argument, 185-86, 189
Stringer, Vivian, 138
Strom, Alfred, 10
Structural Transformation of the Public Sphere, 189-90
Stupid Black Men, 105
Suarez, Ray, 91
Sudden Infant Death Syndrome, 136
Sunday Morning, 125
Supreme Court of Missouri, 46
Supreme Court of the U.S., 66, 67, 109, 113, 119, 130, 181, 214, 216, 223
Supreme Court of Washington, 173
Survival Seed Bank, 31
Sweet Jesus, I Hate Bill O'Reilly, 65
Swim against the Current, 85
Swindall, Pat, 90
Syracuse University, 7, 26, 76, 146-47

"Take a Loved One to the Doctor Day," 96
Talbot, Stephen, 53
Taliaferro, Ray, 92
Taliban, 116
Talk of the Nation, 91
Talk Radio (movie), 16
Talk Radio (play), 16
Talk Radio and the American Dream, 3
Talk radio influence on voters, 170
Talk Radio Network, 9, 114, 131
Talk Radio Research Project, 12, 18-19
Talk to Me, 80
Talkers, 12, 14, 15, 18, 20, 46, 67, 110, 111, 117, 121, 139, 177, 221, 222, 223
TalkUSA Network, 219
Tammy Bruce Show, The, 118
Tavis Smiley Center for Professional Media Studies, 96
Tavis Smiley Foundation, 96
Tea parties, 211
Teachers unions, 101
Temple University Law School, 66
Ten Commandments, 62
Tennent, Rose, 143, 208

Tennessee church shooting, 123
Terrible Truth about Liberals, The, 102
Testimonials, 185
Texas A&M University, 100
Texas Observer, 85
Texas Railroad Commission, 85
Texas Southern University, 96
The Nation, 216
There's Nothing in the Middle of the Road but Yellow Stripes and Dead Armadillos, 85
Thieves in High Places, 85-86
Thomas, Clarence, 54, 113
Thompson, Fred, 9, 71, 197
Thompson, Jeri, 71
Thompson, Richard, 135
Thompson, Robert, 7, 26, 76, 146-47
Those Who Trespass, 60
Time, 65, 106, 136, 194, 202
Times-Mirror Survey, 166
To Renew America, 40, 169
Tolson, Andrew, 194
Tolz, Alan, 170, 209-10
Tom Joyner Morning Show, The, 95
Tom Joyner Presents How to Prepare for College, 96
Torricelli, Robert, 171
Toulmin Model, 190-92
Toulmin, Stephen, 190-92
Toward a Civil Discourse, 59, 176
Town square metaphor, 5, 192-94
TownHall.com, 200
Trainwreck, 94
Transfer, 185
Transportation Security Administration, 5
Travolta, John, 163
Treasury Department, 183-84
Tribune Media Services, 70
Truman, Harry S., 115
Truth at Last, The, 129
Tse Tung, Mao, 208
Turck, Frank, 152-53
Turner Diaries, The, 15
Turner, Hal, 139-40
Turner, Tina, 52, 101
Tuskegee Institute, 95
Twain, Mark, 183
Twenty-seventh Amendment, 178
Twitter, 6

Uncle Henry, 25, 26, 154, 175
United Arab Emirates, 181
United Nations, 106, 129
United Nations Commission on the Status of Women, 121
University of Alabama, 153
University of California, 131
University of Chicago, 194
University of Colorado, 80
University of Georgia, 120
University of Illinois, 42
University of Maryland, 109
University of Miami, 80
University of North Carolina at Wilmington, 6
University of North Texas, 85
University of Pennsylvania Law School, 147
University of Pennsylvania, 13, 170, 176
University of Santa Barbara, 58
University of Southern California, 150
University of Tennessee women's basketball team, 138
University of the Pacific, 119
University of Virginia Law School, 94
University of Virginia, 7
University of West Florida, 7
USA Today, 53, 69, 101, 107, 138, 176, 189, 203, 224

Vietnam War, 2, 3, 86, 90, 130, 157, 197, 216
View, The, 138-39
Virginia Technological Institute, 102-3

WABC, 2, 43, 44, 45, 58, 67, 119, 143, 160, 172
Waco standoff, 68, 150
Walden, Greg, 219-20, 225
Walden-Pence Broadcaster Freedom Act, 225
Wall Street Journal, 40, 218
Wal-Mart, 29
Walsh, Ken, 18, 23, 158-59
Walt Disney Corporation, 85
WAMU, 22, 119
War on Choice, The, 11-12, 224
War on Christmas, 62
War Room, The, 208

Ward, Artemus, 182
Ward, Bernie, 92
Warren, Donald, 127
Washington Post, 13, 20, 53, 176, 204, 215, 218
Washington Times, 40, 197-98
Waterboarding, 107-8
Watergate, 3
Waterkeeper Alliance, 94
Way Things Ought to Be, The, 46
WBAP, 108-9
WBBM, 42
WBZ, 9-10, 108, 184
WCAU, 66-67
WCOA, 19, 31, 146, 157, 178
WDUN, 120
We Are Family Foundation, 65-66
We the People, 90
Weapons of Mass Distortion, 8-9, 76
WEBY, 18, 157-158
WECR, 153
Weicker, Lowell, 90, 173
Weiner, Michael Alan, 131
Weiskopf, Michael, 21
Weisman, Steven J., 221
Weld, William, 91
West, Michael J., 167, 170
Westwood One, 9, 35, 72, 166
WFLZ, 107
WFTS, 18
WFTW, 31, 158-59
WGBC, 129-30, 215-16
WGCI, 95
WGIL, 150
WGST, 58, 90
Wharton, David, 13
What's Race Got to Do with It?, 105
WHDH, 108
White House, 183
White, Steve, 152
Whitewater, 49
Whitlock, Jason, 138
Whitman, Christine Todd, 43
Who's Looking Out for You?, 62, 63
WHUR, 112
Wilbur, Kirby, 163, 173
Wilcox, Mary Rose, 142
Wilder, Douglas, 90
Will, George, 221
Williams, Armstrong, 69-70

Williams, Bruce, 19
Williams, Jerry, 91, 109-10, 173
Williams, Michelle, 7
Williams, Rob, 145, 155-57
WILM, 2
Wilson, Brian, 183
Windsor, Dave, 31, 157
Winfrey, Oprah, 112, 154
Winter Olympics (1994), 160
WISN, 161
WJR, 127
WKRI, 152
WKRP in Cincinnati, 163
WKXW, 172
WLW, 140-41, 199
WMCA, 79
WNBC, 79, 135-36
WNEW, 131
WNRP, 31
WNTM, 78, 153-54
WNWS, 151
WOL, 78-79, 112
Wolff, Michael, 209, 210
Women in talk radio, 111-21
Women's movement, 2
Woodward, Bob, 13, 175
Woolley, Lynn, 75-76, 207, 222
WOR, 43, 36-37, 78, 107, 134, 160
World and I, 220
World Court, 177
World War II, 79, 111-12, 124, 130, 184
World Wide Web, 13, 30, 31, 110, 114, 118, 134, 135, 140, 184, 214
WPGA, 90
WPHT, 148
WPOJ, 86-87
Wright, Jeremiah, 189, 196
Wright, Jim, 178
WRKO, 108, 109, 163
WSB, 58, 93, 100
WSVU, 74
WTKS, 145
WTMJ, 21, 41, 176
WVNN, 58
WVON, 97
WWDB, 34, 147, 148
WWHG, 109
WWRC, 77
WWTN, 149

WXXM, 146
WYLL, 120
Wyman, Jane, 56

Yale Law School, 179
Yale University, 49, 105
Yamaguchi, Kristi, 160

Yardley, Jonathan, 20
Your Turn, 158

Zappa, Frank, 130
Ziegler, John, 26, 126-27, 149-50
Zimmer, Richard, 171
Zoller, Martha, 111, 120

About the Author

Randy Bobbitt is an assistant professor in the Department of Communication Arts at the University of West Florida. In addition to public relations, he has taught courses in journalism, communication law, and communication ethics. Prior to going to UWF, he taught at the University of North Carolina at Wilmington, Marshall University, and the University of South Florida.

His research interests include public relations, political communication, popular culture, and communication law and ethics. Prior to college teaching, he worked professionally in both journalism and public relations. He is a past president of the West Virginia Chapter of the Public Relations Society of America and is a frequent speaker at professional and student public relations conferences. He holds a Ph.D. in communication law and policy from Bowling Green State University.

In addition to *Us against Them*, his other monographs include *A Big Idea and a Shirt-Tail Full of Type: The Life and Work of Wallace F. Stovall* (1995), *Who Owns What's Inside the Professor's Head: Universities, Faculty, and the Battle over Intellectual Property* (2006), and *Lottery Wars: Case Studies in Bible-Belt Politics* (2007). His textbooks include *Developing the Public Relations Campaign* (2005 and 2009, coauthored with Ruth Sullivan), *Exploring Communication Law* (2007), and *Decisions, Decisions: Case Studies in Communication Ethics* (2009). He is currently working on a new book, *The Writing on the Wall*, which explores the 1950s Hollywood blacklist.

Books by Randy Bobbitt

A Big Idea and a Shirt-Tail Full of Type

Developing the Public Relations Campaign
(coauthored with Ruth Sullivan)

Who Owns What's Inside the Professor's Head?

Lottery Wars

Exploring Communication Law

Decisions, Decisions

Us against Them

The Writing on the Wall